Rereading Aphra Behn

HISTORY, THEORY, AND CRITICISM

D1215823

Feminist Issues: Practice, Politics, Theory
Alison Booth and Ann Lane, Editors

Carol Siegel
*Lawrence among the Women: Wavering Boundaries
in Women's Literary Traditions*

Harriet Blodgett, Editor
*Capacious Hold-All: An Anthology of
Englishwomen's Diary Writings*

Joy Wiltenburg
*Disorderly Women and Female Power in the Street
Literature of Early Modern England and Germany*

Diane P. Freedman
*An Alchemy of Genres: Cross-Genre Writing
by American Feminist Poet-Critics*

Jean O'Barr and Mary Wyer, Editors
Engaging Feminism: Students Speak Up and Speak Out

Kari Weil
Androgyny and the Denial of Difference

Anne Firor Scott, Editor
Unheard Voices: The First Historians of Southern Women

Anne Wyatt-Brown and Janice Rossen, Editors
Aging and Gender in Literature: Studies in Creativity

Alison Booth, Editor
Famous Last Words: Changes in Gender and Narrative Closure

Marilyn May Lombardi, Editor
Elizabeth Bishop: The Geography of Gender

Heidi Hutner, Editor
Rereading Aphra Behn: History, Theory, and Criticism

Rereading Aphra Behn

HISTORY, THEORY, AND CRITICISM

Edited by

Heidi Hutner

University Press of Virginia

Charlottesville and

London

The University Press of Virginia
Copyright © 1993
by the Rector and Visitors
of the University of Virginia

First published 1993

Library of Congress Cataloging-in-Publication Data

Rereading Aphra Behn : history, theory, and criticism / edited by
Heidi Hutner.
    p.   cm. — (Feminist issues)
    Includes index.
    ISBN 0-8139-1442-6 (cloth). — ISBN 0-8139-1443-4 (pkb.)
    1. Behn, Aphra, 1640–1689—Criticism and interpretation.
2. Feminism and literature—England—History—17th century.
3. Women and literature—England—History—17th century.
I. Hutner, Heidi.   II. Series: Feminist issues (Charlottesville, Va.)
PR3317.Z5R47   1993
822'.4—dc20   93-12243
                                                                    CIP

Printed in the United States of America

For my mother and father,
and for Keni

Contents

HEIDI HUTNER
Rereading Aphra Behn: An Introduction   1

Beginnings and Endings

LAURIE FINKE
Aphra Behn and the Ideological Construction
of Restoration Literary Theory   17

JESSICA MUNNS
"Good, Sweet, Honey, Sugar-Candied Reader":
Aphra Behn's Foreplay in Forewords   44

Drama

CATHERINE GALLAGHER
Who Was That Masked Woman? The Prostitute and
the Playwright in the Comedies of Aphra Behn   65

JANE SPENCER
"Deceit, Dissembling, all that's Woman": Comic Plot and
Female Action in *The Feigned Courtesans*   86

HEIDI HUTNER
Revisioning the Female Body:
Aphra Behn's *The Rover,* Parts I and II   102

SUSAN GREEN
Semiotic Modalities of the Female Body in
Aphra Behn's *The Dutch Lover*   121

Fiction

ELLEN POLLAK
Beyond Incest: Gender and the Politics of Transgression in Aphra
Behn's *Love-Letters between a Nobleman and His Sister*   151

Contents

ROS BALLASTER
"Pretences of State": Aphra Behn and the Female Plot   187

CHARLOTTE SUSSMAN
The Other Problem with Women: Reproduction and
Slave Culture in Aphra Behn's *Oroonoko*   212

JACQUELINE PEARSON
The History of *The History of the Nun*   234

RUTH SALVAGGIO
Aphra Behn's Love: Fiction, Letters, and Desire   253

Poetry

JUDITH KEGAN GARDINER
Liberty, Equality, Fraternity: Utopian Longings
in Behn's Lyric Poetry   273

ROBERT MARKLEY AND MOLLY ROTHENBERG
Contestations of Nature: Aphra Behn's "The Golden Age"
and the Sexualizing of Politics   301

Contributors   325

Index   329

Acknowledgments

My heartfelt thanks go to Robert Markley, my dissertation advisor at the University of Washington, who introduced me to Aphra Behn. Without his expert advice and generous support, this collection would not have come to fruition. I am grateful as well to the feminist scholars who offered advice and support: Deborah C. Payne, Pat Gill, Laurie Finke, and Cynthia Caywood. Special thanks go to Dale Spender for suggesting that I put this collection together.

Kenneth Fine, my husband, helped me at every stage of this project; this book is dedicated to him, and to the loving memory of my parents, Shirley and Bernard Hutner.

Rereading Aphra Behn

HISTORY, THEORY, AND CRITICISM

HEIDI HUTNER

Rereading Aphra Behn:
An Introduction

*R*ereading Aphra Behn investigates the ways in which Behn is now entering the canon of English literature. It explores the significance of her work in the contexts of both seventeenth-century English literature and of contemporary debates in critical and feminist theory. After being largely ignored by literary critics and historians for nearly two hundred years, Behn has recently received a great deal of attention; during the past twenty years feminist critics have resurrected her as the foremother of British women's writing, and other scholars have studied *Oroonoko* as a crucial text in the development of the novel. To some extent, however, these recent critical efforts have limited our understanding of Behn's work. The essays in this volume demonstrate that we cannot fully understand Behn's writing without recognizing the ideological complexities of, and ambiguities in, her texts: she is a Tory apologist and a proponent of women's freedom, as well as an early abolitionist. They argue that we cannot uncritically revalue Behn's work and attach it to an otherwise unchanged Restoration literature, as some recent critics attempt to do, because her work challenges traditional literary values and destabilizes traditional aesthetic and historical assumptions about the literary culture of the English Restoration. Given the breadth of Behn's work in drama, the novel, and poetry, and given her prominence as a political writer in the 1680s, the contributors to this volume, taken together, suggest that an in-depth theoretical, historical, and critical rereading of Behn's work is essential to the reassessment of Restoration literary culture.

Since her death in 1689 Aphra Behn's work has been marginalized and dismissed. Though many of Behn's male contemporaries respected her—she kept company with wits such as Rochester, Otway, Dryden, Lee, Buckhurst, and Sedley and gained the patronage of James II and the Duke of Buckingham—and despite the fact that, next to Dryden, she may have been the most prolific writer of her day, until the mid–twentieth century Behn has been repeatedly repudiated as a morally depraved minor writer by the majority of her male critics. In the eighteenth century Thomas Brown (1703), William Wycherley (1704), and Richard Steele (1711) attacked Behn and her writing as lewd;[1] Alexander Pope (1737) wrote the now-famous lines: "The stage how loosely does Astrea tread, / Who fairly puts all characters to bed!"[2] John Duncombe (1754) maintained that Behn was the friend of moral depravity and the foe of female virtue, and the *London Chronicle* (1757) attacked the loose morality of *The Rover*.[3] In the nineteenth century, the attacks on Behn increased: Mary Hays (1803), Matilda Betham (1804), Alexander Dyce (1827), Jane Williams (1861), and Julia Kavanagh (1862) agreed that Behn's writing was corrupt and deplorable—unfit to be read.[4] The dramatic scholar John Doran (1865) asserted that Behn "might have been an honour to womanhood—she was its disgrace. She might have gained glory by her labors—she chose to reap infamy." In "Literary Garbage" (1872), an anonymous critic wrote that "if Mrs. Behn is read at all, it can only be from a love of impurity of its own sake, for rank indecency of the dullest, stupidest, grossest kind, unrelieved by the faintest gleam of wit and sensibility."[5] Even those critics who believed that Behn was an important writer—such as Leigh Hunt (1828), William Forsyth (1871), and William Henry Hudson (1897)—generally apologized for the alleged moral depravity of her life and work.[6] Yet despite the endless attacks on Behn's morals, her biography was written and rewritten throughout the years, and it provided endless fascination for critics such as "One of the Fair Sex" (1698), Dyce (1827), Edmund Gosse (1884), Ernest Bernbaum (1913), Montague Summers (1915), Vita Sackville-West (1928), Virginia Woolf (1928),

George Woodcock (1948), William J. Cameron (1961), and Frederick Link (1968), among others.[7] Only *Oroonoko* was treated with any seriousness by literary scholars; from the late eighteenth century until the present it has been regarded by some as the first abolitionist and humanitarian novel and as a precursor to Jean-Jacques Rousseau's *Discourses on Inequality*. Behn's other fiction, however, has been largely ignored by critics, as have many of her plays, most of her poetry, and all of her translations.[8]

Significantly, however, in the past twenty years, with the great feminist critical wave, Behn has resurfaced as a major woman writer. Maureen Duffy (1977) and Angeline Goreau (1980) have written feminist biographies of her; Ruth Perry (1980), Hilda Lee Smith (1982), Moira Ferguson (1985), Jane Spencer (1985), Dale Spender (1986), Elaine Hobby (1988), and Janet Todd (1989) include information on Behn's life in their accounts of seventeenth- and eighteenth-century women writers;[9] Gilbert and Gubar (1985), Katharine M. Rogers and William McCarthy (1987), and Germaine Greer (1988) include her writing in anthologies of early women writers.[10] A small portion of Behn's work is finally becoming available and affordable: *The Rover* was edited in 1967, *Oroonoko* in 1973, *Love-Letters between a Nobleman and His Sister* in 1987, and *The Lucky Chance* in 1988. In addition, Janet Todd has recently edited a complete edition of Aphra Behn's work—the first of its kind since Montague Summers's incomplete 1915 edition.[11]

Yet while Aphra Behn is finally gaining recognition from literary critics, they still tend to read her work—as earlier critics did—as an embellishment of her sensationalized biography. Until very recently, the vast majority of critical studies on Behn have been dominated by the premise that understanding her biography is a surefire means to understanding her work. By now, anyone familiar with Behn knows that she probably traveled to Surinam (the setting for *Oroonoko*), was married briefly to an unknown "Mr. Behn," spied for Charles II in Holland, was imprisoned at least twice, socialized with the male writers of her day, loved the bisexual John Hoyle, became one of the leading propagandists for the Tories during the Exclusion Crisis and, against all odds, earned her living by her pen. The mostly hypothesized details of her devil-may-care and incomparable life, however, often have precluded critics from seeing Behn as a serious writer and thinker; in effect, biography has functioned in lieu of interpretation. Even well-intentioned contemporary feminist critics such as Goreau (1980), Ferguson (1985), Spender (1986), and Mary Ann O'Donnell (1989), to name a few, have focused on the details of Behn's life rather than on her work.[12] This biographical emphasis seems particularly ironic to me because Behn appears deliberately to have left us so little information about her personal life; as Todd argues (alluding to Angellica's self-advertisement in *The Rover*), Behn "did not hang out herself, but a sexual, social, historical and artistic artifact"—she both played to and frustrated cultural constructions of herself as a woman and a writer.[13]

How, then, do we account for the obvious disregard and marginalization of the work of a writer who was recognized as an important literary figure in her day? One obvious answer is that Behn was historically outcast because she was a woman, a Tory, and quite possibly a Catholic. But the crux of the matter, I would argue, is that Behn's work is often ignored, dismissed, or simply misunderstood because her literary vision challenges traditional critical assumptions about Restoration literature and culture. More specifically, Behn's discourses resist modern conceptions of subjectivity derived from what Michel Foucault describes as the "repressive hypothesis" constructed in the seventeenth and eighteenth centuries.[14] As Robert Markley astutely observes, Behn's "vision challenges the Puritan ideology of self-denial . . . the masculinizing of desire—the creation of women as other and as object—that is crucial to a social ideology which insists on the indivisibility of feminine chastity and feminine identity."[15] Behn's complex combination of royalism and feminism may then be seen as a form of resistance to Puritan rational thought and the new individualism, which was, as Foucault argues, an ideology of internalized (sexual) discipline, a strategy in which the self regulates the self and in which women are objectified and female desire is denied (*History of Sexuality*). As Markley and Molly Rothenberg argue further in their essay in this volume,

> as a professional woman writer, a proponent of women's sexual freedom, and a Tory apologist, Behn must draw upon a variety of incommensurate discursive strategies and political values to ground her critique of repression. . . . Therefore [her work] does not and cannot exhibit either a formal aesthetic unity or a co-

herent political ideology; in fact, its theoretical and historical significance lies in its disclosure of the necessarily fragmentary ideological conditions of its production, its registering of the discursive crises within late-seventeenth-century constructions of nature, politics, and sexuality.

Behn's work, therefore, cannot be adequately understood within mutually exclusive feminist or historical contexts. Her writing, as Markley and Rothenberg suggest, is intensely and complicatedly political, registering the fissures and discontinuities in late-seventeenth-century English culture. The tendency for most critics has been to simplify or to ignore the complexities of Behn's work, to choose one of "the incommensurate discursive strategies" Markley and Rothenberg identify to promote their own "authoritative" reading of a particular text or texts.

Yet, significantly, despite the recent revisionist analyses of Restoration literary culture by Micheal McKeon (1975), Laura Brown (1981), Nicholas Jose (1984), Markley (1988), Felicity Nussbaum (1990), Julie Stone Peters (1990), and Richard Kroll (1991),[16] among others, a theoretically based, new historical, and/or feminist "systematic method of inquiry without closure that is always subject to revision, a mode of questioning the status quo" in Restoration and eighteenth-century literary studies, as Nussbaum and Brown argue in their introduction to *The New Eighteenth Century* (1987), remains a tentative project. As Nussbaum and Brown point out, the opposition to the inclusion of theory in the criticism of Restoration and eighteenth-century literature results from the fear of dismantling the pure "aesthetic value of 'literature.'"[17] But given the political implications of the repression of and resistance to Behn's writing throughout the centuries, the dismantling of the pure aesthetic value of literature might be just what critics of the Restoration and eighteenth century need to do. As Laurie Finke argues in this volume, if we are to treat women writers seriously and not just as political stalking horses, we must find new methods of reading, new grounds for what constitutes valuable literature. It comes as no surprise, then, that of the critics who are writing on Behn's work at the present time, many of them use theoretically informed methods: Brown explores the conjunction of gender and race in her essay on *Oroonoko* (1987); Elin Diamond reads the construction of gender through a Marxian-Lacanian lens in her article on *The Rover* (1990); Rosalind Ballaster analyzes the discordant relationship between feminism and new historicism in her essay on *Oroonoko* (1992); and Markley analyzes the constructions of gender, nature, and politics in Behn's Tory plays of the 1680s (1993).[18] The theoretically engaged directions of this recent critical work suggest that rereading Behn may destabilize traditional notions of what constitutes literature, language, and art and, as Finke argues, "restore to [the literature of this period] its history of conflict, contradiction, political debate, and turbulence."

Rereading the Restoration and ressurrecting lost women writers and Aphra Behn in particular, then, involves far more than some feminist critics at first may have imagined. Behn's work revises dominant models of the literary canon, and it is engaged in a number of complex ways in the socioeconomic discourses of the Restoration. Most of the contributors to this volume, therefore, utilize nontraditional, theoretically engaged methods to analyze Behn's work. Rather than arguing for a single new interpretation of her work, the essays in this volume represent a multiplicity of interpretative strategies: historical, theoretical, and critical. Their objective, in part, is to diversify the debate in Behn studies beyond the discussion of her biography in order to examine ideological complexities in her writing and to demonstrate how the discourses of gender, race, and class interpenetrate in her work. These essays, then, deconstruct or at least destabilize what seem, at first glance, straightforward categories such as feminism, abolitionism, or Toryism. In mapping out the politics of a feminist literary practice, Annette Kolodny (1980) suggests that feminist critics should not attempt to formulate any one

> reading method or potentially Procrustean set of critical procedures nor, even less, the generation of prescriptive categories for some dreamed-of-non-sexist literary canon . . . [O]ur task is to initiate a playful pluralism, responsive to the possibilities of multiple critical schools and methods, but captive of none, recognizing that the many tools needed for our analysis will necessarily be largely inherited and only partly of our own making. Only by employing a plurality of methods will we protect ourselves from the temptation of so oversimplifying any text. . . . And if feminists openly acknowledge ourselves as pluralists, then we do not give up the search for patterns of opposition and connection . . . ; what we give up is simply the arrogance of claiming that our work is either exhaustive or definitive.[19]

In this regard, this volume contains a "playful plurality" of readings—a variety of critical and theoretical perspectives—not "prescriptive categories" for analyzing Behn's work. *Rereading Aphra Behn*, then, does not present itself as "a last word on the subject" of Behn studies but "as one of the first."[20]

Judith Kegan Gardiner and Jacqueline Pearson, for example, offer historically grounded interpretations of Behn's feminism. In her analysis of Behn's poetry, Gardiner argues that Behn laments the powerlessness of women in late-seventeenth-century society and imagines a new social order, "free of Capitalistic interest," in which women and men are equals. In Behn's poetry, she asserts, "traditional tropes of heterosexual love present a longing for community, for a society in which the radical values of liberty, equality, and fraternity would be possible for women and defined in women's terms. . . . Behn mythologized her family of origin, her personal past, and her nation's history; her poetry created a world in which a woman like herself could flourish." Thus Behn's method of mythologizing the past is part of her royalist vision of freedom, as her poem "The Golden Age" demonstrates. Gardiner's argument calls attention to the complexities of this process of idealization, a topic that Markley and Rothenberg also address in their essay. In her analysis of "The History of *The History of a Nun*" Pearson compares Behn's construction of femininity to those of Jane Barker and Thomas Southerne in their revisions of Behn's novella. Pearson demonstrates that Behn presents a feminist ideal of a woman who is "free-speaking, assertive, and professional," an ideal that Barker, Southerne, and other eighteenth-century writers attempt to erase or to deny.

Other essays in this volume examine the discontinuities in Behn's feminist agenda in regard to the problematic of female representation. Catherine Gallagher, Jane Spencer, Susan Green, and Ellen Pollak examine the paradoxes of female masking and dissembling in Behn's work. Gallagher asserts that in her prefaces Behn capitalized on the symbol of "the professional writer as a newfangled whore." In effect, Behn (like her female characters) is empowered through self-alienation—fracturing her identity and selling it "piecemeal." But, as Gallagher astutely implies, this process of female self-ownership through the "fracturing and multiplication of the self" is also problematic because there are "moments when the veiled woman confronts the impossibility of being, finally, perhaps, gratified." This fracturing of female identity, then, quite possibly elides female desire because the female character only achieves self-possession "through her nullity, her nothingness." In her analysis of *The Feigned Courtesans* Jane Spencer suggests that the act of female dissembling, and in particular, the donning of the mask of the courtesan, "celebrates women's . . . actions in pursuit of their desires." However, Spencer points out that the veil of the prostitute does not, finally undermine the equation of female worth and sexual virtue and therefore this attempt ultimately "reinscribes female desire within a patriarchal text." Ellen Pollak suggests that female dissembling is empowering to the female character in Behn's *Love-Letters between a Nobleman and His Sister*. For Pollak, although the incest plot of *Love Letters* does not write women out of the oppressive oedipal dyad, the female character's recognition that she is a "a representation within a homosocial matrix of desire" allows her to move "beyond the limits of the typical love plot" and beyond the limits of patriarchal law. In "Semiotic Modalities of the Female Body in Aphra Behn's *The Dutch Lover*," Susan Green uses Griemas's semiotic square to study the "representability of the [female] body and its unrepresentability" in Behn's comedies. Green determines that while Behn's female character has "no lever" with which "to pry apart the veil that covers her," Behn, as her female creator, does. Green thus argues that "in narrativizing the female body . . . Behn also shows us how women, in fact, do represent themselves."

Exploring the significance of Behn's neglected contributions to criticism, Jessica Munns and Laurie Finke discuss the transgressive rhetorical strategies in her prefaces, prologues and epilogues. Munns asserts that while Behn refuses to play traditional female games in her discourse, "Behn can use no voice except one that will both assert and erase her sexuality. . . . Behn was caught between monstrosity and immodesty, and the dialogic of assertion and denial, the only moves open to her, which locks her into an unending titillating foreplay that can never climax, in which, in fact, climax must be denied." For Munns, Behn's voice functions deconstructively; Behn becomes "elusive, and almost invisible," because she must construct multiple identities. Finke, taking a different approach, argues that Behn's criticism destabilizes traditional notions of patriarchal literary authority. She suggests that Behn has been excluded from the canon of literary criticism because her

Introduction

depiction of the theater contrasts markedly with the more static [and dominant] view of "dramatic poesy." . . . In this view, critics' apparent concern for the rules of classical decorum—and for reproducing the ideologies of their classical educations—makes the drama seem almost disembodied. The drama is not produced by specific economic and social practices, but rather by the "genius" of the individual creator. . . .

Behn's literary criticism, by contrast, does not lend itself to such a characterization; thus it can potentially expose the cultural work that enables and perpetuates these values, work that is never purely artistic but that implicates art in both economics and politics and in the social lives of both its producers and consumers.

In contrast to those modern, aestheticized constructions of Dryden (and of other Restoration critics such as Thomas Rymer and John Hughes), Finke emphasizes that Behn's work "is an agent of both social and cultural behavior, a producer of—as well as a product of—social meanings." Thus, Finke concludes, the rereading of the "epistles, dedications, and prefaces to Behn's plays, poems, and novels" as literary criticism necessarily leads to the destabilization of the monologic model of the "timeless, universal vacuum that continually validates the doctrines of liberal individualism" of traditional literary theory. Behn's work, then, becomes a crucial means to rehistoricizing Restoration literary criticism.

Other essays in *Rereading Aphra Behn* analyze the conflicting semiotics of gender, race, and class in Behn's writing. Ros Ballaster and Ruth Salvaggio both examine female desire in Behn's fiction. Salvaggio suggests that Behn turned to fiction writing as a means to express her deep "dissatisfaction with the plot of the conventional love story," and she therefore attempted to make women into desiring subjects "through varied and fantastic expressions of female desire." In her chapter on Behn's "Female Plot," Ballaster complicates Salvaggio's thesis; she suggests that because Behn, as a woman, could not directly advocate her Tory position (and earn her money by it, as her experience in Antwerp illustrates), she utilized the more accepted written form for women writers of amatory fiction as a vehicle through which she could both articulate her Tory views and still earn her bread. Ballaster further points out that in Restoration literature the sign of the woman represented a new ideal of passive masculinity, devoid of the violence of political rebellion. This construction of woman as a representative of a new kind of man, Ballaster argues, maintained female subordination. Therefore, "Behn's narrative strategies, whereby woman is represented as simultaneously subject (the female writer) and subjected (the female character) within the social order, are a register of this confusion, as well as an attempt to resolve it." For Ballaster, Behn's conflicted representation of women as both subject and subjected registers her own ambivalent position in Restoration society. Charlotte Sussman finds this narrative—of the female character as both "subjected" and a "subject"—troubling, specifically in regard to the question of women and race. In analyzing *Oroonoko,* Sussman asserts that the "white woman speaks in the novel literally over the body of a black woman." In my analysis of *The Rover,* parts I and II, I argue that because of Behn's frustration with the traditional archetypes of the female character as whore or virgin, she constructed "other" women—the monster Jewesses—who resist being controlled by traditional love plots that define women as objects of male desire and commodification. In *The Rover,* parts I and II, as in the poem "The Golden Age," Behn stakes out idealized alternative positions for women in order to resist the repression and denial of female power and desire. And, in regard to the intersecting ideologies of sex and class, Markley and Rothenberg argue that the classist biases that underwrite Behn's vision of prelapsarian nature in her poem "The Golden Age" function both to celebrate and to constrain female desire. The authors point out that Behn's representation of female sexuality in the Golden Age "reinforces an idealized image of an aristocratic patrilineal society that must seek both to control feminine desire . . . and to naturalize the coercive means by which the exploitation of labor and natural resources maintains the hierarchies of class and gender."

To emphasize the scope of Behn's canon, the essays in this volume are divided into categories of genre rather than theoretical method. However, these divisions are intended to be neither exhaustive nor definitive (absent from the list are translations and letters, for instance). These essays demonstrate how Behn's vision provides important alternatives to the dominant monologic models of generic development—not only in the drama, for which Behn is most well-known, but also in the novel, poetry, and literary criticism. The combination of a theoretical rereading of Behn's work, as well as in-depth exploration of her suppressed genres, then, will enrich and expand our critical reassessment and revision of the Restoration and the literary canon. Like Angellica's admirers in *The Rover*, we may never know the "original" signifier of the author or her work, "but we may gaze on . . . the Shadow of [that] fair Substance . . . for nothing."[21] Yet this gazing is no more innocent in the twentieth century than it was in the seventeenth. What is at stake in rereading Behn are the ways in which we (re)construct literary history and the uses to which we put those historical (re)constructions.

Notes

1. [Thomas Brown], "From Worthy Mrs. Behn the Poetess, to the Famous Virgin Actress" and "The Virgin's Answer to Mrs Behn," in *A Continuation or Second Part of the Letters from the Living by Mr. Thomas Brown, Capt. Ayloff, Mr. Henry Barker, etc.*, ed. Arthur C. Hayward in numerous editions of collected works (1703 n.p.; rpt. London: Routledge, 1927), pp. 435–42. William Wycherly, "To the Sappho of the Age. Suppos'd to Ly-In of a Love-Distemper, or a Play," in *Miscellany Poems* (London, 1704). [Steele, Richard], *The Spectator* 51 (April 28, 1711).

2. Alexander Pope, "The First Epistle of the Second Book of Horace Imitated," in *The Poems of Alexander Pope*, ed. John Butt (New Haven: Yale Univ. Press, 1963), lines 290–91.

3. John Duncombe, *The Feminiad: A Poem* (1754; rpt. Los Angeles: William Andrews Clark Memorial Library, Univ. of California Press, 1981), p. 207; "The Theatre," from the *London Chronicle, Or Universal Evening Post* 1, no. 24 (February 1757): 22–24.

4. Mary Hays, "Aphara Behn," in *Female Biography; Or Memoirs of Illustrious and Celebrated Woman of All Ages and Countries* (London, 1803); Matilda Betham, "Aphra Behn," in *A Biographical Dictionary of the Celebrated Women of Every Age and Country* (London, 1804); Alexander Dyce, *Specimens of British Poetesses* (London, 1827); Jane Williams, *The Literary Women of England* (London, 1861); Julia Kavanagh, *English Women of Letters: Biographical Sketches* (Leipzig, 1862), pp. 1–23.

5. John Doran, "Their Majesties' Servants," in *Annals of the English Stage, from Thomas Betterton to Edmund Kean* (New York, 1865), p. 239; "Literary Garbage," *Saturday Review* 27, (January 1872): 109–10.

6. Leigh Hunt, "Poetry of British Ladies," *The Companion* 19, (May 14, 1828): 268–69; William Forsyth, *The Novels and Novelists of the Eighteenth Century, in Illustration of the Manners and Morals of the Age* (London: J. Murray, 1871); William Henry Hudson, "Two Novelists of the English Restoration," in *Idle Hours in a Library* (San Francisco, 1897), pp. 125–78.

7. One of the Fair Sex, "The History of the Life and Memoirs of Mrs. Behn," in *All the Histories and Novels* (London, 1696), pp. 1–2; Dyce, *Specimens of British Poetesses;* Edmund Gosse, "Mrs. Behn," *Athenaeum* 2967 (September 6, 1884): 304; and Gosse, "Behn, Afra, Aphra, Aphara, or Ayfara (1640–1689)," in *Dictionary of National Biography* (London, 1885), 2:129–31. Ernest Bernbaum, "Mrs. Behn's Biography a Fiction" *PMLA* 28 (1913): 432–53; Bernbaum, "Mrs. Behn's Oroonoko," in *Anniversary Papers by Colleagues and Pupils of George Lyman Kittredge* (Boston: Ginn Press, 1913), pp. 419–35; Montague Summers, "Memoir of Mrs. Behn," in *The Works of Aphra Behn,* ed. Summers, 6 vols. (1915; rpt. New York: Benjamin Blom, 1967), 1:15–61; Vita Sackville-West, *Aphra Behn: The Incomparable Astrea* (London: Gerald Howe, 1927); Virginia Woolf, *A Room of One's Own* (New York: Harcourt, Brace, and World, 1957); George Woodcock, *The Incomparable Aphra* (London: T. V. Boardman, 1948); William J. Cameron, *New Light on Aphra Behn* (Auckland: Univ. of Auckland Press, 1961); Frederick Link, *Aphra Behn* (New York: Twayne, 1968).

8. The disregard of Behn's work has been noted by several critics, including Summers, "Memoir of Mrs. Behn," p. ix, and Maureen Duffy, *The Passionate Shepherdess: Aphra Behn, 1640–89* (London: Methuen, 1989), p. 23.

9. Duffy, *The Passionate Shepherdess;* Angeline Goreau, *Reconstructing Aphra: A Social Biography of Aphra Behn* (New York: Dial Press, 1980); Ruth Perry, *Women, Letters, and the Novel* (New York: AMS Press, 1980); Hilda Lee Smith, *Reason's Disciples: Seventeenth-Century English Feminists* (Urbana: Univ. of Illinois Press, 1982); Moira Ferguson, *First Feminists: British Women Writers, 1578–1799* (Bloomington: Indiana Univ. Press, 1985); Jane Spencer, *The Rise of the Woman Novelist: From Aphra Behn to Jane Austen* (Oxford: Basil Blackwell, 1986); Dale Spender, *Mothers of the Novel: 100 Good Women Writers before Jane Austen* (London and New York: Pandora, 1986); Elaine Hobby, *Virtue of Necessity: English Women's Writing, 1649–1688* (Ann Arbor: Univ. of Michigan Press, 1988); Janet Todd, *The Sign of Angellica: Women, Writing, and Fiction, 1660–1800* (New York: Columbia Univ. Press, 1989).

10. Sandra M. Gilbert and Susan Gubar, *The Norton Anthology of Literature by Women: The Tradition in English* (New York: Norton, 1985); Katharine M. Rogers and William McCarthy, *The Meridian Anthology of Early Women Writers: British Literary Women from Aphra Behn to Maria Edgeworth, 1660–1800* (New York: Meridian, 1987); Germaine Greer et al., eds., *Kissing the Rod: An Anthology of Seventeenth-Century Women's Verse* (London: Virago, 1988).

11. Aphra Behn: *The Rover,* ed. Frederick M. Link (Lincoln: Univ. of Nebraska Press, 1967); *Oroonoko,* ed. Lore Metzger (New York: Norton, 1973); *Love-Letters between a Nobleman and His Sister,* ed. Maureen Duffy (London: Virago, 1987); *The Lucky Chance,* ed. Fidelis Morgan (New York: Methuen, 1984); *Complete Works of Aphra Behn,* vol. 1, ed. Janet Todd (Columbus: Ohio State Univ. Press, 1992) (vols. 2–6 forthcoming).

12. Goreau, *Reconstructing Aphra;* Ferguson, *First Feminists;* Spender, *Mothers of the Novel;* Mary Ann O'Donnell, "Tory Wit and Unconventional Woman," in *Women Writers of the Seventeenth Century.* ed. Katharina M. Wilson and Frank J. Warnke (Athens and London: Univ. of Georgia Press, 1989), pp. 341–73.

13. Todd, *The Sign of Angellica,* p. 10.

14. See Michel Foucault, *The History of Sexuality,* vol. 1: *Introduction,* trans. Robert Hurley (New York: Vintage, 1980).

15. Robert Markley, " 'Be impudent, be saucy, forward, bold, touzing, and leud': The Politics of Masculine Sexuality and Feminine Desire in Behn's Tory Comedies," in *Revisionist Readings of the Restoration and Eighteenth-Century Theatre,* ed. J. Douglas Canfield and Deborah C. Payne (forthcoming).

16. Michael McKeon, *Politics and Poetry of Restoration England: The Case of Dryden's Annus Mirabilis* (Cambridge: Harvard Univ. Press, 1975); Laura Brown, *English Dramatic Form, 1660–1760: An Essay in Generic History* (New Haven: Yale Univ. Press, 1981); Nicholas Jose, *Ideas of the Restoration in English Literature, 1660–71* (Cambridge: Harvard Univ. Press, 1984); Robert Markley, *Two-Edg'd Weapons: Style and Ideology in the Comedies of Etherege, Wycherly, and Congreve* (Oxford: Clarendon Press, 1988); Julie Stone Peters, *Congreve, the Drama, and the Printed Word* (Stanford: Stanford Univ. Press, 1990); Felicity Nussbaum, "The Politics of Difference: Introduction," *Eighteenth-Century Studies* 23 (1990): 375–86; Richard W. F. Kroll, *The Material Word: Literate Culture in the Restoration and Early Eighteenth Century* (Baltimore: Johns Hopkins Univ. Press, 1991).

17. Felicity Nussbaum and Laura Brown, "Revising Critical Practices: An Introductory Essay," in *The New Eighteenth Century: Theory * Politics * English Literature,* ed. Nussbaum and Brown (New York: Methuen Press, 1987), pp. 1, 13.

18. Laura Brown, "The Romance of the Empire: *Oroonoko* and the Trade in Slaves," in *The New Eighteenth Century,* pp. 41–61; Elin Diamond, "*Gestus* and Signature in Aphra Behn's *The Rover,*" *Eighteenth-Century Literary History* 56 (1989): 519–41; Ros Ballaster, "New Histericism: Aphra Behn's *Oroonoko:* The Body, the Text, and the Feminist Critic," in *New Feminist Discourses,* ed. Isobel Armstrong (New York: Routledge, 1992), pp. 283–95; Markley, " 'Be impudent, be saucy.' "

19. Annette Kolodny, "Dancing through the Minefield," in *The New Feminist Criticism: Essays on Women, Literature, and Theory,* ed. Elaine Showalter (New York: Pantheon, 1985), p. 161.

20. Nussbaum and Brown, "Revising Critical Practices," p. 4.

21. Aphra Behn, *The Rover; or the Banished Cavaliers,* pt. 1, in *The Works of Aphra Behn,* 1.2.21–27.

Beginnings
and Endings

LAURIE FINKE

Aphra Behn and the Ideological Construction of Restoration Literary Theory

> I am not content to write for a Third day only. I value
> Fame as much as if I had been born a Hero.
>
> —Aphra Behn, Preface, *Lucky Chance*

Although feminist literary critics in the last two decades have rediscovered previously "lost" female writers in almost every period, including the Restoration, women still seem to be almost entirely absent from the history of literary criticism. In fact, Lawrence Lipking has noted that Hazard Adams's standard anthology of literary criticism, *Critical Theory since Plato,* "does not find room for a single woman in its 1249 double-columned small-printed pages."[1] Yet this exclusion has passed almost unremarked by feminist criticism, a silence that implies that presumably until the second half of the twentieth century women had nothing to say about the nature and function of literary art. To my knowledge, the only study of the subject is Lipking's 1983 essay, "Aristotle's Sister: A Poetics of Abandonment." In it, Lipking assumes that feminist literary criticism has no history before the twentieth century, a deficiency that may be a good thing, because such a tradition would stifle feminist creativity by chaining it to a dead past.

But the assumption that women have no tradition of literary criticism, I would argue, is an illusion created by the particular practices that have constructed this history in the first place. We have simply never thought of as literary criticism Christine de Pisan's contributions to the debate over the *Roman de la Rose,* Anne Finch's introductions to her poems, Eliza Haywood's *Female Spectator,* Fanny Burney's and Charlotte Lennox's dedications to their novels, Mary Wollstonecraft's critique of *Paradise Lost* in *The Vindication of the Rights of Woman,* George Eliot's "Silly Novels by Lady Novelists," to cite only a few examples.[2] Scrutiny of the critical record before the twentieth century suggests not only that women have been writing literary theory all along but that their narratives about women who wrote and about the means by which what is written is given value force us to revise radically our histories of particular periods of literary criticism. It is not enough, therefore, simply to include women in textbooks of literary criticism. Rather, the inclusion of women theorists in the history of criticism before the twentieth century requires changes in our perspectives on the issues that constitute that history. As feminist historians of literary criticism continue to examine more of the documents produced by women, women's roles in shaping the literary tastes of seventeenth- and eighteenth-century England may emerge more clearly. In particular, the conventional notions of what was important to consumers of literature during this period may be radically altered, and we may begin to see the role the woman writer played in the shift in the eighteenth century from a criticism that focused on the moral utility of literature to one investigating the sources of aesthetic pleasure.[3]

My test case for this argument that the inclusion of women in the history of criticism will fundamentally alter the way in which we write such histories is Aphra Behn. This essay explores Behn's contributions to seventeenth- and eighteenth-century debates about literature, poetry's imitation of Nature, and the moral utility of poetry. I argue that Behn's and other contributions by women have been erased from the history of literary criticism by the particular ideological construction of the field in twentieth-century universities—itself a construction of the particular histories of eighteenth- and nineteenth-century literary criticism. The first Englishwoman to write professionally, Behn was the most prolific writer of the Restoration after John Dryden. This essay asks what difference it makes to the history of literary criticism if we read the epistles, dedications, and prefaces to Behn's plays, poems, and novels next to, against, and in conjunction with canonical works from the same period, like, say, Dryden's "Essay of Dramatic Poesy." Do these occasional pieces constitute a coherent body of criticism? Does that criticism engage the same issues, the same debates as more canonical criticism? Does it offer the same answers? Or does it invite us to rethink these debates, to contextualize them in radically different ways and so to reconceptualize the history of seventeenth-century literary criticism itself? The remainder of the essay focuses on these questions, arguing that Behn's exclusion from literary criticism has been the result of a politically motivated set of beliefs about the nature and purpose of literary criticism.

I

More than any literary critic of the seventeenth century, Behn reveals in her critical writing the difficulties faced by a practicing dramatist in the Restoration theater, particularly one who must operate outside of proper society while at the same time striving to gain a place in it. Her prefaces are peopled by theater managers and licensors who threaten to suppress her plays, critics who find them obscene, audiences who shout them down, directors who rewrite her lines, and actors who mangle them. Her writing undermines the commonplaces of seventeenth-century criticism as they have been perceived by twentieth-century accounts of the Restoration by setting her practical experience as a playwright against the "rules" of neoclassical orthodoxy. In Behn's prefaces, the theater emerges as a cultural activity—a set of practices full of conflict, collaboration, competition, politics, and even gossip. It is an agent of both social and cultural behavior, a producer of—as well as a product of—social meanings.

Behn's depiction of the theater contrasts markedly with the more static view of dramatic poesy articulated by twentieth-century textbook representations of her contemporaries. In this view, critics' apparent concern for the rules of classical decorum—and for reproducing the ideologies of their classical educations—makes the drama seem almost disembodied. The drama is not produced by specific economic and social practices, but rather by the genius of the individual creator. The Dryden that most of us read, for instance in "An Essay of Dramatic Poesy," seems primarily concerned with abstractions like the imitation of nature or with the poet—Shakespeare, Jonson, Beaumont and Fletcher, all conceived as the lone producers of meaning in their works—struggling with and against the classical rules to create a regular play. Literary value as it is constructed by the tradition must be transcendent, the result of an author's successful negotiation of the rules of classical decorum. Although Dryden was, in fact, like Behn, an astute observer of political and religious contention, an effective polemicist, and an accomplished satirist, histories of literary criticism characteristically suppress historical contingency in his accounts of dramatic poesy.[4]

Behn's literary criticism, by contrast, does not readily lend itself to such abstraction; thus, it can potentially expose the cultural work that enables and perpetuates these values, work that is never purely artistic but that implicates art in both economics and politics and in the social lives of both its producers and consumers. I would emphasize here that I am not suggesting that Behn's critical statements, unlike Dryden's, somehow magically remain free from any hegemonic contamination, providing us with some privileged access to a true critical practice. Rather I wish to foreground in Behn's writing what I have called elsewhere the noise of culture and history, those narratives that have been excluded as nonmeaningful in the construction of the literary tradition.[5] The inclusion of such noise can never be simply additive, nor can it provide a privileged position from which to evaluate truth claims; instead, it enables us to imagine more complex and multifaceted representations of our past.

Dryden's inclusion in and Behn's exclusion from the history of literary criticism, then, is the result of a particular construction of criticism that serves the ideological end of maintaining an absolute distinction between literature, which is valued for its universality and timelessness, and the historically contingent events and phenomena that form a backdrop or context against which these works emerge. Our own notions of literary criticism, at least since Matthew Arnold, have been dominated by a belief that literary criticism is the "disinterested endeavor to learn and propagate the best that is known and thought in the world, and thus to establish a current of fresh and true ideas." That belief shapes our reading of the critical record of the past. Literary criticism must disinterestedly pursue its task of describing the nature and function of literature without reference to practical considerations or to the merely political disputes between liberals and conservatives, Whigs and Tories, or men and women: "A polemical practical criticism makes men blind even to the ideal imperfection of their practice, makes them willingly assert its ideal perfection, in order the better to secure it against attack."[6] Art (and by extension the criticism of art) must be supremely unaware of politics and economics or of the social life of its producers and consumers. Its subject must be the art object and its presiding genius—its maker—both of them transcending the circumstances of its production. Literary criticism, then, plays itself out in a timeless, universal vacuum that continually validates the doctrines of liberal individualism.

In keeping with this general aim, the literary criticism of the past reproduced in anthologies takes as its ideal genre the essay or treatise. The objectivity and disinterestedness of these essays is enhanced by the semiotics of anthology production. The essays' modalities[7]— their status as self-evident and factual statements—are increased when they are reprinted as a succession of virtually oracular statements without reference to any practical motives that might have prompted their writing. Any allusions to the historical or sociopolitical events or relations that might have shaped these essays—and thus undermined their modality—are suppressed.

The body of work I am designating as Aphra Behn's literary criticism—the dedicatory epistles and prefaces to her plays, poems, and novels—must seem by such Arnoldian standards of disinterestedness highly interested, their objectivity called into question by their ultimate aim to curry favor either with the fashionable nobility or with the often unruly and hostile audiences of her plays. Indeed, in her preface to *The Dutch Lover,* Behn rejects outright the stance of disinterested objectivity as so much posturing. The genres in which Behn produced her literary criticism—the epistle dedicatory in particular—cannot live up to the standard of disinterested inquiry demanded by twentieth-century notions of literary criticism, simply because the epistle dedicatory's practical function of soliciting patronage, makes it susceptible to charges of gross flattery, dishonesty, or mercenary intent. Behn is all too aware of judgments that question the disinterestedness of this speech genre. In dedicating *The Round-*

heads (1681) to Henry Fitz-roy, the king's illegitimate son, she writes "Dedications which were Originally design'd, as a Tribute to the Reverence and just esteem we ought to pay the *Great* and *Good;* are now so corrupted with Flattery, that they rarely either find a Reception in the World, or merit that Patronage they wou'd implore. But I without fear Approach the great Object, being above that mean and mercenary Art."[8] In this passage, Behn undercuts her own disinterestedness by recognizing the interestedness of dedications. She at once asserts and denies her desire for patronage. Most of her dedicatory epistles display this anxiety that her appeal for patronage will be construed as merely flattery, vitiating the sentiments expressed therein. At the same time, however, she is also expressing the anxieties of the age in which the "mercenary Art" involved in patronage relationships seems much more transparent—because more marginal—than in an earlier age.

Behn is astutely aware that the dedication and the symbolic exchange it signifies militates against any pose of disinterested objectivity. Dedications during the Restoration increasingly implicate all writers in the exchanges of goods and services that patronage is designed to mask. In a dedication to Sir William Clifton in 1685 she writes

> every Mans Vertue is measured according to the sence another
> has of it, and not by its own intrinsic value, so that if another
> does not see with my Eyes and judge with my Sence, I must be
> Branded with the Crime of Fools and Cowards; nor will they be
> undeceived in an Error that so agreeably flatters them, either by
> a better knowledge of the Person commended, or by a right un-
> derstanding from any other Judgment; they hate to be convinced
> of what will make no part of their satisfaction when they are so,
> for as 'tis natural to despise all those that have no vertue at all,
> so 'tis as natural to Envy those we find have more than our selves
> instead of imitating 'em. (6:365)

What she fears in her own dedications—that they will be dismissed as mere flattery, as empty rhetoric—she sees as fundamental to the genre. "Intrinsic value"—whether in individuals or in literary works —is formed, deformed, and reformed not only by the whims of individual "Fools and Cowards" who live by flattery, but also (and perhaps more significantly) by the complex network of loyalties and rivalries that constituted literary patronage in late-seventeenth-century England.

No doubt the sentiments expressed in these dedications are conventional to the genre of the epistle dedicatory. But this very conventionality suggests its participation within a system of patronage relationships. Epistles of dedication were a common practice throughout the Restoration; nearly half of all the plays published bore dedicatory letters. The widespread practice of dedicating literary works to aristocratic patrons attests to the importance of patronage in the literary world of the Restoration. Almost all the canonical writers of the Restoration participated in the practice. Deborah C. Payne argues that the patronage involved in such dedications had less to do with the exchange of material resources or financial support (which was usually negligible) than with the exchange of what Pierre Bourdieu has called "symbolic capital."[9] The aristocratic patrons addressed in these dedications provided access to marketplaces, protection from enemies and competitors, and, most importantly in the theaters, introductions to the managers of the two theaters (and after 1682 the one) who monopolized the means of theatrical production. Without the protection and access provided by aristocratic patrons, it seems unlikely that any writer would have long survived the partisan atmosphere of late-seventeenth-century letters. Yet it takes the observations of someone like Behn, who, because she was a woman, was marginal to the system (at least early in her career) and thus anxious about her position within it, to expose the self-interest masked by the disinterested and easy role of client adopted by someone—say, Dryden, the poet laureate—more comfortably situated within this patronal system.

"An Essay of Dramatic Poesy," long considered a central document in the history of English criticism,[10] is dedicated to Dryden's frequent patron Charles Sackville, Lord Buckhurst, although, in keeping with the semiotics of anthology production, that dedication is rarely anthologized along with the essay. If Dryden's language in this dedication seems less anxious than Behn's typically does, it is perhaps because Dryden approached his friend and patron on more nearly equal terms as a fellow wit. Yet the marks of the unequal exchange between patron and client are nonetheless present. Dryden is engagingly self-deprecating; he calls his critical efforts "rude and indigested," a trifle prompted by the closing of the theaters during the plague. Buckhurst, on the other hand, is compared to Achilles; there is "no person amongst our young Nobility, on whom the eyes of all men are so much bent." His Lordship "imitate[s] the course of Nature, who gives us the flower before the fruit."[11] The exchange of symbolic capital is clear. Dryden's reputation as a poet will enhance Buckhurst's poetic efforts: Dryden praises, perhaps a bit too excessively, Buckhurst's *Pompey* and laments his patron's withdrawal from the stage. In return, Buckhurst's reputation as an aristocratic rake and wit enhances Dryden's own aspirations in that area, as his offhand, if painfully studied remark that he engaged in the essay "with the same delight with which men think upon their absent Mistresses" (17:3) might suggest.

Dryden himself seems fully aware that his criticism is hardly disinterested. Indeed he sees it as part of an intensely partisan set of debates into which he willingly enters because they are part of the court culture of "Wit and Quality" in which Dryden desired recognition, as well as social and financial advancement. These literary debates involved conflicts of class and national loyalty. "An Essay of Dramatic Poesy," which was written "chiefly to vindicate the honour of our English Writers, from the censure of those who unjustly prefer the French before them" (17:7), dramatizes a fictional dialogue set during the Dutch Wars on a barge floating in the Thames in the midst of a naval battle.[12] I can think of no other reasons for such a bizarre and inappropriate setting for a discourse on "dramatic poesy" except that Dryden wished to emphasize the nationalistic fervor that prompted this essay championing *English* drama over its political and cultural competitor, the *French,* whose monarch was happy to see Charles impoverish himself fighting the Dutch.

Dryden's choice of interlocutors in the debate further emphasizes his interested participation in the patronal system based on class distinctions and hierarchies. All the participants in the debate have been fairly positively identified. Crites is Sir Robert Howard, Dryden's brother-in-law, Eugenius is Dryden's patron, Lord Buckhurst, Lisideius is Sir Charles Sedley. Neander is Dryden, the "new man" and the only nonaristocrat among them. It is clear that although he gets the last word, he relates to the other three as a client to his patrons, who are introduced using a language that makes clear the patron-client relationship between them. They are "persons whom their wit and quality have made known to all the town; and whom I have chose to hide under these borrowed names, that they may not suffer by so ill a relation as I am going to make of their discourse" (17:8). As in his dedication to Buckhurst, Dryden makes clear the inequalities that mark their positions by deprecating his own literary abilities while praising theirs.

Dryden's "Essay of Dramatic Poesy" seems as much designed to show his solidarity with the royalist and aristocratic program of "wit and quality" as to establish disinterestedly a "current of fresh and true ideas." "Who," Behn asks in a 1685 dedication to the Earl of Salisbury, "should one celebrate with Verse and Song, but the Great, the Noble, and the Brave?" (6:115). Given the tenor of his own dedications, there is no reason to believe that Dryden and most of his male contemporaries did not share these same interested sentiments.

II

Behn can expose the cultural work and partisan interestedness masked by the abstractions of seventeenth-century critical ortho-doxies because her position as a writer within that culture is (ambigu-ously) nonhegemonic.[13] She was not simply an outspoken critic of female oppression and of those who would exclude women from the profession of writing, as some feminist critics have contended.[14] Rather, her attitude toward the hegemonic culture was riven by contradictions that we might probe as a means of exposing the ideological gaps within seventeenth-century literary culture.

The woman who lived a public life in the seventeenth century, whether as a publishing writer, a playwright, or an actress, was sexually suspect, as available for hire as any prostitute because she was not the exclusive *private* property of a man. "The woman who shared the contents of her mind instead of reserving them for one man was literally, not metaphorically, trading in her *sexual* prop-erty."[15] Throughout her career Behn inveighed against the unfairness of a public that condemned her plays as obscene and promiscuous simply because they were written by a woman. In the preface to *Sir Patient Fancy* she writes "I Printed this Play with all the impatient haste one ought to do, who would be vindicated from the most unjust and silly aspersion, Woman could invent to cast on Woman; and which only my being a Woman has procured me; *That it was Baudy, . . .* [and] *from a Woman it was unnaturall"* (4:7). Her criticisms here and in the preface to *The Lucky Chance* attack the sexual ideology that holds that "the Woman damns the Poet" (3:186). In these declarations, Behn exposes what Mary Ellmann has called criticism by sexual analogy, in which "books by women are treated as though they themselves were women, and criticism embarks, at its happiest, upon an intellectual measuring of busts and hips."[16]

Yet, at the same time she exposes the sexualization of women's writing, she can also exploit it for her own uses, poaching on the very ideologies that oppressed women by constantly making them objects of sexual consumption.[17] Her dedication of *The Young King* to "Philaster" (quite possibly her lover, John Hoyle), for instance, speaks of the play as a "Dowdy Lass," "a Virgin-Muse, harmless and unadorn'd, unpractis'd in the Arts to please." Philaster is the first "whose Person and Merits cou'd oblige her to yield her ungarded self into his protection" (2:105). In this tongue-in-cheek dedication, in which the play becomes a simple virgin offering herself up into the somewhat dubious protection of the rake hero, Behn calls attention to the metaphorical connections that link the sexual promiscuity of the libertine to the linguistic promiscuity that philosophers since Plato have accused poets of indulging.[18] The unstated anxieties Behn's playful metaphor probes link the fear of sexual license uncontrolled by the reproductive disciplines of marriage with the fear of linguistic excess undisciplined by the demands of referentiality and Truth.

Payne has argued that Behn's later writing abandons this sexually teasing tone once she has secured patronage and a more assured position within the theatrical world.[19] Yet, as late as 1686, in the prologue to *The Lucky Chance*, Behn writes

> Since with old Plays you have so long been cloy'd,
> As with a Mistress many years enjoy'd,
> How briskly dear Variety you pursue;
> Nay, though for worse ye change, ye will have New.
> (3:188)

Near the end of her career, Behn is still exploiting the sexual analogy that linked the fashionable pose of the libertine with the production of a new play. In this prologue, her play is the new sexual conquest that will satisfy the jaded libertine's unending, repetitive quest for variety, for new conquests and new diversions. She adapts to her own ends the subject positions available to her as a woman and an outsider; she plays off the shady lady against the proper lady.[20]

At the heart of Behn's sexualization of her writing is her embracing of royalist politics and the fashionable pose of sexual libertinism that accompanied it after the Restoration. This pose was epitomized by the restored monarch, Charles II, and by the Earl of Rochester, whom Behn greatly admired; Rochester elevated frivolity, sexual promiscuity, drunkenness, and the pleasures of the senses to a form of political rebellion that, to us at any rate, seems to contradict his hegemonic and even powerful position.[21] Yet, the roles of the libertine and his conquest could not simply be reversed to put the female in the position of sexual predator. Behn could not position herself as a female rake without exposing the unequal class and gender relations obscured by the rake's easy and glib wit. The pose had a very different valence for a woman, who had little to gain from this libertinism and much to lose. The libertine pose presupposes the impossibility for a woman of a truly *sexual* conquest: "for the doing of the deed would be the undoing of her power."[22] The Restoration rake desired the chaste beauty as the object of his pursuit and enjoyment. But once she gave herself sexually she ceased to be desirable, cast off in an endless search for variety and change. The title of Behn's most well-known play, *The Rover,* describes both the hero's peripatetic life-style during the Interregnum and the restlessness of his affections. The fate of the courtesan Angellica Bianca suggests what happens to the female libertine once she has given herself sexually. Once the object of desire is possessed, she ceases to hold his interest and indeed she may be despised for her capitulation.[23] For this reason, a woman could never achieve a sexual conquest, because her only power lay in withholding sex. The only exception was the whore, who parcelled her sexuality out piecemeal at a very high rate of exchange while withholding her identity, her self, which is what Angellica Bianca does until she gives herself to Willmore. Any woman attempting sexual conquest not tied to this fragmented monetary exchange would find herself in the position of cast-off mistress or abandoned wife.

The reason for the asymmetry in the libertine pose, for the impossibility of conceiving a truly female libertinism, is the contradiction at heart of the libertinism itself as a form of political or ideological rebellion. After the restoration of the monarchy, the rake's cultivation of sexual profligacy runs counter to the stake he has as a royalist or an aristocrat in a patrilineal ideology that keeps aristocratic estates intact and heirs legitimate by controlling sexuality—women's sexuality. For all his rebellious promiscuity, the aristocratic rake believed in the ideology that promoted patriarchy, primogeniture, and legitimate monarchy. Within this ideology a woman's desire is taboo because it threatens the legitimate and orderly transfer of property from father to eldest son. This contradiction explains the anxiety of royalists over Whig attempts to promote the succession of Charles's illegitimate son, the Duke of Monmouth, over the legitimate heir, the Catholic Duke of York. It suggests why, unlike Henry VIII and in spite of his many mistresses, chance affairs, and illegitimate children, Charles never got rid of his barren wife. The contradiction between the rake's promiscuity and his stake in legitimate succession is resolved by requiring the chastity and constancy of women. Ideally, women must preserve and give themselves intact and wholly to their husbands to preserve property intact and whole.

Behn's articulation of a "woman's version of sexual conquest," a female libertinism, does not attempt to counter this contradiction but to embrace it and exploit it. How, Catherine Gallagher asks, does a woman engage in sexual conquest and still keep desire alive? Behn has her female characters engage in sexual conquests and keep their lovers' desire alive by linking sexuality and wit. The analogy between the sexually available woman ("the newfangled whore") and the woman playwright (who has "mastered" language) is crucial to her appropriation of the libertine pose. The female playwright, Gallagher writes, "will not be immediately conquered and discarded because she will maintain her right through her writing. The woman's play of wit is the opposite of foreplay; it is a kind of afterplay specifically designed to prolong pleasure, rescucitate desire and keep a woman who has given herself sexually from being traded in for another woman."[24] This strategy is articulated by Hellena, Behn's heroine in *The Rover,* who achieves her conquest of Willmore through linguistic manipulation by refusing to give herself completely and wholly to him. "I am as inconstant as you, for I have considered, Captain, that a handsom Woman has a great deal to do whilst her Face is good, for then is our Harvest-time to gather Friends; and should I in these days of my Youth catch a fit of foolish Constancy, I were undone; 'tis loitering by day-light in our great Journey: therefore declare, I'll allow but one year for Love, one year for Indifference, and one year for Hate—and then—go hang yourself—for I profess myself the gay, the kind, and the unconstant—the Devil's in't if this won't please you" (1:48). The creation of the persona of the female rake by both Behn and her character Hellena depends, as Jessica Munns has suggested, not on a version of theatrical cross-dressing, not merely on asserting "my Masculine Part, the Poet in me," but in a kind of "double-dressing," in pressing the claims of both masculinity and femininity in a single body.[25] The rake heroine claims both her femininity and her right to masculine self-assertion. This strategic doubleness was recognized by many of Behn's contemporary readers as characteristic of her style. For example, in poems prefacing Behn's "Poems on Several Occasions" both "J.C." and J. Adams refer to her possessing "A Female Sweetness and a Manly Grace." Adams proclaims:

> Yet neither sex do you surpass alone,
> Both in your Verse are in their glory shown,
> Both Phoebus and Minerva are your own.
> (6:119, 120)

This double-dressing, Behn's strategy of exploiting and confounding traditional gender roles within a single persona, enables her to play with the radical pose of the libertine—even if it provides at best an unstable poetic moment—that was the source of so many creative possibilities for male writers of the period. In fact, the pose's very instability may have been the source of its creative power.

I have recapitulated Gallagher's and Munns's arguments at some length so that I might examine how Behn's sexualization of her writing enables her to approach obliquely and from a rather unique perspective the critical issues that occupied late-seventeenth-century literary critics, in particular, questions about the poet's imitation of Nature and poetry's moral utility. At the same time Behn's critical writing eroticizes the relationships between a female playwright and a male audience, it also exposes the eroticism underlying the relationships between male poets and a female Nature that is so disturbing to late-seventeenth-century literary critics (who are, not incidentally, usually male). The problem of defining the poet's imitation of Nature dominated English literary criticism from the Renaissance until the end of the eighteenth century. No aesthetic writing of this period, either on the Continent or in England, fails to mention this problem. Indeed Behn may well be one of the few seventeenth-century critics to have anything really new to say about the subject. Her writing unmasks a fundamental set of analogies that link the sexual, political, economic, philosophic, and literary to seventeenth-century anxieties about the nature of Nature, anxieties that have their roots both in the political turbulence that accompanied the English Civil War and its debates about monarchy and political order and in the tensions between new scientific knowledge and received philosophical and religious ideals.

Both Evelyn Fox Keller and Carolyn Merchant examine the gendered concepts of nature in seventeenth-century science and culture.[26] Merchant in particular argues that the scientific revolution and the rise of market culture undermined the close organic connection between women and Nature that characterized preindustrial organic societies. My analysis of late-seventeenth-century conflicts about Nature differs somewhat from Merchant's in that I would argue that the need to gender Nature as female arose not from some intrinsic and necessary connection between women and Nature that made preindustrial cultures ecologically healthier than industrial ones, but rather from anxieties about a political order that, especially after the Civil War, seemed increasingly in danger of fragmentation and chaos. The monarchial political order that was restored after 1660 required, but was increasingly anxious about, patrilineage, an order specifically dependent on the control of female sexuality and on the naturalization of that control. In this regard, then, I am interested in the ways in which talk that connects Nature and female sexuality can and must be talk about politics.

Because Behn's position as a woman libertine is not symmetrical with the male playwright's libertinism, she can call attention to those places where the linkages among sexuality, economics, politics, and art are erased—most notably in the critical commonplace that sees art as the imitation of Nature, the same Nature that in Merchant's history of science is increasingly mechanized and fragmented. The anxieties Behn plays on in her dedications and epistles linking the female playwright with the "newfangled whore" that female chastity and female identity might be fragmented and bartered piecemeal are directly linked, I would argue, to the anxieties expressed by many seventeenth-century critics that poetry—and by extension all literature—will fragment Nature and barter it piecemeal by creating endlessly reproducible simulacra. This anxiety fuels the debate about Nature in "An Essay of Dramatic Poesy," and indeed all Dryden's work seems representative of how this anxiety was managed by the seventeenth-century male critic. All the interlocutors agree that a play is—or ought to be—a "lively imitation of Nature" (17:44), although they do not agree on what they mean by it. All feel the need to reassert the truth of a providential design that orders and controls Nature, making it whole and organic. Neander sees dramatic poetry as reproducing an ideal Nature whole, intact, and complete, but also heightened: "Nature wrought up to a higher pitch." Crites, however, worries that Nature is "torn and ill represented" on the contemporary stage: "the ancients have handed down to us a perfect resemblance of her; which we, like ill Coyers, neglecting to look on, have rendered monstrous and disfigur'd" (17:16). Lisideius criticizes Shakespeare because what he does is not "to imitate or paint Nature, but rather to draw her in miniature, to take her in little; to look upon her through the wrong end of a Perspective, and receive her Images not only much less, but infinitely more imperfect than in life: this, instead of making a Play delightful, renders it ridiculous" (17:36). Their concerns about incomplete and fragmented representations of Nature are echoed in other critical statements by Dryden that suggest the difficulties of representing "Nature in disorder," a more chaotic and less idealized version of Nature. In his dedication of *The Rival Ladies* to Orrery, Dryden conceives of Nature as "a thing so almost Infinite, and Boundless, as can never fully be Comprehended, but where the Images of all things are always present" (8:97). Like women, Nature is so chaotic that the poet cannot simply describe "her" but must "constitute it as a complex entity which must be brought into line with his critical and ideological values."[27] In much the same way, Merchant argues the mechanists had to suppress views of nature that stressed its disorder, anarchy, change, uncertainty, and unpredictability in favor of those that were compatible with order, control, and manipulation.[28]

Dryden's use of the pronoun "her" in "An Essay of Dramatic Poesy" makes manifest what is otherwise implicit in most seventeenth-century pronouncements about Nature: the Nature poets imitate and scientists scrutinize is female and anxieties about Nature being fragmented and incompletely reproduced correspond to anxieties about women's identities and bodies being fragmented and exchanged in "a gender specific version of possessive individualism."[29] Nature intact means hymens intact, which will preserve estates intact; the debate over the poetry's imitation of Nature naturalizes socially mandated gender roles in the service of a distinct political and economic agenda. This complex series of historical connections is erased in the seventeenth-century literary criticism reproduced in most anthologies, which abstract criticism from the matrix of social institutions, cultural conflict, and discursive heteroglossia that produced it. In the final section I examine the sociopolitical contexts that framed these politically charged debates and the grounds on which the meanings of the key terms of late-seventeenth-century literary criticism—imitation, nature, and moral utility—were contested.

III

It is not enough, however, to consider Behn's literary criticism only synchronically, as of a piece throughout a career that lasted nearly two decades. Some diachronic analysis is required to show the ways in which her thinking about her art and about the debates that fueled seventeenth-century criticism developed and changed. As Deborah C. Payne has argued, Behn's career as a literary critic falls roughly into two periods, divided by the Exclusion Crisis and marked respectively by her two most sustained pieces of critical writing: the "Epistle to the Reader," which prefaces *The Dutch Lover* (1673), and the prefatory material (both dedication and preface) to *The Lucky Chance*, written toward the end of her career (1686).[30] In these two texts we can chart the development of Behn's critical attitudes toward the fashionable literary debates of her day; in particular we may begin to see the political connections she forges between debates about the imitation of nature and the claims for poetry's moral utility.

The "Epistle to the Reader," a preface to Behn's third play, dates from the period of her life in which Behn was attempting to establish a name for herself in the extremely competitive world of the theater without the support of a powerful patron.[31] In this work she takes advantage of her position as a marginalized outsider—both because of her sex and because of her lack of patronage—to criticize the newly emerging avocation of criticism and the proliferation of critics, those "whiffling would-be Wits of the Town, . . . whose Business it is to find Fault" (1:222). She lampoons them with withering scorn in the character of "a long, lither, phlegmatick, white, ill-favour'd, wretched Fop" (1:223) who attempts to cry down her play and who becomes the image for all the hostility directed toward it. She uses her witty address to the "good, Sweet, Honey, Sugar-Candied Reader" both to mock the hypocrisy of poets' claims of moral utility and to proclaim her loyalty to the libertine philosophy of pleasure.

The opening passages begin the task of undercutting, with savage irony, the lofty claims of the fashionable literary theory of the day. The wheedling address to the "good, Sweet, Honey, Sugar-Candied Reader" is turned back on itself; Behn has no intention of attempting to ingratiate herself into her readers' good graces. Instead she punctures their self-importance. Her treatise will not divert them from more important intellectual pursuits because "I presume you have not much to do and therefore are to be obliged to me for keeping you from worse employment." She parodies the philosophically dense and incomprehensible language of fashionable intellectual debate.

> Indeed, had I hung a sign of the Immortality of the Soul, of the Mystery of Godliness, or of Ecclesiastical Policie, and then had treated you with Indiscerpibility and Essential Spissitude (words, which though I am no competent Judge of, for want of Languages, yet I fancy strongly ought to mean just nothing) with a company of Apocryphal midnight Tales cull'd of the choicest Insignificant Authors; if I had only proved in Folio that Apolonius was a naughty knave, or had presented you with two or three of the worst principles transcrib'd out of the peremptory and ill-natur'd (though prettily ingenious) Doctor of Malmsbury [Hobbes] undigested and ill-manag'd by a silly, saucy, ignorant, impertinent, ill educated Chaplain I were then indeed sufficiently in fault (1:221)

The "Epistle" exposes the aristocratic and elitist ideologies underpinning of literary theory because, at this point in her career, Behn has no stake in upholding them. Unlike Dryden, who, in "An Essay of

Dramatic Poesy," charts the evolution of the modern stage from classical antiquity, sprinkling his argument liberally with Latin and Greek quotations, Behn had everything to gain from separating her profession—the writing of plays—from literary activities that required a university education and knowledge of Greek and Latin, knowledge from which she was barred by her sex. "For waving the examination why women having equal education with men, were not as capable of knowledge, of whatsoever sort as well as they: I'll only say as I have touch'd before, that Plays have no great room for that which is men's great advantage over women, that is Learning" (1:224).[32] If Behn could not have access to the kind of education that would enable her to enter debates about poetry's utility on the intellectual terms set by the classical tradition, she could attempt to reposition the argument of her own terms, dismissing her "want of letters" as irrelevant.

She rejects the extravagant intellectual and moral claims made for poetry: "I would not undervalue Poetry, so neither am I altogether of their judgement who believe no wisdom in the world beyond it" (1:221). Perhaps the most outrageous claim made for the drama, she argues, is that of its moral utility. As a response to attacks on the immorality of the theater, Restoration critics attempted to use the authority of classical texts to defend the theater from charges that it was obscene and blasphemous. The authority for this position was located in Horace's *Art of Poetry:* "The aim of the poet is to inform or delight, or to combine together in what he says, both pleasure and applicability to life." This statement—that the purpose of literature is to delight and instruct (*dulce et utilite*)—has been repeated so often in the history of Western criticism that it has come to be known as the Horatian platitude. Certainly by the seventeenth century it had attained the status of an unexamined axiom; it is cited by virtually every literary critic of the period. Yet such commonplaces about the moral utility of literature obscure their own complicity in defining what "morality" is and how it is deployed. It is worth noting that Horace was more forthright about the economic and material basis of his advice than most of his English and Continental followers. In a less-well-known passage from the *Art of Poetry,* a few lines after the platitude, he writes that a book that both instructs and delights "is the sort of book that will make money for the publisher."[33] But because Behn had been denied access to the education that would have indoctrinated her into this "educated" view of literature, she can expose the economic underpinnings of the seemingly simple and presumably inoffensive statement that literature should instruct and delight. "I am myself well able to affirm that none of all our English Poets, and least the Dramatique (so I think you call them) can be justly charg'd with too great reformation of men's minds or manners, and for that I may appeal to general experiment, if those who are the most assiduous Disciples of the Stage, do not make the fondest and the lewdest Crew about this Town" (1:222). She continues, "I will have leave to say that in my judgement the increasing number of our latter Plays have not done much more towards the amending of men's Morals, or their Wit." In this indictment of those who hide behind the emptiness of the Horatian platitude rather than acknowledge their political interestedness, Behn exposes seventeenth-century criticism's reliance on the imitation and appropriation of received authorities, particularly the master texts of classical antiquity, which presented arguments about literature and morality that buttressed the ideologies of the educated and ruling elite, an elite to which Behn desired access in spite of her exclusion from it. Knowledge of Greek and Latin was a mark of membership in this class. As both a woman and, at this point in her career, a socially marginal professional writer, Behn did not have access to the classical education that would have given her an ideological investment in the Horatian argument about literature's moral utility.[34] She was, however, able to see the political purposes "instruction" could be made to serve.

She could also see that the debate over poetry's moral utility connected with arguments about the poet's imitation of Nature as both became the signs of membership in a ruling elite. For the classically educated seventeenth-century critic, the Nature the poet imitated was the ideal, not the real. Nature corresponded to God's providential plan. Sir Philip Sidney, for instance, writes in "An Apology for Poetry" that "right poets" "imitate to teach and delight, and to imitate borrow nothing of what is, hath been, or shall be; but range, only reined with learned discretion, into the divine consideration of what may be or should be."[35] This view of imitation argues that the purpose of the poet is ultimately to affirm the providential rule of justice and order and by extension the justice and order of the ruling class. In her discussion of imitation, Behn argues that the "Nature" displayed by playwrights is neither ideal nor worthy of imitation. Of tragedy she says "You'll find their best of Characters unlikely patterns for a wise man to pursue," primarily because far from imitating Nature, these characters are wildly improbable. Of comedy she writes "The finest folks you meet with there are still unfitter for your imitation (1:223). For Behn drama is about neither the imitation of Nature nor the reformation of morals; it is finally about pleasure: "In short, I think a Play the best divertisement that wise men have: but I do also think them nothing so who do discourse as formallie about the rules of it, as if 'twere the grand affair of human life" (1:223). The "musty rules of Unity" (1:224) that are the subject of so much debate in "An Essay of Dramatic Poesy" she dismisses as meaningless. She strips away the "Academick frippery" that surrounded the debate over the three unities, reminding us that far more important than the structural unity of a play's plot is the competence of the actors who perform it. The material practices of the theater—from the patron who promises an epilogue to an actor who "spoke but little of what I intended for him" (1:224)—that transform a play from an inscription to a performance are in Behn's preface as fit a subject for criticism as the "musty rules of Unity."

Moving from the witty assertiveness of this preface to the dedication of Behn's *Lucky Chance* to Laurence Hyde, Earl of Rochester, thirteen years later, one is struck by the difference in tone. Gone is the bantering wit, which would, of course, be unseemly in a serious dedication. Gone also is the devotion to the politics of libertine pleasure (despite the bawdiness of the play itself, which is probably one of Behn's most cynical comedies). In the dedication Behn links her play to the "Ancient and Honourable" history of the theater, placing it within a distinctly classical tradition of civic virtue—of "the most Illustrious Persons of *Greece* and *Rome*"—the very tradition she had rejected in her preface to *The Dutch Lover.* The Horatian platitude and the notion of poetic justice that Behn had criticized as hypocrisy in the earlier preface dominate this dedication. Plays are not simply amusements but "the Schools of Vertue, where Vice is always either punish't or disdain'd." They are "secret Instructions to the People" (3:183).

Two events might account for Behn's more orthodox and less

irreverent tone in this dedication. The first is that by 1686 Behn was simply a less-marginal playwright than she had been earlier in her career; the woman writer less a novelty. She was both successful and prolific despite her sex and despite the financial difficulties that caused the two London theaters to merge in 1682. Behn had secured the favor of more powerful patrons, who, judging from her dedications, included the Duke of York, the King's illegitimate son Henry Fitz-roy, Nell Gwyn, and the Earl of Rochester. The second cause of this change in tone is that Behn had undoubtedly been chastened by her experiences of the political witch-hunts that accompanied the Exclusion Crisis. In 1682 Behn had been briefly arrested for an epilogue she had written chastising the Duke of Monmouth for his desertion of his father, the king.[36] Like many of her contemporaries, she had learned the dangers of writing politically charged invective.

In her preface to the play, Behn's primary defense of her comedies and those of her contemporaries against the charge that they were obscene is to resort to what Harriet Hawkins has called the "example theory" of literature.[37] As I suggested earlier, during the seventeenth century all literary critics who had received a classical education argue that poetry must serve some moral agenda. Literature, however, to imitate Nature most fully, must represent not only the good, the beautiful, and the true, but also the wicked, the ugly, and the cruel. The latter often manage to capture readers' sympathies and imaginations more effectively than the former. Defenses against the charge that literature makes evil seem attractive usually take the form of redirecting that evil to serve moral ends. Evil is as much a part of life as good and so must be represented, but only as part of a larger vision in which good is ultimately rewarded and evil punished. Although in the preface to the *Dutch Lover* Behn rejected this appeal to the morality of proper imitation, in this later preface she turns to the example theory as a means to justify her comic practice, which she says is "proper to the Characters"; "they so naturally fall into the places they are designed for, and so are proper for the Business that there is not the least Fault to be found with them" (3:186). At this point in her career, it serves her purpose of defending "my Masculine part, the Poet in me" to characterize herself as the equal of her male contemporaries and to place herself within a long and primarily classical tradition of dramatic criticism.

Still, it would be a mistake simply to read this dedication as a retreat to a complacent orthodoxy. Behn's articulation of the Horatian platitude that literature must delight and instruct only *seems* to bring her criticism in line with the more conventional concerns of late-seventeenth-century criticism, at least as they have been defined by twentieth-century histories of criticism. Behn does not, for instance, lay claim to the disinterested objectivity—the role of detached observer—that has been the hallmark of European literary criticism,[38] nor does she argue in favor merely of a kind of abstract and watered-down moral instruction. The purposes to which plays must be put are, for Behn, still primarily political and highly interested: "Plays have been ever held most important to the very Political Part of Government." It is their function to strengthen the state by inculcating political and civic virtues. "'tis Example alone that inspires Morality, and best establishes Vertue, I have my self known a Man, whom neither Conscience nor Religion cou'd perswade to Loyalty, who with beholding in our Theatre a Modern Politician set forth in all his Colours, was converted, renounc'd his opinion, and quitted the Party" (3:183). For Behn, then, literature is part of a self-conscious program of political indoctrination that creates better citizens whose primary virtue is their loyalty to king and country.

In the preface to *The Lucky Chance,* Behn's most orthodox statement about literature, in which she declares her desire to "tread in those successful Paths my Predecessors have so long thriv'd in, to take those Measures that both the Ancient and Modern Writers have set me" (3:187), Behn reveals most fully the interested ends of disinterested criticism. She directly links the argument that literature serves moral ends to the institution of patronage, demonstrating the ways in which the drama served the moral ends of the ruling elites; because "Plays and publick Diversions were thought by the Greatest and Wisest of States, one of the most essential Parts of good Government, and in which so many great Persons were interested. . . . By right of Antient Custom, the Patronage of Plays belong'd only to the Great Men, and chiefest Magistrates" (3:183). Both drama and the patronage that supports it are important, because both serve the public good, reproducing and reinforcing existing power relations. Although common sense (or, more likely, the ideological division of labor between creative and critical writing) may suggest that criticism is secondary, a supplement to the drama, the preface to *The Lucky Chance* exposes the intricate web of exchanges among drama, the criticism of drama, and the patronage of drama, each circularly producing and being produced by the other two.

Behn's prefaces and dedications do represent, then, a coherent, if dynamic and changing, body of literary criticism. They show that the literary culture of the late seventeenth century, far from being a "disinterested endeavor to learn and propagate the best that is known and thought," was a thoroughly political and highly interested institution, completely involved in the political intrigues of the day. The drama, and criticism of it, served as an arena of cultural conflict, and Behn, far from being an anomaly because of her sex, in fact, participated in the very same debates and conflicts that occupied her male contemporaries, even if, because her sex positioned her differently, she approached those debates from a very different perspective. Behn's criticism, however, has not proven as amenable as that of her contemporaries, like Dryden, to appropriation by twentieth-century productions of literary criticism's tradition because her work does not lend itself easily to the tradition's erasure of historical contingency. Behn's literary criticism, then, becomes a means not only of countering women's silencing in literary theory but also of restoring to literary criticism its own history of turbulence, conflict, struggle, and ideological and political debate, a much-needed antidote to the static histories of criticism so prominent in contemporary anthologies. This history of literary criticism I am proposing, although certainly messier than the one traditionally taught, might also be more interesting and less dead.

Notes

1. Lawrence Lipking, "Aristotle's Sister: A Poetics of Abandonment," *Critical Inquiry* 10 (1983): 61; Hazard Adams, *Critical Theory since Plato* (New York: Harcourt Brace Jovanovich, 1971). Lipking writes, "Adams assures me that any future edition of this anthology will contain at least one woman" (p. 79 n. 2). The new edition (1992) now includes two women before 1900: Mary Wollstonecraft and Madame de Staël. The perusal of several other recent anthologies yields little more. The second edition of Charles Kaplan's *Criticism: The Major Statements* (New York: St. Martin's Press, 1986) includes only one

woman between the fifth century B.C. and the twentieth century who made a "major statement" about literature: Adrienne Rich. The third edition (1991) includes several twentieth-century women who have contributed to literary criticism, from Virginia Woolf to Barbara Johnson, but no women before the twentieth century. Another St. Martin's anthology, *The Critical Tradition: Classic Texts and Contemporary Trends,* ed. David H. Richter, (New York: St. Martin's Press, 1989) includes only Madame de Staël before the twentieth century.

2. For an anthology of literary criticism that attempts to reconceptualize this exclusion, see Robert Con Davis and Laurie Finke, eds., *Literary Criticism and Theory: The Greeks to the Present* (New York: Longman, 1989).

3. James Engell, *Forming the Critical Mind: Dryden to Coleridge* (Cambridge: Harvard Univ. Press, 1989).

4. For another view of Dryden's literary criticism that stresses his immersion in the literary, political, and religious anxieties of his day, see Robert Markley, *Two-Edg'd Weapons: Style and Ideology in the Comedies of Etherege, Wycherley, and Congreve* (Oxford: Clarendon Press, 1988), pp. 78–99. It is worth pointing out that to argue this point of view Markley must turn to those critical documents that have most often been excluded from traditional histories of criticism: the preface to *An Evening's Love* and "Annus Mirabilis" and his dedication of *Rival Ladies* to Orrery.

5. Laurie Finke, *Feminist Theory, Women's Writing* (Ithaca: Cornell Univ. Press, 1992), pp. 22–28.

6. Matthew Arnold, "The Function of Criticism at the Present Time," in Davis and Finke, *Literary Criticism and Theory,* pp. 513, 507.

7. By modality I refer to the linguistic markers that designate the status, authority, and reliability of an utterance, those markers that confer or deny the truth of the utterance; see Robert Hodge and Gunther Kress, *Social Semiotics* (Ithaca: Cornell Univ. Press, 1988), pp. 121–61.

8. All citations to Behn's prefaces are from the edition prepared by Montague Summers, *The Works of Aphra Behn,* 6 vols. (1915, rpt. New York: Benjamin Blom, 1967), 1:337. Subsequent references to this edition will be cited parenthetically in the text by volume and page number.

9. Pierre Bourdieu, *Outline of a Theory of Practice,* trans. Richard Nice (Cambridge and New York: Cambridge Univ. Press, 1977), p. 178. Deborah Payne revises Paul Korshin's argument that patronage was being replaced in the late seventeenth and early eighteenth centuries by a market system of literary production by showing that the resources patrons provided for their clients were less financial than symbolic, but that such "symbolic capital" was an essential ingredient for success in the theatrical world of the Restoration. For an analysis of the symbolic economies at work in the dedicatory epistle during the Restoration see Deborah C. Payne, in "The Restoration Dramatic Dedication as Symbolic Capital," *Revisionist Readings of the Restoration and Eighteenth-Century Theatre,* ed. J. Douglas Canfield and Deborah C. Payne (forthcoming); Paul Korshin, "Types of Eighteenth-Century Literary Patronage," *Eighteenth-Century Studies* 7 (1973–74): 453–73.

10. This phenomenon is evidenced by its nearly universal inclusion in anthologies of literary criticism; I have not found a single anthology of the history of criticism that does not include Dryden's "An Essay of Dramatic Poesy."

11. John Dryden, "An Essay of Dramatic Poesy," in *The Works of John Dryden,* ed. H. T. Swedenberg, Jr., et al., 19 vols. (Berkeley: Univ. of California Press, 1971), 17:5. Subsequent references to this edition will be cited parenthetically in the text by volume and page number.

12. It is worth remembering that at about the same time (the period of the Dutch Wars), Aphra Behn was serving in Holland as a spy for Charles II under the direction of Thomas Killigrew.

13. The term (ambiguously) *nonhegemonic* is used by Rachel Blau DuPlessis to describe women's ambiguous participation in patriarchy; see "For the Etruscans: Sexual Difference and Artistic Production," in *The Future of Difference,* ed. Hester Eisenstein and Alice Jardine (Boston: G. K. Hall, 1980), pp. 128–56. Women remain "outside of the dominant systems of meaning, value, and power" (p. 147). Yet, because of the nature of hegemony, women are frequently internally oriented toward hegemonic norms in what DuPlessis calls a "painful double dance." This doubleness, I would argue, characterized Behn's critical perspectives.

14. As, for instance, Angeline Goreau maintains in her biography of Behn, *Reconstructing Aphra: A Social Biography of Aphra Behn* (New York: Dial Press, 1980).

15. Catherine Gallagher, "Who Was That Masked Woman? The Prostitute and the Playwright in the Comedies of Aphra Behn," *Women's Studies* 15 (1988): 27. (This essay is reprinted below in this volume.) Several other feminist scholars of seventeenth-century literature have also pointed this out. See Katherine Eisaman Maus, " 'Playhouse Flesh and Blood': Sexual Ideology and the Restoration Actress," *ELH* 46 (1979): 595–617; Goreau, *Reconstructing Aphra,* pp. 23–42; and Jessica Munns, " 'I by a Double Right Thy Bounties Claim': Aphra Behn and Sexual Space," in *Curtain Calls: British and American Women and the Theater, 1660–1820,* ed. Mary Anne Schofield and Cecelia Macheski (Athens: Ohio Univ. Press, 1991), pp. 193–210.

16. Mary Ellmann, *Thinking about Women* (New York: Harcourt, Brace, and World, 1968), p. 29.

17. The term *poaching* is Michel de Certeau's and describes the ways in which individuals subjected to practices designed to oppress them manipulate and shape those practices to their own ends by seeming to conform to them; see *The Practice of Everyday Life,* trans. Steven F. Rendall (Berkeley: Univ. of California Press, 1984). Gallagher has made this argument about Behn's exploitation of the connection between playwright and prostitute ("Who Was That Masked Woman?" pp. 23–30); see also Deborah C. Payne, " 'And Poets Shall by Patron-Princes Live': Aphra Behn and Patronage," in *Curtain Calls,* ed. Schofield and Macheski, pp. 111–14, 116–17, for a critique of Gallagher's argument.

18. For an analysis that links sexual promiscuity and linguistic excess, see Howard Bloch, "Medieval Misogyny," *Representations* 20 (1987): 1–14.

19. Payne, "'And Poets Shall by Patron-Princes Live,'" pp. 116–17.

20. See Mary Poovey, *The Proper Lady and the Woman Writer: Ideology as Style in the Works of Mary Wollstonecraft, Mary Shelley, and Jane Austen* (Chicago: Univ. of Chicago Press, 1984), and Nancy Cotton, *Women Playwrights in England c. 1363–1750* (Lewisburg, Pa.: Bucknell Univ. Press, 1980).

21. On the political, historical, and sexual aspects of the rake, see James G. Turner, "The Properties of Libertinism," *Eighteenth-Century Life* 9 (1985): 75–87, and Randolph Trumbach, "Sodomy Transformed: Aristocratic Libertinage, Public Reputation, and the Gender Revolution of the 18th Century," *Journal of Homosexuality* 19 (1990): 105–24.

22. Gallagher, "Who Was That Masked Woman?" p. 24.

23. Goreau describes in detail in *Reconstructing Aphra* the grim alternatives for a woman's response to libertinism. She cites the example of the actress Elizabeth Farley, who "caught the King's eye" and ended up as a notorious and impoverished prostitute (pp. 173–74), as well as Behn's own troublesome affair with John Hoyle (pp. 191–206). Wives fared little better. Goreau also describes the fate often suffered by wives during the Restoration who, having bartered themselves away to husbands in legal marriage, found themselves immured alone on country estates while their husbands caroused in London (p. 176).

24. Gallagher, "Who Was That Masked Woman?" p. 25.

25. Munns, "'I by a Double Right Thy Bounties Claim,'" pp. 195–96.

26. See especially Evelyn Fox Keller, *Reflections on Gender and Science* (New Haven: Yale Univ. Press, 1985), and Carolyn Merchant, *The Death of Nature: Women, Ecology, and the Scientific Revolution* (San Francisco: Harper and Row, 1980).

27. Markley, *Two-Edg'd Weapons*, p. 79.

28. Merchant, *Death of Nature*, pp. 194–95.

29. Gallagher, "Who Was That Masked Woman?" p. 29.

30. Payne, "'And Poets Shall by Patron-Princes Live,'" pp. 109–10.

31. Ibid., pp. 110–11.

32. For a description of the kind of education received by most women during the seventeenth century, see Goreau, *Reconstructing Aphra*, pp. 24–40.

33. Davis and Finke, *Literary Criticism and Theory*, pp. 99–100.

34. Nonetheless, Behn points out that it would not require an education in the classics to articulate the position (1:121). Her verses to Thomas Creech on his translation of Lucretius's *De Rerum Natura*, however, reveal something of her anxieties about the inadequacy of her education:

> Till now, I curst my Birth, my Education,
> And more the scanted Customes of the Nation:
> Permitting not the Female Sex to tread,
> The mighty Paths of Learned Heroes dead.
> The God-like *Virgil* and great *Homers* Verse,
> Like Divine Mysteries are conceal'd from us.
> We are forbid all greateful theams
> No ravishing thoughts approach our Ear,

The Fulsome Gingle of the times,
Is all we are allow'd to understand or hear. (6:220)

35. Sir Philip Sidney, "An Apology for Criticism," in Davis and Finke, *Literary Criticism and Theory,* p. 203.

36. Payne, "Aphra Behn and Literary Patronage," pp. 114–16, and Goreau, *Reconstructing Aphra,* p. 251.

37. Harriet Hawkins, "The 'Example Theory' and the Providentialist Approach to Restoration Drama: Some Questions of Validity and Applicability," *Eighteenth Century: Theory and Interpretation* 24 (1983): 103–14.

38. Kristina Straub, "Women, Gender, and Criticism," in Davis and Finke, *Literary Criticism and Theory,* pp. 855–76.

JESSICA MUNNS

"Good, Sweet, Honey, Sugar-Candied Reader": Aphra Behn's Foreplay in Forewords

"**G**ood, Sweet, Honey, Sugar-Candied Reader": immediately after this honeyed salute in the "Epistle to the Reader" prefixing the published text of *The Dutch Lover* (1673), Behn adds, "which I think is more than anyone has called you yet."[1] As she continues the opening sentence, she makes it clear that her flattering address was a ruse: "I must have a word or two with you before you do advance into the Treatise." It is not a "Treatise," however, that the reader will advance into, but a comic play, and, having caught the reader's attention with a series of misleading signals, Behn now moves into the attack. She will not "beg your pardon for diverting you from your affairs" and instead urges readers with something better to do to "get you gone about your business." If, however, no such business calls, the reader is "obliged to me from keeping you from worse employment." Explaining jokes is always a pedantic process guaranteed to remove all humor, but if this first sentence is unpacked, it discloses a complex series of rhetorical gestures and cultural assumptions—as is true of any piece of writing—that sustain and characterize the flirtation and irony of Behn's approach.

I

The very form of address, "Good, Sweet, Honey, Sugar-Candied Reader," draws attention to itself initially by its inappropriateness. It is always difficult to assess the precise tenor of informal language, but this, if not the language of the boudoir, is certainly familiar in tone. In contrast, the final term, "Reader," introduces an unfamiliar and unknown quantity where we might expect Tom, Dick, or even Harry to be recipient of the author's affectionate salutation. The greeting signals a mild social and rhetorical transgression, which is the very stuff of wit and flirtation. The follow-up, in which the writer points out that this is an unusual, if not unique form of address, draws attention to the transgression and proceeds to set other processes in motion. If the come-on of the affectionate address is a tickle, the blunt statement that the reader has not been called this term before is in the nature of a slap and suggests that the reader probably does not deserve affection. The next phrase, "I must have a word or two with you before you do advance," reveals that the whole structure has been a delaying device, which in turn discloses the writer's belief that unusual means are necessary to get the reader's attention. From opacity and pretence the author moves to apparent transparency and honesty. As a part of this move, the writer strips off a layer of her rhetorical clothes and invites a new intimacy given that we all recognize what she is doing and why.

The final part of the sentence takes the reader a long way from the initial caress. Behn moves from an importunately overfamiliar address to a stranger, which would put her in the reader's debt, to the assertion that the very fact of reading these words indicates our need for her and our obligation to her. In fact, far from being a close friend or lover, the reader is being constituted as an adversary, more mildly, as a careless, easily bored and hasty reader who tends to skip things like epistles and prefaces moving straight to the main text and neglecting the foreplay of forewords. The epistle insists that a preliminary skirmish or two is desirable, that the reader—first addressed as an intimate then revealed as a stranger—must, bit by bit, be made into an acquaintance.

I come now to a significant aspect of the author's voice in these opening moves: it is a woman's voice, and, as such, is both playing and refusing to play traditional female games. The over-affectionate baby talk address is female in its winsome sweetness and sues for attention through flattery, but the follow-ups all undo the saccharine opening and move the female author from below to, as it were, on top of the reader. The reader, I suggest, is not only constituted in the terms I have already suggested, as a possible adversary, but as male. A male reader might like to pretend that he is reading a "Treatise," not an idle play, or might like to believe that he has "business" he could attend to (and only men have business), or might, as the epistle later indicates, like members of the initial audience, condemn the work because it was written by a woman. Gendering the reader, Behn also genders herself in a reaction formation that allows her to flatter and insult her reader-victim. In playing the overly affectionate female card and then reversing it, however, Behn is not merely surprising her reader out of male complacency but also flirting in approved Restoration style, in which insults and reversals, masking and unmasking, are essential elements in sex-war titillation.[2]

After the initial attention-grabbing opening sentence, Behn produces a long-winded philosophical series of clauses moving from the "Immortality of the Soul" to "Indiscerpibility and Essential Spissitude" to illustrate subjects on which she has *not* written. After the latter phrase she inserts a parenthetical comment and describes these as "words, which though I am no competent Judge of, for want of Languages, yet I fancy strongly ought to mean just nothing." Of course she is a perfectly competent judge, with or without the male insignia of learning, languages (i.e., Latin and Greek, the learned languages), and as she denies her adequacy, she asserts it.[3] Behn frequently refers to her female ignorance: she will not absolutely assert that poetry was in ancient times the form in which science was expressed because "my want of letters makes me less assured of [this] than others happily may be." But since it turns out that all poetry did was "propagate so many idle superstitions," Behn has postulated the preeminence of poetry over science only to deflate both forms. Similarly, she will not list the subjects studied at university "lest I misspell them" (1:221–22)—but because it turns out that academic study is absurd, what would be the virtue in correctly spelling nonsense? Behn indicates that being gendered out of the arena of learned debate is no loss—yet the repetitious, if mocking, references to her inability to enter the male debates remain in place, even as Behn does, in fact, enter the debates of the arts and the sciences, the universities and the world. The author dances lightly on the margins, making her occasional forays into the center only to deny its centrality. The whole process of debate is turned into a flirtation of reversals, as she denies that she is serious and then denies that the serious is serious.

Behn constructs a similar double assertion-denial stance as she claims that her work is not like the learned works she has indicated in her mimic male and serious language. Her work is inscribed on the title page as a "comedy," and therefore the reader may "guess pretty nearly what penny-worths you are like to have." But in a countermove she also asserts that she "would not yet be understood to lessen the dignity of Playes," and she claims for plays "a place among the middle if not better sort of Books." This is indeed the margin making claims to the center, to the middle ground, but that in itself is not enough for Behn, who goes on to argue (and who are we to deny it) that "most of that which bears the name of Learning . . . and continually employs so many ignorant, unhappy souls for ten, twelve, twenty years in the University (who yet poor wretches think they are doing something all the while) . . . are much more absolutely nothing than the errantest Play that e'er was writ" (1:221).

Not content with claiming a space in the middle ground of "better books," Behn displaces the learning emanating from the exclusively male universities, characterizing it as insubstantial, pathetic, and misguided. In many ways, she is on safe ground here: The ignorant gownman, as opposed to the worldly Londoner, was a standard satiric-comic figure. But my concern is less with the "safeness" of her targets, the dowdy, foolish scholar or, later, an ignorant and arrogant fop, than with her rhetorical manipulations as she shifts categories of gender and "high" and "low," polite and vulgar discourses, across invisible but palpable lines of demarcation.[4] These shifts produce surprises and reversals that both valorize and diminish Behn's claim to a place in the literary marketplace.

Having mocked the "Academick frippery" that lays claim to a privileged position in the discourse of learning, we expect the poet to defend poetry. Far from doing so, Behn denies the classical defense of poetry as the sugar pill for moral precepts, stating dryly, "I am myself well able to affirm that none of all our English Poets, and least the Dramatique (so I think you call them) can be justly charg'd with too great reformation of men's minds or manners" (1:222). The denial of drama's moral authority, although it weakens the status of the genre in which Behn works, strengthens her claim to its practice. With all the retreats into mock-modest parentheses, reversals, disclaimers, and asides, Behn's rhetorical postures move her to the position in which she can assert that the aim of drama is entertainment and that as a woman she is as well equipped to provide such entertainment as anyone else.

It is in Behn's interest to deny academic pretension to drama even as she must also assert the viability of drama as a literary form. In a typically convoluted sentence in which the disclaimed represents the central issue of how gender is constructed, Behn argues that "waving the examination why women having equal education with men, were not as capable of knowledge, of whatsoever sort as well as they: I'll only say as I have touch'd before, that Plays have no great room for that which is men's great advantage over women, that is Learning" (1:224). Later in the same paragraph, Behn mocks male attempts to mystify and appropriate drama to learning with "their musty rules of Unity, and God knows what besides" and asserts that "if they meant anything, they are enough intelligible and as practible by a woman." Behn is not content, however, merely to establish drama as an area of literary practice unmarked by the characteristics of male discourse, classical learning, and a high moral tone. She also argues that if "Plays have not done much more towards the amending of men's Morals, or their Wit," then neither has "the frequent Preaching, with which this last age hath been pester'd with" (1:222). Once again, the play is set against the category of the serious in an apparent distinction that is quickly erased.

Behn needed to confuse categories and seduce her readers. *The Dutch Lover* had been unsuccessful in performance. Nancy Cotton has noted that Behn did not have any plays produced, at least not under her name, for the next three years.[5] Behn explains that the play was badly dressed and incompetently acted and complains that a particularly foolish and offensive male member of the audience, whom she refers to as a "thing," remarked "that they were to expect a woeful Play, God damn him, for it was a woman's" (1:224). For all its jauntiness, anger and anxiety mark the prefatory epistle to *The Dutch Lover,* as Behn works to cancel out the remark made by the "thing." His remark, almost buried in the description of his pitiful vanity and stupidity, is the true pretext of this pre-text. As in a dream, the most significant material is buried but also surfaces in different but related forms at all points as Behn plays with her and our sex, moving restlessly between the cultural inscriptions of gender that prompted and enabled the remark. What we are reading, the epistle, and what we will read, the play, are written by a woman.

And, writing within this reading, Behn takes us on a circular tour: Women are not educated and plays are not learned; men are educated and academic treatises are learned; but educated men are also ignorant and academic discourse is absurd. Plays are as good as treatises—but treatises are not very good. Plays entertain and sermons preach—but neither improve morals. Women are denied education, and if they had it they would be as clever as men—but educated men are not, after all, very clever. The circularity of the arguments and their constant doubling back into themselves take us to a point of aporia: in terms of language and logic/illogic, which is all we have, we can go no further. It is perhaps the essence of flirtation that it is a come-on with no coming.[6] Yet this foreplay does lead to a play: in her final sentence, Behn wishes the reader an airy "adieu" and admits that she has now "eas'd her mind"—a verb that suggests evacuation—and the reader is released, a little less sugar-candied than before, to the play text. Whether or not the reader is satisfied, the author is sated.

Behn's prologues similarly employ strategies of seduction. A prologue must soften up and please the audience, and coquettish insults—whether written by a man or a woman—as much as lavish flattery, are undoubtedly typical of the mode.[7] Prologues are more specifically directed, more goal oriented, however, than prefatory remarks, which allow the author a range of digressions and personal reflections inappropriate to the purposes of settling an audience in their seats.[8] Behn's dedicatory epistles to aristocratic patrons, which are dominated by the correct and civil address used for members of the nobility, are also less personal and less outrageous than her general prefaces. Even so, when not laying the flattery on with a trowel, the epistle dedicatory of *The Lucky Chance* (1687) takes the occasion to address Lawrence Hyde, Earl of Rochester, with a discourse on the status of plays in the ancient and modern world before going on in a general preface to discuss the prejudices the woman writer faces. Dedications to less elevated figures allow for more wit, free play, and sexuality, as in the sprightly dedication of *The Young King; or, the Mistake* (1679) to "Philaster" or the rather weary dedication of the prose fiction, *The Fair Jilt* (1688), to Henry Paine, which begins "Dedications are like Love, and no Man of Wit or Eminence escapes them" (5:70).[9] It is, however, in the general prefaces and epistles to readers that Behn's prefatory writing has most scope, urgency, and energy.

In later epistles to readers, we can hear more anger and frustration and less flirtation and persuasion than in the epistle to *The Dutch Lover,* as Behn struggles with the absurd sexual dialectics and economic constraints of her position. Despite the success of a play like *The Rover* (1677), whose combination of lively action and adroit cavalier flattery allowed Behn to dedicate the follow-up, *The Rover,* part II (1681), to the Duke of York, consistent court patronage eluded her. Without private means and some regular patronage, courtly or otherwise, a writer of this period was obliged to keep up a high rate of literary production. The writer could hope for good third-night receipts at the theater, a few guineas from the bookseller for printing, and a few more for obliging friends with prologues and epilogues or contributing to miscellaneous collections and undertaking translations. But prior to the development of a voracious print culture and some copyright safeguards for producers, a writer could barely hope to live by producing and selling books to booksellers.

The writer's relationship to the reader is often an uncomfortable and ambiguous one. The reader has not greatly, if at all, contributed to the writer's wealth, but the disapprobation of the reader can contribute to the writer's decline. There is much to lose but not much to gain from pleasing the reader. And these considerations, which affect all professional writers of the period, are in Behn's case further complicated but also rendered enabling by the gender violation of publicity/publication, which makes her noteworthy but freakish.[10] Her public and promiscuous flirtations, general epistles and prefaces, after all, are addressed to all who care to read them. Only prostitutes, vizard masks, flirt and send out challenges to all comers. This point has been developed by Catherine Gallagher, who comments on Behn's seductive stylistics in the prologue to *The Forced Marriage*. Gallagher argues that Behn accepts and works with the identity of woman writer as whore and utilizes the implications of fragmentation that result from barter and exchange. If the writer is not trying to retain, whole and chaste, a singular identity, she can "repeat the act of self-alienation an unlimited number of times" and "regenerate, possess, and sell a series of provisional, constructed identities."[11]

I will return to the issue of writer as whore, but at this point Gallagher's insight into Behn's "provisional, constructed identities" is relevant to Behn's ongoing rhetorical practices in her general prefaces, where arguments and argumentative positions shift ground with dazzling rapidity. More specifically, a characteristic of the many identities Behn displays in her prefatory rhetorics—an outrageous flirt, a learned academic, a theater critic, a masculine poet, a hard-working woman, a dedicated poet, a bruised victim of unjust sneers—is the way the identities cancel each other out. The many identities, so rapidly shuffled around, render the author elusive and almost invisible—as in the sudden disappearance from the text which she effects at the end of the prefatory epistle to *The Dutch Lover*.

Keeping up with the author can be a problem, as in the single-page address to the reader prefixed to *Sir Patient Fancy* (1678), which Behn claims to have written in "impatient haste," and certainly Behn's assertions and denials follow each other with such speed that the effect is almost dizzying, as one is caught up in ever-decreasing circles. Her indignation focuses on disapproval by female members of the audience who found the play obscene: "The most unjust and silly aspersion, Woman could invent to cast on Woman; and which only my being a Woman has procured me; *That it was Baudy*, the least and most Excusable fault in the Men writers, to whose Plays they all crowd, as if they came to no other end than to hear what they condemn in this: *But from a Woman it was unnaturall*" (4:7).

Behn also claims that either on the stage or on the page her play would not give "the most innocent Virgins . . . cause to blush." Certainly the virgins would have to be very innocent, as the play is as bawdy as most Restoration comedies. In two (very lengthy) sentences, Behn claims a right to write sexually explicit drama and then denies that she has done so. Arguing that women read their own obscene imaginations into her text, Behn insists that if the same women would read her text again they would find it chaste. But if the obscenity is there, even if no worse than in male texts, there is nothing she can do to protect her text; if the obscenity comes from the imagination, not from her text, then there is again nothing she can do to protect her text. The powerlessness of Behn's position with regard to her audience/readers, condemned if she does as others do, condemned even if she does not, is inscribed in the long concluding sentence, which similarly whirls around contradictory positions, insults, and supplications.

Behn asserts that the play's "loss of Fame with the Ladies" has not hurt it much—yet this female disapproval provoked the whole angry preface. Interestingly enough, Behn appears to be at her most incoherent and to use an old English word, flummoxed, when the subject—if not, perhaps, the object—of her address is other women. Although bisexuality was not beyond Behn's range, it is not so easy for her as a woman to deal flirtatiously with the criticisms of other women.[12] Men can be flattered and jeered at, cooed over and insulted, and either or both modes of discourse register inside the conventions of sexual play. And male dramatists defending themselves against female criticism can resort to misogyny, fraternal bonding, and sexual jokes that place the aroused and angry female audience inside the male triangulated economy of desire as they speak through women about men.[13] These options are not open to Behn. Rallying wit would be inappropriate, and misogyny, albeit female misogyny, is what she suffers from here. To imply that women are, in fact, creatures of obscene imaginations, which she does briefly, is a self-destructive tack. Instead, despite the implication of her earlier stance that her work is not to be judged as a woman's, she strikes an unusually pathetic, defenseless, female note.

Other women "ought to have had good Nature" and watching the play they should have "attributed its faults to the Authours unhappiness, who is forced to write for Bread." However, the uncharacteristic pathos of this is swiftly undone as she adds that she is "not ashamed to owne it." This is followed by a statement of her obligation as a working professional playwright to "write to please" the "Age," which one may take to include the right to write bawdily

(4:7). If this is assertive and, with the capitalized "Age," even heroic, this in turn is undone.[14] Behn remarks that "this way of writing," and the demonstrative is unclear referring either to playwriting in general or to writing in a racy manner, is "a way too cheap for men of wit to pursue who write for Glory" (4:7). Finally, she both excludes and includes herself in the categories of wit and glory as she concludes that the kind of popular writing she produces "even I despise as much below me" (4:7). Behn associates her gender with an economic necessity that forces her to write against the implications of her gender, but the kind of writing she would like to produce, that of "men of wit," can only be characterized in terms that would involve her in a violation of her gender.

This conundrum is addressed in the by-now famous concluding paragraph of the preface to *The Lucky Chance* (1687). Behn claims "Priviledge for my Masculine Part the Poet in me" and states that she values "Fame as if I been born a *Hero*" (3:187). There are no terms available for her to use in her defense as a writer except the very terms of masculine achievement that cancel her out. Behn can use no voice except one that will both assert and erase her sexuality. And the popular, rather than lyric and ladylike, forms she works in mean that she must attack the middle ground even as she lays claim to it or, as in the epistle prefixing *Sir Patient Fancy,* situate herself above and below it. Behn was caught between monstrosity and immodesty, and the dialogic of assertion and denial, the only moves open to her, which locks her into an unending titillating foreplay that can never climax, in which, in fact, climax must be denied.

As a woman writer, Behn had and did not have place and space to maneuver. The very fact of her literary activity grounded her authority, but it was an authority always open to attack on the grounds of her gender. Behn was always doing the one thing she was supposed not to be doing, and, as she was well aware, the more effectively she did it, the less she should be doing it. The more feminine she sounds, the less readers/auditors should be reading/hearing her voice, and the less feminine she sounds the even less they should be hearing/reading her. In asserting her "Masculine Part," as in the preface to *The Lucky Chance,* she is claiming a part she does not literally possess, and in revealing her female parts she is revealing that which should be concealed.

II

The foreword, in the form of epistles, dedications, and prefaces, is an appropriate place for Aphra Behn's very particular voice to be heard and for her very particular dilemma to be inscribed, because if her voice is itself marginal and contradictory, so too is the form in which it is heard. As Gayatri Chakravorty Spivak has pointed out in her preface to *Of Grammatology,* "as it is commonly understood, the preface harbors a lie. 'Prae-fatio' is 'a saying before-hand,' "[15] yet prefaces are, in fact, retrospections, postscripts, and afterwords. To continue my sexual metaphors, these are, in fact, postcoital discussions, words composed *after* the event, and although they are placed before the main text/play, they preface and post-date an already extant text and event. As we saw with Behn's elaborate prefatory discourse to *The Dutch Lover,* the foreplay that arrests and occupies the reader is predicated on the existence of the play and aims to mediate the reactions that will follow a reading of the play. Whether the writer is writing a preface to his or her own or another's work, the work itself already exists. The words that prepare one for the text inevitably work within this double focus, belonging to something that is completed and also preparing the reader for something new and unread or about to be reread, which is always different from the first reading. Displacing and delaying reading, the preface becomes itself both the sign and the performance of difference, destabilizing the identities of writer and reader, rocking the status of the main text and raising questions of what is primary and what is secondary.

To quote Spivak again, "A written preface provisionally localizes the place where, between reading and reading, book and book, the inter-inscribing of 'reader(s)' and 'writer(s),' and language is forever at work."[16] Is the prefatory voice the authoritative voice, parent to the child text, or is the main text the parent giving birth, as an afterthought, to the preface? And if either the preface or the main text is offspring, of what gender is the author who gives birth to both, and who is in charge of what? And, turning to the reader, as in the issue constantly in debate in the preface to *The Dutch Lover,* is the reader who has paid for the text in control, or is the writer controlling the reader: who is in whose debt? Further, in the case of forewords to plays, the preface frequently insists on the difference between the text as written and the text as performed, in a further destabilization that even as it attempts control, gestures in fact to the implausibility of the project.[17] The play foreword constitutes a political, economic, and sexual space, in which authority, control, gender, and status are at issue but are irresolvable. If this indeterminacy can constitute an embarrassing and irritating space for male writers, it is precisely the space in which the female writer, who is necessarily violating gender conventions and asserting areas of control and authority that are societally denied, is located.

Despite claims to authority, the supplicatory and submissive posture of the writer of forewords, who exhibits wares and sues for readers and favors, can never be entirely erased.[18] The prefatory remarks must please, flatter, intrigue, and excite the reader/dedicatee and are, in a sense, writing in a feminine mood. The femininity, however, is that codified as prostitution, for if the main text is the object of circulation, something that will be bought and sold, used and abused, prefatory remarks function, like all advertisements, as titillations, encouragements to purchase, to spend, and, in a sense, are the encouragements of bawds. For the male writer of forewords the dilemma is acute, because at these points he enters a textual space in which his cultural hegemony is undermined by the supplicatory, defensive, and uncertain status of a form whose supplementary status is always ambiguous.

The costs of production to the author obliged to wine and dine the cast; playhouse finances; the existence of printers, patrons, and booksellers; third-night receipts; and rival playhouses are frequently mentioned in forewords, indicating the corporate and economic realities of writing plays.[19] The preface/dedication is an uneasy textual transaction in which the realities of cultural production surface through fissures in the fictions of artistic autonomy and male control. These fictions were actively being constructed at this time in a possessive individualism or individuated possession of the text. This is signaled as much in denunciations of actors' deviations from the text and in denials (usually untrue) of plagiarism as in assertions, like Behn's, of her gender and her aspirations to erase gender. The cultural imperatives of authorial authority and autonomy impel Behn to her acts of self/textual possession even as the same cultural imperatives, in which the man and not the woman is constituted as the active autonomous subject, turn such acts of assertion and possession into a problematic.

The ultimate possessive authority of gestation and birth involves male writers in an uneasy gender reversal, and for a woman writer the cliches of artistic birth strike an almost too appropriate note that raises again the issue of promiscuity. In her dedication to *The Young King; or the Mistake* (1679) Behn refers to it as "the first Essay of my infant-Poetry" (2:105), while the epilogue to *The False-Count; or, a New Way to Play an Old Game* (1681) describes the work as "a slight Farce, five days brought forth with ease" (3:175). The metaphors of motherhood for a woman were, however, vulnerable to abuse, to transformations, as it were, into the boasts of Mother Midnight, as in Thomas Brown's invective against Behn; "How could you do otherwise than produce some wit to the world, since you were so often plough'd and sow'd by the kind husbandmen of Apollo?"[20] If the female writer can be accused of textual/sexual promiscuity, the male writer has the strange and not entirely comfortable privilege of a kind of bisexual relationship to his text.

In an obvious appropriation of female creativity, Behn's friend and contemporary Thomas Otway asserts a masculine/paternal control over his texts in his preface to *Don Carlos* (1676) and his dedication of *The Souldiers Fortune* (1680). In the former, Otway depicts himself as a "bashful young Lover" who "never durst venture on my Muse" until in "private I had Courage to fumble, but never thought she would have produc't anything, till at last I know not how, e're I was aware, I found myself Father of a Dramatique birth."[21] He becomes, as it were, both father and mother of his play, impregnating himself and, in understandably mysterious ways, having a fatherly birth. In more overtly and carelessly fatherly tones, the dedication to *The Souldiers Fortunes* dismisses the birth of the play: "I must confess my self a very unnatural Parent, for when it is once brought into the World, E'en let the Brat shift for itself."[22] Nevertheless, in both cases the play is the author's child and the male author has brought it into the world, and no amount of swagger quite displaces the fact of the central female metaphors of gestation, labor, and birth and the implied—if denied—follow-up of nurture and concern.

If prefatory remarks to the main text, characterized as offspring, can move male authors into an uneasy collusion with the processes of female creativity, they can also associate writer and text with prostitution, generally, if unfairly, regarded as a uniquely female practice. All writing can carry the possibility of prostitution; as "Critick" explains in *A Comparison between the Two Stages* (1702), the Muses are female, "not because the Sex had any thing to do with Poetry, but because in that Sex they're much fitter for prostitution."[23] Prefatory remarks calling for reader approval and purchase or acknowledging that gifts or cash have been received intensify the financially transactive and promiscuous relationship between author and his or her offspring, who is up for sale.

William Wycherley exploits a range of sexual possibilities in the dedication of his play, *The Plain-Dealer* (1676), to the famous brothelkeeper "Mother" Bennet. In a discourse that is marked throughout by sexual language and misogyny, Wycherley closely associates writing and prostitution: "I think a poet ought to be as free of your houses as of the playhouses, since he contributes to the support of both."[24] This witty and obscene discourse situates the dedication at the margins of the play, the playwright at the margins of society, and the whorehouse at the margins of sexuality in a series of interacting homologies and also, like Behn's prefatory discourses, uses concepts of exclusion and marginality to deny and displace the rejecting center.

In a similarly aggressive dedication, Otway signaled a recognition and rejection of the supplicatory and financially dependent position of the writer when he dedicated *The Souldiers Fortune* to his bookseller, Mr. Bentley, who, unlike aristocratic patrons, pays "honestly for the Copy."[25] In both cases, Wycherley's dedication to a whore and Otway's to a bookseller, the prefatory site offers the writers a space to display an apparently metatextual awareness of the actual processes of cultural production. Similarly, Behn's forewords, be they charming, argumentative, breathless and angry, or all of these things, bring to the surface the problematics of the production in terms of gender, genre, and finance. Forewords can constitute a place to foreground unease, becoming a species of cultural deconstruction, supplements that are both nugatory and essential in their relationships to more opaque main texts that conceal their specific dependencies and masquerade as autonomous. In the very process of asserting authorial identity and artistic control, the form, placing, and function/s of forewords undo or render problematic these assertions.

It seems appropriate to discuss briefly what seems to be the exception to the manifestations of unease, indeterminacy, and transgressive wit in prefatory practices. Dryden's prefaces, dedications, and epistles are the most well-known examples of the prefatory genre. Dryden used the preface to argue for critical positions, define critical-theoretical formulations, and attack friends, enemies, and relations who disagreed with him. In doing so, Dryden, who was notoriously uncomfortable with the supplicatory mode (and did his best to turn it into the subtle insult), was firmly gendering the preface and erasing textual unease. In his hands, the preface becomes just the kind of discourse of high masculine academic seriousness, complete with classical references and the formulation of rules, that Behn mocks in her denials of drama's claims to elevation rather than amusement.[26]

In Dryden's elevating practice, the practice of a gentleman, poet-landowner, and son-in-law to an earl, the popular dramatic form that is to follow the prefatory remarks becomes the supplement. The preface, drawing on the conventions of academic discourse, rendered palatably urbane and witty, becomes a place in which serious men talk to serious men. Dryden places the flirtatious, outrageous, and metatextual in the prologues and epilogues that frame his plays and can become part of the moments of dramatic enactment.[27] His prefatory remarks move further away from the play texts to become quite separate critical essays, which have been, quite suitably, anthologized and collected in editions separate from the plays, where they are read as part of the history of English criticism rather than in terms of their specific textual position.[28] Dryden invests the prefatory mode with a singular, masculine, and confident presence and moves the preface, as critical discourse, into the public sphere. However, Dryden's strongly singular practice, as much as subversive forewords, like Otway's growling dedication to his bookseller or Wycherley's elaborately courtly insults to a whore, can be seen as indications of male unease with a form that invokes a double and indeterminate voice.

Forewords represent a space marked by sexual indeterminacy in which there is more than usual room for free play and transgressive wit. Ambiguous in gender characteristics and uneasy in terms of status and relationship to the reader/dedicatee, forewords negotiate a series of boundaries—those of gender, of pre-text and text, of leisure and commerce, and of authority and subservience. They also conflate the intimacy of private reading and the publicity of publication and, in the case of play texts, contrast the page and the stage. The foreword, especially from a woman who is herself a question mark inside the question mark of the foreword, is a place of contradiction and doubleness where, in Spivak's words, "responsibility must cohabit with frivolity."[29]

It is not surprising, then, that forewords constitute a special place in which Behn can articulate her problematic voice. Behn was always gendered out of the fiction of singular masculine authority, and she clearly knew that her gender provoked a double focus on the reading (or watching).[30] In response, multiplicity and playfulness become appropriate and necessary rhetorical strategies, along with the inscription of the reader, "Sugar-candied" or adversarial, as a participant in the processes of production. It is in these forewords that Behn found a place to reveal and, indeed, revel in her position on the boundaries of gender and genre. While her plays, despite their warm sympathy to bold heroines, whores, and unhappy wives, can be reasonably regarded as conventional exercises in a male-dominated mode, these prefaces and forewords are places where she assumes responsibility for her own discourse as a woman—even, of course, as she labors to undo the gendering of her discourse. The discomforts of the mode are her discomforts, the discomforts of any woman in the patriarchy who must tease, disconcert, flatter, provoke, and seduce her way into the brokerage of power. And, removing the prefix, these are also the comforts of the mode, the strategies of discontinuity, doubleness, and desire. Play is easy, and coming only leads to going, but foreplay is the art of the possible, the provisional, the ongoing, and the inconclusive.

Notes

1. All citations from Behn's works are taken from *The Works of Aphra Behn*, ed. Montague Summers, 6 vols (1915; rpt. New York: Benjamin Blom, 1967), 1:221. Subsequent references to this edition will be cited parenthetically by volume and page number.

2. For an interesting discussion of sexuality in Behn's rhetoric, see Catherine Gallagher's essay, "Who Was That Masked Woman? The Prostitute and the

Playwright in the Comedies of Aphra Behn," *Women's Studies,* 15 (1988): 23–
42. This essay is reprinted below in this volume. See also Deborah C. Payne's
discussion of Behn's sexual innuendos in her forewords in " 'And Poets Shall by
Patron-Princes Live': Aphra Behn and Patronage," in *Curtain Calls: British and
American Women and the Theater, 1660–1820,* ed. Mary Anne Schofield and
Cecilia Macheski (Athens: Ohio Univ. Press, 1991), pp. 105–19.

3. Behn's concern over her lack of Latin was later expressed in her verses to
Thomas Creech on his translation of Lucretius's *De Rerum Natura* (1682): She
celebrates the idea that with access to the classics in translation women become
equal to men.

4. For a useful discussion of cultural intersections impelled by "the demar-
cating imperative," see Allon White's and Peter Stallybrass's *The Politics and
Poetic of Transgression* (Ithaca: Cornell Univ. Press, 1986), p. 191.

5. Nancy Cotton, *Women Playwrights in England c. 1363–1750* (Lewisburg, Pa.: Bucknell Univ. Press, 1980), p. 72.

6. Catherine Gallagher has argued that "the woman's play of wit is the
opposite to foreplay; it is a kind of afterplay specifically designed to prolong
pleasure, resuscitate desire and keep a woman who has given herself sexually
from being traded in for another woman" ("Who Is That Masked Woman?"
p. 25). Essentially I believe our positions, if not our placing, are similar. I stress
deferral and delay of climax and Gallagher stresses revival and resuscitation: we
both agree on the prolongation of play as a female sexual characteristic that is
replicated in textual rhetorical strategies. Before or after, the effort is to hold
onto the male (reader) whose tendencies and privileges are to stray, to close
down, and to move out. My later discussion also makes it clear (I hope) that
before and after are precisely the sorts of terms that get unfixed.

7. Commenting on Dryden's prologues and epilogues, James Sutherland
notes sadly that "the conscious, calculated obscenity of such writing is its worst
feature; the jest that might pass in a momentary sally becomes less tolerable
when it is deliberately produced" ("Prologues, Epilogues, and Audience in the
Restoration Theatre," in *Of Books and Humankind: Essays and Poems Presented to Bonamy Dobree,* ed. John Butt [London: Routledge and Kegan Paul,
1964], pp. 37–54, 47). Calculated obscenity comes with the turf, as the writer
quite deliberately produces arousal effects.

8. For a discussion of the uses and functions of prologues and epilogues, see
David M. Vieth's "The Art of the Prologue and Epilogue: A New Approach
Based on Dryden's Practice," *Genre* (1972): 271–92.

9. See Deborah C. Payne's discussion of Behn's relations to her patrons and
the way that flirtatious dedications, such as the one to "Philaster," possibly
Behn's lover John Hoyle, "diminish the play's virginal status" and reduce the patron's "distanced authority" (" 'And Poets Shall by Patron-Princes Live,' ") p. 112.

10. For a discussion of seventeenth-century attitudes toward women and
writing, see Angeline Goreau's *Reconstructing Aphra: A Social Biography of
Aphra Behn* (New York: Dial Press, 1980). See also, Patricia Crawford's short
and sensible essay, "Women's Published Writings, 1600–1700," in *Women in*

English Society 1500–1800, ed. Mary Prior (London and New York: Methuen, 1985), pp. 211–82.

11. Gallagher, "Who Was That Masked Woman?" p. 28.

12. I refer to Behn's lesbian love poem "To the Fair Clarinda, who made Love to me, imagin'd more than a Woman," *Works*, 6:363, see also Behn's "The Golden Age," 6:138–44.

13. See Wycherley's dedication, referred to later, to *The Plain-Dealer*. For a discussion of female criticism of the theater, see David Roberts, *The Ladies: Female Patronage of Restoration Drama, 1660–1700* (Oxford: Clarendon Press, 1989).

14. Such capitalization may reflect the printer's conventions rather than Aphra Behn's intentions, but left with the printed text, that is what I will adhere to.

15. Gayatri Chakravorty Spivak, "Translator's Preface," to Jacques Derrida's *Of Grammatology* (Baltimore and London: Johns Hopkins Univ. Press, 1976), p. x.

16. Ibid., p. xii.

17. Roger Chartier provides an insightful discussion of the complex cultural practices and strategies produced in the interrelationship of readers, writers, and pre-texts in "Texts, Printing, Readings," which takes as its starting point a discussion of Fernando de Rojas's prologue to *Celestina* (Saragossa, 1507) (in *The New Cultural History*, ed. Lynn Hunt [Berkeley, Los Angeles, London: Univ. of California Press, 1989], pp. 154–75).

18. Forewords, especially dedicatory forewords, often express this unease in terms of a rueful acknowledgment that the address and the author may be unwelcome. This possible reception for a dedication is referred to in *The Way of the World*. Witwoud compares the letter from his country brother to "a panegyric in a funeral sermon, or a copy of commendatory verses from one poet to another. And what's worse, 'tis as sure a forerunner of the author, as an epistle dedicatory" (*The Way of the World*, ed. Kathleen M. Lynch, Regents Restoration Drama Series [Lincoln: Univ. of Nebraska Press, 1965], act 1, lines 271–274).

19. See Elkanah Settle's description in his dedicatory epistle to *The Empress of Morocco* (1673) of the processes of selling a play (Settle's play is one of the works in *Five Heroic Plays*, ed. Bonamy Dobree [London: Oxford Univ. Press, 1960], pp. 99–100); or George Farquhar's gleeful reference to the fact that the first night performance of his play detracted from the third-night takings of Thomas Durfey's play at the rival Haymarket theater, *The Recruiting Officer* (1706), ed. Michael Shugrue, Regents Restoration Drama Series (London: Edward Arnold; Nebraska: Univ. of Nebraska Press, 1966), p. 4. *A Comparison between the Two Stages* contains a hair-raising account of the costs to the author of putting on a play, whittling down third-night takings from seventy to fifteen pounds (London, 1702), p. 10.

20. Thomas Brown, *The Works of Mr. Thomas Brown*, 2 vols. 9th ed. (London, 1790), 2:154–55.

21. Thomas Otway, *The Works of Thomas Otway*, ed. J. C. Ghosh, 2 vols. (Oxford: Clarendon Press, 1932), 1:173.

22. Ibid., 2:91.

23. *A Comparison between the Two Stages* (London, 1702), p. 26.

24. William Wycherley, *The Plain-Dealer,* in *The Plays of William Wycherley,* ed. Peter Holland (Cambridge and New York: Cambridge Univ. Press, 1981), p. 351.

25. Otway, *Works,* 2:91.

26. Such prefatory mannerisms are also mocked but used by Wycherley when he excuses his quotations to "Mother" Bennet, "There's Latin for you again, madam; I protest to you, as I am an author, I cannot help it" (*Plays,* p. 351).

27. Most famously, in the epilogue to *Tyrannick Love* (1669), Nell Gwyn leaps off her funeral bier to berate the bearers and delivers a witty speech that interweaves the part she played on stage and the part she is deemed to have played in life as Dryden draws together into a complex and interreferential manner text, posttext, and extratextual representation.

28. See, for instance, J. W. H. Atkins's discussion of Dryden's criticism in *English Literary Criticism: Seventeenth and Eighteenth Centuries* (London: Methuen, 1966).

29. Spivak, Preface to *Of Grammatology,* p. xiii.

30. To double up on this point, see my discussion of Behn's double-dressing in "'I by a Double Right Thy Bounties Claim': Aphra Behn and Sexual Space," in *Curtain Calls,* ed. Schofield and Macheski, pp. 193–210.

Drama

CATHERINE GALLAGHER

Who Was That Masked Woman?
The Prostitute and the Playwright
in the Comedies of Aphra Behn

Everyone knows that Aphra Behn, England's first professional female author, was a colossal and enduring embarrassment to the generations of women who followed her into the literary market-place. An ancestress whose name had to be lived down rather than lived up to, Aphra Behn seemed, in Virginia Woolf's metaphor, to obstruct the very passageway to the profession of letters she had herself opened. Woolf explains in *A Room of One's Own*, "Now that Aphra Behn had done it, girls could go to their parents and say, You need not give me an allowance; I can make money by my pen. Of course the answer for many years to come was, Yes, by living the life of Aphra Behn! Death would be better! and the door was slammed faster than ever."[1]

It is impossible in this brief essay to examine all the facets of the scandal of Aphra Behn; her life and works were alike characterized by certain irregular sexual arrangements. But it is not these that I want to discuss, for they seem merely incidental, the sorts of things women writers would easily dissociate themselves from if they led pure lives and wrote high-minded books. The scandal I would like to discuss is, however, with varying degrees of appropriateness, applicable to all female authors, regardless of the conduct of their lives or the content of their works. It is a scandal that Aphra Behn seems quite purposely to have constructed out of the overlapping discourses of commercial, sexual, and linguistic exchange. Conscious of her historical role, she introduced to the world of English letters the professional woman writer as a newfangled whore.

This persona has many functions in Behn's works: it titillates, scandalizes, arouses pity, and indicates the vicissitudes of authorship and identity in general. The author-whore persona also makes of female authorship per se a dark comedy that explores the bond between the liberty the stage offered women and their confinement behind both literal and metaphorical vizard masks. This is the comedy played out, for example, in the prologue to her first play, *The Forced Marriage,* where she announces her epoch-making appearance in the ranks of the playwrights. She presents her attainment, however, not as a daring achievement of self-expression, but as a new proof of the necessary obscurity of the "public" woman.

The prologue presents Aphra Behn's playwrighting as an extension of her erotic play. In it, a male actor pretends to have escaped temporarily the control of the intriguing female playwright; he comes on stage to warn the gallants in the audience of their danger. This was a variation on the Restoration convention of betraying the playwright in the Prologue with an added sexual dimension: the comic antagonism between playwright and audience becomes a battle in the war between the sexes. Playwrighting, warns the actor, is a new weapon in woman's amorous arsenal. She will no longer wound only through the eyes, through her beauty, but will also use wit to gain a more permanent ascendency. Here, woman's playwriting is wholly assimilated to the poetic conventions of amorous battle that normally informed lyric poetry. If the male poet had long depicted the conquering woman as necessarily chaste, debarring (and consequently debarred from) the act of sex itself, then his own poetry of lyric complaint and pleas for kindness could only be understood as attempts to overthrow the conqueror. Poetry in this lyric tradition is a weapon in a struggle that takes as its most fundamental ground rule a woman's inability to have a truly *sexual* conquest: for the doing of the deed would be the undoing of her power.

Aphra Behn's first prologue stretches this lyric tradition to incorporate theater. However, the woman's poetry cannot have the same *end* as the man's. Indeed, according to the prologue, ends, in the sense of terminations, are precisely what a woman's wit is directed against:

> Women those charming victors, in whose eyes
> Lie all their arts, and their artilleries
> Not being contented with the wounds they made,
> Would by new stratagems our lives invade.
> Beauty alone goes now at too cheap rates
> And therefore they, like wise and politic states,
> Court a new power that may the old supply,
> To *keep* as well as gain the victory:
> They'll join the force of wit to beauty now,
> And so *maintain* the right they have in you.[2]

Writing is certainly on a continuum here with sex, but instead of leading to the act in which the woman's conquest is overturned, playwrighting is supposed to extend the woman's erotic power beyond the moment of sexual encounter. The prologue, then, situates the drama inside the conventions of male lyric love poetry but then reverses the chronological relationship between sex and writing; the male poet writes before the sexual encounter, the woman between encounters. She thereby actually creates the possibility of a woman's version of sexual conquest. She will not be immediately conquered and discarded because she will maintain her right through her writing. The woman's play of wit is the opposite of foreplay; it is a kind of afterplay specifically designed to prolong pleasure, resuscitate desire, and keep a woman who has given herself sexually from being traded in for another woman. If the woman is successful in her poetic exchange, the actor warns the gallants, then they will no longer have the freedom of briskly exchanging mistress: "You'll never know the bliss of change; this art Retrieves (when beauty fades) the wandring heart."

Aphra Behn, then, inaugurated her career by taking up and feminizing the role of the seductive lyric poet. The drama the audience is about to see is framed by the larger comedy of erotic exchange between a woman writer and a male audience. That is, this prologue does what so many Restoration prologues do, makes of the play a drama within a drama, one series of conventional interactions inside another. But the very elaborateness of this staging of conventions makes the love battle itself (the thing supposedly revealed) seem a strategic pose in a somewhat different drama. After all, what kind of woman would stage her sexual desire as her primary motivation? The answer is a woman who might be suspected not to have any—a woman for whom professions of amorousness and theatrical inauthenticity are the same thing: a prostitute. Finally, just in case anyone in the audience might have missed this analogy, a dramatic interruption occurs, and the prologue stages a debate about the motivation behind all this talk of strategy. The actor calls attention to the prostitutes in the audience, who were generally identified by their masks, and characterizes them as agents of the playwright, jokingly using their masks to expose them as spies in the amorous war.

> The poetess too, they say, has spies abroad,
> Which have dispers'd themselves in every road,
> I'th'upper box, pit, galleries; every face
> You find disguis'd in a black velvet case.
> My life on't; is her spy on purpose sent,
> To hold you in a wanton compliment;
> That so you may not censure what she's writ,
> Which done they face you down 'twas full of wit.

At this point, an actress comes on stage to refute the suggestion that the poetess's spies and supporters are prostitutes. She returns, then, to the conceits linking money and warfare and thus explicitly enacts the denial of prostitution that was all along implicit in the trope of amorous combat. Unlike the troop of prostitutes, she claims,

> Ours scorns the petty spoils, and do prefer
> The glory not the interest of war.
> But yet our forces shall obliging prove,
> Imposing naught but constancy in love:
> That's all our aim, and when we have it too,
> We'll sacrifice it all to pleasure you.

What the last two lines make abundantly clear, in ironically justifying female promiscuity by the pleasure it gives to men, is that the prologue has given us the spectacle of a prostitute comically denying mercenary motivations. The poetess like the prostitute is she who "stands out," as the etymology of the word *prostitute* implies, but it is also she who is masked. Indeed, as the prologue emphasizes, the prostitute is she who stands out by virtue of her mask. The dramatic masking of the prostitute and the stagey masking of the playwright's interest in money are exactly parallel cases of theatrical unmasking in which what is revealed is the parallel itself: the playwright is a whore.

This conclusion, however, is more complex than it might at first seem, for the very playfulness of the representation implies a hidden "real" woman who must remain unavailable. The prologue gives two explanations for female authorship, and they are the usual excuses for prostitution: it alludes to and disclaims the motive of money; it claims the motive of love, but in a way that makes the claim seem merely strategic. The author-whore, then, is one who comically stages her lack of self-expression and consequently implies that her true identity is the sold self's seller. She thus indicates an unseeable selfhood through the flamboyant alienation of her language.

Hence Aphra Behn managed to create the effect of an inaccessible authenticity out of the very image of prostitution. In doing so, she capitalized on a commonplace slur that probably kept many less ingenious women out of the literary marketplace. "Whore's the like reproachful name, as poetess—the luckless twins of shame,"[3] wrote Robert Gould in 1691. The equation of poetess and "punk" (in the slang of the day) was inescapable in the Restoration. A woman writer could either deny it in the content and form of her publications, as did Catharine Trotter, or she could embrace it, as did Aphra Behn. But she could not entirely avoid it. For the belief that "Punk and Poesie agree so pat, / You cannot well be *this,* and not be *that*"[4] was held independently of particular cases. It rested on the evidence neither of how a woman lived nor of what she wrote. It was, rather, an a priori judgment applied to all cases of female publication. As one of Aphra Behn's biographers, Angeline Goreau, has astutely pointed out, the seventeenth-century ear heard the word *public* in *publication* very distinctly, and hence a woman's publication automatically implied a public woman.[5] The woman who shared the contents of her mind instead of reserving them for one man was literally, not metaphori-cally, trading in her *sexual* property. If she were married, she was selling what did not belong to her, because in *mind and body* she should have given herself to her husband. In the seventeenth century, "publication," Goreau tells us, also meant sale due to bankruptcy, and the publication of a woman's mind was tantamount to the publication of her husband's property. In 1613 Lady Carey published (anonymously, of course) these lines on marital property rights, publication and female integrity:

> Then she usurps upon another's right,
> That seeks to be by public language graced;
> And tho' her thoughts reflect with purest light
> Her mind, if not peculiar, is not chaste.
> For in a wife it is no worse to find
> A common body, than a common mind.[6]

Publication, adultery, and trading in one's husband's property were all thought of as the same thing as long as female identity, selfhold, remained an indivisible unity. As Lady Carey explained, the idea of a public mind in a private body threatened to fragment female identity, to destroy its integrated wholeness:

> When to their husbands they themselves do bind,
> Do they not wholly give themselves away?
> Or give they but their body, not their mind,
> Reserving that, tho' best, for other's prey?
> No, sure, their thought no more can be their own
> And therefore to none but one be known.[7]

The unique, unreserved giving of the woman's self to her husband represents the act that keeps her whole. Only in this singular and total alienation does the woman maintain her complete self-identity.

We have already seen that it is precisely this ideal of a totalized woman, preserved because *wholly* given away, that Aphra Behn sacrifices to create a different idea of identity, one complexly dependent on the necessity of multiple exchanges. She who is able to repeat the action of self-alienation an unlimited number of times is she who is constantly there to regenerate, possess, and sell a series of provisional, constructed identities. Self-possession, then, and self-alienation are just two sides of the same coin; the alienation verifies the possession. In contrast, the wife who gives herself once and completely disposes simultaneously of self-possession and self-alienation. She has no more property in which to trade and is thus rendered whole by her action. She *is* her whole, unviolated womanhood because she has given up possessing herself; she can be herself because she has given her *having* herself. Further, as Lady Carey's lines make clear, if a woman's writing is an authentic extension of herself, then she cannot have alienable property in that without violating her wholeness.

Far from denying these assumptions, Aphra Behn's comedy is based on them. Like her contemporaries, she presented her writing as part of her sexual property, not just because it was bawdy, but because it was hers. As a woman, all of her properties were at least the potential property of another; she could either reserve them and give herself whole in marriage, or she could barter them piecemeal, accepting self-division to achieve self-ownership and forfeiting the possibility of marriage. In this sense, Aphra Behn's implied identity fits into the most advanced seventeenth-century theories about self-hood; it closely resembles the possessive individualism of Locke and Hobbes, in which property in one's self both entails and is entailed by the parcelling out and serial alienation of one's self. For property by definition, in this theory, is that which is alienable. Aphra Behn's, however, is a gender-specific version of possessive individualism, one constructed in opposition to the very real alternative of staying whole by renouncing self-possession, an alternative that had no legal reality for men in the seventeenth century. Because the husband's right of property was in the whole of the wife, the prior alienation of any part of her had to be seen as a violation of either actual or potential marital propriety. That is, a woman who, like Aphra Behn, embraced possessive individualism, even if she were single and never bartered her sexual favors, could only do so with a consciousness that she thus contradicted the notion of female identity on which legitimate sexual property relations rested.

Publication, then, quite apart from the contents of what was published, ipso facto implied the divided, doubled, and ultimately unavailable person whose female prototype was the prostitute. By flaunting her self-sale, Aphra Behn embraced the title of whore; by writing bawdy comedies, which she then partly disclaimed, she capitalized on her supposed handicap. Finally, she even uses this persona to make herself seem the prototypical writer, and in this effort she certainly seems to have had the cooperation of her male colleagues and competitors. Thus, in the following poem, William Wycherley wittily acknowledges that the sexual innuendos about Aphra Behn rebound back on the wits who make them. The occasion of the poem was a rumor that the poetess had gonorrhea. Wycherley emphasizes how much more public is the "Sappho of the Age" than any normal prostitute, how much her fame grows as she looses her fame, and how much cheaper is the rate of the author-whore than her sister punk. But he also stressed how much more power the poetess has, since in the world of wit as opposed to the world of sexual exchange, use increases desire, and the author-whore accumulates men instead of being exchanged among them:

> More Fame you now (since talk'd of more) acquire,
> And as more Public, are more Mens Desire;
> Nay, you the more, that you are Clap'd to, now,
> Have more to like you, less to censure you:
> Now Men enjoy your Parts for Half a Crown,
> Which, for a Hundred Pound, they scarce had done,
> Before your Parts were, to the Public known.[8]

Appropriately, Wycherley ends by imagining the whole London theatrical world as a sweating-house for venereal disease.

> Thus, as your Beauty did, your Wit does now,
> The Women's envy, Men's Diversion grow;
> Who, to be clap'd, or Clap you, round you sit,
> And, tho' they Sweat for it, will crowd your Pit;
> Since lately you Lay-in, (but as they say,)
> Because, you had been Clap'd another Way;
> But, if 'tis true, that you have need to Sweat,
> Get, (if you can) at your New Play, a Seat.

If Aphra Behn's sexual and poetic parts are the same, then the wits are contaminated by her sexual distemper. Aphra Behn and her fellow wits infect one another: the theater is her body, their wits are their penises, the play is a case of gonorrhea, and the cure is the same as the disease.

Given the general Restoration delight in the equation of mental, sexual, and theatrical "parts" and its frequent likening of writing to prostitution and playwrights to bawds, one might argue that if Aphra Behn had not existed, the male playwrights would have had to invent her in order to increase the witty pointedness of their cynical self-representations. For example, in Dryden's prologue to Behn's

The Widow Ranter, the great playwright chides the self-proclaimed
wits for contesting the originality of one another's productions and
squabbling over literary property. Drawing on the metaphor of literary paternity, he concludes:

> But when you see these Pictures, let none dare
> To own beyond a Limb or single share;
> For where the Punk is common, he's a Sot,
> Who needs will farther what the Parish got.[9]

These lines gain half their mordancy from their reference to Aphra
Behn, the poetess-punk, whose offspring cannot seem fully her own,
but whose right to them cannot be challenged with any propriety. By
literalizing and embracing the playwright-prostitute metaphor, therefore, Aphra Behn was distinguished from other authors, but only as
their prototypical representative. She becomes a symbolic figure of
authorship for the Restoration, the writer and the strumpet muse
combined. Even those who wished to keep the relationship between
women and authorship strictly metaphorical were fond of the image:
"What a pox the women to do with the muses?" asks a character in a
play attributed to Charles Gildon. "I grant you the poets call the nine
muses by the names of women, but why so? . . . because in that sex
they're much fitter for prostitution."[10] It is not hard to see how much
authorial notoriety could be gained by audaciously literalizing such a
metaphor.

Aphra Behn, therefore, created a persona that skillfully intertwined the age's available discourses concerning women, property,
selfhood, and authorship. She found advantageous openings where
other women found repulsive insults; she turned self-division into
identity.

The authorial effect I'm trying to describe here should not be confused with the plays' disapproving attitudes toward turning women
into items of exchange. *The Lucky Chance,*[11] which I am now going
to discuss, all too readily yields a facile, right-minded thematic analysis concerning women and property exchange. It has three plots that
can easily be seen as variations on this theme: Diana is being forced
into a loveless marriage with a fop because of her father's family
ambition. Her preference for the young Bredwell is ignored in the
exchange. Diana's father, Sir Feeble Fainwood, is also purchasing

himself a young bride, Leticia, whom he has tricked into believing that her betrothed lover, who had been banished for fighting a duel, is dead. Julia, having already sold herself to another rich old merchant, Sir Cautious Fulbank, is being wooed to adultery by her former lover Gayman. That all three women are both property and occasions for the exchange of property is quite clear. Diana is part of a financial arrangement between the families of the two old men, and the intended bridegroom, Bearjest, sees her merely as the embodiment of a great fortune; Leticia is also bought by "a great jointure," and though we know, interestingly, nothing of Julia's motives, we are told that she had played such a "prank" as Leticia. It is very easy, then, to make the point that the treatment of women as property is the problem that the play's comic action will set out to solve. Whether she marries for property, as in the cases of Leticia and Julia, or she is married *as property* (that is, given, like Diana, as the condition of a dowry), the woman's identity as a form of property and item of exchange seems obviously to be the play's point of departure, and the urge to break that identification seems, on a casual reading, to license the play's impropriety. One could even redeem the fact that, in the end, the women are all given by the old men to their lovers by pointing out that this is, after all, a comedy and hence a form that requires female desire to flow through established channels.

Such a superficial thematic analysis of *The Lucky Chance* fits in well with that image of Aphra Behn some of her most recent biographers promote: an advocate of "free love" in every sense of the phrase and a heroic defender of the right of women to speak their own desires. However, such an interpretation does not bear the weight of the play's structure or remain steady in the face of its ellipses, nor can it sustain the pressure of the play's images. For the moments of crisis in the play are not those in which a woman becomes property but those in which a woman is burdened with a selfhood that can be neither represented (a self without properties) nor exchanged. They are the moments when the veiled woman confronts the impossibility of being represented and hence of being desired and hence of being, finally, perhaps, gratified.

Before turning to those moments, I'd like to discuss some larger organizational features of the play that complicate its treatment of the theme of women and exchange. First, then, to the emphatic way in which the plots are disconnected in their most fundamental logic.

The plots of Diana and Leticia rely on the idea that there is an ir-
reversible moment of matrimonial exchange after which the woman
is "given" and cannot be given again. Thus the action is directed
toward thwarting and replacing the planned marriage ceremony, in
the case of Diana, and avoiding the consummation of the marriage
bed, in the case of Leticia. Julia, however, has crossed both these
thresholds and is still somewhat free to dispose of herself. The logic
on which her plot is based seems to deny that there are critical or
irremediable events in female destiny. Hence in the scene directly
following Leticia's intact deliverance from Sir Feeble Fainwood's bed
and Diana's elopement with Bredwell, we find Julia resignedly urging
her aged husband to get the sex over with and to stop meddling with
the affairs of her heart: "But to let us leave this fond discourse, and, if
you must, let us to bed" (p. 135). Julia proves her self-possession
precisely by her indifference to the crises structuring Diana's and
Leticia's experiences.

On the one hand, Julia's plot could be seen to undercut the
achievement of resolution in the other plots by implying that there
was never anything to resolve: the obstacles were not real, the crises
were not crises, the definitive moment never did and never could
arrive. Julia's would be the pervasive atmosphere of comedy that
keeps the anxieties of the more "serious" love plot from truly being
registered. But on the other hand, we could argue that the crisis plots
drain the adultery plot not only of moral credibility but also of
dramatic interest, for there would seem to be simply nothing at stake
in Julia's plot. Indeed, Julia's plot in itself seems bent on making this
point, turning as it so often does on attempts to achieve things that
have already been achieved or gambling for stakes that have already
been won. These two responses, however, tend to cancel one another,
and we cannot conclude that either plot logic renders the other
nugatory. *The Lucky Chance* achieves its effects, rather by alternately
presenting the problem and its seeming nonexistence. The imminent
danger of becoming an unwilling piece of someone else's property is
at once asserted and denied.

The alternating assertion/denial emphasizes the discontinuity between the two "resolutions" of the woman's sexual identity that I
discussed earlier: one in which the giving of the self intact is tantamount to survival; the other in which an identity is maintained in a
series of exchanges. This very discontinuity, then, as I've already

pointed out, is part of an overarching discursive pattern. The proof of self ownership is self sale; hence, Julia has no exculpatory story of deceit or coercion to explain her marriage to Fulbank. But the complete import of what she does, both of what she sacrifices and what she gains, can only be understood against the background of a one-time exchange that involves and maintains the whole self.

The disjunction between the plot exigencies Leticia is subjected to and those that hold and create Julia (our inability to perceive these plots within a single comic perspective) reveals the oppositional relationship between the two seventeenth-century versions of the female as property. Built into this very disjunction, therefore, is a complicated presentation of the seeming inescapability for women of the condition of property. In the play, the exchange of women as property appears inevitable, and the action revolves around the terms of exchange. The crisis plots, of which Leticia's is the most important, posit wholeness as the precondition of exchange and as the result of its successful completion. The unitary principle dominates the logic of this plot and also, as we are about to see, the language of its actors and its representational rules. Julia's plot, on the other hand, assumes not only the fracturing and multiplication of the self as a condition and result of exchange, but also the creation of a second order of reality: a reality of representations through which the characters simultaneously alienate and protect their identities.

This split in representational procedures can be detected in the first scene, where it is associated with the characters of the leading men. In the play's opening speech, Bellmour enters complaining that the law has stolen his identity, has made him a creature of disguise and the night. His various complaints in the scene cluster around a central fear of de-differentiation, of the failure properly to distinguish essential differences. Thus it is the

> rigid laws, which put no difference
> 'Twixt fairly killing in my own defence,
> And murders bred by drunken arguments,
> Whores, or the mean revenges of a coward.
> (p. 76)

that have forced his disguise, his alienation from his own identity. That is, the denial of the true, identity-insuring, difference (that

between duelers and murderers) necessitates false differences, disguises, and theatrical representations that get more elaborate as the
plot progresses. The comedy is this series of disguises and spectacles,
but its end is to render them unnecessary by the reunion of Bellmour
with his proper identity and his proper wife.

The very terms of Bellmour's self-alienation, moreover, are iden-
titarian in their assumption that like must be represented by like. Bellmour has taken a life in a duel, and for that he is deprived of the life he
thought he would lead. He has destroyed a body with his sword, and
for that a body that belongs to him, Leticia's, will be taken from him
also through puncturing. Even the comic details of Bellmour's reported death are consonant with this mode of representation:

> RALPH: Hanged, Sir hanged, at The Hague in Holland.
> BELLMOUR: For what, said they, was he hanged?
> RALPH: Why, e'en for high treason, Sir, he killed one of their kings.
> GAYMAN: Holland's a commonwealth, and is not ruled by kings.
> RALPH: Not by one, Sir, but by many. This was a cheesemonger, they
> fell out of a bottle of brandy, went to snicker snee, Mr. Bellmour
> cut his throat, and was hanged for't, that's all Sir. (p. 81)

The reductio ad absurdum of like representing like is the commonwealth in which everyone is a king. It is within this comically literalist
system of representation that Bellmour is imagined to have had his
neck broken for slitting the throat of a cheesemonger. It is no wonder
that the climax of Bellmour's performance is a simulation of the
exchange of like for like. As Sir Feeble Fainwood approaches the bed
on which he intends to deflower Leticia, asking her, "What, was it
ashamed to show its little white foots, and its little round bubbies?,"
Belmour comes out from between the curtains, naked to the waist.
And, all the better to ward off that which he represents, he has
Leticia's projected wound painted on his own chest and a dagger
ready to make another such wound on Sir Feeble. The whole representational economy of this plot, therefore, has an underlying unitary
basis in the notion that things must be paid for in kind. Even Leticia's
self-sale seems not to be for money but for the jewelry to which she is
often likened.

Like Bellmour, Gayman also enters the first scene in hiding,
"wrapped in his cloak," but the functional differences between the

two kinds of self-concealment are soon manifested. The end of Gay-man's disguises is not the retrieval of his property, but the appropria-tion of what he thinks of the property of others: "Are you not to be married, Sir," asks Bellmour. "No Sir," returns Gayman, "not as long as any man in London is so, that has but a handsome wife, Sir" (p. 77). His attempts are not to reestablish essential differences, but rather to accelerate the process of de-differentiation. "The bride-groom!" exclaims Bellmour on first seeing Sir Feeble. "Like Gorgon's head he's turned me into stone." "Gorgon's head," retorts Gayman, "a cuckold's head, 'twas made to graft upon" (p. 79). The dizzying swiftness with which Gayman extends Bellmour's metaphor speaks the former's desire to destroy the paired stability of exchanges. Look-ing at the bridegroom's head, Bellmour sees an image of destructive female sexuality, the Gorgon. Thus, the bridegroom represents the all-too-available sexuality of Leticia. Gayman's way of disarming this insight is to deck it with horns, to introduce the third term, taking advantage of Leticia's availability to cuckold Sir Feeble. But for Bellmour this is no solution at all, since it only further collapses the distinction between lover and husband, merging him with Sir Feeble at the moment he alienates his sexual property: "What, and let him marry her! She that's mine by sacred vow already! by heaven it would be flat adultery in her!" (p. 80). "She'll learn the trick," replies Gayman, "and practise it the better with thee." The destruction of the "true" distinctions between husband and lover, cuckold and adul-terer, proprietor and thief is the state for which Gayman longs.

Bellmour's comedy, then, moves toward the reestablishment of true difference through the creation of false differences; Gayman's comedy moves toward the erasure of true differences through the creation of false and abstract samenesses. Gayman is in disguise because he cannot bear to let Julia know that he is different from his former self. He wishes to appear before her always the same, to hide the new fact of his poverty. He tries to get money from his landlady so that he can get his clothes out of hock and therefore disguise himself as himself in order to go on wooing Julia. On the same principle of the effacement of difference, Gayman later tries to pass himself off as Julia's husband when he, unbeknownst to her, takes the old man's place in bed.

Moreover, just as the false differences of Bellmour's comedy conformed to a unitary like-for-like economy of representation, the false sameness of Gayman's plotting is governed by an economy of representation through difference. The most obvious example of this is the use of money. Money in this plot often represents bodies or their sexual use, and what is generally emphasized in these exchanges are the differences between the body and money. For example, in the scenes of Gayman's two prostitutions (the first with his landlady and the second with his unknown admirer), the difference between the women's bodies and the precious metals they can be made to yield is the point of the comedy. The landlady is herself metamorphosed into iron for the sake of this contrast: she is an iron lady who emerges from her husband's blacksmith's shop. She is then stroked into metals of increasing value as she yields 'postle spoons and caudle cups that then exchange for gold. However, Gayman's expletives never allow us to forget that this sexual alchemy is being practiced on an un-sublimatable body that constantly sickens the feigning lover with its stink. Even more telling is the continuation of this scene, in which Gayman receives a bag of gold as advance payment for the assigna-tion with an anonymous woman. Here the desirability of the gold (associated with its very anonymity) immediately implies the un-desirability of the woman who sends it:

> Some female devil, old and damned to ugliness,
> And past all hopes of courtship and address,
> full of another devil called desire,
> Has seen this face, this shape, this youth,
> And thinks it's worth her hire. It must be so.
>
> (p. 94)

Of course, as this passage emphasizes, in both cases the women's money stands for Gayman's sexual worthiness, but as such it again makes a difference, the difference in the desirability of the bodies to be exchanged. Hence the unlike substance, gold, marks the inequality of the like biological substances.

The freedom and the perils, especially the perils for women, that this comedy of representation through difference introduces into erotic life are explored in the conflict between Julia and Gayman. And this conflict returns us to the issue of authorial representation. Julia, like many of Aphra Behn's heroines, confronts a familiar predicament: she wishes to have the pleasure of sexual intercourse with her lover without the pain of the loss of honor. Honor seems to mean something wholly external in the play; it is not a matter of conscience since secret actions are outside its realm. Rather, to lose honor is to give away control over one's public representations. Hence, in the adultery plot, as opposed to the crisis plot, women's bodies are not the true stakes; representations of bodies, especially in money and language, are the local points of conflict.

Gayman's complaint against Julia, for example, is that she prefers the public admiration of the crowd, which she gains through witty language ("talking all and loud," p. 99) to the private "adoration" of a lover, which is apparently speechless. Julia's retort, however, indicates that it is Gayman who will betray the private to public representation for the sake of his own reputation. It is Gayman who will "describe her charms,"

> Or make most filthy verses of me
> Under the name of Cloris, you Philander,
> Who, in lewd rhymes, confess the dear appointment,
> What hour, and where, how silent was the night,
> How full of love your eyes, and wishing mine.
>
> (p. 99)

(We have just, by the way, heard Gayman sing a verse about Cloris's wishing eyes to his landlady.)

To escape being turned into someone else's language, losing the ability to control her own public presentation, Julia subjects herself to a much more radical severance of implied true self from self-representation than Gayman could have imagined. At once to gratify her sexual desire and preserve her honor, she arranges to have Gayman's own money (in some ways a sign of his desire for her) misrepresented to him as payment for sexual intercourse with an unknown woman. That is, Julia makes the anonymous advance earlier discussed.

Julia, then, is hiding behind the anonymity of the gold, relying on its nature as a universal equivalent for desire, universal and anonymous precisely because it doesn't resemble what it stands for and can thus stand for anything. But in this episode, she becomes a prisoner of the very anonymity of the representation. For, as we've already seen,

Gayman takes it as a sign of the difference between the woman's desirability and his own. Apparently, moreover, this representation of her undesirability overwhelms the private experience itself, so that when the couple finally couples, Gayman does not actually experience Julia, but rather feels another version of his landlady. As he later reluctantly describes the sightless, wordless encounter to Julia (whom he does not suspect of having been the woman), "She was laid in a pavilion all formed of gilded clouds which hung by geometry, whither I was conveyed after much ceremony, and laid in a bed with her, where, with much ado and trembling with my fears, I forced my arms about her." "And sure," interjects Julia aside to the audience, "that undeceived him." "But," continues Gayman "such a carcass 'twas, deliver me, so shrivelled, lean and rough, a canvas bag of wooden ladles were a better bedfellow." "Now, though, I know that nothing is more distant than I from such a monster, yet this angers me," confides Julia to the audience. "'Slife, after all to seem deformed, old, ugly." The interview ends with Gayman's final misunderstanding, "I knew you would be angry when you heard it" (p. 118).

The extraordinary thing about this interchange is that it does not matter whether or not Gayman is telling the truth about his sexual experience. The gold may have so overwhelmed his senses as to make Julia feel like its opposite: a bag of wooden ladles rather than precious coins; and, indeed, the continuity of images between this description and Gayman's earlier reactions to women who give him money tends to confirm his sincerity. The bag of ladles reminds us of the landlady, who was also a bag, but one containing somewhat more valuable table utensils: 'postle spoons and caudle cups. However, Gayman may be misrepresenting his experience to prevent Julia's jealousy. Either way, Julia was missing from that experience. Whether he did not desire her at all or desired her as someone else is immaterial; what Julia experiences as she sees herself through this doubled representation of money and language is the impossibility of keeping herself to herself and truly being gratified as at once a subject and object of desire.

By participating in this economy of difference, in which her representations are not recognizably hers, then, Julia's problem becomes her state of unexchangeability. The drive for self-possession removes her "true" self from the realms of desire and gratification. Because she has not given herself away, she finds that her lover has not been able to take her. Surprisingly, however, the play goes on to overcome this difficulty not by taking refuge in like-for-like exchanges but by remaining in the economy of difference until Julia seems able to adjust the claims of self-possession and gratification.

The adjustment becomes possible only after Julia has been explicitly converted into a commodity worth three hundred pounds. The process leading up to this conversion merits our scrutiny. Gayman and Sir Cautious are gambling: Gayman has won 300 pounds and is willing to stake it against something of Sir Cautious's

> SIR CAUTIOUS: I wish I had anything but ready money to stake: three hundred pounds, a fine sum!
> GAYMAN: You have moveables Sir, goods, commodities.
> SIR CAUTIOUS: That's all one, Sir. That's money's worth, Sir, but if I had anything that were worth nothing.
> GAYMAN: You would venture it. I thank you, Sir. I would your lady were worth nothing.
> SIR CAUTIOUS: Why so, Sir?
> GAYMAN: Then I would set all 'gainst that nothing.

Sir Cautious begins this dialogue with a comical identification of everything with its universal equivalent, money. Everything he owns is convertible into money; hence, he believes that money is the real essence of everything that isn't money. Hence, everything is *really* the same thing—money. For Sir Cautious the economy of difference collapses everything into sameness. The only thing that is truly different, then, must be "nothing," a common slang word for the female genitals. One's wife is this nothing because in the normal course of things she is not a commodity. As Sir Cautious remarks, "Why, what a lavish whoremaker's this. We take money to marry our wives but very seldom part with 'em, and by the bargain get money" (p. 126). Her normal nonexchangeability for money is what makes a wife different from a prostitute; it is also what makes her the perfect nothing to set against three hundred pounds. We could say, then, that Julia is here made into a commodity only because she isn't one: she becomes the principle of universal difference and as such, paradoxically, becomes exchangeable for the universal equivalent.

The scene provides a structural parallel for the scene of Gayman's prostitution, in which, as we have seen, money also marks difference. But the sequels of the two scenes are strikingly dissimilar. Gayman is once again back in Julia's bed, but his rather than her identity is supposedly masked. Whereas in the first encounter, Gayman went to bed with what he thought was an old woman, in the second, Julia goes to bed with what she thinks is her old husband. But the difference between these two scenes in the dark as they are later recounted stems from the relative inalienability of male sexual identity. Even in the dark, we are led to believe, the difference of men is sensible; Gayman says,

> It was the feeble husband you enjoyed
> In cold imagination, and no more.
> Shyly you turned away, faintly resigned . . .
> Till excess of love betrayed the cheat.
>
> (p. 139)

Gayman's body, even unseen, is not interchangeable with Sir Cautious's. Unlike Julia's, Gayman's body will undo the misrepresentation; no mere idea can eradicate this palpable difference and sign of identity, the tumescent penis itself. Hence, when Gayman takes Sir Cautious's place in bed, he does not really risk what Julia suffered earlier: "after all to seem deformed, old, ugly." Gayman's self will always obtrude into the sphere of representation, another version of the ladle, but one that projects from the body instead of being barely discernible within it.

This inalienable masculine identity, although it seems at first Gayman's advantage, is quickly appropriated by Julia, who uses it to secure at once her own good reputation and complete liberty of action. Once again we are given a scene in which the speaker's sincerity is questionable. When Gayman's erection reveals his identity, Julia appears to be outraged at the attempted deception: "What, make me a base prostitute, a foul adult'ress? Oh, be gone, dear robber of my quiet" (p. 139). We can only see this tirade as more deceit on Julia's part, since we know she tricked the same man into bed the night before. But since her deceit was not discovered and his was, she is able to feign outrage and demand a separation from her husband. The implication is, although, once again, this cannot be represented, that Julia has found a way to secure her liberty and her "honor" by maintaining her misrepresentations.

It is, then, precisely through her nullity, her nothingness, that Julia achieves a new level of self-possession along with the promise of continual sexual exchange. But this, of course, is an inference we make from what we suspect Julia of hiding: her pleasure in Gayman's body, her delight that she now has an excuse for separating from her husband, her intention to go on seeking covert pleasure. All of this is on the other side of what we see and hear.

It is this shady effect, I want to conclude, that Aphra Behn is in the business of selling. And it is by virtue of this commodity that she becomes such a problematic figure for later women writers. For they had to overcome not only her life, her bawdiness and the author-whore metaphor she celebrated, but also her playful challenges to the very possibility of female self-representation.

Notes

This chapter appeared in *Last Laughs: Perspectives on Women and Comedy,* ed. Regina Barreca—copyright © 1988 by Gordon and Breach Science Publishers—and is reprinted here by permission of the publisher.

1. *A Room of One's Own* (New York: Harcourt, Brace and World, 1957), p. 67. Woolf here no doubt exaggerates the deterrent effects of Behn's scandal. We know that hundreds of women made some sort of living as writers in the late seventeenth and early eighteenth centuries. Indeed, there was no consensus that Behn was infamous until the second half of the eighteenth century. Nevertheless, in an age that loved scandal, she seems willingly to have obliged her audience's taste.

2. "Prologue," *The Forced Marriage; or, the Jealous Bridegroom* (London, 1671), n.p.

3. This quotation is from Robert Gould's *Satirical Epistle to the Female Author of a Poem* called "Sylvia's Revenge" (London, 1691). The poem acknowledges that the lines are a paraphrase from Rochester's "Letter from Artemisia in the Town to Chloe in the Country." The sentiment is presented as a commonplace.

4. Ibid.

5. This discussion is heavily indebted to Angeline Goreau's *Reconstructing Aphra: A Social Biography of Aphra Behn* (New York: Dial Press, 1980), especially pp. 144–62. Goreau has gathered much of the evidence on which I draw; however, we reach very different conclusions on the basis of the evidence.

Goreau writes that Behn "savagely resented" the charge of immodesty and makes no references to the playwright's own sly uses of the author-whore metaphor. For a discussion of Behn's self-presentation that recognizes her use of this trope, see Maureen Duffy, *The Passionate Shepherdess: Aphra Behn, 1640–89* (London: Jonathan Cape, 1977), especially pp. 94–104.

6. Lady Elizabeth Carey, *The Tragedy of Mariam, the Fair Queen of Jewry* (London, 1613), act 3 (unpaginated), quoted in Goreau, *Reconstructing Aphra,* p. 151.

7. Ibid.

8. William Wycherley, *Miscellany Poems,* vol. 3 in *The Complete Works of William Wycherley,* ed. Montague Summers (Soho: Nonesuch, 1924), pp. 155–56.

9. John Dryden, Prologue to Aphra Behn, *The Widdow Ranter: or, the History of Bacon in Virginia* (London, 1690), n.p. The prologue was, in fact, first spoken to Shadwell's comedy *The True Widow* in 1678, yet another reminder that the author-whore metaphor was ready-made for Behn's appropriation.

10. Quoted at the opening of Fidelis Morgan, *The Female Wits: Women Playwrights on the London Stage, 1660–1720* (London: Virago, 1981), n.p.

11. Aphra Behn, *The Lucky Chance; or, the Alderman's Bargain* (performed first in 1686), in Morgan, *The Female Wits,* p. 76. All further quotations are from this edition of the play, and page numbers are given in the body of the essay.

JANE SPENCER

"Deceit, Dissembling, all that's Woman": Comic Plot and Female Action in *The Feigned Courtesans*

In the second scene of *The Rover*, an exchange between hero and heroine shows them as rival interpreters and reveals some of the constraints on and opportunities for an activity in which both heroine and playwright are engaged: attempting a woman's version of stories shaped by men. Willmore, the Rover, has just met Hellena in her gypsy disguise. As they flirt, she tells him that she is going to be put in a nunnery and that if he wants her he will have to storm the convent walls. His reaction is very enthusiastic: "A nun! Oh how I love thee for't! There's no sinner like a young saint. Nay, now there's no denying me; the old law had no curse to a woman like dying a maid: witness Jephtha's daughter." Hellena replies: "A very good text this, if well handled; and I perceive, Father Captain, you would impose no severe penance on her who were inclined to console herself before she took orders."[1] The story of Jephtha's daughter (Judges 11:37–40) is one of the most brutal fables of patriarchal power in the Bible. Jephtha kills his daughter to fulfil his vow to sacrifice to God the first creature he sees on his homecoming after God has delivered the Ammonites into his hands. When he gets home, his daughter comes out to greet him and so becomes the sacrifice for her father's success in battle. Not only is all this done according to the law, what is considered most worthy of lament is the fact that she dies a virgin (and hence has not fulfilled her true sexual and reproductive role). Her father allows her two months before the sacrifice to go up into the mountains and "lament her virginity." Willmore's ability to make comic use of this story reveals how far the old law of the Old Testament is still the law of the society for which Behn writes: for a woman, security and status are still gained by losing her virginity in the approved manner, in marriage. The plot of this comedy, as of many others, leads to the marriage of the virginal heroine. Willmore, of course, is a devil quoting scripture for his own purposes; offering a libertine gloss on the biblical text, he makes the curse of virginity serve his turn as an argument for seduction. That he can use it in this way suggests, in the context of Restoration comedy with its stories of successful seduction, that the apparently lawless rake with his free-love philosophy is in reality upheld by the old law. Both society's laws and libertine lawlessness assume that a woman's purpose is contained in her sexuality.

Hellena's response to this is not the angry one that we might expect from a spirited heroine, but a provisional acceptance: "A very good text this, *if well handled*" (my emphasis). Her handling of the text seems at first the same as his: her reference to consoling herself before she takes orders leads Willmore to expect that his seduction will succeed, and it is only later that she lets him know that she is going to insist on marriage. Then, helped by her birth and large fortune, she succeeds in trapping the Rover. Her victory is conventional and entirely within the old law that sees marriage as woman's success, virginity as her failure. Yet for all Hellena's inability to escape from the text cited by Willmore, she does try to handle it differently—to read the text according to her own desires. In her case the patriarchal law, represented by her brother, because her father, though his commands are mentioned, never appears on stage), wants to insist on her continued virginity, saving on costly dowry by sending her to a nunnery. Hence, for her purposes the story of Jephtha's daughter is a good text, if well handled, if taken as a warning not to lament her virginity in passive acquiescence but to take active steps to get rid of it on her own terms.

Jane Spencer

Hellena's acceptance of—and reinterpretation of—the patriarchal text might be seen as a paradigm for the author's own endeavors as a woman dramatist in the Restoration period. Behn was a popular dramatist during the 1670s and the 1680s, producing both tragedies and comedies but particularly famed for (and priding herself on) her comedies. She was the only woman whose plays were regularly performed on the London stage in these years; the only one then, successfully to cater to public taste at a time when a male monopoly on all aspects of the theater—writing for it, acting in it, managing it—was only just beginning to be challenged. Women had been writing plays in England for many years before this: Margaret Cavendish wrote a large number in the 1650s and 1660s, published in 1662 and 1668; they were often explicitly feminist in content and tone. As closet dramas they did not have to pass the test of audience approval. Katherine Philips had two heroic dramas, *Pompey* and *Horace,* performed in the 1660s. Frances Boothby's *Marcelia: or the Treacherous Friend* was staged at the Theatre Royal in 1669, and Elizabeth Polwhele's *The Faithful Virgins* at Lincoln's Inn Fields in 1670, the year in which Behn's first play, *The Forced Marriage,* appeared in the same theater. Behn, however, was the only one to continue writing plays and having them performed. Not until a few years after Behn's death did other women become regular and notable writers for the stage. From 1695 a new group of women—"Ariadne," Catharine Trotter, Delariviere Manley, Mary Pix, and, in 1700, Susannah Centlivre—brought female authorship of plays on the English stage to record levels. These women were writing in a new climate of growing sentimentalism and concern for reform of the stage, in which it was possible to lay claim to what the age perceived as a properly feminine viewpoint. "The ladies" were supposed to dislike bawdry and support plays that presented exemplary morality: Mary Pix in particular offered them "good examples," eschewed "loose expressions," and concentrated on the tender emotions of her female characters.[2]

Behn, on the other hand, provided the bawdy writing that the earlier period demanded. Her success depended on appealing to the audience's tastes, and these, in the 1670s, ran strongly in favor of sex comedies, with rakish heroes and bawdy jokes. She succeeded and was popular, though, as she bitterly observed, she had to contend

88

with the double standard that condemned in women what was applauded in men. She wrote that she had her comedy *Sir Patient Fancy* (1678) printed "with all the impatient haste one ought to do, who would be vindicated from the most unjust and silly assertion, Woman could invent to cast on Woman; and which only my being a Woman has procured me; *That it was Baudy,* the least and most Excusable fault in the Men writers, to whose Plays they all crowd, as if they came to no other end then to hear what they condemn in this: *but from a Woman it was unnaturall.*"[3]

The typical sex comedy of the 1670s was a story of masculine dominance and sexual success. The hero was a libertine who dominated the action of the play through his clever tricks and its rhetoric through his witty repartee. His control of his social world was seen most strikingly in his sexual exploits. He generally seduced one of the female characters during the course of the play; perhaps also managed gracefully to get rid of a mistress no longer desired; often ended up marrying a rich and virginal heiress; and, most importantly, was not punished for his rakishness except to the extent that marriage might be seen as a comic curb on his future freedom. Famous rake heroes include Horner of Wycherley's *The Country Wife* (1675), who follows a happy career as a cuckold-maker and gets off scot-free, escaping matrimonial fetters; and Dorimant of Etherege's *The Man of Mode* (1676) who gets rid of an old mistress, seduces a new one, and keeps his options open to continue the affair as he moves toward marriage with a third woman more desirable than either because she is a wealthy virgin and herself a woman of wit. Criticism of these plays has been divided as to the attitude an audience is supposed to take to the rake hero—whether lighthearted acceptance, moral indignation, or perhaps more likely an ambivalent response. But there is no doubt that his power, particularly over women, gives him his glamour, and is central to the play.[4] Clearly this was a mode created by men and pandering to their fantasies; there was little room on the London stage of the 1670s for an alternative, female viewpoint. In *The Rover* Behn presented, in some respects, the typical rake hero, who seduces a woman, deserts her, and marries another; Behn's work has sometimes been seen as successful only because it pandered so well to prevailing masculine tastes.[5] Yet Behn shifts the balance of

power between hero and heroine, treating her rake hero more indul-
gently, perhaps, but also granting him much less control over the
action, which tends to be initiated by the women of the play.[6]

Recent work on women's drama in the Restoration has suggested
that it distinguishes itself from men's not necessarily by stronger
statements of direct feminist protest but by its emphasis on various
strategies to empower female characters. Jacqueline Pearson's line
counts on one hundred plays by women and one hundred by men in
the period 1640–1740 show, for example, that in women's plays
women tend to be given more lines to speak than in men's; there are
more women characters and more women-only scenes; and women
are more often given the opening scene of a play, thus establishing a
woman's viewpoint on the action as central.[7] Behn shares these
strategies: her particular position as *the* woman dramatist of the
1670s and 1680s means not that she possesses a completely different
outlook from her female successors in the 1690s but that she has a
particular set of problems and solutions.

Comedy becomes increasingly sentimental in the 1690s and after,
and Behn's successors tend to create their woman's viewpoint on
the basis of a sentimental view of womanhood. Toward the end of the
century, tragedy came to be viewed as the form most suited to the
ladies of the audience and most fitted to the expression of a female
point of view. Mary Pix, for example, pleads for women to support
her work because of its old-fashioned ideals of love and fidelity (the
opposite of the cynicism of sex comedy) and because of its modesty.
For her, the moral idealism that she provided for the ladies could best
be realized in tragedy, but her version of heroic tragedy is deliberately
angled away from the masculine concern with battle and toward the
feminine one of love and suffering. As the prologue to one of her
plays puts it:

> To please your martial men she [i.e., the author] must despair,
> And therefore Courts the favour of the fair:
> From huffing Hero's she hopes no relief,
> But trusts in *Catharine's* love, and *Isabella's* grief.[8]

Pix is writing the pathetic tragedy, or "she-tragedy," that is prominent around the turn of the century, enshrining an idealised view of
women as naturally inclined to virtue, modest, full of passionate

feeling, and apt to be a suffering victim—a view that became dominant in eighteenth-century literature. It's not surprising that some
women dramatists should have been attracted to this idea of womanhood, which attributed to women dignity and heroism and allowed
for the expression of dissatisfaction with women's lot.

For eighteenth-century writers tragedy was the woman's genre,
the genre that gave her dignity and seemed most to reflect her interests. We only need to think of Samuel Richardson's tragic novel
Clarissa, seen by its author and many of its early female commentators as a work that exalted femininity and supported women. In
Clarissa the struggle between Lovelace and Clarissa is expressed in
terms of generic conflict. He believes himself to be a latter-day Restoration rake living in a comedy called "The Quarrelsome Lovers" that
will end happily in marriage and male domination. Clarissa is compared by Belford to the heroine of Nicholas Rowe's she-tragedy, *The
Fair Penitent,* and in practically willing her own death she is insisting
that Lovelace's actions have had a tragic meaning. The vindication of
Clarissa's virtue and heroism is also the victory of tragedy.

The dangers of a feminism based on tragic exaltation of female
suffering are obvious. Yet it is not always recognized that the early
women dramatists also used—to very good effect—an alternative
way of presenting a woman's viewpoint. Behn's comedies and those
of some of the women who succeeded her increased the role and
importance of women in the comic plot. *She Ventures and He Wins*
(1695), a comedy by a woman known as "Ariadne," gives the heroine
an unusually dominant role in the plot. Some of Susannah Centlivre's
comedies center on women and give them an active role, especially
The Wonder: A Woman Keeps a Secret (1714). For these writers,
comedy can be the woman's genre, the genre in which women tend to
take control of the action, disguise themselves and play tricks on the
other characters, and actively pursue their own desires. If Behn takes
this view in *The Rover,* which is her adaptation of a man's comedy—
Sir Thomas Killigrew's *Thomaso*—about a successful rake, she does
so even more markedly in *The Feigned Courtesans,* the plot of which
is original to her. It is the meanings of female action within the comic
plot of *The Feigned Courtesans* that I intend to explore here.

The Feigned Courtesans was first acted at the Duke's Theatre in
Dorset Garden in 1679. Behn was already a well-known dramatist by

this time, and the first part of *The Rover,* her most popular play, had been first produced at the same theater two years earlier. *The Feigned Courtesans* is a comedy with some similarities to the earlier play: both depict young women outwitting their male guardians, adopting disguises including masculine attire, and pursuing the men they have chosen to marry; both contrast a witty pair of lovers (Hellena and Willmore in *The Rover,* Cornelia and Galliard in *The Feigned Courtesans*) with a more serious couple (Florinda and Belvile in *The Rover,* Marcella and Fillamour in *The Feigned Courtesans*); and in both the witty heroine has to win her lover from a rival. Unlike the earlier comedy, though, *The Feigned Courtesans* is not based on any particular known source, though it is part of a general tradition of English comedies modeled on Spanish intrigue comedy. It was well acted (with the famous actress Elizabeth Barry playing Cornelia) and favorably received, but it never achieved the big success of *The Rover.*

One reason for this lack of success is no doubt the difficulties that the London theaters faced in 1679 and for the following few years. The political furor over the Popish Plot had begun in 1678, and the next few years were dominated by the Exclusion Crisis. The insecurity of the times greatly reduced theater audiences, many fewer new plays were produced, and one of the theatrical companies, the King's Company, suffered so badly that it was forced to merge with its rival in 1682.[9] The prologue to *The Feigned Courtesans* refers to the difficulties the Popish Plot caused actors and playwrights in 1679: "The Devil take this cursed plotting Age, / 'T has ruin'd all our Plots upon the Stage."[10] Behn, as an ardent supporter of the succession of James, Duke of York, entered the political arena in some of her work (notably *The City Heiress,* a 1682 comedy that contained a satirical portrait of the Whig leader Shaftesbury), but *The Feigned Courtesans* has no such prominent political message. One of Behn's biographers, Maureen Duffy, suggests that at this difficult time for James's supporters—the early stage of the Popish Plot—Behn was deliberately being "almost apolitical."[11] R. D. Hume considers that after the failure of *Sir Patient Fancy,* with its bawdy farce, in early 1678, she returned to the safer ground of intrigue comedy (which operated under chaste conventions, characters often appearing in compromising situations but never being allowed to take their love affairs to the point of consummation).[12] Whatever the reason, for this play

Behn adopted one of her favorite modes, one that allowed her to develop an important comic theme—women's clever trickery—from a woman's point of view.

A simplified outline of the complicated plot runs as follows: Two sisters, Marcella and Cornelia, have fled to Rome to avoid the forced marriage of Marcella to Octavio. They pretend to be courtesans and call themselves Euphemia and Silvianetta. They are pursued by Octavio and by their uncle, Count Morosino. Their brother, Julio, also turns up in Rome, as do two Englishmen, Fillamour and Galliard. Laura Lucretia, Octavio's sister, is also trying to avoid an arranged marriage, in her case to Julio. There follow two basic tangles, the contest between Laura Lucretia and Cornelia for Galliard's love, and Marcella's test of Fillamour's constancy (as Euphemia, she tries to seduce him and is pleased when she fails). The situation is further complicated by the antics of a foolish young English traveller, Sir Signal Buffoon, and his hypocritical Puritan tutor, Tickletext, both of whom, separately, try to get assignations with one of the supposed courtesans and are tricked out of their money by the heroines' servant. In the end, after many complications, all identities are revealed and the characters are paired off.

To get an idea of the play's swift-moving succession of comic incidents it is best to look closely at a particular scene. In act 5, scene 2, the sexual comedy of four characters' continued and continually interrupted pursuit of their desires is created through a series of tricks, countertricks, and mistakes. Some characters know more than others, but none of the four knows the true identity of all of the other three; that pleasure is reserved for the audience. Laura Lucretia is planning the seduction of Galliard, whom she has been pursuing all through the play. Her latest ploy is to send him a message as from an unknown lady, inviting him to her chamber. Galliard, always ready to bed a new woman, arrives promptly, but while he is waiting for the lady his friend Julio appears. Julio is returning to the scene of an earlier—also interrupted—encounter with Laura Lucretia. At that time he believed her to be the courtesan la Silvianetta, while she believed him to be Galliard. She has now discovered her mistake, but when she enters she does not recognize Julio as the man who visited her before; she thinks of him merely as a stranger who must be maneuvered out of the way. "Help me, Deceit, Dissembling, all that's

Woman," she cries (2:395). In answer to her prayer, a new strata-
gem immediately occurs to her. She greets Galliard as her long-lost
brother, feared dead, and when he denies this, she claims that she
made a mistake, that her brother must, then, have been murdered,
and that Julio is, or looks like, the murderer. She does not realize that
the stranger she accuses is Julio, the man she has been, against her
will, contracted to marry; and although he recognizes her as the
woman he met last night, he does not know that she is Laura Lucretia, the woman his uncle has arranged for him to marry. For the
audience, there are abundant indications that Laura Lucretia's deceit
and dissembling will soon backfire on her, but she gains her immediate point. Julio withdraws, leaving her alone with the bemused but
eager Galliard. A second interruption, however, immediately intervenes. Cornelia, who also loves Galliard—and who, in her disguise
as the courtesan la Silvianetta, has already aroused his desires—is
determined to spoil his assignation with another woman. She has
followed him to Laura's house in her present disguise as a boy; once
there she recognizes Laura as the woman betrothed to her brother,
Julio (but Julio himself she does not recognize, as he has been away
from home for years). Pretending to be Julio's servant, she delivers a
message designed to let Galliard know that the woman who is seducing him is his friend's fiancée. Her device fails, as Galliard does not
believe her—he has only just parted from Julio. (This should alert
Laura but does not—she thinks Galliard is lying to get rid of the boy).
Cornelia, desperate, tries to get Galliard to fight, but he scorns the
"boy's" challenge, and Laura Lucretia calls her servants to throw
"him" out. Triumphant—for the moment—Laura Lucretia retires
with Galliard.

   Such a complex web of mistaken identities is typical of the
intrigue comedy, based on Spanish models and very popular during
the Restoration in England. Behn was particularly fond of the form,
which is not usually much valued by modern critics.[13] Plots patently
constructed for their possibilities of intricate complication—rather
than to embody a particular moral or satiric outlook on contemporary life—are judged not worthy of serious attention, and the preference for comedy that offers a dazzling display of verbal wit detracts
from the appreciation of what we might call the structural comedy of
the intrigue form. The humor of the exchanges between Laura Lu-

cretia, Cornelia, and Galliard in the scene discussed above, for instance, depends not on the wit of the speeches but on the audience's consciousness of the intricate pattern of relationships among the speakers, a pattern of which they themselves are ignorant. When Galliard tells Cornelia "let your Master know he'll find a better welcome from the fair vain Curtezan, *la Silvianetta,* where he has past the Night, and given his Vows," both women comment on his speech in an aside, one pleased, the other not. Both assume he is lying. Laura Lucretia thinks he is playing her game of thinking up tales to get rid of an intruder, while Cornelia thinks he has recognized her, under her boy disguise, as la Silvianetta—her courtesan disguise. Both asides take the audience into the character's confidence but leave the audience's superior awareness intact. We know that, in fact, Galliard is telling the truth—as far as he knows it. The woman he thinks of as la Silvianetta is not the same as the "la Silvianetta" Julio reported spending the night with. Both false la Silvianettas are, unknown to him, with him at that moment, and quite unknown to him (and unknown to one of the contestants) both women are struggling for possession of him. Confusing to read and difficult to summarize, *The Feigned Courtesans* offers comic pleasures of a kind easily grasped in performance.

As well as its considerable entertainment value, though, intrigue comedy as produced by Behn incorporates a cool and clever reexamination of the roles allotted to women in her society. In *The Feigned Courtesans* women initiate the action, the heroines Marcella and Cornelia by running away and pretending to be courtesans, Laura Lucretia by taking a house near the supposed courtesans to further her pursuit of Galliard. Laura Lucretia might well call on "Deceit, Dissembling, all that's Woman" to help her: The three principal women all adopt multiple disguises during the course of the action, each pretending in turn to be a courtesan and to be a boy. The point, of course, is that both disguises offer a relative freedom of speech and action that the modest woman, who proves her virtue by silence and seclusion, cannot easily claim in her own person. Laura Lucretia, in equating women with deceit, is voicing a traditional misogynist complaint, but its significance has shifted because of the context. Complaints about the evil of deception and the particular deceitfulness of women are typical of antitheatrical literature. From early Christian days to the Renaissance, women and the theater had alike been attacked for deceitfulness.[14] Behn is using the supposed link between women and deceit for her own purposes. The women in her play are the better actors in all senses—better at dissembling than the men and more actively shaping the plots of their lives. In comedy, power and audience sympathy are usually with the trickster. Laura Lucretia's remark in this context is not a misogynist statement but a witty reversal of one.

In their various disguises, the women can enter forbidden areas of action. In act 2, scene 1, for example, when Octavio attacks Fillamour and his bravos attack Galliard, "the Ladies run off," but Laura Lucretia, dressed as a man, can enter the fight on Galliard's side and is rewarded by his embrace as he thanks her: "This Bravery, Sir, was wondrous" (2:336). She soon realizes the inadequacy of her male disguise to gain her what she really wants from Galliard, though: "But Oh, how distant Friendship is from Love," she laments, "That's all bestow'd on the fair Prostitute!" (2:346). In act 5, scene 2, as we have seen, Laura Lucretia, pretending to be a prostitute, will have the edge over her rival, who is pretending to be a boy. An unwritten rule for male disguise in the play seems to be that it allows women to fight successfully when they are engaged in helping their lovers but not when they attempt to challenge their lovers' power. Thus, not only does Laura Lucretia go to Galliard's rescue, Marcella, in a later scene (act 2, scene 1), takes up her sword to protect Fillamour. But Cornelia's last-ditch attempt to stop Galliard from going off with Laura Lucretia by challenging him with her sword (act 5, scene 2) is scorned. Marcella's behavior in act 5, scene 3 provides a good example both of the way multiple disguises allow women to run rings around unsuspecting lovers and of the unspoken but strict limits imposed on action in disguise. Pretending to be her brother, Julio, Marcella challenges Fillamour to a duel claiming that "Julio" is punishing Fillamour for neglecting Marcella in favor of the courtesan Euphemia; Marcella, of course, provided the temptation herself in her disguise as Euphemia. But she does not actually fight him; they are interrupted by the appearance of her real brother, Julio, whose own challenge to Fillamour—for having (as Julio believes) injured his honor by running away with his sister—supercedes hers. Marcella is reduced to sending the servant after Fillamour to protect him.

Petro, the heroine's servant, is crucial to the action and a constant reminder that women are not the only tricksters in the comedy. A version of the traditional clever servant of comedy, he adopts a dazzling variety of disguises, sometimes appearing "like a Barber," sometimes as a "civility master." Part of the fun of the play is in witnessing his versatility: as Galliard appreciatively remarks, Petro "is capacitated to oblige in any quality" (2:314). It is important, though, that he is obliging not just an audience but the heroines. When they pretend to be courtesans, he pretends to be their pimp, and in this capacity he tricks Sir Signal Buffoon and Tickletext into paying for sexual services from la Silvianetta, which, of course, neither ever receives. In this way Petro provides the heroines with a means to live without resorting in actuality to their pretended prostitution, and he draws attention to the paradoxical honesty of his tricks: "I doubt not to pick up a good honest painful livelihood, by cheating these two Reverend Coxcombs," he remarks (2:315). However much disguise and deception in the play are designed for our enjoyment, we are constantly reminded that they are adopted through necessity. Male servants are traditional comic tricksters; if heroines, in this play, get to share their pleasures, it is because they also share the subordinate position that makes trickery necessary. In this play, true to the conventions of intrigue comedy, honor is a concept that much preoccupies the male leads. When Fillamour is challenged by Marcella-as-Julio and accused of neglecting Marcella to visit Euphemia, he sticks proudly to the truth: "I scorn to save my Life by Lyes or Flatteries" (2:401). If this nobility is made to seem slightly ridiculous in context (we know, as he does not, who is really challenging him), it is also one of the qualities which makes him the man Marcella loves. The attitude Fillamour expresses here is one that only a man of quality can afford to take—the woman he so reveres has to practice various kinds of lying throughout the play.

Yet, because of the different conventions governing male and female honor, Marcella's lies do not compromise her honor. Despite all the comic delight in women's deceit and dissembling offered by the play, it is important that the female characters are not, in the last analysis, false, and their truth consists in their chastity. Laura Lucretia, who slips into deception with the fewest qualms and most relish, is also the one least careful of her chastity. During the action we are twice led to believe that she is about to have sex, first with Julio (with whom she spends a night, thinking he is Galliard) and then with Galliard, but in both cases we hear afterwards that the would-be lovers have remained "innocent." Yet because Laura Lucretia (unlike the other women) would be willing to compromise her chastity, the plot punishes her: She is the only one of the three women who fails to gain her heart's desire at the end. She loses Galliard to Cornelia and has to agree to marry Julio after all.

Cornelia and Marcella, on the other hand, are rewarded by the plot partly for taking on a disguise to pursue their desires—and partly for doing so only reluctantly. Marcella in particular plays her part with misgiving, shrinking from the very sound of the word *courtesan*. The livelier Cornelia teases her, "Can you be frighted with the Vizor, which you your self put on?" (2:328). The play juggles with the notions of deceit within deception involved in falsely adopting a vizard. The vizard or mask worn by the prostitute was synonymous with her: In the Restoration, a courtesan was a mask. So, of course, is an actor. But a feigned courtesan, like Marcella, adopts the mask to hide—or shelter—her truth—the truth of her virginity and her true love for Fillamour. The dilemmas of the feigned courtesans are the subject of many jokes in the play. Cornelia quips that they are in danger of losing their reputations as courtesans because of their commitment to chastity: "Our Lovers begin to suspect us for some honest Jilts" (2:329). Later, Galliard, punning on two senses of the word honest, exclaims to her:

No Curtezan! hast thou deceiv'd me then?
Tell me, thou wicked honest cozening Beauty,
Why didst thou draw me in . . .
What honest Whore but wou'd have scorn'd thy Cunning?
(2:380)

His wordplay, like much else in the play, depends on the notion that honesty in women is entirely different from that in men: In women it means chastity, in men (and as Galliard implies, in whores, who have lost woman's proper honor) it means telling the truth. Women in this play have to violate honesty in the masculine sense if they are to preserve it in the feminine sense; therefore, whatever they do is dishonest by one or the other criterion. This is made clear in act 2, scene 1, when Cornelia reminds Marcella of their difficult financial position. Marcella has a fortune, but her uncle controls it. The sisters cannot afford, then, to be only feigned courtesans for long; Cornelia points out that they will have to agree to become, respectively, Octavio's wife (Marcella) and a nun (Cornelia). Forced marriage is therefore seen as an equivalent to, indeed a less desirable form of, prostitution. At the moment, Marcella's pretense of being a whore is her only way to avoid actually becoming one. Even Cornelia is concerned to make it clear that she is willing to sport with her reputation but not the reality of her chastity: "A little impertinent Honour, we may chance to lose, 'tis true: but our down-right Honesty I perceive you are resolv'd we shall maintain through all the dangers of Love and Gallantry" (2:329).

Heroines who deceive only to be true begin to sound rather Richardsonian, and indeed the beginnings of a shift to a more sentimental view of womanhood might be discerned in *The Feigned Courtesans*. We should not forget, though, the different angle of view on the question of truth that would have been provided for the audience by the original theatrical context. In the Restoration, when (for the first time on the London stage) women are playing the female roles, there is the idea that once a woman is revealed under male disguise, the truth has been revealed, the truth of the body adumbrating the truth of the narrative. But when the chaste heroine adopts the courtesan's mask, the layers of deceit may be more complex. It is well known that the Restoration audience would tend to equate actress with courtesan, and it was a time when the relatively small group of actors and the audience knew each other well and when there was a personality cult surrounding leading actors and actresses. Thus, the actress's sexual reputation might figure more largely in the minds of an audience than that of the character she played.[15] The chaste and rather straitlaced Marcella was originally played by Betty Currer, who refers to her own offstage reputation in the prologue. After complaining that no one is interested in plots on the stage because of Popish Plots elsewhere, the actress complains that all her lovers have "turned saints" and are neglecting her. In the perception of the original audience, then, the feigned courtesan was being played by a real one, and this surely twists any moral about female truth and honor that the play might express.

The Feigned Courtesans, then, certainly throws into question the woman's proper role of silence and submission, celebrating women's deceitful, dissembling actions in pursuit of their desires. It does so, though, without really undermining the equation of woman's worth with her sexual virtue. It is an attempt to inscribe female desire within a patriarchal text, and in our reading of it we need to give weight both to the attempt and to its inevitable limitations. Behn is unable to escape the constraints of Restoration comedy, but within them she allows the fullest possible scope to female action; she uses the carnival atmosphere of comedy, which briefly licenses role reversal, to allow her audience glimpses of female power.

Notes

Some of the ideas in this essay were developed in an unpublished paper, "Women's Drama in the Restoration," given at a joint meeting of the British Society for Eighteenth-Century Studies and the Women's Studies Group 1500–1825 in January 1990. I would like to thank all those who heard the paper and offered me their comments and suggestions.

1. Aphra Behn, *The Rover,* ed. F. M. Link (Lincoln: Univ. of Nebraska Press, 1967), act 1, scene 2, lines 176–82. All further references to the play are to this edition.

2. See the prologue and epilogue to Mary Pix's *The False Friend* (London, 1699).

3. "To the Reader," *Sir Patient Fancy: A Comedy. As it is Acted by the Servants of his Royal Highness.* Written by A. Behn. London, 1681. sig. A1r.

4. For a discussion of critical reactions to these plays, ranging from John Palmer's opinion that *The Country Wife* is "a whirlwind of inspired buffonery" to Bonamy Dobree's belief that it exhibits "deep pessimism," see R. D. Hume, *The Development of English Drama in the Late Seventeenth Century* (Oxford: Clarendon Press, 1976), pp. 86–104. Hume's own view is that these plays contain satire but do not present consistent or profound moralizing. Laura Brown presents a good case for considering these plays as serious social satire, arguing that the disjunction between a moral view of the heroes (which must condemn them) and an audience's tendency to enjoy their social success is itself the basis of the plays' dramatic satire. See her *English Dramatic Form, 1660–1760: An Essay in Generic History* (New Haven and London: Yale Univ. Press, 1981), pp. 43–55.

5. This view is argued in Katharine M. Rogers, *Feminism in Eighteenth-Century England* (Urbana: Univ. of Illinois Press, 1982), pp. 97–100.

6. For a discussion of "the domination and control of the women and the

relative passivity of the men" in *The Rover,* see Jacqueline Pearson, *The Prostituted Muse: Images of Women and Women Dramatists, 1642–1737* (London: Harvester, 1988), pp. 152–54.

7. Ibid., pp. 63–70, 254–55, 266–69.

8. *Queen Catharine: or, The Ruines of Love* (London, 1698), prologue.

9. See Hume, *Development of English Drama*, pp. 318–28, and ch. 8, "The Political Eighties."

10. *The Feigned Courtesans,* in *The Works of Aphra Behn,* ed. Montague Summers, 6 vols. (1915; rpt. New York: Benjamin Blom, 1967), 2:307. Subsequent references to this edition will be cited parenthetically in the text by volume and page number.

11. Maureen Duffy, *The Passionate Shepherdess: Aphra Behn, 1640–89* (London: Jonathan Cape, 1977), p. 174.

12. Hume, *Development of English Drama*, pp. 328–29.

13. R. D. Hume is one of the few critics to value the intrigue form, as his appreciative discussion of Sir Samuel Tuve's "Spanish" intrigue, *The Adventures of Five Hours* (1663) shows; see Hume, *Development of English Drama*, 73–78. One recent historian of Restoration and eighteenth-century drama, R. W. Bevis, sums up Behn's and Thomas Durfey's intrigue comedies as "brisk stage business and easy laughs." He adds that "it is easy to condescend to Behn's texts, forgetting their theatrical appeal." See *English Drama: Restoration and Eighteenth Century, 1660–1789* (London and New York: Longman, 1988), p. 90. Laura Brown offers a very interesting reading of *The Rover* but seems to consider that its "Spanish effects of disguise, mistaken identity, honor duels, and nighttime escapades" detract from its importance; see Brown, *English Dramatic Form,* p. 60.

14. See the discussion in Elin Diamond, "*Gestus* and Signature in Aphra Behn's *The Rover*," *ELH* 56 (1989): 519–41.

15. See Katharine Maus, "'Playhouse Flesh and Blood': Sexual Ideology and the Restoration Actress," *ELH* 46 (1979): 595–617.

HEIDI HUTNER

Revisioning the Female Body:
Aphra Behn's *The Rover,*
Parts I and II

Aphra Behn's *The Rover,* parts I and II is a recognizable revision of Thomas Killigrew's *Thomaso, or the Wanderer,* a two-part, ten-act play that was written during the Interregnum. Indeed, *The Rover,* parts I and II resembles *Thomaso* enough that Behn was compelled to defend herself against critics who felt she had stolen the play.[1] The rewriting of *Thomaso* may have appealed to Behn in part because it offered, as Maureen Duffy suggests, an opportunity for a "celebration of [her] cavalier childhood heroes."[2] The leading male characters of both plays, Thomaso and Willmore, share the ruthless and seductive qualities of a Rochester. Yet the differences between *Thomaso* and *The Rover* are striking, particularly in regard to the construction of femininity. Killigrew's female characters are depicted either as prized, angelic virgins or as deformed and grotesque "others."[3] His women are treated solely as the property of men and suffer repeated physical and emotional abuse. In contrast, Behn's play rebukes the patriarchal concept of women and "others" as property. As in her other works, such as *Oroonoko* and *The Widow Ranter,* which examine gender and racial stereotypes, Behn develops strategies of resistance in *The Rover,* part II to counter puritanical constructions of woman as object, commodity and "other." [4] Behn's presentation of the body of woman as a prelapsarian ideal—free from sociopolitical and ideological codes of honor and restraint—becomes a means to resist late-seventeenth-century repressions of feminine nature, as her poem "The Golden Age," at least in some respects, suggests. In *The Rover,* parts I and II, the chaotic, unrepressed "other" body of woman is similarly idealized to allow Behn to express a cultural longing for a prelapsarian golden age in which the sexes love mutually and women are desiring subjects rather than passive objects.[5] *The Rover,* part I shows us that Hellena, the virgin heiress, attempts to turn her world upside down—to transgress class and gender boundaries—but she is eventually and willingly brought back into the patriarchal fold. In *The Rover,* part II, however, men and women are matched as equals, and the body of the "other" woman, as we shall see, resists patriarchal control. Behn's resistance to repressive strategies of control is evident in the two parts of *The Rover* in the move from the prostitute as outsider to the prostitute as heroine: Angellica loses Willmore to the virgin heiress Hellena in part I, but La Nuche wins Willmore over Ariadne in part II.

Much of the recent criticism of *The Rover* has focused on the problem of the author's dialectically self-constructed image as the female writer-whore. Elin Diamond and Catherine Gallagher, for instance, argue that Behn portrays Angellica Bianca as a universal symbol of female oppression.[6] In my view, however, Behn utilizes the construction of the sexualized whore to subvert the ideology of passive, self-controlled, and commodified womanhood. Moreover, aside from Robert Markley, these critics have examined only part I of the play. In this essay I shall suggest that a more accurate reading of *The Rover* calls for a critique of all of its ten acts. Read as a ten-act play, we shall see that it is through the celebration of the "other" woman that Behn resists the Puritan ideology of rational thought, sexual repression, and the masculinization of desire. While *The Rover,* part I ends with a traditional set of upper-class marriages and the apparent restoration of patriarchal authority, *The Rover,* part II undermines the ideology evident in these conclusions.

In a brilliant analysis of three of Behn's Tory comedies of the Exclusion Crisis, Markley suggests that Behn's conflicted configurations of female desire and the male libertine are ideologically rather than psychologically constructed. He argues that Behn's "utopian vision challenges Puritan ideology of self-denial[,] . . . the masculinizing of desire—the creation of women as other and as object—that is crucial to a sexual ideology which insists on the indivisibility of feminine chastity and feminine identity." Markley further asserts that Behn's "idealized vision of a golden age of unrepressed sexuality . . . is produced by a political ethos of idyllic royalism against the economies of exile and repression symbolized by Roundheads and Whigs. . . . Behn seeks to demasculinize desire, to find contemporary equivalents—in her Tory heroes and the women who love them—for the nymphs and shepherds of the golden age."[7] Behn's resistence to sexual repression signifies her aversion to the increasing dichotomization of public and private worlds and the promotion of self-regulation and self-control.[8] Although I am greatly indebted to Markley's argument, my purpose here will be different from his; rather than looking at the royal rake as a model of the social freedoms to which Behn wishes to return or as an ideal that her heroines long to become, I shall demonstrate that it is through the body of the "other" woman that Behn articulates her resistance to late-seventeenth-century denials of feminine desire.[9] Through the discourse of colonialism, therefore, Behn attempts to subvert the construction of woman as a self-policing and passive commodity. The merging of the colonial female, the upper-class European female, and the white European prostitute in *The Rover,* part II is a counter-ideological strategy that Behn uses to overturn what Michel Foucault describes as the "repressive hypothesis."[10]

For Foucault, the repression of the body is crucial to the dissemination and instantiation of reason and modern conceptions of civilized sociality that emerge in the seventeenth and eighteenth centuries. The body as a site of desire and potential transgression disappears, as the powers of the state and family begin to monitor the individual through discursive strategies rather than by means of physical force. Hence, he argues, the negation of the body and the repression of sexuality promote the construction of the self-policing individual who internalizes the ideology of regulation and prohibition. In effect, the eye of what Foucault describes as the gaze of power controls and contains the body of difference.[11] In the literature of the Renaissance and Restoration, therefore, we see, as M. M. Bakhtin points out in *Rabelais and His World,* the denigration of the human, and more specifically, female, body.[12] The advent of new strategies in the seventeenth and eighteenth centuries to celebrate and to repress the body seeks to negate a feminized chaos and excess.

Behn's plays show us again and again how the ideology of passive and commodified womanhood and the dialectical construction of woman as both virgin and whore constitutes the repression of feminine desire. In part II of *The Rover,* though, Behn goes further than in her earlier comedies; in exploding the trope of the contained virgin body as an ideal of feminine virtue, she posits the celebratory body of the "other" as an alternative model of femininity free from sexual repression, self-restraint, and oppressive patriarchal law. In part II, the "other" women—the whore and the Jewish "monsters"—assert an idealized and powerful feminine authority that potentially subverts the construction of femininity we have seen in part I.

I

One of the few names Behn retains from *Thomaso* is Hellena. *Thomaso's* Hellena is an old courtesan—"an *old decayed blind, out of Fashion whore* . . . that has neither teeth nor eyes" (1:363, part I.4.2.153–54); she approaches the mountebank to be made fifteen and beautiful again.[13] The older Hellena's body is described in terms that render her powerless; her lack of desirability is conflated with her physical decay and moral corruption. Killigrew's portrait of the old courtesan implies that feminine sexual desire and freedom are corrupt and promote (bodily) deterioration. She comes to the mountebank/father to be granted a youthful and beautiful body that can once again function as a commodity. In "rescuing" Killigrew's Hellena—transforming her into the leading lady who opens *The Rover,* part I—Behn undermines the ideological constructions of the virgin as the ideal embodiment of virtue and the whore as base and corrupt. Behn's Hellena desires and loves—she leaves her father's house of her own volition and enters the carnival in masquerade. She is young, attractive, and witty, modeled on Killigrew's two characters who, like young Hellena, are to be sent to a nunnery but refuse the calling, the virgin Serulina and the prostitute Paulina. Like Behn's Hellena, Serulina refuses to be sent to a monastery, dons a mask, and pursues

her wanderer, but her pursuit occurs late in *Thomaso;* Behn significantly highlights the heroine's self-assertiveness by making Hellena's
refusal of the nunnery, masquerade, and pursuit of love the very first
events in *The Rover.* Notably, the other character who refuses to be
sent to a monastery in *Thomaso* is the good whore, Paulina, who
saves Thomaso from the rage of his female enemies (part II.4.2). By
conflating and fusing virgins and whores—Serulina, Paulina, and the
old Hellena—into the sexually desirous yet virginal Hellena, Behn
emphasizes the limited choices available to women of her age: the
nunnery, where female sexuality lies buried behind the monastery
wall, or prostitution, in which female sexuality represents itself for
male pleasure. Behn's revision of Hellena ironically collapses the
distinction—in terms of virtue and therefore moral power—between
virgin and whore; neither the old nor the young Hellena is able
transgressively to turn her world upside down.

Unlike *Thomaso,* which is set entirely in Madrid during the
Spanish Inquisition, part I of *The Rover* takes place during carnival, a
discursive setting that Peter Stallybrass and Allon White refer to as a
"*catalyst* and *site of actual and symbolic struggle.*"[14] Behn's Hellena
appropriates the bawdy language of the carnival when she dons the
mask. She asserts, "I'm resolv'd to provide my self this Carnival, if
there be e'er a handsome Fellow of my humour above Ground, tho I
ask First" (1.1.40–42). Dressed in costume, Hellena claims she will
appeal to her man first. And, rather than follow her brother's designs
for a husband, she haughtily tells him, "I care not, I had rather be a
Nun, than be oblig'd to marry as you wou'd have me, if I wer design'd
for't" (1.1.157–58). In an aside she says, "I'll have a Saint of my own
to pray to shortly, if I like any that dares venture on me" (1.1.164–
65). When her servant asks Hellena what she will do in the carnival,
she exclaims, "That which all the World does, as I am told, be as mad
as the rest, and take all innocent Freedom—Sister, you'll go too, will
you not? come prithee be not sad—We'll out-wit twenty Brothers, if
you'll be ruled by me—Come put off this dull humour with your
Clothes, and assume one as gay, and as fantastick as the Dress my
Cousin Valeria and I have provided, and let's ramble" (1.1.195–
202). Hellena's donning of the mask is a form of resistance to the
repression of feminine desire. Masked, she believes she will rule
herself. Hellena convinces Florinda of the potential joys of the car-

nival—transformation and control of her own destiny. The assumption of a new and different identity, as Hellena suggests, will bring the women together in an act of rebellion against those aspects of patriarchal law that they experience as repressive. Significantly, however, Hellena and Florinda do not attempt to cross class boundaries.

In *The Rover,* part I, the masquerade gives young women freedom to ramble: to leave the house, to speak their minds, to approach men of their choice. But it also exposes them to grave danger and ridicule, as the gypsied Hellena asks Willmore: "Why must we be either guilty of Fornication or Murder, if we converse with you Men?—And is there no difference between leave to love me, and leave to lie with me?" (1.2.214–17). Conversation with men, then, even if a woman is masked, substantiates her role in the carnival as an object of desire. Willmore is attracted to the gypsy costume, but he is equally attracted to all pretty women, particularly pretty pictures of women. He aptly asserts, "I long to see the Shadow of the fair Substance [Angellica], a Man may gaze on that for nothing" (2.1.21–22). He wants to look and lie with the prostitute but not pay for sex, lie with Hellena when she is disguised as a gypsy but not marry her. Like a clever merchant, he wants to get the most from the female goods with as little out of his own pocket as possible. When Willmore hears of Hellena's large fortune, he tellingly says, "Ha, my Gipsy worth two hundred thousand Crowns!—oh how I long to be with her—pox, I knew she was of Quality" (4.2.200–202). In a patriarchal society, landed money heightens the value and desirability of the female object. The female disguise, therefore, promises freedom, but that freedom only functions within the context of the seventeenth-century marriage market and its class-based assumptions about feminine value.

Angellica, like Hellena, attempts to turn sexual politics—the role of woman as the object of the gaze—on their head. She has set her picture before the male public and named a high price. Her desire and her political and economic control of her body, Angellica believes, lie in the reversed double gaze—watching men watch her. Her reversed double gaze symbolizes the dynamic and contested field of power between the sexes. When Angellica's servant reports how the men admire "Beauty only" and "past-off" the picture as they laugh at the large sum required for her purchase, Angellica smugly replies: "No matter, I'm not displeas'd with their rallying; their Wonder feeds my Vanity, and he that wishes to buy, gives me more Pride, than he that gives my Price can make me Pleasure" (2.1.129, 131; 2.1.132–35). Angellica is coopted into the masculinist ideology symbolized by the "Wonder" of the men, however; it supposedly gives her pleasure to be admired, regardless of what she earns, but male desire holds her fixed in her oppressed role as courtesan because ultimately she is not empowered by the reverse double gaze—Willmore breaks her heart. She believes Willmore loves her, but he merely ignites her passion to appropriate her power. His ultimate pleasure lies not in the sexual conquest itself but in duping her. As Foucault suggests, "The pleasure [is] fed back to the power that encircled it."[15] The veil only encourages the gazer to do the unveiling; it leads Willmore through the foreplay of the masquerade to the abduction—at first stealing her small picture, the shadow, and ultimately the unrequited love he has encouraged.

Both Angellica and Hellena dress as males to assert their wills. Angellica wants to seek revenge upon Willmore by her own hand, so she dresses as a man and attempts to kill him with a pistol; the weapon is symbolic of her attempt to usurp phallic control. Significantly, Angellica does not succeed in killing him, and she is led back into her role as courtesan by Pedro. Hellena does—temporarily—win her Rover at the end of part I by imitating his language and behavior (5.1.522, 532–33). Yet, when Hellena attempts to obtain the object of her desire by dressing as a male page who will lead the Rover away from Angellica, Willmore discovers the phallic disguise and turns it against her. He tells the jealous Angellica: "This small Ambassador comes not from a Person of Quality, as you imagine, and he says; but from a very errant Gipsy, the talkingst, pratingst, cantingst little Animal thou ever saw'st. . . . Thou may'st as well be jealous of thy Monkey, or Parrot as her" (4.2.353–57, 361–62). Notably, Willmore attempts to mislead Angellica as well as abuse Hellena—they are therefore doubly abused. The metaphorical implications of this passage are merely another means to disrupt the female character's act of self-assertion. The (male) costume, therefore, is not empowering for Hellena or Angellica in this royalist satire. Willmore's attacks upon the multiplicity of female identities—the masks of the gypsy and the male page—force Hellena and Angellica into traditional roles as disempowered objects of male desire (the wife and the prostitute). Moreover, this dichotomy reinforces the class distinctions between the two women. Later, when Angellica tries to move from the role of prostitute to lover, she tellingly is abandoned by the very man who encouraged the crossing. Angellica's servants try to prevent her from falling in love with an aristocrat— they know, perhaps better than those of the upper class, how difficult and dangerous it is to transgress those boundaries of class and of feminine honor that constrain and define her.

Florinda is Behn's revision of Killigrew's Serulina, the only "bright star of female virtue" in *Thomaso* (part II.5.10.125). What makes Florinda markedly different from Serulina is her choice of a lover. The virgin Serulina is also virtuous, but her lover is not; her goodness is supposed to reform him. Belvile, in contrast, is Florinda's equal, not her opposite. Behn's revision implies that if women are to be virtuous, men must be virtuous too. Florinda is stereotypically good—unappropriative, passive—but so is Belvile.

However, despite Florinda's passive sexual nature and her choice of Belvile because of his genuinely good character (as opposed to Hellena's and Angellica's passionate desire for and self-destructive choice of the untrustworthy Willmore), she must, like all women in *The Rover,* part I, "traverse the whore's marketplace." Throughout the play Florinda is subject to a series of attempted rapes, first by Willmore, then by Blunt and Frederick, and finally by a group of men, including her own brother, Pedro. Thus, in her voyage into the carnival in search of her Prince Charming, Florinda becomes the object of pursuit. Pedro and Willmore chase after her, she enters the doors of a house to find shelter from them, and she encounters another man who wants to rape her.

Blunt is angry because he has been stripped of his masculine garb; Lucetta—a lower-class petty thief and prostitute—has pretended to seduce him to steal his belongings. Lucetta has stripped him of his clothes/costume, reversing the traditional seduction (like that of Angellica Bianca by the Rover) in which the woman, as the object of desire, is seduced and abandoned. The masked and innocent Florinda, seeking shelter, enters Blunt's lair while trying to escape her brother. Blunt, who is tellingly another good friend of Belvile's, blames all women for his being duped; he sees woman as one mass body to be taken, beaten, or abducted as a man desires, although he later accepts the class distinction between a woman of quality and a whore. He wants to "pull off their false Faces," just as his mask has been removed (5.1.604). He tells Florinda, "I will kiss thee all over; Kiss, and see thee all over; thou shalt lie with me too, not that I care of the Injoyment, but to let you see I have ta'en deliberated Malice to thee, and will be revenged on one Whore for the Sins of another. . . . Therefore prepare for both my Pleasure of Enjoyment and Revenge, for I am resolved to make up my Loss here on thy Body, I'll take it out in Kindness and in beating" (4.3.143–47, 176–79). In effect, Behn suggests that Blunt finds it necessary to master a woman because he cannot master himself. In order for the duped Blunt to regain his manly authority, he attacks a woman—any woman. Punning on the image of the highly priced portrait of Angellica, which none of the cavaliers can afford, Blunt then says he will strip Florinda "stark naked" and hang her out his window "by the Heels, with a Paper of scurvey Verses fasten'd to [her] Breast, in praise of damnable Women" (4.3.150–53). For Blunt, whore and virgin are interchangeable in the market of the patrilineal masquerade—they are "as much one as t'other" (4.3.136). Behn comically disrupts the masculinist discourse of the masquerade, however, by putting it in the mouth of Blunt, the powerless fool with the "old rusty sword," whom the banished cavaliers associate with only for his money (1:81).

Despite Florinda's traditionally feminine passive nature, she is ultimately subject to the same verbal and physical abuse and condemnation by the masculinist ideology of her culture as Hellena and Angellica—the desiring women who love a rake. Confronted by the would-be rapists in act 5, including Florinda's brother, who preys unknowingly upon his sister, the circling wolves ironically decide to let the man with the "longest Sword carr[y] her" (1.5.108–9). As it turns out, her brother, "Pedro, being a Spaniard, ha[s] the longest" phallus/sword, and he wins Florinda (1:89). Willmore suggests that Pedro allow the "lady to . . . chuse her Man," however (1.5.134). The mask allows Florinda to appear to make this decision at least because Pedro does not realize the effect of what he has done when he says, "I am better bred, than not to leave her Choice Free" (1.5.135). Yet, significantly, what Pedro offers his sister is no free choice at all: Pedro does not know who Florinda is when he makes this offer; as far as he is aware, he merely allows a nameless and faceless whore/ woman to choose her own rapist. Thus Florinda's less aggressive and, hence, more morally correct character (according to the patrilineal economy that constrains and confines her), ultimately affords her no freedom or protection from men's violation and abuse. In this manner, Behn demonstrates that in a patriarchal economy virgin and whore are equally subject to male domination.

In *The Rover,* part I, women who attempt to resist the repression of their autonomy and express their desires are reincorporated into the masculinist economy that constructs and constrains them. Angellica's attempt to transgress the role of the prostitute is thwarted by the very man who encouraged the crossing, and at the end of the play she unhappily returns to her role as prostitute. While Hellena wins the Rover, believing she will achieve her freedom through him, he has chosen her at least in part for her money, and their union is short-lived—as we shall see in part II. Moreover, Behn's juxtaposition of the attempted gang-rape of Florinda immediately prior to the wedding ceremonies at the end of the play undermines the moral code that marriage supposedly embodies; thus, Florinda's fairy-tale union with the Prince Charming Belvile is depicted as disturbing and fictional. In part I, Behn thus implicitly suggests that roles for women other than virgin and whore must be sought in order to achieve the feminization of desire.

II

In part II of *The Rover* the male gaze turns back upon itself and disarms the disciplinary powers of the masculinist ideology of part I.[16] In act 1, scene 1 of part II, Willmore pretends "*sham Sadness*" in recalling the recent death of Hellena (1:122). The desiring woman, one who is beautiful, sexually desiring, and honorable, has died after one month of marriage. As Willmore says, albeit jokingly, Hellena "was too good for Mortals" (1.1.144). In contrast to his prototype in Killigrew's play, the Rover has not been reformed by his marriage to the honorable woman—he already plans his new conquests. Hence, the triumphant marriage that supposedly "fixt the Wanderer" in *Thomaso* is rendered irrelevant (part II.5.10.126). Killigrew's play stereotypically and conveniently ends with a redeeming marriage—

redeeming for the man—while Behn strategically alludes to what happens to women after the wedding. Hellena has died at sea, and Willmore has already spent all of her fortune. In Behn's vision, marriage is displayed as merely a means of transmitting property from one male to another, not as the blissful ordering of the social misrule of the carnival that Killigrew implies. In other words, Behn unmasks as ideology what Killigrew portrays as a conventionally happy ending.

Not surprisingly, the Rover's shamming continues throughout part II. One of the few characters to go unmasked in part I, Willmore puts on the mask of the Mountebank in part II. In *Thomaso* the Mountebank is presented as a real magician, not a fake. His primary function in *Thomaso* is to make women physically conform to the dominant ideal of beauty, thereby enhancing the value of the female as a commodity. In contrast to Killigrew's portrait of the Mountebank who successfully alters and mutilates the bodies of the female characters, in *The Rover* the "other" women whom the Mountebank/Willmore tries to control resist his attempts to constrain them and subvert his authority to confine and to repress feminine desire. Although the Rover lures La Nuche into seeking his advice while disguised as the Mountebank, for example, his manipulative discourse is undermined by her self-determination. In telling La Nuche her fortune, Willmore, as a mountebank, asserts that "not all [La Nuche's] Vows, [her] Wit, [her] resolution, or [her] Cunning can hinder him from conquering absolutely" (3.1.246–48); he states that she will relinquish her "mercenary" pursuits for the Rover, and although Willmore does not love her, La Nuche is "destin'd his, and to be ruin'd." La Nuche notably responds with "No,—I will controul my Stars and Inclinations; . . . I will be Mistress of my fixt Resolves" (3.1.249, 251, 255). She is ultimately united with Willmore at the end of part II, not for any reasons out of her power, as the Mountebank/Willmore suggests, but because she has chosen to love. If La Nuche is ruined, by loving Willmore, it is not because she is sexually experienced but because she gives up her fortune for passion.

Behn's revision of Killigrew's Jewesses further overturns the masculinist ideology that attempts to erase difference and repress female desire; *The Rover*'s Jewish female monsters are powerful women whose bodies cannot be dominated and controlled. *Thomaso*'s monster Jewesses are never seen onstage; they are only spoken of by the male characters. The "other" is, in effect, marked by her absence. If the female body is discursively depicted as invisible or nonexistent, then female desire is denied. In bringing the female monsters onstage, therefore, Behn promotes the expression of female desire through the representation of the "other" female body. Further, not only are Killigrew's Jewish monsters never seen, but they are physically and mentally abused and destroyed—"boyl'ed away" and "cast into an evil mould"—by the Mountebank's baths of reformation (part II.5.5.86, 92). In contrast, Behn's powerful Jewish women are never physically controlled or repressed.

Behn's and Killigrew's use of the term *reformation* (in reference to the Mountebank's baths) suggests the ironic connections among the attempt to convert or displace the Jews during the Spanish Inquisition and the subsequent development of the puritanical repression of sexuality during the seventeenth-century. In particular, Behn's use of *reformation* links the sociohistorical expurgation of racial and religious difference to the repression of sexuality. Although Behn does not directly contest the anti-Semitic construction of the Jewish women who cannot intermarry "for fear of a Race of Giants . . . Pigmies and Fairies . . . worse than the Invasion of the *Moors*," she subverts these racially derogatory remarks by changing the meaning of difference and deformity (3.1.210, 134, 210–11). For Behn, the different body is a celebration, reminiscent of a lost golden age when the body and nature were alive, interconnected, and free from repression. The giant hopes that she will "meet [her] Match, and keep up the first Race of Man intire: But . . . this scanty World affords none such" (3.1.97–99). Confronted by men who act like mice, she boldly states: "I'll marry none whose Person and Courage shall bear some Proportion to mine" (3.1.82–83). Behn's female monsters are thus hierarchically elevated; the men do not measure up to these extraordinary "others"—just as Hellena was too good for the mortal Willmore. Behn's giant, the "other" woman, demands her equal, and, with her sister, rejects the two fools, Blunt and Fetherfool, in favor of Shift and Hunt, who, like the Rover, are displaced cavaliers. Moreover, Hunt must try to reform himself into a giant; he stands on the shoulders of another man to achieve her height. The ironic implication of this visual gag is that it takes two men to equal one woman.

Not only does Behn construct "other" women who refuse to be reformed, but it is the mouse-like men who must try to reconstruct themselves in order to match up to the strong women. Unlike Killigrew's silent and invisible "others," Behn's Jewish women can never be "boyl'ed away" in the baths of ideological repression because they voice and act upon their desires.[17]

In part II of *The Rover*, Behn clears a new space for the utopian woman—the "other" "Amazonian Princess"—whom man cannot possibly mutilate, alter, or appropriate (3.1.107). Killigrew's vision of the "other" woman, in contrast, is repressive and appropriative of difference and female sexuality. He presents the "other" female body as a metaphorically fecund land that deserves to be appropriated and commodified. The two male characters who pursue the monsters—Edwardo and Ferdinando—intend to marry the Jewish women only to steal their fortunes and abandon their monster wives. When Edwardo and Ferdinando attempt to reform their wives' bodies in the Mountebank's baths, one of the Jewesses is boiled to the size of a tiny diamond, while her sister is driven insane (part II.5.5.89). The Jewesses' guardian then forces Edwardo and Ferdinando to return the women's "money and Jewels" because they won their wives with "witchcraft" and therefore "rob the true Heires of the Estate" (part II.5.5.99, 101, 104). For Killigrew, however, Edwardo's and Ferdinando's abusive treatment of the Jewesses' is justified because, the Jewish women "are as rich as *Peru;* . . . the Jews their Parents couzen'd the poor of a Nation to give it to these Monsters" (part II.4.10.9, 11–12). And, because the female monsters are destroyed, Killigrew avoids the problem of intermarriage and the feared hybrid races of "giants" and "pigmies." In response to their (financial) losses, the disappointed Edwardo and Ferdinando claim they will go to the New World, where they will use the Mountebank's magical powder to seduce and rob "other" women:

> EDW[ARDO]: Yes [we will go to] the Indies; where we are promis'd
> six black wives a piece, smooth and comely beauties, naked truths,
> *Eves*, in the state of inocence, Girles that will neigh and fight for
> my bed. . . .
> FERD[INANDO]: Hunt their hunt, we are resolv'd, Sir; six plump,
> smooth pregnant Girles a piece is the bargain, with flat-noses all,
> for conveniency of kissing, with brave swell'd lips, *Cupids*

Cushions; so soft and sweet . . . ; their very sweat Aromatique and
Balsam'all; . . . and I warrant thee the feed will thrive.

EDW[ARDO]: Your *Fourbisher,* your *Magellan,* your *Drake* and
Rawley; all content your Moors woman has no fellow in nature;
she's your black Garden-mould, the same rich earth Adam digg'd
in, so full of nature and strength the Sun dwells in her; and will
send forth such Clustes of Boys and Girles, such straw, and such an
ear, so full, so clean, the Cradles will not hold the Barnes: our barren cold red and white clay knows no such harvest; all the streams
the Sun sucks from the parch'd earth you will find in the woman
there, as full and luscious as the Greek Vine; and 'tis true pleasure
to pluck a Girle there, so full of juyce she'l fill the Press; and there
women show their true virtue and their use.

(part II.5.7.56–58, 61–79)

Killigrew's portrayal of the "other" woman thus evokes the appropriative discourses of colonial power. The black woman is depicted as
the soil of the New World and of Eden: she will be tamed, molded,
and put to proper "use." Her rich body will bear the white man's
fruit. She increases his phallic and material power; he has six wives
and will have six children—one by each wife. Her earth is rich, "full
of juyce," his to control, dominate, and commodify. Particularly
significant is the timing of Edwardo's and Ferdinando's dialogue,
which comes directly after losing their potential wealthy, though
monstrous, Jewish wives. In effect, if Edwardo and Ferdinando cannot have the riches of the Jewesses, they can fantasize a feminized
land that they may appropriate and economically exploit—the body/
property of the black woman.

Edwardo's speech about appropriating the black woman's body
is not reworked in *The Rover.* Behn's play retains traces of the
metaphor of the "other" female body as representative of the material riches of New World, however. Her use of the metaphor of La
Nuche's and Ariadne's jewels in the love plots implicitly recalls
the colonization, appropriation, and commodification of the female
body/land of the New World. La Nuche's and Ariadne's jewels are
repeatedly referred to throughout the last acts of part II. The elderly
Petronella steals La Nuche's jewels so that she can seduce and win
Blunt (1:203). In offering herself, Ariadne significantly brings her
"basket" of "ten thousand Pound in ready Jewels" to Willmore,

England's royalist representative (5.3.235). As Carolyn Merchant points out, nature and the female body were viewed similarly in the seventeenth-century; mining the earth—both in England and in the colonies—was symbolically identified with the invasion of the female body.[18] The relationship between woman as sexual and material commodity—jewels as a metaphor for the sexual organs—is not new, but Behn gives a twist to the traditional images of masculine appropriation of woman as commodity and of female virginity as a jewel. Because women are presented as identical to the property/land of the New World, Behn symbolically links the repression of sexuality and the construction of woman-as-object to the economy of colonial power. The Jewesses, for example, are said to have acquired their wealth in Mexico, a country known to be filled with gold, silver, and gems and colonized specifically for its mineral wealth. Mexico was also land colonized by Spain, England's competitor in imperial expansion. For Behn as well as Killigrew, then, the acquisition of women's gems and bodies are conflated with mining the riches of the New World and the body/land of the "other."

However, in Behn's vision of female colonization the gaze of the white male turns back on itself. In *Thomaso*, after the Jewesses have been destroyed by the Mountebank's baths, Ferdinando and Edwardo are told by the guardian of the Jewesses that they must return the women's jewels. Yet we never see or hear of their return in Killigrew's comedy. In contrast, Behn emphasizes the necessity for the return of the Jewesses' property. At the end of *The Rover*, part II, when all of the stolen jewels have been restored to their rightful female owners, a necklace belonging to the Jewish giant has yet to be returned. Afraid that the monster would "devour him" (3.1.54), Fetherfool has symbolically eaten the powerful woman by swallowing the "delicious row of Pearls" around her neck (5.3.96). The exiled royalists, Shift and Hunt, force Fetherfool to return the female goods. In *The Rover*, therefore, the traditional invasion of the female body/land is reversed: Fetherfool's body must be "dissected"—opened up and specularized. He must go to the doctor, who will "redeem him [and] glyster him soundly" so that the giant's pearl will be retrieved and returned (1:211). The male body is invaded and observed, made to yield up its stolen riches. Fetherfool is literally punished for invading the female body and appropriating her jewels—he is forced to play the traditional passive female role, to undergo a symbolic rape so that her stolen property may be returned. In effect, then, Behn utilizes the restoration of the Jewish women's jewels as a strategy to subvert the ideology of the passive, colonized, and commodified woman who is gazed upon, invaded, and controlled by men. In Behn's utopian vision, the female body/land can never be appropriated and controlled.

The final love match between La Nuche and Willmore further demonstrates Behn's idealistic celebration and promotion of feminine desire in *The Rover,* part II. In part II, the prostitute and desiring woman gains the authority that both Hellena and Angellica sought and lost in part I. Along with the Jewish monsters, La Nuche presents an alternative model to that of the passive and commodified seventeenth-century woman. At the end of the play she is neither whore nor virgin; she cannot be confined by these categories. In part II, it is Ariadne who shares Angellica's fate; this time the virgin heiress loses Willmore—fortunately, in one sense, because he is attracted to her only for her fortune. Instead, La Nuche (Angellica's and Hellena's double) and Willmore unite in a nonlegal relationship outside of the traditional institution of marriage and its concerns with the transmission of property from one male to another. In the original productions of the two parts of *The Rover,* Elizabeth Barry played both Hellena and La Nuche, which, Peter Holland argues, stresses the inevitability of the love match between La Nuche and the Rover.[19] I think Behn self-consciously meant for us to perceive the likeness between the heroines and, hence, to read the relationship between La Nuche and Willmore as a more positive alternative to the legal marriage, which, symbolically at least, leads to Hellena's death. Both Willmore and La Nuche ultimately learn to reject money for love and, hence, economic power for equality between the sexes. In Behn's final vision, then, the female body escapes (at least temporarily) the repressive strategies of Church and state.

It is difficult to accept Behn's utopian vision as a valid political strategy for female emancipation if we believe that the desire for the golden age and a sociality free from sexual repression is, as Foucault argues in his *History of Sexuality,* also a fiction. But when we consider that, like her monsters, Behn herself was an extraordinary outsider, it is clear that the author's struggle for the expression of feminine desire was not merely theatrical. Behn's vision, while indeed fantastic, is an attempt to demystify the strategies of discursive power, to make visible what puritanical ideology subsumed into language—nature, women, people of color—and transformed into an economy of discipline and power. By recovering the absent "other" body, Behn subverts the male observer's strategy of repression and appropriation. The voices of the so-called outsiders are a necessary addition to cultural studies of the Restoration. *The Rover,* parts I and II demonstrate the resistance of the "other" body—colonial, grotesque, female—to the Whig ideology that we have inherited.

Notes

1. Aphra Behn, "Post-Script," *The Rover; or the Banish'd Cavaliers,* Parts I and II, in *The Works of Aphra Behn,* ed. Montague Summers, 6 vols. (1915; rpt. New York: Benjamin Blom, 1967), 1:107. Subsequent references to this edition will be cited parenthetically in the text by volume and page and/or line numbers. Maureen Duffy notes that Behn must have had Killigrew's consent to rewrite the play "even though she doesn't allude to it in her note to the published edition where she rebuts the . . . charge of plagiarism," in *The Passionate Shepherdess: Aphra Behn, 1640–89* (London: Methuen, 1989), p. 153.

2. Duffy, *The Passionate Shepherdess,* p. 153. As Duffy points out, the celebration of the "banished cavaliers" (the subtitle of *The Rover* as well) would "evoke a certain nostalgia, a remembrance of things past. . . . What lads we were; how clever, how brave, how irresistable. It was good propaganda too, a rallying for the faithful when the first romance of the King's return had worn thin and the country was again divided into factions" (p. 153).

3. For a different reading of *Thomaso* and *The Rover,* see Jones De Ritter, "The Gypsy, *The Rover,* and the Wanderer: Aphra Behn's Revision of Thomas Killigrew." *Restoration* 10 (1986): 82–92. See also Nancy Copeland, "Once a whore and ever"? Whore and Virgin in *The Rover* and Its Antecedents." *Restoration* 16 (1992): 20–27.

4. In "New Histericism: Aphra Behn's *Oroonoko:* The Body, the Text, and the Feminist Critic" (in *New Feminist Discourses,* ed. Isobel Armstrong [New York: Routledge Press, 1992], p. 292), Rosalind Ballaster argues that the white narrator in *Oroonoko* "cannot, or rather will not, identify with nor appropriate . . . the black woman." As a result, Ballaster claims, we should not read the novel as deconstructive of colonial power. I read the relationship between the white narrator and Imoinda quite differently. Behn's position is clearly ambivalent toward rather than simply constitutive of racial and colonial stereotypes. In *The Rover,* for example, there are a number of stereotypically anti-Semitic

remarks spoken by the male and female characters; and yet, ironically, it is her Jewish women who embody the potentially subversive and idealized female excessivity and freedom from the masculinist gaze.

See also Laura Brown, "The Romance of the Empire: *Oroonoko* and the Trade in Slaves," in *The New Eighteenth Century: Theory * Politics * English Literature,* ed. Felicity Nussbaum and Laura Brown (New York: Methuen Press, 1987), pp. 41–61, and Laura Brown "Reading Race and Gender: Jonathan Swift," *Eighteenth-Century Studies* 23 (1990): 425–43. I agree with Brown's premise that European women are made to bear the responsibility for mercantile capitalism—particularly in the works of male writers of the late seventeenth and early eighteenth centuries. However, I read Behn's conflation of the female European self and colonized "other" as a strategic attempt, at least, to resist the masculinization of desire and, hence, the oppression of women of all races.

5. See my "Aphra Behn's *Oroonoko:* The Politics of Gender, Race, and Class," in *Living by the Pen: Early British Women Writers,* ed. Dale Spender (New York: Teachers College Press, Columbia Univ., 1992), pp. 39–51.

6. Elin Diamond, "*Gestus* and Signature in Aphra Behn's *The Rover,*" *ELH* 56 (1989): 519–41, and Catherine Gallagher, "Who Was That Masked Woman? The Prostitute and the Playwright in the Comedies of Aphra Behn," *Women's Studies* 15 (1988): 77–83. This essay is reprinted above in this volume. Diamond suggests that Behn is portraying herself in the character of Angellica Bianca. She also asserts that all of the female characters in *The Rover* find they must "traverse the whore's marketplace. . . . They will market themselves as she does, compete for the same male affection, suffer similar abuse." Gallagher similarly asserts that Behn "introduced to the world of English letters the professional woman writer as a newfangled whore." For a refutation of Gallagher's argument, see Deborah C. Payne " 'And Poets Shall by Patron-Princes Live': Aphra Behn and Patronage," in *Curtain Calls: British and American Women and the Theater, 1660–1820,* ed. Mary Anne Schofield and Cecilia Macheski (Athens: Ohio Univ. Press, 1991), pp. 105–19. Payne asserts that Behn dropped the role of the writer-prostitute—specifically in the prologues and epistles to her plays—as soon she gained court patronage in 1680. Payne suggests that Behn sought a means of self-representation that "seemed more authentic, more 'real' than this self-abnegating pose" (p. 117).

7. Robert Markley, " 'Be impudent, be saucy, forward, bold, touzing, and leud': The Politics of Masculine Sexuality and Feminine Desire in Behn's Tory Comedies," in *Revisionist Readings of the Restoration and Eighteenth-Century Theatre,* ed. J. Douglas Canfield and Deborah C. Payne (forthcoming).

8. For more on Michel Foucault's "repressive hypothesis" and the construction of femininity in the eighteenth century, see Nancy Armstrong, *Desire and Domestic Fiction: A Political History of the Novel* (New York: Oxford Univ. Press, 1987), especially chapters one and two.

9. Judith Kegan Gardiner, "Aphra Behn: Sexuality and Self-Respect," *Women's Studies* 7 (1980): 69.

10. Michel Foucault, *The History of Sexuality:* vol. 1, *An Introduction,* trans. Robert Hurley (New York: Vintage Books, 1980).

11. For more on the gaze, see Michel Foucault, "The Eye of Power," in *Power/Knowledge: Selected Interviews and Other Writings, 1972–1977,* ed. Colin Gordon, trans. Colin Gordon et al. (New York: Pantheon Books, 1980), pp. 146–65.

12. Mikhail Bakhtin, *Rabelais and His World,* trans. Helene Iswolsky (Cambridge: MIT Press, 1968).

13. Thomas Killigrew, *Thomaso, or, The Wanderer: A Comedy,* Parts I and II, (Henry Herringman, 1663). Subsequent references to this edition will be cited parenthetically in the text by line or page number.

14. Peter Stallybrass and Allon White, *The Politics and Poetics of Transgression* (Ithaca: Cornell Univ. Press, 1986), p. 14.

15. Foucault, *History of Sexuality,* pp. 44–45.

16. See Homi K. Bhabha's "Of Mimicry and Man: The Ambivalence of Colonial Discourse" (*October* 28 [1984]: 125–33) in which he asserts that "the dominant strategic function of colonial power, intensifies surveillance, and poses an immanent threat to both 'normalized' knowledges and disciplinary powers" (p. 126). In effect, the gaze of power doubles back upon itself, alienates the disciplinary gazer, and the "observer becomes observed" (p. 128).

17. See Dianne Dugaw, *Warrior Women and Popular Balladry, 1650–1850* (Cambridge and New York: Cambridge Univ. Press, 1989). She argues that the woman warrior in popular balladry functioned to provide a positive model of femininity. As Dugaw asserts, "the Female Warrior Ballads propose . . . not only that woman *could* play the part of a man, could step out of her 'female identity,' and thus subvert any notion of its immutability, but that, in fact, women should be encouraged to do so." These powerful women assert a "remarkable premodern ideal of womanhood" (p. 5).

18. Carolyn Merchant, *The Death of Nature: Women, Ecology, and the Scientific Revolution* (San Francisco: Harper and Row, 1980).

19. Peter Holland, *The Ornament of Action: Text and Performance in Restoration Comedy* (Cambridge and New York: Cambridge Univ. Press, 1979), p. 67.

SUSAN GREEN

Semiotic Modalities of the Female Body in Aphra Behn's *The Dutch Lover*

The possibility of any radical constructionism can only be built on the foundations of a hidden essentialism.

—Diana Fuss, *Essentially Speaking: Feminism, Nature, and Difference*

We cannot know in advance the precise intersection (if any) of questions of sexuality with questions of the body with respect to any particular issue.

—Beverley Brown and Parveen Adams, "The Feminine Body and Feminist Politics"

In this essay I will explore the sense in which the female body on Aphra Behn's comic stage parallels the problem of the female body in contemporary feminist theory.[1] To the extent that current feminist theory often suggests a body split between its materiality and its knowledge of itself as a subject, so too Behn's drama stages both the representability of the female body and its unrepresentability. In other words, in Behn's theatrical practice, as in contemporary feminist theory, the female body constitutes itself in a kind of theater of reference and association. I focus on the way feminism creates a drama out of the epistemological value of the female body in much the same way that Behn creates her drama.

To understand how Behn's plays spring from a central concern about the possibilities for representing the female body, I will distinguish between a biological body and an essentialized one in the present context. Behn certainly did not employ the word *essential* to designate her deployments of dramatic form in relation to the female body under the particular conditions of the English theater in the 1670s and 1680s, and I do not wish to unnecessarily extend some of the rancorous feminist debates that have surrounded this word over the past few years.[2] On the contrary, I want to show how Behn's plays offer representations of the female body that both incorporate and exhaust discursive essentializations that can be produced on behalf of that body. In other words, I am not using the term *essential* to apply to distinctions of the body in nature such as chromosomal, hormonal, or primary and secondary sexual characteristics. Rather, I am pointing to the female body as that which is posited as female from within feminist arguments that appeal to a difference of women (whether seen as a "natural" difference or a historical one) or from within a theatrical practice that required women to play women's roles (as in Behn's case). For purposes of my argument I will say that the female body becomes, in these discursive arrangements, essentialized—seen to contain within a particularly female form a female content.

In spite of the useful assertion in Beverley Brown and Parveen Adams's statement that heads this essay that "we cannot know in advance" the meaning of the body in any particular discursive deployment, they make no distinction between a female body and a feminine one.[3] Brown and Adams argue that the feminine body is the only natural body available for a feminist politics that necessarily must then deconstruct the essentialization. I want to describe how Behn employs two of the newest features of the Restoration theater, female actresses and movable scenery, to dramatize the discrepancy between what we might call a constructed femininity and the particular female body that tries to take its place within that construction.[4] Her play *The Dutch Lover,* performed disastrously in 1673 for only one night, offers Behn's fullest enactment of the disjunction felt by women when the lived experience of their bodies comes into conflict with discursive modalities of the female body.[5] The play's opening night failure (with Charles II attending) as a result of bad costuming and bad acting prompted Behn's vehement defense in her "Epistle to the Reader" appended to the play upon publication later in 1673. The epistle has become widely anthologized and commented upon in recent years for its forthright statement about women's right to cultural authority as well as for presenting a formative theory of drama and of comedy.[6] The importance of Behn's epistle, then, might prompt us to think more seriously about what she was doing in the play itself—even to the extent that it be performed again, if not in a theater, at least in our critical imaginations.

In addition to comparing the deployment of the female body on Behn's stage to concerns about the body in contemporary feminist theory, my analysis of *The Dutch Lover* demonstrates as well some significant aspects of Restoration drama in the 1670s. This discussion follows the arguments of Eric Rothstein and Frances Kavenik, who suggest that the comedies of the 1670s offer "different provisional images to different members of the same audience" (p. 7). A play's determinacy, then, rests more with the responses of the audience—in what they desire to see, rather than in what they resist seeing—than in any formal resolution provided by the plot's closure.[7] In Rothstein and Kavenik's view, such a model of comedy fosters "ideological discrepancy" within the plays such that the plots of the 1670s comedies were not simply vehicles for "satire and energy," as was more general with the more ideologically conservative plays of the 1680s. In other words, the highly politicized comedy plots of the 1670s worked semiotically in ways that I describe in reference to *The Dutch Lover,* where mutually exclusive interpretative possibilities resist synthetic conceptualization. To begin my analysis, however, it is important to look back to the very different conditions of the Elizabethan theater to see that the question Behn's drama poses most forcefully—the question of how a female body can represent itself— was massively elided by Elizabethan theatrical practice.

Recent scholars may be arriving at a consensus that the homoerotics of the Elizabethan theater were based on fear of women, while, at the same time, the radical instability of human essence was assumed.[8] Stephen Orgel finds the Elizabethan sense of the protean nature of human essence particularly apparent in the easy reversibility of genders in the plays.[9] At the level of enunciation, boys represent women; at the level of fiction, the romantic heroines must make a passage through masculinity to establish their distinction as women. But, as Orgel notes, this is a differentiation Shakespeare sometimes does not fully grant to his women characters, as when Viola, still dressed as a boy at the end of *Twelfth Night,* says she cannot become a woman until her women's clothes have been re-covered, or when the boy actress playing Rosalind undoes the con-struction of Rosalind "as a woman" effected by the play, revealing that she has been played all along by a boy—a revelation made in the epilogue to *As You Like It*. In an important sense, then, Shake-spearean drama plays itself out within the contradiction that, given the permeability and flexibility of human essence, the act of repre-senting a self may result in men becoming women, particularly if boys alone could make those representations. As I have argued elsewhere, Shakespeare and Fletcher in their jointly written play, *The Two Noble Kinsmen,* explicitly confront the generative consequences of a possi-ble fear on the part of men that their theatrical practice profoundly compromises what is natural about their gender.[10]

Perhaps these contradictions within Shakespearean drama prompted Behn to evoke the erotic, pleasurable dimension of her illustrious predecessor's plays when she defended her play in her "Epistle to the Reader" of *The Dutch Lover*. When Behn vigorously argues for her woman's right to a public, theatrical discourse, she claims for herself all the prerogatives of playwrighting accorded to "the immortal Shakespeare . . . who was not guilty of much more [learning] than often falls to women's share."[11] For Behn, drama as a genre has "no great room for that which is men's great advantage over women, that is Learning" (p. 123). In her mind, the most basic response to theater is emotional and erotic—plays "exercise men's passions not their understandings." Both her comedy and Shake-speare's offer, above all else, erotic, pleasurable experience; but, considering the very different status of the female body on their stages, we might well ask whose passions are represented and what pleasures are evoked on their stages. We can approach an answer to this complex question if we see the similarities between Behn's nar-rativizations of women's bodies and those found in some contempo-rary feminist theories.

At the risk of importing a too-technical and too-bulky theoretical apparatus to present my argument, let me schematize the possibilities for the representation of the female body in the form of a semiotic square.[12] It is beyond the scope of this article to explain all the complex rhetorical relations involved in Greimas's square, but it does prove useful, I think, in discussing Behn's representation of women and in dislodging feminist arguments caught within opposing dualities in language when discussing the female body. As Diana Fuss points out, feminist arguments too often posit an overdetermined binarity in which essentialist and constructivist positions are mutually exclusive; Fuss argues that essentialism is not always reactionary and that even constructivism depends on a "hidden essentialism" that may be "quietly doing its work elsewhere."[13] The advantage of employing Greimassien semiotics in an analysis of the discourse surrounding the female body is that it can give language to that "elsewhere" of essentialism's political investments. Greimas constructs a model of the production of meaning in which semantic and social bonds advance in a narrative whose terms are produced in a double relation of disjunction and conjunction. Within the relationships among each of the four terms that Greimas posits as necessary to any fully semiotic understanding (the first term, the second term as its contrary nonterm, the third term as its negative or doubly positive term, and the fourth term as a negative nonterm or a doubly negative term), logical possibilities for producing meaning are exhausted, yet the importance of the semantic exchange is that it presupposes change, content, and an ideological investment. Behn's attention to how the female body acquires its significance and comes to represent a particular female content by means of its particularly female form follows these same semiotic processes, as we shall see in the narrativization of the female body that constitutes her play *The Dutch Lover.*[14]

Before discussing that extremely complex play (whose plot is so intricate as to be barely able to be summarized), it will be helpful to see that the representability of the female body may be understood as falling within the semiotic relation illustrated in figure 1.

Within this model of the female body:

$fb1$ = sexualized/politicized body—a self-giving or self-evident body constituted by language as self-performance. Sexual differentiation has already occurred, that is, place is already given for the body as, for example, on the Restoration stage, where women were required to take women's roles. This body functions in feminist theory when the place from which a woman

FB
Representability

fb1
Essentialist Body
(Self-evident,
Sexualized/Politicized)

fb2
Constructivist Body
(Desiring)

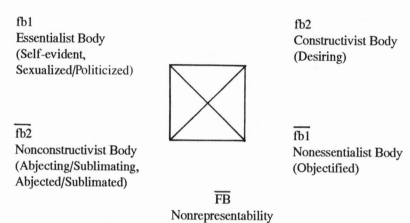

$\overline{fb2}$
Nonconstructivist Body
(Abjecting/Sublimating,
Abjected/Sublimated)

$\overline{fb1}$
Nonessentialist Body
(Objectified)

$\overline{FB}$
Nonrepresentability

Figure 1: Model of the representability of the female body.

speaks—her epistemological standpoint—is emphasized. By means of this body, a woman takes up a political position about what she wants, speaking as a woman enacting her right to agency in language.

fb2 = desiring body—a body wholly taken up into language and therefore a body continually being put into place. The question of the representability of female desire has received a great deal of attention from poststructural psychoanalytic theorists. It is not the purpose of this essay to delineate all those arguments. Within the context of desire, I consider that a female body is construed as a feminine body—a body with an active drive but a passive aim. In a basic sense, the feminine body only wants to watch itself being watched, but strategies for understanding how the feminine body may also speak its own complex desires have been advanced by Luce Irigaray, for example, who proposes that to speak their desires women must mimic the hysteria that constitutes the feminine in language.[15] Hélène Cixous suggests that we gaze at the terrifying, laughing face of the Medusa—the dark, destructive side of the feminine—until we can see her smile.[16] In any case, theorists agree that "the feminine" offers women a treacherous, labyrinthine access to representation of their desires, an aspect of the problem of representation encountered by women that Behn's drama fully explores. I place this body on the constructivist corner of the square because, even though some psychoanalytic theories are accused of essentialism, no one suggests that a desiring body is anything but a body constituted in language.[17]

$\overline{fb}1$ = objectified body—the body of the "other," speaking the solipsistic language of the objectifying subject. Because this body is only surface and shape, it can be thought of as nonessential. On the Elizabethan stage, for example, boy actors objectified the women's bodies they played, but they were not essentially women. In an oversimplified sense, the objectified female body is the one most reviled by feminist theorists, the one most abjected in feminist theory, we might say. But feminist discourse, like any other discourse, needs to recognize that its desires, as with all desires, presuppose an objectified body—one, in feminist analysis, that is often female. Two feminist critiques of feminist discourse that deconstruct feminist desire by locating the objectified female body upon which it rests are Margaret Atack's "The Other: Feminist," which shows how the feminist "herself" becomes objectified in Julia Kristeva's work.[18] Meaghan Morris analyzes Mary Daly's construction of a female "other"—the mindless, male-identified fembot that becomes the objective necessity underlying Daly's feminist analysis.[19]

$\overline{fb}2$ = abjecting/sublimating body—a prelinguistic, gestural body situated on the border between space and place. Kristeva's discussion of the abject offers feminists an important place from which to analyze how women delimit their world through processes of abjection and sublimation. Her analysis of the maternal body describes a body undergoing a fundamental division that occurs without a phallic signifier to structure the event. Thus, Kristeva embarks on a theory of a subject that does not yet project an object. The preoedipal site of such a subjectivity (if it can be called subjectivity) is only intelligible retroactively through representation. In language, Kristeva identifies "the *semiotic*" as the preoedipal divisions within and from the maternal that are apprehended in rhythms, punning, prosody, slips of the tongue—aspects of language existing outside the domain of structural linguistics. Although it is not my purpose here to outline the implications for women and for the representation of women that such a theory of the abject holds, I do suggest that feminists could profit from a more politicized analysis of abjection and sublimation.

For purposes of this essay, I make a distinction between the abjected body and the abjecting body as they differ in narrativization.

The maternal may be narrativized as the abjected body of preoedipal reaction formations, as in Kristeva's analysis, but we also have to account for the other side of abjection—the sublime. A sufficient analysis of a female sublime would posit another body—a female body from within its own abjection, receiving and inscribing its own sublimity, tracing out its own sublimations. Kristeva attempts such a discussion in her widely anthologized essay, "Stabat Mater," but there is a reactionary allure within the maternal sublime that requires a further, more politicized, historicized analysis. Patricia Yaeger's article entitled "Toward a Female Sublime" provides a good place to begin such an exploration, as does the work of Behn, as I will demonstrate in this essay.[20]

The abjecting/sublimating body is positioned on the square at the corner that Ronald Schleifer emphasizes as the most "explosive" of all the modalities—the corner from which movement and change can occur.[21] Because abjection locates the moment when a preoedipal not-yet-subject sets the limits of its world—expelling the unclean and improper so as to create a place for the emergence of the ego with its array of desired objects, logics, and representations, and so forth, the processes of abjection locate a profoundly liminal area from which, one might claim, all of culture arises. Hence, abjection's location at the most protean position on the semiotic square.

In specifying these modalities of the female body, I want to emphasize that I am not imagining an array of separate bodies available for women that are divided up between discourses or among characters in a play (though the ensuing analysis might lead to that conclusion). Rather, I am describing a division of the female body in its subjugation to signification. This division is felt most acutely at moments when discursive stability moves into crisis. In *The Dutch Lover* I am interested in the moments when articulation of the female body moves between designations in place in the theatrical space (or scene) and designations in language. This movement is particularly crucial in act 2, scene 2 and act 4, scene 3, which I will discuss in some detail. Because I argue that Behn's theater explores the discrepancy between a constructed femininity in language and an essentialized female body that tries to take its place within that construction, I will turn now to her plays to continue the discussion.

If Behn's drama is about the epistemological value of the female body—what we can learn from efforts to represent women in their embodied specificity—one way to approach that analysis would be to ask how Behn's heroines know what they know. Catharine Gallagher analyzes what Behn's heroines learn and what they do with that knowledge.[22] Gallagher argues that in Behn's play, *The Lucky Chance* (1686), Julia learns she cannot represent herself as self-alienated without being considered damaged property on the marriage market. But, even more, Julia learns how to appropriate the masculine advantage in representation. This advantage is signified when Julia's lover, Gayman, has a second erection during their night of lovemaking. The problem is that Gayman had won the night by winning a wager with Julia's husband, Sir Feeble, to take his place in bed. But Gayman's "excess of love" betrays his identity. Until that moment, Gayman tells Julia, accusingly: "It was the feeble husband you enjoyed/In cold imagination, and no more."[23] The narrative implies Gayman's advantage in representation. When his body reveals his identity, the implication is that his sexual powers are inalienable; he cannot be anything other than who he is. His stake in representation secured, the essentialism of his body is absolute. Julia, on the other hand, operates from within a more "shady effect," as Gallagher calls it.

Behn presents a perfect asymmetry regarding men and women within her representational scheme. The night before Gayman's escapade, Julia had conspired to spend the night with him. Unbeknownst to Gayman, Julia secretly supplied money to his landlady to pay his debts and to take his landlady's place in bed with Gayman, who had offered his sexual services in place of his rent money. During that night, Gayman never suspects that it is Julia in bed with him. In fact, we are to imagine that he would never suspect he had slept with Julia except that he is conducted to her same bedroom on the next night after he wins his wager with Sir Feeble. When Julia accuses him of not having known her the night before, Gayman does not need to admit this is true. Instead, he slyly denies that he recognized her the night before when he insists that in his imagination he was making love to his awkward landlady: "A canvas bag of wooden ladles were a better bedfellow" (p. 43). The implication is, of course, that female sexuality is wholly an effect of men's imaginations. Gayman is decisive in promoting the insinuation that a woman can never be anything except the figure her male partner imagines her to be. As Gallagher argues, a woman of Julia's class may be self-alienated, she may be sexually distinct from other women, but she cannot represent herself as such and retain her social standing. In fact, Behn implies that she may not be able to represent herself as distinguishable from other women at all because men's ability to represent themselves seems absolute and takes into its domain the representability of the female. In such a scheme, Julia can only appropriate the male advantage in representation. Her feigned moral outrage that her husband has sold her sexually to another man (even though she duped him herself the night before), gives her the socially sanctioned reason she needs to leave Sir Feeble, making her available to marry Gayman, whom she loves.

Without the ability to distinguish herself from other women, any representation Julia may make about herself cannot be done as a woman. Put another way, under the representational scheme Behn both employs and critiques in this play, history cannot produce a heterogeneously gendered subject because veiled women (discernable because concealed) cannot achieve any distance from themselves that can become a representable distance. As Luce Irigaray explains, the contradiction for women in representational systems in which they must be veiled is that woman, separated off and distinguished as the difference from man, cannot give form to matter because she must stand for matter.[24] She is said not to have essence but to be essence. Hence, Julia cannot distinguish herself sexually from the woman of Gayman's imagination without sacrificing her entire social identity. Veiled as the essence of woman, she cannot get out of her constructed social self to have access to essence as form, i.e., identify with herself as same. If Julia could do this, it would mean that she could posit an essentiality to her female body and identify with other women (as same) to create form out of the infinite differences that could be articulated through that primary identification. Without a stake in representation, no lever to pry apart the veil that covers her, Julia represents herself only through appropriation.

But Behn is not Julia. In narrativizing the female body as she does, Behn also shows us how women, in fact, do represent themselves as women. Behn stakes an idea of a specifically female consciousness over and against the idea of the specifically female body. I think we are only recently able to see Behn's theatrical practice in this way, such has been the power of the veiled woman of the male imaginary to obscure the female body's status as a historicized and politicized body with a capacity to signify something particular about female consciousness. Both Irigaray and Behn imagine that such a discursive body is available if there is a need for one, and they create one to expose the conditions of representation that would deny a specifically female access to form.

Gallagher's analysis brilliantly observes that Behn's drama narrativizes the moment when a woman realizes the problems inherent in the representation of her desires. Although we can see that Behn's plays thematize what her heroines learn and what they do with that knowledge, an analysis like Gallagher's, which articulates the plane of content in Behn's plays, does not address the question of how the female body becomes invested with epistemological value on her stage. As Gallagher describes, Behn's narrativization locates Julia's resources in representation within the hidden or the suppressed middle term that the pure syntax of the binary essence vs. construction cannot articulate. As essence, Julia cannot distinguish herself from Gayman's landlady; she becomes instead pure construction. Yet, from within this mutual exclusivity, Julia maneuvers to achieve her aims, which cannot be represented or else they cannot be achieved.

As valuable as this insight into Behn's theatrical practice is, I think we can see in the excessive narrativizations of Behn's *The Dutch Lover* that her understanding of the semiosis of the female body goes beyond the syntactical possibilities for women in the binary essence vs. construction. We should consider, too, that *The Lucky Chance* (1686) and *The Dutch Lover* (1673) were produced under different historical circumstances. I would argue that the more restricted representational possibilities for women that Behn hilariously exposes in *The Lucky Chance* reflect the later decade's more conservative performance conditions. In her earlier play, under a more ideologically configured and formative theatrical practice, Behn attempts to account for the signification of the female body—how it produces meaning, not just that it does.

It helps my analysis that *The Dutch Lover* tells the interconnected story of four heroines. If we place these heroines on the corners of the semiotic square I described earlier, we can see how *The*

Dutch Lover plays out the representability of the female body in the form of a semiotic square. In other words, the play dramatizes how the female body derives epistemological value. On the plane of content, this value crucially determines a primary cultural division of women articulated in this play by the complimentary questions: How do men know who their sisters are? How do women know who their brothers are?

Superimposing the four heroines onto the semiotic square introduced earlier, *The Dutch Lover*'s plot and its representation of women exist within the following semiosit relation illustrated in Figure 2.

Euphemia   Clarinda

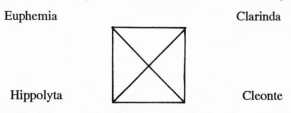

Hippolyta   Cleonte

Figure 2: Model of the semiotic relations among the heroines of *The Dutch Lover* (to be superimposed onto *Figure 1* above)

Euphemia's privileged position in the narrative as the woman who inaugurates the plot indicates that she functions semantically as an essentialized/politicized female force. She not only decides to woo the stranger, Alonzo, rather than wed the Dutchman, Haunce (as her father has arranged), she stage manages all the transactions necessary to marry the man she chooses. She even persuades Alonzo to disguise himself as Haunce to fool her family into thinking she is marrying as she ought.

Tracing Alonzo's relationship to the four heroines helps delineate the semiosis of the female body in this play. If Euphemia is the woman who can ask Alonzo to marry her, Clarinda is the woman who asks him to be her brother and give her protection. In fact, as he later learns, she is his sister and, thus, is the one woman on the stage whom he cannot marry. Euphemia and Clarinda function as contraries to each other in this regard and in other ways as well. For example, Euphemia actively pursues the man she wants to marry, but Clarinda merely waits for her lover, Marcel, to come to her. While Euphemia promotes herself from within a sense of scene or place that she stage manages, Clarinda inscribes herself within language. As desiring subject, she waits for Marcel to meet her at night: "And now when I have done this, and am all trembling with fear and shame (and yet an infinite desire to see him too)" (p. 148). When desire fails to give her the identity she wants, she makes a verbal agreement with Alonzo to be his "sister." Thus, she occupies the constructivist corner of the square.

If Clarinda is the woman who most cultivates the construction of her desires within language, Cleonte becomes the most objectified figure in the play. Rather than securing the alliance of a brother, Cleonte suffers from a mistake about whom her brother is. She thinks her brother is Silvio, the man who professes his love for her. In the most extreme objectification in the play, Silvio can only respond to Cleonte (who he, likewise, thinks is his sister) by vacillating between the impulses of rape and murder.

Cleonte functions like a complex positive term in the semiosis in that she participates both in Clarinda's narrative functions and in Euphemia's. As I have pointed out, Cleonte and Clarinda both are ignorant about whom their brothers are. (Cleonte mistakenly thinks Silvio is her brother; Clarinda does not realize that Alonzo is hers.) Alonzo, in fact, is the male figure whose relations with these heroines most clearly traces out the dimensions of the semiosis. He mediates between Cleonte and Clarinda, bringing Clarinda to Cleonte's home for protection when Marcel becomes angry after he thinks Clarinda is meeting his rival, Silvio, rather than waiting for him. As I mentioned, Silvio is not in love with Clarinda but with Cleonte. His attention to Clarinda is merely to hide from the world his true feelings for the woman he thinks is his sister—Cleonte. So, in a sense, Silvio, like Alonzo, also mediates between the two women. In fact, a great deal of the play circles around the men's inability to sort out their relationships to Clarinda and Cleonte. Are they sisters or potential lovers?

While Cleonte and Clarinda both have a hidden relation to men that must be revealed, both Cleonte and Euphemia suffer from too much objectification by men. Silvio dangerously creates Cleonte solely as the object of his desire while Haunce's misogynistic objectification of Euphemia is more covert, less deadly, but hardly less violent. "I'll manage her that must be my wife, as I please, or I'll beat her into fashion," (p. 169), he says as he prepares to woo Euphemia even though he is drunk. But Euphemia has already shown herself capable of manipulating her own objectified image. She presents herself "veiled" to Alonzo at their first meeting (act 1, scene 3), then stages an elaborate "unveiling," creating an image of herself to secure his attention. Thus, between what might be seen as a binary relation between Euphemia's essentialized, active assertions and Clarinda's constructed, passive femininity appears Cleonte, the more complex combination of them both. She suffers objectification, as does Euphemia but without Euphemia's politicized participation in that process. Like Clarinda, her hopes for marrying the man she loves are entangled in the problem of knowing her real relation to her brother. For Cleonte, that entanglement means she is confused about her desires for Silvio, with whom she is falling in love, although she thinks he is her brother, both protecting and menacing her. Clarinda, on the other hand, knows she desires Marcel, but she is threatened by Marcel's sexual aggressiveness because she lacks a brother to insist that Marcel marry her.

Hippolyta casts her shadow across all these relations. Because she has acknowledged her sexual relationship to Antonio when she is supposed to be waiting for her betrothed, Alonzo, to arrive and marry her, for Marcel she is the sister whose honor requires his protective revenge. Marcel would ravage Clarinda, yet he must avenge Hippolyta's ravagement. He understands how Hippolyta has placed him in this doubly negative position. "I either must my shameful love resign,/Or my more brave and just revenge decline" (p. 142), he says as he prepares for the night in which he is to meet his lover yet must redress his sister's dishonor.

Like the negative complex term of the semiotic square, Hippolyta creates a different context through which to reconsider the semantic opposition set up by the contrary relation at the upper level. This is especially evident in Hippolyta's relationship to Euphemia. Hippolyta has rejected Alonzo, the man Euphemia wants to marry, but, like Euphemia, who aggressively courts Alonzo, Hippolyta risks becoming a courtesan. Although the plot requires that male characters learn their correct social relation to Cleonte and Clarinda, male confusion over Hippolyta's and Euphemia's identities are more complexly (and negatively) related to issues about the representability of the female body.

A mysterious moment in which discursive instability evokes these more troubling relations occurs in act 2, scene 2. Euphemia takes refuge in what she thinks is a bawdy house (actually the house where Antonio has lodged Hippolyta after spreading rumors that she is a courtesan, although Hippolyta does not yet know this). There Euphemia is presented to Marcel, who is heavily cloaked and whom everyone thinks is Alonzo coming to marry her. Alonzo sees Marcel enter the house and thinks he has a rival for Euphemia's attentions. Marcel mistakes Euphemia for Hippolyta, although Alonzo does not yet realize Marcel's mistake. When they are about to fight, three nearly simultaneous actions occur creating in the performance a moment much like the moment of Angellica Bianca's appearance in Behn's *The Rover,* which Elin Diamond describes as a Brechtian *gestus*—the moment that "makes visible the contradictory interactions of text, theater apparatus, and contemporary social struggle."[25] Those three simultaneous actions are that Euphemia calls for help, her veil falls off, and Hippolyta enters dressed like a courtesan. The stage directions indicate how complex this moment becomes for Marcel: "Marcel stands gazing on both with wonder" (p. 145). The confusion, he says, has been absolute: "I've lost the power of striking where I ought" (p. 145). Although the narrative instantly makes clear to Marcel and to the audience what his error has been, we learn later that from Hippolyta's point of view things have not become so transparent. In this regard, Hippolyta functions at a more complex narrative level than even Euphemia, with whom she was confused in this scene and who, as I have suggested, acquired considerable narrative stature when she initiated the play's action by choosing to woo Alonzo in act 1, scene 1—the very man, of course, whom Hippolyta has rejected.

Hippolyta's representation arises from a more protean narrative level than is true of any other character in the play. Her fluid identity merges easily with others. In her first scene, as I explained earlier, she is mistaken for Euphemia. Antonio spreads rumors that she is a courtesan, and she even appears dressed as one in the scene just discussed. Narrative resolution occurs when her identity is revealed beneath the male disguise she adopts when she seeks revenge against Antonio. (Significantly for the semiosis of the play, she disguises herself as Alonzo, the male character whose relations with women, I argue, trace out the dimensions of the semiosis I describe.)

I have indicated that the semiotic modality indexed by Hippolyta's representation is best thought of in its relation to what Kristeva calls the abject. If abjection is the process of a pre-oedipal splitting of the not-yet-subject from the not-yet-object, all that Hippolyta does in act 3, scene 3 when she weeps over Antonio's sleeping (and wounded) body while she contemplates both suicide and murder can be seen as partaking of abjection. In other words, the scene enacts Hippolyta's struggle at the boundary of what she will claim as proper to herself. Antonio's doubly wounded, sleeping body functions as the object, which is not yet "other" enough to permit a full emergence of her ego.

> Why should this villain sleep, this treacherous man—
> Who has for ever robbed me of my rest?
> Had I but kept my innocence entire,
> I had out-braved my fate, and broke my chains,
> Which now I bear like a poor guilty slave.
>
> (p. 170)

Her abjection arises from her acknowledgment that she is bound by "loathed fetters" but still must "love on, in spite of me." When Antonio sees that he is in danger, he woos her again to get her dagger from her hand, then turns on her and taunts her with the knowledge that he has only compromised her honor in revenge against her brother Marcel, who destroyed his hopes with Clarinda. It is significant that this male narrative emerges with clarity at the same time that Hippolyta struggles to distinguish herself. Is she simply the prop in a male revenge plot? Is "loving on" her only option as she attempts to preserve her class status and not be thought a courtesan?

As the scene progresses, abjection circles around again, so that when Antonio taunts her by revealing his manipulations in advertising her as a courtesan, she answers

> Dost think I did not understand the plot?
> Yes, and was mad till some young lovers came.
> But you had set a price too high upon me,
> No brisk young man durst venture,
> I had exposed myself at cheaper rates.
>
> (p. 173)

Hippolyta adopts an abject version of Euphemia's more overtly politicized strategy in an effort to solve the narrative contradictions that mark her as the boundary delimiting a male dispute over honor. Hippolyta counters Antonio's revelation by saying she had offered herself to anyone who would kill him: "He that durst say Antonio lives no more,/Should have possest me *gratis*" (p. 173). Because this is the first we have heard of Hippolyta's plot, its veracity is in doubt. Much better, Hippolyta's words here inscribe into the representation a critique of Euphemia's politics. Hippolyta's rhetorical move shows how dangerous it can be when a woman imagines that she can simply appropriate her image, as it is constructed within male narrative, for her own political ends. Upon saying these words, Hippolyta is threatened with rape.

The scene dramatizes Hippolyta's abjection of Antonio at the point where she struggles to move out of the abjectifications of an underlying (or competing) male narrative that would overwhelm her. To complete her revenge against Antonio (she plans to kill him), she disguises herself as a man—Alonzo. "'Tis an act too horrid for a woman" (p. 171), she says.

It is useful to see that she takes up male disguise under an entirely different semiosis than does a Shakespearean comic heroine. In short, when Shakespeare's heroines take on male disguise, it always works; for Behn's heroines, it never does. Imogen, Viola, and Rosalind wear men's clothes to protect themselves from male sexual aggression when they venture into strange societies outside the immunity their families would normally give them. Unprotected by male family members, these women's bodies would signal sexual vulnerability. Men's clothing covers them, buys them time while they assess the political situation and find a way to enter, as a woman, what might otherwise be a dangerous world for them.

When Behn's heroines operate in drag, doing so offers them little protection. Their real female selves are always discovered by men— sometimes, as in Hippolyta's case, after the women have been wounded in swordplay. Furthermore, in Behn's dramas women adopt other disguises besides male ones. They often disguise themselves across class, as Hippolyta and Euphemia do when they flirt with identities as courtesans. In fact, female disguise across class lines works for Behn's heroines better than disguise across gender lines. Often male characters become confused about women's identities when women cross-dress across class. Men's inability to identify women's class status is often what allows women characters to explore their identities outside male-defined class restrictions. Thus, discovery of the female occurs under different terms in Behn's drama and in Shakespeare's.

In Shakespearean drama, the discovery of the woman occurs circuitously—much like the discovery of feminine desire in language. That this should be so makes some sense considering that on Shakespeare's stage, feminine desire in language is the only resource available for the representation of women, because, with women absent, a semiotics of the female body specifically does not function as an aid in the representation of women's gender. Thus, gender difference in Shakespeare's plays is articulated almost entirely through reference to the male. It is as if a whole world had to come into a new realignment for the woman to take effect. Shakespearean lovers are blocked until the play finds a way to represent to themselves and the audience the profoundly absent female body so that sexual arousal can take place. The discovery of Behn's heroines, on the other hand, occurs over and over again because the female body, signified by the female actresses themselves, is always, and perhaps awkwardly, present to her audience. Thus, Behn's couples are blocked while they negotiate how to represent the female body that already has a place on the stage.

The semiotics of discovery scenes on the Restoration stage are crucially tied in Behn's theatrical practice to issues about the representability of the female body.[26] In *The Dutch Lover,* there are five discovery scenes. Act 1, scene 3, mentioned earlier, discovers Euphemia "veiled." Act 2, scene 6 discovers Cleonte in her nightgown undressing. Act 3, scene 3 (discussed above), in which Hippolyta sings and weeps over Antonio's wounded, sleeping body, is also a discovery scene. We can note that Shakespeare's open theater required repeated emptying of the stage so that place had to be created out of theatrical space (over and over again) through the dramatic use of an embodied language. On the Restoration stage, place could be discovered—as if it were already there—by means of an elaborate system of opening and closing a series of painted screens spaced some feet apart from one another and preset in accordance with the sequence of scenes the play required. The screen was divided in the center so that each half moved in from the two wings to close over the figures of the actors. Or, the screen could split down the center and move apart to reveal actors in place behind the screen. I would argue that the conditions of Elizabethan drama emphasize the putting into place of sexual difference. On Behn's stage, because there is already place on the stage in an important sense because of the moveable scenery, we can understand that sexual differentiation has already occurred. The female body is given as present with everyone in the theater knowing at the start that women are playing women's roles. Thus, in Shakespeare's comedies, characters move toward sexual arousal, while Behn's characters seem aroused before the play even begins.[27]

It is significant, too, that in Shakespearean drama intercourse rarely if ever occurs within the action of the play (or it becomes the site of massive speculation, as in *Othello*).[28] In *A Midsummer Night's Dream,* we are invited to imagine an interspecies liaison when Bottom, disguised as an ass, spends the night with Titania. In *All's Well that Ends Well* and *Measure for Measure* the bed tricks function very differently than in Restoration drama, because Helena and Marianna maneuver to obtain their rightful, even lawful, sexual rights. By contrast, extramarital intercourse is a regular feature of Behn's plots. *The Amorous Prince* begins with Cloris and Frederick getting out of bed after spending the night together. Angellica and Willmore in *The Rover* negotiate a sexual encounter that Willmore will not have to purchase. As I already noted, Julia in *The Lucky Chance* manages to sleep with Gayman, who may not ever have to acknowledge he knows it was she in bed with him. But it is Behn's treatment of Hippolyta's sexual circumstances that pushes the semiotic possibilities of Restoration theater to the limit of what can and cannot be represented regarding the female body. When that limit is reached, men and women can know who their brothers and sisters are and who their lovers may be.

I want to focus now on act 4, scene 3, where Hippolyta's identity undergoes a series of discoveries while she is disguised as Alonzo. The first revelation comes after Hippolyta is wounded in a four-way (semiotically squared) swordfight among herself (disguised as Alonzo), Alonzo himself, Marcel, and Antonio. Although Antonio does not recognize Hippolyta, as soon as she is wounded he pleads for his life so that he can "repair [his] injuries" to her. Antonio's conversion, in which his sympathies and even his love turn to Hippolyta, comes, then, without an overt revelation that the figure before him is, indeed, Hippolyta. Thus, the most significant recognition of a woman by a man in this play, the recognition upon which all the other alliances between men and women depend, is evoked in this mysterious reversal of Antonio's feelings under the effects of Hippolyta's wounding. Alonzo wants to continue the fight with Marcel to redress Marcel's false petition in offering the now-wedded Hippolyta as his bride. This prompts Hippolyta to emerge from beneath her disguise, although she is not discovered by all the men at once. Her words to Alonzo equivocate her identity:

> Hold, hold, brave man, or turn your sword on me.
> I am the unhappy cause of all your rage:
> 'Tis I, generous Alonzo, that can tell you
> What he's ashamed to own,
> And thou wilt blush to hear.
>
> (p. 201)

Marcel, recognizing her, instantly tries to kill her but is stopped by Antonio, who claims her as his wife. But Alonzo, the man whose response to the women characters most indicates the terms of their representability, voices the play's final statement about what is representable or not representable about the female body:

> I understand no riddling; but whoever thou be'st
> Man or woman, thou'rt worth our care—
>
> (p. 201)

With this, Hippolyta faints. Her gender identity is no longer significant. Alonzo and the others are ready to accept her in her figuration, whoever she may be. The narrativization of the female body in this play is here cancelled, and that cancellation is signaled by Hippolyta's faint.

More is indicated about the terms of the representability of the female body than the end to its potential for narrativization. While her fainting signals the exhaustion of representational possibilities for the female body on the stage, Hippolyta's wounding in this scene signifies the moment of discursive instability upon which the representational scheme of the play depends and which it must repair narratively. I have argued that Behn dramatizes the instability of that moment when the female body moves between designations in theatrical place to designations in language within a semiosis that uses up the logical possibilities for the representation of women at the same time that it semantically opens up possibilities for transformation and reevaluation of those conditions of representability. Hippolyta is wounded because she has crossed all the categories constructed to produce representational stability. At the level of enunciation she is a female actress representing a woman disguised as a man; at the level of the fiction, she is a woman dressed as a man, she is a sister who enacts her own revenge, she is a betrothed who may be already wed, she is an honorable woman who may be a courtesan, she is the abjected figure of male narrative who can also perform her own abjections. In fact, the narrativization of her body seems to be the sole reason that the plot should get so complicated. She faints when the narrative can go no further. But she is wounded because her narrative crossings have exhausted the logic of her representability— a logic that has become the very grounds of representability both in the fictional world of the play and in terms of the theatrical apparatus Behn employs to represent her. By comparison, the resolution of all the other plot complications that are revealed in act 5 follow logically from new information that is given about the representability of the female body in this scene. Alonzo learns he is Clarinda's brother; Silvio learns Cleonte is not his sister. In act 5, Hippolyta and Antonio are the first to marry; all other marriages depend on theirs. Marcel indicates the seriousness of their union to their most basic social arrangements,

> Don Antonio has by marrying her,
> Repaired the injury he did us all,
> Without which I had killed him.
> (p. 214)

Antonio's marriage to Hippolyta in the final act is more than a narrative resolution secured by a patriarchal endowment. Rather, the narrativization of Hippolyta's body becomes the vehicle for questioning and transforming all other representations of women in the play. The severe objectification of Cleonte ceases; Euphemia no longer has to maneuver from within her objectification by Alonzo; Clarinda, the woman who most located her desires and her politics within language, now has a place in the society.

Because the heroines of Behn's *The Dutch Lover* dramatize a synchronism of possibilities for representing the female body, we can observe in this play a process through which women assess how the female body derives epistemological value. Finally, I think we can see that Behn's semiosis of the female body offers more maneuvers for a feminist politics than the binary of essentialism and constructionism. Yet we should take Behn's own assessment of her play in her famous "Epistle" as well and acknowledge that "comedy was never meant, either for a converting or a confirming ordinance" (p. 122). I would argue that like comedy, feminism is also neither a converting or a confirming process. Rather, Behn's play may suggest to us that we can formulate a feminist politics that does not necessarily know in advance, as Brown and Adams suggest in the quotation that heads this essay, precisely what the intersection between questions of the body and questions of sexuality will be. If we locate our politics within a semiotics of the female body rather than being confined to what have become our customary binarities, then, perhaps like Hippolyta's, our narratives can exhaust themselves in transformations that question all others.

Notes

An earlier version of this paper was presented to the Shakespeare Association of America's seminar on "Renaissance Women as Readers and Writers" at the April 1990 national convention in Philadelphia. My thanks to Deborah C. Payne and to Ronald Schleifer for helpful conversations when I was revising the paper. Thanks also to participants in the faculty workshop at the University of Oklahoma, where this paper was discussed during revision. Also thanks to Robert Con Davis for help with editing.

1. Diana Fuss's *Essentially Speaking: Feminism, Nature, and Difference* (New York: Routledge, 1989) argues that essentialist and constructionist positions in contemporary feminist theory have come to be seen as mutually exclusive. Her arguments have been useful in understanding Behn's deployment of essentialism in her plays.

2. See Teresa de Lauretis's discussion of the use of the terms *essentialist* and *anti-essentialist* in contemporary feminist theory in "Upping the Anti (sic) in

Feminist Theory" in *Conflicts in Feminism,* ed. Marianne Hirsch and Evelyn Fox Keller (New York: Routledge, 1990), pp. 255–70. See also Gayatri Spivak, *In Other Worlds: Essays in Cultural Politics* (New York: Methuen, 1987), which simultaneously critiques and endorses a "strategic use of positivist essentialism in a scrupulously visible political interest" (p. 207) when considering the work of the Subaltern Studies group. Fuss thinks that the determining factor in deciding the political effectiveness of deploying essentialism rests with an analysis of who is taking the risk and why.

3. Beverley Brown and Parveen Adams, "The Feminine Body and Feminist Politics," *m/f* 3 (1979): 35–50.

4. Although it is not known for certain, it is likely that the first English actress played the role of Desdemona in a production of *Othello* for the King's Company in November or December 1660. See John Harold Wilson, *All the King's Ladies: Actresses of the Restoration* (Chicago: Univ. of Chicago Press, 1958). See Stephen Orgel, "Nobody's Perfect; or Why Did the English Stage Take Boys for Women?" *South Atlantic Quarterly* 88 (1989): 7–30, for details about female actresses from the Continent performing in England before 1660. Robert W. Lowe, *Thomas Betterton* (London: Kegan Paul, Trench, Trübner & Co., 1891) describes the brief period of time at the early onset of female actresses when boys (and aging boys) continued to play female roles. Katharine Eisaman Maus, "'Playhouse Flesh and Blood': Sexual Ideology and the Restoration Actress," *ELH* 46 (1979): 595–617, provides the most thorough argument for the historical appearance of the actress on the English stage.

Regarding movable scenery on the Restoration stage, scholars have noted what Peter Holland calls Behn's "obsessive" use of discovery scenes. See Peter Holland, *The Ornament of Action: Text and Performance in Restoration Comedy* (Cambridge and New York: Cambridge Univ. Press, 1979). Richard Southern in his *Changeable Scenery: Its Origin and Development in the British Theater* (London: Faber and Faber, 1952) claims that Behn invented the use of a theatrical space for the discovery of a woman in her bedroom or a woman in her nightgown in a chamber. See his analysis of *Sir Patient Fancy* in his article, "Aphra Draws off a Scene," *Life and Letters Today* 31 (1941): 106–14. John Dennis in his 1725 essay, "The Causes of the Decay and Defects of Dramatick Poetry, and of the Degeneracy of the Publick Taste" claims that at the Restoration, dramatists "altered all at once the whole Face of the stage by introducing scenes and women;—which added probability to the Dramatick Action and made every thing look more naturally." In *The Critical Works of John Dennis,* ed. Edward Niles Hooker, (Baltimore: Johns Hopkins Univ. Press, 1943). Henry Allen Hargreaves, "The Life and Plays of Mrs. Aphra Behn" (Ph.D. Diss., Duke University, 1960), notes Behn's experiments with the "limits of the stage" in her extensive use of stage directions and manipulation of the four scenic flats.

5. Little has been written about *The Dutch Lover.* The only discussion I have found is in George Woodcock, *Aphra Behn: The English Sappho* (Montreal:

Black Rose Books, 1989), previously published under the title *The Incomparable Aphra* (London: T. V. Boardman, 1948), pp. 67–79.

6. See Jessica Munns, "'I by a Double Right Thy Bounties Claim': Aphra Behn and Sexual Space," in *Curtain Calls: British and American Women and the Theater, 1660–1820*, ed. Mary Anne Schofield and Cecilia Macheski (Athens: Ohio Univ. Press, 1991), pp. 193–210. See also Robert D. Hume, "Theory of Comedy in the Restoration," *Modern Philology* 70 (1973): 302–18, and his *The Development of English Drama in the Late Seventeenth Century*, (Oxford: Clarendon Press, 1976).

7. See Eric Rothstein and Frances M. Kavenik, *The Designs of Carolean Comedy* (Carbondale: Southern Illinois Univ. Press, 1988). See particularly their analysis of the four potential readings of *The Man of Mode* (pp. 9–10), which suggests to me the kind of semiotically squared representation I detect in *The Dutch Lover*.

8. See particularly Lisa Jardine, *Still Harping on Daughters: Women and Drama in the Age of Shakespeare* (Sussex: Harvester Press, 1983) who notes the logic of boys taking women's roles because they are both in subordinate positions to men. Laura Levine, "Men in Women's Clothing: Anti-Theatricality and Effeminization from 1579–1642," *Criticism* 28 (1986): 121–43, brilliantly argues that the essentialism deployed by both anti-theatricalists and antifeminists is "used as a defense against the fear that there is no such thing as a fixed self" (p. 139). Although this may be true in the antitheatrical tracts Levine studies, I argue that Behn's theatrical practice posits an essential female body, then makes a drama out of its representability. See also Orgel, "Nobody's Perfect." Although Orgel admits he cannot answer his own question, his very useful article offers that the Elizabethan use of boy actresses for women's roles has to do with "culture-specific attitudes toward women, and toward sexuality" (p. 18). See also Stephen Greenblatt, "Fiction and Friction," in *Reconstructing Individualism: Autonomy, Individuality, and the Self in Western Thought*, ed. Thomas C. Heller et al. (Stanford, Conn.: Stanford Univ. Press, 1986), pp. 30–52. Greenblatt argues that "a conception of gender that is teleologically male and insists upon a verifiable sign to confirm nature's final cause finds its supreme literary expression in a transvestite theater" (p. 47). See also Maus, "Playhouse Flesh and Blood," which argues that the eagerness of Restoration audiences to see female actresses in male disguise was "rooted in the same attitudes that make the boy impersonators seem obsolete" (p. 615). The unmasking of women characters in men's disguise on Restoration stages "reinforces a histrionic appeal which depends upon the seductive appeal of female difference" (p. 615). Although I agree with her analysis, I am interested in what it means to these representational imperatives that the foremost woman Restoration dramatist creates women characters who become conscious of their status as nonrepresentable.

9. See Orgel, "Nobody's Perfect." Discussion of the boy actress on the Elizabethan stage provides its own kind of ideological index. Some critics read the image of the woman on the stage uncritically in terms of gender construction, seeing only a woman there. For this point of view, see Paula S. Berggren, "The

Woman's Part: Female Sexuality as Power in Shakespeare's Plays," in *The Woman's Part: Feminist Criticism of Shakespeare,* ed. Carolyn Ruth Swift Lenz, Gayle Greene, and Carol Thomas Neely (Urbana: Univ. of Illinois Press, 1980), pp. 17–34; Juliet Dusinberre, "On Taking Shakespeare's Women for Granted," *Shakespeare Newsletter,* April 1978, p. 18; Peter Hyland, "Shakespeare's Heroines: Disguise in the Romantic Comedy," *ARIEL: A Review of International English Literature* 9 (1978): 23–39; Michael Jamieson, "Shakespeare's Celibate Stage: The Problem of Accommodation to the Boy Actress in *As You Like It, Antony and Cleopatra* and *The Winter's Tale,* in *Papers, Mainly Shakespearean,* ed. G. I. Duthie (Edinburgh: Oliver and Boyd, 1964), pp. 21–39. Other critics observe problems in constructing the image of a woman through the body of the boy actor. J. W. Binns, "Women or Transvestites on the Elizabethan Stage?: An Oxford Controversy," *Sixteenth Century Journal* 5 (1974): 95–120, finds in a controversy over transvestite actors at Oxford University in the later sixteenth century all the arguments necessary for closing the theaters in 1642. Phillip Traci, "*As You Like It:* Homosexuality in Shakespeare's Play," *College Language Association Journal* 25 (1981): 91–105, argues that confusion over sexual identity is part of the "delightful" quality of the play.

10. See Susan Green, "'A mad Woman! We are made, boys!': The Jailor's Daughter in *The Two Noble Kinsmen*," In *Shakespeare, Fletcher, and 'The Two Noble Kinsmen',* ed. Charles Frey (Columbia: Univ. of Missouri Press, 1989), pp. 121–31.

11. The "Epistle to the Reader" and *The Dutch Lover* appear in *Selected Writings of the Ingenious Mrs. Aphra Behn,* ed. Robert Phelps (1950; rpt. New York: Greenwood Press, 1969), pp. 119–221. Subsequent references to this edition will be cited parenthetically by page number.

12. The usefulness of the semiotic square in describing the appearance of the female body on Behn's stage was suggested to me by Wladimir Krysinski's article, "Semiotic Modalities of the Body in Modern Theater," *Poetics Today* 2 (1981): 141–61, as my title and use of some of his semiotic designations may suggest. Umberto Eco considers that the basic problems of the theater are directly linked to the basic problems of general semiotics in that theatrical performance poses a crucial semiotic question: Is there a difference between natural and artificial signs? I am suggesting that Behn creates her drama out of this question, which she translates into a question about the female body: Are Restoration actresses natural or artificial signs? See Umberto Eco, "Semiotics of Theatrical Performance," *Drama Review* 21 (March 1977): 107–17. Of course, Keir Elam's *The Semiotics of Theatre and Drama* (London and New York: Methuen, 1980) may be consulted, although he never addresses the question of the semiotics of the body in relation to gender. For a helpful explanation of Greimas's square, see Ronald Schleifer, *A. J. Greimas and the Nature of Meaning: Linguistics, Semiotics, and Discourse Theory* (Lincoln: Univ. of Nebraska Press, 1987), especially pp. 25–33.

13. One place to observe this argument is in the British and American reception of Luce Irigaray's *Speculum of the Other Woman,* trans. Gillian C. Gill

(Ithaca: Cornell Univ. Press, 1985) and her *This Sex Which Is Not One,* trans. Catherine Porter (Ithaca: Cornell Univ. Press, 1985). Initial responses to Irigaray focused on her alleged essentialism. See Christine Fauré. "The Twilight of the Goddesses, or the Intellectual Crisis of French Feminism," *Signs* 7 (1981): 81–6; Carolyn Burke, "Irigaray Through the Looking Glass," *Feminist Studies* 7 (1981): 288–306; Monique Plaza, " 'Phallomorphic Power' and the Psychology of 'Woman,' " *Ideology and Consciousness* 4 (1978): 57–76; Toril Moi, *Sexual/ Textual Politics: Feminist Literary Theory* (London and New York: Methuen, 1985). Defenders of Irigaray against charges of essentialism include Jane Gallop, "Quand nos levres s'ecrivent: Irigaray's Body Politic," *Romantic Review* 74 (1983): 77–83; Margaret Whitford, "Luce Irigaray and the Female Imaginary: Speaking as a Woman," *Radical Philosophy* 43 (1986): 3–8; and, most recently, Fuss, *Essentially Speaking.*

14. Nancy Armstrong discusses the semiotic square as a narrative production in her article, "Inside Greimas's Square: Literary Characters and Cultural Restraint," in *The Sign in Music and Literature,* ed. Wendy Steiner (Austin: Univ. of Texas Press, 1981), pp. 52–66.

15. See Irigaray, *The Sex Which Is Not One.*

16. See Hélène Cixous, "The Laugh of the Medusa," in *New French Feminisms: An Anthology,* ed. Elaine Marks and Isabelle de Courtivron (New York: Schocken Books, 1980), pp. 245–64.

17. The debate about whether psychoanalytic theories of the feminine are essentialist is by now extensive and has been divisive. Claire Pajaczkowska, "Introduction to Kristeva" *m/f* 5–6 (1981): 149–57, offers a clear argument against locating Kristeva's work as essentialist by identifying a crucial misreading of Kristeva in Beverly Brown and Parveen Adams, "The Feminine Body." Pajaczkowska argues that Kristeva is not identifying the semiotic modality of language as a form of female sexuality as Brown and Adams suggest; rather, Kristeva's project is to describe the construction of subjectivity within signification, language, and discourse.

18. Margaret Atack, "The Other: Feminist," *Paragraph* 8 (1986): 25–37.

19. The argument appears in the chapter "A-mazing Grace: Notes on Mary Daly's Poetics," in Meaghan Morris, *The Pirate's Fiancée: Feminism, Reading, Postmodernism* (London and New York: Verso, 1988), pp. 27–50.

20. See Patricia Yaeger, "Toward a Female Sublime," in *Gender and Theory: Dialogues on Feminist Criticism,* ed. Linda Kauffman (Oxford and New York: Basil Blackwell, 1989), pp. 191–212.

21. See Schleifer, *A. J. Greimas,* on the significance of the position of the negative complex term on the square (pp. 25–33).

22. Catherine Gallagher's "Who Was That Masked Woman? The Prostitute and the Playwright in the Comedies of Aphra Behn," *Women's Studies* 15 (1988): 23–42. (This essay is reprinted above in this volume.)

23. Aphra Behn, *The Lucky Chance; or, the Alderman's Bargain,* ed. Fidelis Morgan (London and New York: Methuen, 1984), p. 64. Subsequent references to this edition will be cited parenthetically in the text by page number.

24. Irigaray, *Speculum*, p. 224.

25. Elin Diamond, "*Gestus* and Signature in Aphra Behn's *The Rover*," *ELH* 56 (1989): 519–41.

26. Scholars have noted what Peter Holland calls Behn's "obsessive" use of discovery scenes. See Peter Holland, *The Ornament of Action: Text and Performance in Restoration Comedy* (Cambridge and New York: Cambridge Univ. Press, 1979). Richard Southern, in his *Changeable Scenery*, claims that Behn invented the use of a theatrical space for the discovery of a woman in her bedroom or a woman in her nightgown in a chamber. See his analysis of *Sir Patient Fancy* in his article "Aphra Draws off a Scene," *Life and Letters Today* 31 (November 1941): 106–14. Hargreaves, "The Life and Plays of Mrs. Aphra Behn," notes Behn's experiments with the "limits of the stage," her extensive use of stage directions, and her manipulation of the four scenic flats.

27. See Martin Ellenhauge, *English Restoration Drama: Its Relation to Past English and Past and Contemporary French Drama, from Jonson via Molière to Congreve* (Copenhagen: Levin and Munksgaard, 1933), who argues that in Restoration drama, men's and women's minds are wholly sexualized. See also Greenblatt, "Fiction and Friction," in which he argues that Shakespeare's comedies "entailed above all the representation of the emergence of identity in the experience of erotic heat" (p. 48).

28. See Alfred Harbage, *Shakespeare and the Rival Traditions* (1952; rpt. Bloomington: Indiana Univ. Press, 1972). He points out that in "32 of Shakespeare's 38 plays no act of fornication or adultery occurs within the course of the action." See his appendix C, "Shakespeare as Expurgator," for a complete listing.

Fiction

ELLEN POLLAK

Beyond Incest: Gender and the Politics of Transgression in Aphra Behn's *Love-Letters between a Nobleman and His Sister*

If subversion is possible, it will be a subversion from within the terms of the law, through the possibilities that emerge when the law turns against itself and spawns unexpected permutations of itself. The culturally constructed body will then be liberated, neither to its 'natural' past, nor to its original pleasures, but to an open future of cultural possibilities.

—Judith Butler, *Gender Trouble*

The *appearance of substance* is precisely that, a constructed identity, a performative accomplishment which the mundane social audience, including the actors themselves, come to believe and to perform in the mode of belief. . . . The possibilities of gender transformation are to be found precisely in the arbitrary relation between such acts, in the possibility of a failure to repeat, a deformity, or a parodic repetition that exposes the phantasmatic effect of abiding identity as a politically tenuous construction.

—Judith Butler, *Gender Trouble*

So well he dissembled, that he scarce knew himself that he did so.

—Aphra Behn, *Love-Letters between a Nobleman and His Sister*

Expressly incestuous and deeply embedded in the politics of regicide and political rebellion, Aphra Behn's *Love-Letters between a Nobleman and His Sister* is also a text insistently preoccupied with questions of gender, identity, and representation. Published in three parts between 1684 and 1687, Behn's novel is based loosely on an affair between Ford, Lord Grey of Werke, and his wife's sister, Lady Henrietta Berkeley, a scandal that broke in London in 1682, when Lady Berkeley's father published an advertisement in the *London Gazette* announcing the disappearance of his daughter. Lady Berkeley had in fact run off with Grey, the well-known antimonarchist figure whom Dryden alluded to as "cold Caleb" in *Absalom and Achitophel* (1681) and who serves Behn here as a model for her character Philander. Prosecuted by Lord Berkeley for abducting and seducing his daughter, Grey was eventually found guilty of "debauchery" but never sentenced.[1] Shortly thereafter, he was also implicated in the Rye House Plot to murder Charles II and was later active in Monmouth's rebellion against Charles's brother, James. In Behn's fiction Grey figures as a political follower and friend of Cesario, the French prince of Condé, whose failed attempt to overthrow his king is modeled on the parallel exploits of Charles's bastard son. Lady Berkeley is Sylvia, the dutiful royalist daughter whom Philander seduces and corrupts. Like the crown for Cesario, she is for Philander a sign of male prerogative and desire, her body the theater across which several dramas of masculine rivalry are played out.

It is not surprising that a text situated so expressly within the political context of the Duke of Monmouth's rebellion against the royal authority of both his father and his uncle should structure itself around the repetition of a series of analogously configured masculine rivalries. Through her elaborate foregrounding of the figure of a woman, however, Behn adds a dimension to this drama of political and familial succession that is manifestly absent from such comparable royalist efforts as *Absalom and Achitophel*. To what extent Behn's choice to develop the love interest here was motivated by her recognition of the greater acceptability for a woman of the role of romance historian over that of political poet, we cannot know for sure;[2] but when Lady Berkeley's father published his advertisement announcing her disappearance and offering £200 for her return, Behn clearly perceived an opportunity to explore the narrative possibilities (as well as discursive instabilities) inherent in comparing stolen daughters with stolen crowns.

Behn incorporates the scandalous historical fact of the Berkeley-

Grey affair into the political, thematic, and figural dimensions of her fiction by situating Philander's justifications for his adulterous and incestuous desire for Sylvia squarely within the context of Restoration debates over the relationship and relative authority of nature and conventional morality. As Susan Staves has amply demonstrated, an increasing dissociation of natural law theory from theology during the second half of the seventeenth century effectively established the conditions both for changes in the institutional treatment of moral crimes and for the emergence of a new brand of heroism in the imaginative literature of the age. Herculean and libertine stage heroes captured the popular imagination through their bold allegiance to a nature defined not in accordance with, but in opposition to, religion, law, custom, and conventional morality. Such heroes appealed to nature to justify a range of behaviors traditionally regarded as crimes against nature as well as God. Along with adultery, sodomy, and parricide, the deployment of incest as a figure for rebellion against traditional forms of authority became a favorite device on the Restoration stage for articulating cultural anxieties and for giving dramatic play to the multiple tensions inherent in contemporary efforts to rethink the connections between the laws of nature, religion, and social morality.[3]

Behn's libertine hero, Philander, fits the profile of this new literary type in his elaboration of natural justifications for his socially criminal desire for Sylvia. From as early as his very first letter, he invokes the liberatory ethos of a return to original pleasures. The legal institutions of kinship and of marriage, he insists, are mere practical creations inspired by material interests, while his own incestuous and adulterous passion has a primacy that transcends the prudent imperatives of tradition. Philander uses the fact that his relation to Sylvia is affinal (a legal relation created through his marriage to her sister) as opposed to consanguineal (a blood relation) to further question the natural basis for the rules that prohibit his having sex with her: "What kin, my charming *Sylvia,* are you to me? No ties of blood forbid my passion; and what's a ceremony imposed on man by custom! . . . What alliance can that create? Why should a trick devised by the wary old, only to make provision for posterity, tie me to an eternal slavery?"[4] In point of legal fact, as Sybil Wolfram's work has shown, because the English concept of marriage in the seventeenth century was based on the legal and religious doctrine of the unity of husband and wife, "intercourse between affinal relations was . . . on a footing with and as much incest as intercourse between close blood relations."[5] But Philander represents an emergent strain of thought that radically questioned the received assumption that incest controverted natural law.

Scripture itself had become a site of theoretical controversy among seventeenth-century moral philosophers, especially at those points where God appeared arbitrarily to command behavior elsewhere prohibited by His law. Staves cites the story of Abraham's divinely ordered murder of Isaac as one scriptural conundrum that seemed to focus the crisis of authority experienced by moralists,[6] but there were also numerous instances of apparent biblical inconsistency regarding the legitimacy of incestuous practices. One of the most pervasively cited involved a perceived discrepancy between the injunctions of Leviticus, which forbade incest, and those of Genesis, which bade Adam and Eve (whom most commentators regarded as siblings) to increase and multiply.

Thus, in 1625 Hugo Grotius asserted that although marriages between brothers and sisters are illegal, they are forbidden by divine command and not (as appeared to be the case with parent-child marriages) by "the pure law of nature."[7] Here Grotius accepts the Jewish teaching that the prohibition against sibling marriage was given to Adam "at the same time with the laws to worship God, to administer justice, not to shed blood, [etc.] . . . ; but with the condition that the laws regulating marriage should not have effect until after the human race had multiplied sufficiently."[8] Jeremy Taylor echoed Grotius thirty-five years later when he asserted that, by contrast to parent-child incest, sibling marriages are only "next to an unnatural mixture"; for "if they had been unnatural, they could not have been necessary" as "it is not imaginable that God . . . would have built up mankind by that which is contrary to Humane Nature."[9] And in 1672, Richard Cumberland took a similarly relative position on the question of sibling incest, arguing that marriages between brothers and sisters "in the first Age of the World" were "*necessary* to propagate that Race of Men, and to raise those Families, which Reason now endeavours to *Preserve,* by *prohibiting.*"[10]

Behn's Philander does not emerge ex nihilo, therefore, when he invokes Genesis to justify his incestuous desires. In a manner typically modern and predictably Whig, he disdains the beaten track of conventional morality to assert the prerogatives of an originary state: "Let us . . . scorn the dull *beaten road,* but let us love like the first race of men, nearest allied to God, promiscuously they loved, and possessed, father and daughter, brother and sister met, and reaped the joys of love without control, and counted it religious coupling, and 'twas encouraged too by heaven itself" (p. 4). As Ruth Perry has observed, Philander speaks for the authenticity of nature over the artifice of social codes. Posing as the ultimate pastoral lover, he emulates the freedom of creatures in the natural world. There is "no troublesome honour, amongst the pretty inhabitants of the woods and streams, fondly to give laws to nature," he insists, "but uncontrolled they play, and sing, and love; no parents checking their dear delights, no slavish matrimonial ties to restrain their nobler flame" (p. 28). Only "man . . . is bound up to rules, fetter'd by the nice decencies of honour" (p. 29).[11]

Given Behn's royalist politics, Philander's defense of incest may seem at first blush a simple alignment of Whiggism with transgression, the act of regicide—as René Girard has noted in another context—constituting an equivalent in the political realm of parricide or incest within the family.[12] Those who violate loyalties to their king, Behn seems to want to say, are also apt to violate the other bonds on which the social order and its civilizing systems of difference depend.[13] Behn's creation of a heroine of royalist birth who draws the better part of her appeal from her success in outdoing Philander at the game of transgressiveness, however, destabilizes this easy, politicized opposition between authority and rebellion and suggests a more complex and heterogeneous notion of transgression than a simply negative political coding would allow.[14] As more than one critic has noted, Behn's treatment of gender often seems to complicate and refract, if not indeed to contradict, her party politics, creating in her work the sense of multiple and incommensurate ideological agenda.[15] *Love-Letters* exemplifies this tendency through its own rhetorical excess, inviting itself to be read with a certain burlesquing tongue-in-cheekiness, as if it wants to make us ask—and it does make us ask—why (if this is first and foremost a political scandal novel) Behn would choose to defend the royal cause through so protracted a portrait of untamed female insubordination.

Is it true, as Janet Todd and Maureen Duffy both suggest, that

Behn wants to promote the values of sincerity and authenticity as they are embodied in the figure of Philander's friend and rival, Octavio, by showing us that Philander's appeal to nature is nothing more than base hypocrisy?[16] Perhaps, at the most manifest level; but why then does her narrative read so much like a celebration of the pleasures and powers of role-playing and artifice whereby the indomitable Sylvia sacrifices Octavio to her revenge against Philander? If, as Perry suggests, Behn's characters are designed to show us "where disrespect for law and order can lead," why does Behn's relation to her heroine's depravity seem so very fraught with irony?[17] The narrator tells us that Sylvia is imperious, proud, vain, opinionated, obstinate, censorious, amorously inclined, and indiscreet (pp. 259–60), and yet Behn seems to revel in the emotional resilience the heroine's duplicity affords. Jane Austen rarely assumes a more heteroglot relation to her heroines than Behn does when, reflecting on the ease with which Sylvia is able to transfer her affection from one lover to the next, she writes: "Nature is not inclined to hurt itself; and there are but few who find it necessary to die of the disease of love. Of this sort was our *Sylvia,* though to give her her due, never any person who did not indeed die, ever languished under the torments of love, as did that charming and afflicted maid" (p. 261). The nature appealed to here is elusively construed, gesturing ironically toward an unstable opposition between female nature and artifice in a world where a natural female impulse toward self-preservation requires the performance, nearly unto death, of the artifice of languishing femininity.[18]

Feminist critics have taken differing positions regarding the significance of the incest in Behn's text. To Janet Todd, it is merely a sensationalist device meant to keep Behn's book in print but not an important theme developed at any length.[19] For Judith Kegan Gardiner, on the other hand, Sylvia's willing participation in an incestuous adultery with her brother-in-law is the paradigmatic instance of her transgressiveness as a heroine and the conceptual point of departure for a complex reconfiguration of literary history.[20] Reading *Love-Letters* as a story of brother-sister incest that does not follow a familiar and traditionally valorized oedipal logic but instead avoids "both father-son and mother-daughter paradigms for a transgressive sexuality in which the woman is not exclusively a victim but a willing and desiring agent,"[21] Gardiner makes the case that a revaluation of the importance of Behn's text in the history of the novel genre opens the way to imagining an alternative paradigm of literary history, one that displaces an oedipal by what she calls "an incestuous model of the novel's origins."[22]

But is Behn's heroine stably figured as a willing agent of incestuous desire? Does the text of *Love-Letters* in fact support Gardiner's assessment that incest functions for Sylvia, as it does for Philander, as the expression of a liberatory eros? Behn may indeed refuse an oedipal model of female desire, but does she therefore necessarily embrace an incestuous ideal of feminine transgression? I shall argue that, on the contrary, far from replacing an oedipal with an incestuous ideal, Behn's narrative effectively displaces the conceptual grounds of a heterosexual matrix of assumptions that encodes incestuous desire as a form of freedom from patriarchal law.

There is a great deal more at stake here than a subtle difference of reading. Where we locate the transgressiveness of Behn's heroine has critical implications not just for the place Behn will occupy in contemporary conceptions of aesthetics and of literary history but also for a feminist analysis of narrative representations of incestuous desire, especially for recent efforts to theorize the role of incest in modern discursive inscriptions of female desire.[23] In making the case for Sylvia's incestuous agency without taking into account how she is located specifically as a female subject in relation both to incest and to the law that produces it as an object of repression—without regard, that is, to the patriarchal power structure within which incest derives its meaning and transgressive force to begin with—Gardiner allows a dangerous slippage to occur in her argument. Assuming that incest always inevitably constitutes transgression (indeed reading incest as the ultimate transgression), she relies on a characteristically modern discursive coding of incestuous desire as natural—an emergent cultural inscription in seventeenth-century England, as we have seen, but one that I would argue Behn's narrative actively refuses to underwrite.

In fact, I would suggest, far from elaborating a simple equivalence or correspondence between incest and transgression, Behn uses both categories to register the shifting positionality of gendered subjectivities, producing a variable model of the transgressiveness of incest and the incestuousness of transgression for her male and fe-

male characters. Rather than inscribing incest as a stable and univo-
cal marker of transgression, she destabilizes incest as a trope of
liberation by exposing the ways it is differently constituted for her
hero and heroine. In the process, she radically problematizes the
question of desire's origins, representing what Gardiner reads as
original desire in Sylvia not as an intrinsic essence but as an effect of
power.[24] Sylvia's transgressiveness as a heroine is situated not in her
incestuous agency but elsewhere; it emerges rather in a conceptual
and performative space made available to her only by the eventual
recognition that Philander's exaltation of incest as a liberation from
prohibitive patriarchal law actually functions as an instrument of
power. Incest operates in Behn's text, in other words, not as a simple
figure for transgression but as a complex discursive site where the
oppositional ideologies of patriarchy and individualism intersect, at
once confronting each other and, in the process, exposing their joint
complicity in (and their shared dependence on) the appropriation
and cooptation of female desire.

This is hardly to revert to Todd's assessment of the essential
insignificance of the incest in Behn's text. On the contrary, it is to read
Sylvia's incest as a necessary part of Behn's complex critique of Whig
libertarian politics. At the level of plot, after all, the incest does take
Sylvia outside her father's house; it thus establishes the conditions
within which Behn is able to show that that outside is always already
inside—always on the verge of reinscribing the very law it would
subvert. To be successfully transgressive on Behn's terms, Sylvia will
have to move beyond the illusory liberation of naturalized incestuous
desire—*outside* the outside of an oedipal dyad in which women are
mere theaters for the playing out of male desire. The serial nature of
Love-Letters allows Behn to effect these consecutive displacements
compellingly, by creating an opportunity for her to write her heroine
out of and beyond the limits of the typical romantic plot.[25]

I. Philander's "Phallic Handshake" and the Limits of the Libertine Critique of Patriarchy

I approach my subject through a reading of several key episodes
that help to establish the context within which the incest in Behn's

narrative acquires meaning. My aim is to illuminate the extent to which the incestuous relation between Philander and Sylvia is conditioned by the dynamics of a system of homosocial exchange in which the daughter's desire functions not as a locus of agency but as a site of confrontation between paternal and fraternal interests. Because familial conflict is coded politically in Behn's novel, this reading also necessarily involves discussion of the way Sylvia's body functions in a double symbolic register as a political as well as familial battleground.

This is not to say that Sylvia entirely lacks transgressive agency. It is rather to suggest that we must first understand the structuring homosocial frame within which her incest is enacted ultimately to appreciate the process whereby she manages to move beyond the possibilities for transgression it delimits into a space subversively generated by a parodic repetition of its terms. For, however paradoxically, it is only after Sylvia comes to recognize her status as a sign within a drama of masculine rivalry, to understand that as a woman she is always already a representation within a homosocial matrix of desire, that she opens herself to the possibility of taking performative control of her enactment of desire and gendered subjectivity.

I take as my point of entry Philander's account of an episode that occurs relatively early in part one, immediately after his first nocturnal tryst with Sylvia. As a dutiful royalist daughter, Sylvia early expresses considerable anguish over Philander's attempts to prevail upon her "honour"; she finally concedes, nevertheless, to a private interview, which she justifies as a trial of her virtue and resolution. And as Philander's letter recounting the details of their first night alone together reveals, Sylvia does remain "a maid" despite the opportunity for physical conquest on his part.

The cause of Philander's forbearance, as he explains, is neither his regard for Sylvia's honor (on the contrary, he says, her resistance inflames him all the more) nor her physical attractions (these, he insists, are overwhelming) but a fit of sexual impotence brought on by a state of overstimulation. Having "overcome all difficulties, all the fatigues and toils of love's long seiges, vanquish'd the mighty phantom of the fair, the giant honour, and routed all the numerous host of women's little reasonings, passed all the bounds of peevish modesty; nay, even all the loose and silken counterscarps that fenced the sacred fort," instead of receiving "the yielding treasure," Philander had fallen "fainting before the surrendering gates," a circumstance he goes on to associate with the weakness of old age. In a rhetorical maneuver that underscores his physical prowess even as it acknowledges a lapse in his "(till then) never failing power," he attributes his attack of impotence to the envy of the gods; one "malicious at [his] glory," he suggests, has left him full of "mad desires," but "all inactive, as age or death itself, as cold and feeble, as unfit for joy, as if [his] youthful fire had long been past, or *Sylvia* had never been blest with charms." Indeed, the excess of passion has so paralyzed Philander that he curses his youth and implores the gods to give him "old age, for that has some excuse, but youth has none" (pp. 50–51).

The dialectic of youthful vigor and old age within which Philander here encodes what amounts to an averted incestuous consummation is, as we have to some extent already seen, precisely the dialectic within which he has attempted to justify his incestuous and adulterous desire from the start. From as early as his very first letter to Sylvia, he has idealized his affection for her by casting the older generation as guardians of a threatened domain of power, invested only in the jealous retention of control over the future. The institutions of kinship and of marriage are mere "trick[s] devised by the wary old" (p. 4), who, like the gods, arbitrarily wield the reins of political power even as they fear and envy Philander's authentic passion and youthful virility.

Philander reproduces this dialectic at a more literal level in his reference later in the same letter to a parallel sexual plot involving another male predator and another "reluctant maid." For even as Philander—"the young, the brisk and gay" (p. 51)—is engineering an interview with Sylvia, Sylvia's father—that "brisk old gentleman" (p. 56)—has been counting on a garden assignation with Melinda, her refreshingly worldly serving maid. Few readers will forget the hilarious "accident" by which plot and comic subplot here intersect, enabling Behn to play irreverently with the ironies, multiple meanings, and shifting power relations produced when the "maid" Sylvia, "mistress" of Melinda, plays "mistress" to Philander while her "maid," Melinda, plays "mistress" to Sylvia's father. Much as Defoe would later point to the ironies inherent in the homonymous relation contained within the honorific *Madam,* Behn here uses the shifting and multiplying of subject positions to baldly expose the illusory forms of power invested in all varieties of mistresses and maids.[26]

According to Philander, no consummation takes place between master and "mistress" here any more than between Philander and Sylvia. Alarmed by a noise that makes the young lovers fear discovery, Philander steals into the garden disguised in Melinda's nightgown and headress, only to be mistaken for Melinda by the eager old gentleman. Here is his account of events as they unfold: "*Monsieur* the Count, . . . taking me for Melinda, . . . caught hold of my gown as I would have passed him, and cried, 'Now *Melinda,* I see you are a maid of honour,—come, retire with me into the grove, where I have a present of a heart and something else to make you' " (p. 55). It is now Philander's turn to play the role of reluctant maid: "With that I pulled back and whispered—'Heavens! Would you make a mistress of me?' —Says he—'A mistress, what woulds't thou be, a cherubin?' Then I replied as before—'I am no whore, sir,'—'No,' cries he, 'but I can quickly make thee one, I have my tools about me, sweet-heart; therefore let us lose no time, but fall to work.' . . . With that he clapped fifty guineas in a purse into one hand, and something else that shall be nameless into the other, presents that had been both worth *Melinda*'s acceptance" (p. 56).

Combining many of the key motifs and topoi of *Love-Letters* (among them masquerade, gender reversal, class and generational encounter, and homosocial exchange of a most literal variety)—all within an epistolary frame—Philander's garden adventure offers a veritable object lesson in the problematics of reading Behn. It is possible to take Philander's narrative at face value, to accept the hero at his word, as Gardiner does when she reads Philander's disguise as providing a sort of comic externalization of his demeaning impotence. Philander, as she sees him here, is a whining buffoon— "a ludicrously declassed and feminized figure"—whose exposure through Behn's publication of his private correspondence realizes his own worst fear, as he expresses it in his letter, of being publicly ridiculed ("Where shall I hide my head when this lewd story's told?" [p. 51]). In Philander's account of his comic adventure with Beralti, Gardiner suggests, Behn not only casts doubt on the virility of the notoriously promiscuous Lord Grey but "undercuts the admiration accorded to Don Juans" generally. His withdrawal from the garden, which leaves his father-in-law in a state of sexual frustration is, Gardiner argues, a burlesque of "his own frustrated romantic seduction of Sylvia."[27]

But Gardiner's reading does little justice to the hermeneutic instabilities generated by the epistolary nature of Behn's text, instabilities that produce the immanent possibility—if not the eminent probability—that Philander is only feigning impotence. The only grounds we have for validating what really happened on that disappointing night are, after all, Philander's words—his own dubious representation of events. And in light of the strategies of seduction he has deployed up to this point, it makes perfect sense to read his attack of impotence not as a fact but as a performance (or what might more appropriately be termed a magnificent antiperformance in this case). Far from constituting a form of humiliation, this episode actually helps Philander to consolidate his power over Sylvia.[28]

Philander's "retreat" from consummation at this moment of peak excitement and opportunity is thoroughly in keeping with the strategies of deferral by which he has gained entry into Sylvia's bedchamber in the first place. From the outset, he has moved with a certain deft belatedness. As early as her third letter, Sylvia pines for word from Philander: "Not yet?—not yet?" she laments, "oh ye dull tedious hours, when will you glide away? and bring that happy moment on, in which I shall at least hear from my *Philander;* . . . Perhaps *Philander's* making a trial of virtue by this silence" (p. 14). In her next, still waiting ("Another night, oh heavens, and yet no letter come!" [p. 16]), she even entertains the thought that Philander may in fact be toying with her: "Is it a trick, a cold fit, only assum'd to try how much I love you?" (p. 16). Predictably, Philander has an excuse, although in presenting it he also betrays a certain disingenuity: "When I had sealed the enclosed, *Brilliard* told me you were this morning come from *Bellfont,* and with infinite impatience have expected seeing you here; which deferred my sending this to the old place; and I am so vain (oh adorable *Sylvia!*) as to believe my fancied silence has given you disquiets; but sure, my *Sylvia* could not charge me with neglect" (pp. 11–12).

It may be revenge for Sylvia's ambivalence about surrendering herself to him, indeed for the tenacity with which she clings to the imperatives of honor, that drives Philander to these delays. For although Sylvia often longs for him, she is just as often grateful for his neglect: "Let me alone, let me be ruin'd with honour, if I must be ruin'd.—For oh! 'twere much happier I were no more, than that I should be more than *Philander*'s sister; or he than *Sylvia*'s brother: oh let me ever call you by that cold name" (p. 14). Philander, however, will be satisfied with gaining nothing less than absolute control over the representation of Sylvia's desire. Early on she describes herself as the very embodiment of disorder and indeterminacy: "Could you but imagine how I am tormentingly divided, how unresolved between violent love and cruel honour, you would say 'twere impossible to fix me any where; or be the same thing for a moment together" (p. 17). Onto this doubt and indecision, Philander fixes his own desire, reading Sylvia as he wishes—like Adam, dreaming her doubt into desire for his advances and then naming it as love (pp. 7–8). "I know you love," writes Philander to Sylvia (p. 24). "He soon taught her to understand it was love," asserts the narrator in the novel's "Argument"; "thou art the first that ever did inform me that there was such a sort of wish about me," writes Sylvia to Philander (p. 61). Such phrases echo as a refrain throughout part one. And Sylvia does at last defer to the authority of Philander's reading of her, both in finally accepting his diagnosis of her alienation from desire and in conceding to his accusations of her fickleness and inconstancy along the way.

In the context of this series of deferrals, Philander's impotence simply constitutes a culminating moment in the production of desire in Sylvia. Although in prior letters she had vacillated wildly between attraction to her brother-in-law and a perfectly catechismal defense of patriarchal honor, in the two letters that she writes in quick succession immediately following Philander's "lapse" in potency, she describes herself as experiencing a degree of desire she has previously not known. "I have wishes, new, unwonted wishes," she writes, "at every thought of thee I find a strange disorder in my blood, that pants and burns in every vein, and makes me blush and sigh, and grow impatient, ashamed and angry" (p. 63). She now further concedes that her previous "coldness" must have been dissembled, as she was "not mistress of" it (p. 63). (This concession by Sylvia is of interest for our reading of Philander, as it admits the possibility that coldness may be feigned.) Sylvia continues, "there lies a woman's art, there all her boasted virtue, it is but well dissembling, and no more—but mine, alas, is gone, for ever fled" (p. 63). In the process of increasingly surrendering to Philander's "cause," Sylvia now begins in several instances to echo his very words and arguments, mirroring his early references to "fond custom" and "phantom honour" as well as the opportunistic and somewhat desperate arguments he had used to justify his commitment to the political interests of the treacherous Cesario. Just as he had there described himself as being "in past a retreat" (p. 40) and declared that "though the glorious falling weight should crush me, it is great to attempt" (p. 41), so Sylvia now casts herself in the role of heroic martyr to her love: "I am plunged in, past hope of a retreat; and since my fate has pointed me out for ruin, I cannot fall more gloriously. Take then, *Philander,* to your dear arms, a maid that can no longer resist, who is disarmed of all defensive power: she yields, she yields, and does confess it too" (p. 65). Sylvia's response to Philander's impotence, in short, is to renounce every doctrine she has hitherto been taught by the "grave and wise" (p. 62). He induces her to give up a "coldness she is not mistress of" by, in effect, being master of his own. One more instance of deferral (occasioned this time by Cesario's calling him away) will secure his romantic victory; to prove his passion, Philander will offer to disregard the summons, but Sylvia—now thoroughly identified with his interests—insists that he respond, promising that Philander's obedience to the commands of Cesario (whom earlier she had regarded as a rival) will be rewarded in her arms (pp. 68–69).

If, as Sylvia is here driven to presuppose, affecting coldness is "a woman's art"—a prerogative or sign of femininity—then feigning impotence is for Philander, in more than one sense, "putting on" the maid. It is a way both of putting Sylvia on (i.e., controlling her through deception) and of doing so by performing a woman's part (affecting coldness), a strategy made literal in Philander's garden performance as Melinda.[29] Appropriating to himself a dissembled coldness that he identifies as a female strategy, Philander does not invite Sylvia to become a better mistress of her own standoffishness, but instead maneuvers her into accepting the coercive fiction of her own natural desire for him. Her longing for him is thus understood not as the effect of a performance on his part but as an essence intrinsic to her, a "natural propensity" (p. 60) poorly masked in her case by a shabby cloak of artificial virtue. As she does at several other points throughout her text, Behn here problematizes the question of desire's origins in depicting Sylvia's grasping after a causal narrative: "I am the aggressor," she declares eventually, "the fault is in me, and thou art innocent" (p. 60).[30] Thus does Philander take control rhetorically of their courtship by inducing Sylvia to own an "unaccountable" passion (p. 61) over which she has neither prior knowledge nor control.

It remains, however, to determine the role of Philander's garden performance as a reluctant maid in his project of displacing all traces of reluctance in Sylvia. I have argued that what to Gardiner is whining and buffoonery on Philander's part can also, if we refuse to assume the hero's authenticity, be understood as a form of strategic self-dramatization whereby Philander acquires power by performing impotence. Philander's account of his "pleasant adventure" in the garden similarly serves his ends with Sylvia by enlisting her collusion as a reader in a comic undermining of paternal authority. By reducing the count to a rather embarrassing travesty of the predatory excesses of youth, it offers a repetition and amplification of Philander's successful manipulation of the signs of impotence and femininity to establish the conditions for sexual victory.[31] It is not just that Philander has prior knowledge from Melinda of Beralti's sexual indiscretions while Beralti himself remains ignorant of Philander's dalliance with his daughter. There is also the fact that the old man is prepared to pay for Melinda's services, a detail that, while it bespeaks Beralti's economic prowess, also makes him compare unfavorably with Philander. The fifty guineas intended for Melinda may stand as a mark of Bellfont's class as well as gender supremacy, but they are also a sign of his maid's affective indifference to him—an indifference that, as we have seen, stands in stark contrast to the passion Philander arouses in Sylvia (despite, if not indeed because of, his temporary lapse in potency). In fact, the comic circumstance of Melinda's physical absence at the moment when the fifty guineas is bestowed makes an utter mockery of the count's physical power over her. The scene in which the father both literally and figuratively attempts to impose the phallus is also the scene in which the paternal phallus is inadvertently exposed, not simply to the laughter of the son-in-law but, through him, to the daughter's laughter too.

But Beralti's garden vigil for the daughter's maid takes place at the very moment when Philander is preparing the stage for the theft of the daughter's maidenhead. The identity of role between Philander and the count as predatory males is thus complicated by their status as rivals. They are not simply mirrors of one another—males in quest of separate objects of desire—but competitors for control of Sylvia. (Could not Beralti's dalliance with the maid in fact be read as a phastasmatic rendering of the eroticized relation between father and daughter that underpins the entire sexual drama of part one?)[32] To the extent that they situate Sylvia's alienation from her father within the context of a drama of masculine rivalry in which she figures not as an agent but a sign, the familial dynamics here are critical. Philander's inclination to flout paternal authority and to infringe upon the father's right of rule is an aspect of his political character as a follower of the regicidal Cesario. But the link does not end there. Like Cesario, Philander functions in the capacity of a son, a role that he has acquired by his marriage to Sylvia's sister, Myrtilla, and one that involves not just the acquisition of certain privileges but also the institution of specific prohibitions. The rules of kinship that give Philander freedom of access to Beralti's daughters also presuppose the assumption of countervailing filial responsibilities. Sylvia alludes to both these prerogatives and their limits when she contemplates the consequences of her father's discovery of their affair: "my father being rash, and extremely jealous, and the more so of me, by how much more he is fond of me, and nothing would enrage him like the discovery of an interview like this; though you have the liberty to range the house of *Bellfont* as a son, and are indeed at home there; but . . . when he shall find his son and virgin daughter, the brother and the sister so retired, so entertained,—What but death can ensue? Or what is worse, eternal . . . confusion on my honour?" (p. 43). In seducing Sylvia (by, in effect, usurping the father's prerogative to dispose of her virginity), Philander violates the authority invested in him as a brother—an "authority" that, as the following passage testifies, Sylvia recognizes as "lawful." Describing herself as impaled by a sense of familial obligation in the face of his advances, as "a maid that cannot fly," she entertains a moment of regret: "Why did you take advantage of those freedoms I gave you as a brother? . . . but for my sister's sake, I play'd with you, suffer'd your hands and lips to wander where I dare not now; all which I thought a sister might allow a brother, and knew not all the while the treachery of love: oh none, but under that intimate title of a brother, could have had the opportunity to have ruin'd me . . . by degrees so subtle, and an authority so lawful, you won me out of all" (pp. 14–15).[33]

Within the discursive economy of Behn's text, in short, Sylvia's honor—represented both by her virgin body and her desire to fulfill her f(am)ilial obligations—becomes Philander's political battleground. As "daughter to the great *Beralti,* and sister to *Myrtilla,* a yet unspotted maid, fit to produce a race of glorious heroes," Sylvia recognizes that all her actions reflect on the honor of "the noble house of the *Beralti"* and that Philander seeks "to build the trophies of [his] conquests on the ruin of both *Myrtilla*'s fame and [her own]" (p. 18). From a political perspective, it is not sufficient that he ruin Myrtilla only, as Sylvia yet remains to "redeem the bleeding [royalist] honour of [her] family" (p. 22). As Myrtilla puts it in her one admonitory missive to her sister, Sylvia is "the darling child, the joy of all, the last hope left, the refuge" of "the most unhappy [family] of all the race of old nobility" (p. 71). Philander's corruption of Beralti's dutiful younger daughter through the illicit appropriation of sexual rights over her in this sense constitutes a Whig usurpation of the royalist right of rule.

One sees here, better perhaps than at any other point in her text, the logic of Behn's interweaving of sexual and political narratives; for what Behn's complex structuring of her tale makes evident is the profound interimplication—indeed the mutually constitutive nature—of sexuality and politics. The relationship between plots here is more than merely analogical, more than the simple matter of a metaphor in which sexual conquest serves as a figure at the level of private life for a more public, political form of victory. It is rather a relationship of discursive interdependence in which the categories of the private and the public, materiality and meaning, desire and the law reveal their inherently contingent and unstable identities. Gardiner accepts the efficacy of a stable distinction between private and public life when she rests her reading on the difference between Philander's positive political power and his lack of familial authority over Sylvia. But this is precisely the distinction Behn destabilizes when she exposes the intensely political nature of individual desire. Philander's binary opposition between private and public life is, she suggests, an illusion created to sustain the liberatory fiction that legitimates the operations of masculine privilege.

Philander represents his incestuous love for Sylvia as an expression of unconstrained desire that marks a liberation from a materialist economy of sexual exchange. Against the institution of marriage—"a trick devised by the wary old only to make provision for posterity" (p. 4)—he urges the authenticity of "pleasures vast and unconfin'd" (p. 20). And eventually, in the invective against marriage to which she devotes her penultimate letter in part one, Sylvia too comes to embrace such a libertine philosophy, asserting that only adulterous love can occasion genuine heterosexual reciprocity ("That's a heavenly match," she writes, "when two souls touched with equal passion meet, . . . when no base interest makes the hasty bargain, . . . and . . . both understand to take and pay" [p. 109]). Ultimately, however, by showing how the very act of erotic transgression that Philander proffers as an individualist solution to the problem of hierarchical repression ultimately reinscribes Sylvia's specular status in reciprocal relations between men, Behn exposes the limits of the libertine critique of patriarchy.

The assymmetrical and nonreciprocal character of Sylvia and Philander's relationship will become increasingly clear, both to Sylvia and to the reader, as the events of parts two and three of the narrative—especially those involving the relationship between Philander and Octavio—unfold. But even within the limits of the love plot of part one, that inadvertent "phallic handshake" between father and son-in-law in the garden—a savage burlesque of the gentleman's agreement by which the gift of the daughter is legitimately exchanged—reveals (even as it figures the bypassing of legitimate succession) the homosocial ground of both patriarchal law and its transgression. Fifty guineas and that "nameless" entity, the father's penis, may be "presents . . . both worth *Melinda*'s acceptance," but only Sylvia—phallic representative of the Father's Name and Law—is worth Philander's. Just as Sylvia's ensuing marriage to Philander's "property," Brilliard, will expose the underlying ironies of the libertine's dependence on the legal artifice of marriage to secure control over the body of his lover, so Behn here shows that an incestuous challenge to the law of patriarchal prerogative does not necessarily constitute a challenge to the law of masculine privilege.

II. Role-Playing, Cuckoldry, and Cross-Dressing: Sylvia's Semiotic Education

It is crucial to recognize the extent to which Philander's performative strategy of playing the maid in part one of Behn's narrative is embedded in the male homosocial dynamics that organize her plot more generally. Abounding in the representation of erotic triangles, *Love-Letters* may be read as a veritable proving ground for analysis of what Eve Kosofsky Sedgwick not long ago identified as the homosocial bases and gender assymmetries of triangular heterosexual desire. Of special relevance here is Sedgwick's analysis of the dynamics of cuckoldry and their relationship to the "masculinizing potential of subordination to a man" as it is elaborated in psychoanalytic accounts of male psychosexual development.[34] Sedgwick quotes Richard Klein's gloss on Freud's account of "the little boy's progress towards heterosexuality" to call attention to the way in which modern constructions of heterosexual masculinity presuppose the existence (and repression) of a prior homosexual stage of feminized subordination to another male. The male child, writes Klein, "must pass . . . through the stage of the 'positive' Oedipus, a homoerotic identification with his father, a position of feminized subordination to the father, as a condition of finding a model for his own heterosexual role."[35]

A dynamic of homoerotic identification similar to the one Freud posits and Klein describes is central to the male relationships represented in Behn's text. It is evident not just in Philander's struggles with his father-in-law, where playing the maid becomes simultaneously the means by which the hero usurps paternal authority and the occasion (however burlesque) for a homoerotic encounter with the father, but also in the prolific instances of cuckoldry recounted elsewhere in the narrative. For Sylvia is not just the space across which Philander aspires to homosocial sameness with "the father"; she is, interestingly, also the conduit whereby he asserts masculine identity with Cesario.

A brief review of the prehistory of the incestuous lovers' affair clearly reveals the extent to which Sylvia functions for Philander simultaneously as a locus of deflected homoerotic love and as a means of resolving his own desire to be like Cesario. The founding circumstance of Sylvia and Philander's love is a prior sexual rivalry between Philander and Cesario over the heart and body of Sylvia's older sister, Myrtilla. After promising to marry the prince, Myrtilla had been drawn instead into a marriage with Philander, only to return at last to an adulterous affair with Cesario. Here again, as in the matter of the affair between Philander and Sylvia, Behn makes the origins of desire problematic, introducing ambiguity in her "Argument" as to whether the impulse toward conjugal infidelity originates in Philander or Myrtilla. Philander nevertheless produces his own causal narrative in an early letter to Sylvia, where he makes the case that Myrtilla was the first to violate her vows. Especially striking here is his response to that alleged betrayal:

> *Myrtilla,* I say, first broke her marriage-vows to me; I blame her
> not, nor is it reasonable I should; she saw the young *Cesario,*
> and loved him. *Cesario,* whom the envying world in spite of prej-
> udice must own, has irresistible charms, that godlike form, that
> sweetness in his face, that softness in his eyes and delicate
> mouth; and every beauty besides, that women dote on, and men
> envy: that lovely composition of man and angel! with the addi-
> tion of his eternal youth and illustrious birth, was formed by
> heaven and nature for universal conquest! And who can love the
> charming hero at a cheaper rate than being undone? And she
> that would not venture fame, honour, and a marriage-vow for
> the glory of the young *Cesario's* heart, merits not the noble vic-
> tim. (p. 9)

Instead of faulting Myrtilla for her disloyalty, Philander identifies with her desire for Cesario. Granted, his letter is part of an elaborate textual strategy of seduction—one that requires that he provide Sylvia with irrefutable justifications for his own adulterous love. But the hyperbolic portrait he paints of Cesario, surpassed in erotic extravagance only by the protracted and probably parodic inventory of Myrtilla's physical attributes in the novel's "Argument," exceeds the demands of Philander's rhetorical project and prepares us for his ensuing account of the "joyful submission" and "shameful freedom" he experiences when Cesario cuckolds him:

> But when I knew her false, when I was once confirmed,—when
> by my own soul I found the dissembled passion of hers, when
> she could no longer hide the blushes, or the paleness that seized
> at the approaches of my disordered rival, when I saw love danc-
> ing in her eyes, and her false heart beat with nimble motions,

and soft trembling seized every limb, at the approach or touch of the royal lover, then I thought myself no longer obliged to conceal my flame for *Sylvia;* nay, ere I broke silence, ere I discovered the hidden treasure of my heart, I made her falsehood plainer yet: even the time and place of the dear assignations I discovered; certainty, happy certainty! broke the dull heavy chain, and I with joy submitted to my shameful freedom, and caressed my generous rival; nay, and by heaven I loved him for it, pleased at the resemblance of our souls; for we were secret lovers both, but more pleased that he loved *Myrtilla;* for that made way to my passion for the adorable *Sylvia!* (pp. 9–10)

At the climax of this passage, it is difficult to disentangle Philander's pleasure from Myrtilla's. But Philander's text ultimately takes a turn whereby its writer comes to occupy more than a single position in the complex network of triangular desire. At one and the same time, he manages to identify with Myrtilla's pleasurable submission to Cesario and, through the mediating figure of Sylvia, with Cesario's position of conquest over him. For Philander, that is, Sylvia is not just a double for Myrtilla (not just another version of prohibited womanhood) but a locus of deflected homosocial love—a substitute, in effect, for Cesario. As in Philander's night of impotence or his garden encounter with Beralti, where playing the maid serves as a strategy for appropriating paternal prerogatives, so here identification with the position of Myrtilla becomes a conduit for his assertion of masculine privilege.[36] By providing the possibility for Philander to occupy multiple subject positions simultaneously, Sylvia creates the conditions whereby he is able to convert his sense of admiration and envy for his rival into a version of identification with him.

" 'To cuckold,' " writes Sedgwick, "is by definition a sexual act, performed on a man, by another man. . . . The bond of cuckoldry . . . [is] *necessarily* hierarchical in structure, with an 'active' participant who is clearly in the ascendancy over the 'passive' one." In the homosocial scheme that underwrites this bond, moreover, "men's bonds with women are meant to be in a subordinate, complementary, and instrumental relation to bonds with other men."[37] The world of *Love-Letters* both exemplifies this ethos and, through the heroine's ability to identify it, provides a critique of its structuring principles.

As Philander notes early on, being cuckolded is hardly an abuse over which it is worth risking one's life, let alone one's friendship with a male rival. "Let the dull, hot-brained, jealous fool upbraid me with cold patience," he writes in defense of his response to Cesario's cuckoldry, "let the fond coxcomb, whose honour depends on the frail marriage-vow, reproach me, or tell me that my reputation depends on the feeble constancy of a wife, persuade me it is honour to fight for an irretrievable and unvalued prize, and that because my rival has taken leave to cuckold me, I shall give him leave to kill me too" (p. 10). Sylvia displays a similar cynicism when she demands in a moment of resistance to Philander, "What husband is not a cuckold? Nay, and a friend to him that made him so?" (p. 18). Philander, of course, claims transcendent passion for Sylvia as grounds for his casual dismissal of Myrtilla, insisting that "only she that has my soul can engage my sword" (p. 10). But his actions in the ensuing narrative will belie these early protestations and expose the deep contradictions inherent in Philander's libertine debunking of the interested codes of patriarchal honor. Sylvia will perceive these contradictions with clarity by the middle of part two, when pregnant and betrayed by Philander after having joined him in his flight to Holland to escape political prosecution (as in real life Henrietta Berkeley had in a similar circumstance followed Grey), she angrily begins a course of increasing cunning and self-sufficiency. Entertaining the advances of another suitor while allowing Philander to continue to believe in her fidelity to him and in her ignorance of his infidelity to her, she will ultimately outstrip Philander at the game of inconstancy. The Dutch nobleman Octavio, illegitimate son of the House of Orange (p. 189) as well as Philander's confidante and friend, fittingly becomes her instrument of revenge.

The ensuing rivalry between Philander and Octavio reproduces the competing demands of love and honor that dominate Philander's seduction of Sylvia, only to recast them in an ironic light. To all appearances, Octavio is the very embodiment of honor and authenticity; but Behn makes a mockery of his honorable punctilios in her portrait of his bumbling efforts to "protect" Sylvia from the secret of Philander's infidelity. Unable to restrain his love for the abandoned Sylvia, Octavio dutifully confesses all in letters to Philander, only to discover that the latter has taken up with Octavio's own virtuous, married sister, Calista, and is altogether willing to surrender Sylvia's body to the encroaching erotic advances of a friend. While Octavio nourishes resentment over the honor of Calista (of whose familial identity Philander yet remains ignorant), he nevertheless resolves that his friendship for Philander will surpass all other ties, including both his duty to his sister and his passion for Sylvia. Finding solace in being able to act honorably toward (i.e., with permission from) his rival in satisfying his desire for his new object, Octavio thus agrees to what amounts to a double transaction with Philander: namely, the prostitution of his sister to gain a lover ("rifle *Calista* of every virtue heaven and nature gave her," he declares, "so I may but revenge it on thy *Sylvia!*" [p. 173]) and the exchange, in effect, of his sister for Philander's. Behn underscores the similarity in difference between incest and exchange here by building a clearly incestuous charge into Octavio's voyeuristic consumption of letters in which Philander elaborately details his erotic encounters with Calista. Through her repeated doubling of the categories of sister and lover, she lodges a deft critique of aristocratic codes of masculine honor that deploy sisters as well as lovers as enabling grounds for the enactment of male prerogative.

Cognizant of the extent to which Octavio and Philander's gentleman's agreement reduces her to a mere object of circulation among men, Sylvia at length confronts Octavio with the double moral standard underlying his devotion to male honor:

> "Oh, you are very nice, *Octavio* . . . in your punctilio to *Philander;* but I perceive you are not so tender in those you ought to have for *Sylvia:* I find honour in you men, is only what you please to make it; for at the same time you think it ungenerous to betray *Philander,* you believe it no breach of honour to betray the eternal repose of *Sylvia.* You have promised *Philander* your friendship; you have avowed yourself my lover, my slave, my friend, my every thing; and yet not one of these has any tie to oblige you to my interest. . . . And here you think it no dishonour to break your word or promise; by which I find your false notions of virtue and honour, with which you serve yourselves, when interest, design, or self-love makes you think it necessary." (p. 192)

Finally, it is neither Sylvia's inconstancy with Octavio nor the latter's erotic rivalry that inspires Philander to raise his sword against his friend; it is rather the perception that, in betraying the "secrets of friendship" to Sylvia (p. 369), Octavio has allowed a heterosexual tie to supercede their homosocial bond. This transgression alone is able to move Philander, as it were, out of the boudoir and onto the battlefield (pp. 369–70).

On the day before he is to take Holy Orders in part three of the narrative, Octavio—now broken by Sylvia's treachery—is visited by Philander, who comes to beg Octavio's pardon for offenses he has committed against him and to persuade him to abandon his determination to retire from the world. Not only has Philander debauched Octavio's sister, who has by now retired pregnant to a convent, but he has ravished from him Sylvia, the very mistress he had not long before abandoned to his friend. As a pledge of his friendship at this critical moment in the text, Philander now assures Octavio that he would never have violated his sister, Calista, had he known of her relationship to him. He would, moreover, as he wryly notes, gladly "quit [Sylvia] to him, were she ten times dearer to him than she was" (p. 393), if doing so would deter Octavio from his desperate intent. Although these protestations of friendship from Philander fail to dissuade Octavio from his resolve, they nevertheless elicit this reciprocal profession of his love:

> "Sir, I must confess you have found out the only way to disarm me of my resentment against you, if I were not obliged, by those vows I am going to take, to pardon and be at peace with all the world. However, these vows cannot hinder me from conserving entirely that friendship in my heart, which your good qualities and beauties at first sight engaged there, and from esteeming you more than perhaps I ought to do; the man whom I must yet own my rival, and the undoer of my sister's honour. But oh—no more of that; a friend is above a sister, or a mistress.' At this he hung down his eyes and sighed." (p. 393)

Uttered on the eve of the hero's initiation into the fraternal order of St. Bernard, this simple maxim—"A friend is above a sister or a mistress"—is perhaps the baldest statement we have of the sexual hierarchies that underpin Behn's plot. Granting the pardon Philander begs, Octavio seals it by taking "a ring of great value from his finger" (p. 394), which he presents to Philander as a pledge of his love, in much the same spirit that Philander had earlier pledged Sylvia. Like the ring, Sylvia is the gift that cements and the token that signifies relations between men.

Sylvia's specular status in relations between men is neatly literalized by her frequent appearances in male attire. It is, in fact, during the first of these episodes of cross-dressing that Octavio initially falls in love with her. Drag enhances Sylvia's attractions as an object of male desire (she "never appeared so charming and desirable" as when dressed as a man [p. 114]) if for no other reason than that it enables her male admirers both to identify with the sexual conquests of the young cavalier whom she impersonates and to experience a certain rivalry with him. These at least are the peculiar pleasures of Octavio's experience: "*Octavio* saw every day with abundance of pleasure the little revenges of love, on those women's hearts who had made before little conquests over him, and strove by all the gay presents he made a young *Fillmond* (for so they called *Sylvia,*) to make him appear unresistible to the ladies; and while *Sylvia* gave them new wounds, *Octavio* failed not to receive them too among the crowd, till at last he became a confirmed slave, to the lovely unknown; and that which was yet more strange, she captivated the men no less than the women" (pp. 118–19).

In the long run, however, cross-dressing has another—a productive as opposed to a merely specular—potential that Sylvia in time learns to exploit with increasing skill and that goes beyond according her that freedom of physical movement and those other "little privileges . . . denied to women" (p. 118).[38] Over the course of her career, Behn's Ovidian letter-writer undergoes a dazzling metamorphosis from corrupted innocence to triumphant depravity—a transformation that culminates in part three of the narrative in an exhilarating escapade in which she elevates the game of sexual conquest from a means of revenge into an art. Having become a consummate fiction-maker and role player (as well as a wealthy courtesan who capitalizes on the weaknesses of unsuspecting men), she here undertakes as a "frolic to divert herself" (p. 403) conquest of the heart of Don Alonzo, a young Spanish-born gentleman distinguished most significantly for being the only man ever to have succeeded in outdoing Philander at the game of inconstancy. When Alonzo boasts of having "reduced . . . to . . . a lover" an unconquerable Dutch countess whose heart even Philander could not command, Sylvia resolves to go him one better by determining to fix his own wandering heart on her (p. 410). She succeeds in her determination by enacting a masquerade in which she plays both male and female parts: a handsome cavalier named Bellumere and his lovely sister, Mme de ———.

By means of a ring that Alonzo gives to Bellumere as a pledge of male friendship and that Mme de ——— later vaunts upon her tour, Sylvia deftly turns Bellumere into a suspected rival of Don Alonzo for her favors. She thus plays an interesting variation on the homosocial code whereby mistresses typically stand in as obligatory heterosexual displacements of prohibited objects of homoerotic male desire. By creating a male version of herself through which to lure her victims into a homoerotic attachment, she paradoxically ensures her own status as a primary object of desire instead of merely an intermediate term in a phallocentric sexual and symbolic economy. In this instance, she also cleverly turns Alonzo's imagined rival into a brother, to whose authority over the disposal of her favors she presents herself as determined to defer. Sylvia imposes her own authority, that is, by means of the pretense of deferring to Bellumere's, thus creating a drama in which she at once reproduces and subverts the hierarchy of authority that informed her early relation with Philander. Both producing and controlling Alonzo's desire for her, she now manages her own circulation as a sign of femininity.

This episode makes stunningly clear the extent to which Sylvia has appropriated Philander's performative strategies of symbolic deferral by the novel's end. As we have seen, the relation between sign and referent in Philander's garden escapade with Beralti following his alleged attack of impotence in part one is neither as stable nor transparent as Gardiner suggests when she reads it as a simple externalization of the hero's demeaning impotence. Nor does it involve a simple masking of the "truth" of Philander's inherent dominance. It is, rather, a productive relation in which Philander consolidates his power by using theater to produce material effects. This, we might say, is his type of sorcery, the basis of that power to charm by which he creates effects in some instances as tangible as those wrought by philtres upon the body of Brilliard or by alchemy on the heart and eyes of Cesario. For Behn, his performances are occasions for displacing the natural ground of the opposition between inner and outer experience, psyches and surfaces, artifice and authenticity. Philander treads an extraordinarily fluid line between role-playing and reality, dissembling so well at times that, as Behn's narrator notes late in the text, "he scarce knew himself that he did so" (p. 355).

By the time Sylvia encounters Don Alonzo, she has learned how to exploit the productive nature of performance so as to move beyond her status as a specular representation of male desire, a mere player in a drama controlled by men, both to create and variously represent herself. She has not, however, always recognized the productive potential of her own radical deracination as a sign (a performer) of femininity. Although she has from the start intuited the insufficiency of the written word to express her soul completely, she is fairly confident initially of its ability to simulate, if not entirely to substitute, for presence. "While I write," she declares in an early letter to Philander, "methinks I am talking to thee; I tell thee thus my soul, while thou, methinks, art all the while smiling and listening by; this is much easier than silent thought, and my soul is never weary of this converse; and thus I would speak a thousand things, but that still, methinks, words do not enough express my soul" (p. 31). Still a fairly naive reader, Sylvia believes this insufficiency can be made up for by the supplement of presence, by merely adding voice to text: "to understand that right, there requires looks; there is a rhetoric in looks; in sighs and silent touches that surpasses all; there is an accent in the sound of words too, that gives a sense and soft meaning to little things, which of themselves are of trivial value, and insignificant; and by the cadence of the utterance may express a tenderness which their own meaning does not bear; by this I wou'd insinuate, that the story of the heart cannot be so well told by this way, as by presence and conversation" (p. 31). A more savvy reader of Philander might by now have recognized the dangers of ventriloquism, which he betrays in his third letter when he describes the emptiness of his public performances: "I move about this unregarded world, appear every day in the great senate-house, at clubs, cabals, and private consultations; . . . I say I appear indeed, and give my voice in public business; but oh my heart more kindly is employed" (p. 12). But Sylvia, though she sometimes doubts his word, still finds Philander's letters more reassuring than ominous. Clinging to an idealized notion of presence, she buys into the rhetorical opposition between private and public life on which Philander erects the fiction of his own sincerity.

While the Sylvia of part one may still believe naively in the possibility of her own and others' authenticity ("I have no arts, heaven knows, no guile or double meaning in my soul, 'tis all plain native simplicity" [p. 16]), her maid and "too fatal counsellor" (p. 22), Melinda, nevertheless detects her mistress's performative potential early on. In the letter she writes to Philander just before his fateful night of impotence, Melinda alludes to the late occurrence of "many ominous things" (p. 46). Among these she cites an incident that has aroused suspicions in Sylvia's mother regarding her daughter's romantic activities. Melinda presumably wants to alert Philander on the eve of his assignation with Sylvia to the perils of heightened parental vigilance, but her letter also provides him with a warning glimpse of Sylvia's budding semiotic education. It shows the heroine's incipient ability to exploit not just the dangerous excesses of script but the dangerous supplementarity of presence and voice itself. Although Sylvia had early lamented the intransigence of her "guilty pen" (p. 26), bemoaning the insidious tendency of writing to betray her best intentions, she here shows an almost instinctive urge to master the treachery of the letter and to exploit its openness as a form of self-defense. Discovered by her mother in the act of writing to Philander, physical evidence in hand, Sylvia brilliantly avoids being implicated in her own guilt through an ingenious act of textual deferral. In the exigency of the moment, she concocts the fiction that she is writing as a surrogate for Melinda to the latter's lover, using pseudonyms to protect that guilty "maid," and she adds demonstrative proof of her claim by, in effect, performing her text aloud with an altered—an essentially ironic—emphasis. As Melinda reports, she "turned it . . . prettily into burlesque love by her *manner of reading it*" (pp. 46–47; italics added).

This cunning transformation of material fact into plausible fiction by creating a multiplicity of referents through the act of reading forms a stark contrast with the later example of Clarissa, who is characteristically victimized by the uncontrollable openness of her own letter texts. When Clarissa finally does learn to exploit the ambiguities of script, moreover, she can do so only by closing them around the referent of the father. Writing to Lovelace that she is "setting out with all diligence for [her] Father's House," in her famous trick of lying truthfully, Clarissa points to a superabundance of father figures not to an open field of interpretive possibility. And indeed one can not help feeling that the imperatives of honesty and sincerity that control Clarissa's writing play a rather sinister role in determining the range of choices she is able to imagine for taking retributive action against Lovelace's treachery.[39] It is not until the topos of the daughter's guilty pen recurs in Frances Burney's *Evelina* or Jane Austen's *Lady Susan* that we again encounter an exploitation of the formal openness of the letter as subtle and subversive as the one Behn offers in this single episode from her text.

This scene, in which Sylvia reads her own love letter as if she were only playacting the lover, resonates in several crucial ways throughout Behn's text. In one sense, it serves as a paradigm in small of Behn's novel as a whole—a figure, as it were, for the distancing effect of parody Behn herself achieves at the level of narration through her characteristic cultivation of rhetorical excess. As the first instance in the narrative when Sylvia instinctively plays the role of "maid," moreover, it foreshadows the freedom she will ultimately realize by abandoning the presupposition that she possesses a natural bedrock of desire and a core of stable self-identity. By introducing the possibility that Sylvia's letter may be itself only a script—that the very text she generates as the sincere expression of her soul may be symptomatic of a role she plays but over which she does not have performative control—it exposes the radically contingent nature of her desire and the performative as opposed to natural basis of her subjectivity.

If Sylvia's original letter text is merely an imitation of originality and if presence and voice are not reliable markers of substance but dangerous forms of supplementarity, then the very possibility of an origin—of an authentic ground from which one's actions and one's utterances proceed—becomes problematic. In the space opened by these unsettling possibilities, Sylvia is freed from the promise of an incestuous fulfillment of original desire into an open field of signifying possibility. Behn gestures toward this openness in the penultimate paragraph of her text, where she sends her heroine daily in search of new conquests "wherever she shews the charmer" (p. 461). The physical body—that most corporeal of figures—finally emerges as the most unstable of all sites of meaning. The ultimate charmer, it obliterates the very ground of truth and falsehood required for the enactment of personal authenticity. In Behn's world of apparently infinite displacements, there is finally no essence or original that is not constituted in the dialogics of performance or the contestations of power politics. Even so allegedly authenticating a gesture as incest is finally exposed as substituting for the law it would subvert.

III. Coda

Libertine rhetoric exalts the female as an iconic substitute for the father-king, promoting the flattering fiction that woman is the source of both desire and prohibition. "Glorious woman was born for command and dominion," declares Philander, "though custom has usurped us the name of rule over all." In fact, he insists, Sylvia's sovereignty is the motivating force for all his political ambitions. He seeks political empire only to be able to trade it for romantic slavery:

> Let me toil to gain, but let *Sylvia* triumph and reign; I ask no more than the led slave at her chariot wheels, to gaze on my charming conqueress, and wear with joy her fetters! Oh how proud I should be to see the dear victor of my soul so elevated, so adorn'd with crowns and sceptres at her feet, which I had won; to see her smiling on the adoring crowd, distributing her glories to young waiting princes. . . . Heavens! methinks I see the lovely virgin in this state, her chariot slowly driving through the multitude that press to gaze upon her, she dress'd like *Venus*, richly gay and loose, her hair and robe blown by the flying winds. (pp. 38–39)

By novel's close, Philander's vision of Sylvia's triumph as spectacle (however disingenuously it has been offered) is realized, as the heroine, "dressed in perfect glory," is pursued by gazing crowds through the streets of Brussels (pp. 436–37), a rival of even Cesario's elegant mistress, Hermione. But unlike Hermione, who invests all her own ambition in Cesario's success only to meet her demise in his defeat, Sylvia does not depend for her glory on Philander's toil and enterprise; she achieves it on her own.[40] She makes the punctilious Octavio an instrument of her revenge against Philander and to that passion she eventually sacrifices him. By the end of the narrative, moreover, she has resourcefully managed to turn even Philander's servant, Brilliard, (originally deployed to maintain Philander's authority over her) to the promotion of her material interests. Now using Brilliard as a prop in her own self-serving schemes, she manipulates him (by once again exploiting a homosocial bond) into extorting an inheritance from the retired Octavio on the spurious promise of her own penitence and retirement. Then, "impatient to be seen on the *Tour,* and in all public places," she promptly furnishes herself with "new coach and equipage, and . . . lavish . . . clothes and jewels" (p. 434).

The irony of Behn's political defense of royalism is that it ends with the triumph not only of the king but also of the woman who most quintessentially embodies unregenerate female defiance of male supremacy. Cesario's rebellion fails and Philander opportunistically embraces monarchy, while in a savagely ironic twist on this double defeat of the Whig cause, Sylvia makes good the libertine promise of female sovereignty. At one level Behn seems to want to point to divinely appointed kingship as the ultimate locus of truth and authority—the original object of worship of which all other objects of desire are failed imitations and empty substitutes. But the figure at center stage in *Love-Letters between a Nobleman and His Sister,* the one that absorbs the reader's gaze, is not the king at all but the spectacularly protean body of Sylvia. That this body is also figured without much comment for the better part of Behn's narrative not as the virgin body Philander invokes but as an eroticized maternal presence, a curiously denaturalized point of physical origin in the shape of a pregnant eros, is perhaps not so very insignificant a detail after all, so thoroughly disruptive as it is of any binary relation between displacement and origin.[41] Much as Sylvia signifies the physical power to generate nameless and presumably endless substitutions, so Behn proliferates meanings beyond the binary frame that constitutes incest as a counter to patriarchal law or legitimate kingship as an ultimate site of meaning and of power.

Notes

1. For further discussion of the Berkeley-Ford affair, see Maureen Duffy, *The Passionate Shepherdess: Aphra Behn, 1640–89,* (London: Jonathan Cape, 1977), pp. 221–24; and Angeline Goreau, *Reconstructing Aphra: A Social Biography of Aphra Behn* (New York: Dial Press, 1980), pp. 273–78. For an

account of the trial, see William Cobbett, *State Trials* (London, 1811), 9:127–86. For the probable identification of Dryden's Caleb as Grey, see Cecil Price, *Cold Caleb: The Scandalous Life of Ford Grey, First Earl of Tankerville, 1655–1701* (London: Andrew Melrose, 1956), p. 71.

2. Ros Ballaster discusses the effect on Behn of conventions regarding "appropriate" female forms in her *Seductive Forms: Women's Amatory Fiction, 1684–1740* (Oxford: Clarendon Press, 1992), pp. 71–81.

3. Susan Staves, *Players' Scepters: Fictions of Authority in the Restoration* (Lincoln and London: Univ. of Nebraska Press, 1979), ch. 5. For other discussions of the dissociation between theology and natural law theory in the seventeenth and eighteenth centuries, see Bruce Boehrer, " 'Nice Philosophy': *'Tis Pity She's a Whore* and the Two Books of God," *SEL* 24 (1984): 355–71; Alfred Owen Aldridge, "The Meaning of Incest from Hutcheson to Gibbon," *Ethics* 61 (1951): 309–13; and W. Daniel Wilson, "Science, Natural Law, and Unwitting Sibling Incest in Eighteenth-Century Literature," *Studies in Eighteenth-Century Culture* 13 (1984): 249–70.

4. Aphra Behn, *Love-Letters between a Nobleman and His Sister*, ed. Maureen Duffy (London: Virago, 1987), p. 4. Subsequent references to this edition will be cited parenthetically in the text by page number.

5. Sybil Wolfram, *In-Laws and Outlaws: Kinship and Marriage in England* (London and Sydney: Croom Helm, 1987), p. 43. On the status of the in-law relationship with respect to incest in England, see also Jack Goody, "A Comparative Approach to Incest and Adultery," *British Journal of Sociology* 7 (1956): 291; and Staves, *Players' Scepters*, p. 304. Behn's Myrtilla in effect assumes affinal as well as consanguineal ties in the in-law relation when she suggests to Sylvia that the existence of her child by Philander strengthens his connections to Sylvia both by relation and by blood. Philander, she writes, "has lain by thy unhappy sister's side so many tender years, by whom he has a dear and lovely offspring, by which he has *more fixed himself to thee by relation and blood*" (p. 70; italics added). The doctrine of "one flesh" that underlay the British concept of marriage became the basis also for arguments regarding the illegality of sexual relations between stepson and stepmother. See, for example, Jeremy Taylor, who argues that "she that is one flesh with my Father is as neer to me as my Father, and thats as neer as my own Mother" (*Ductor Dubitantium: or The Rule of Conscience* [London, 1660] bk. 2, ch. 2, rule 3, n. 29).

6. Staves, *Players' Scepters*, pp. 263–64.

7. Hugo Grotius, *The Law of War and Peace (De Jure Belli ac Paci Libri Tres)*, trans. Francis W. Kelsey (Indianapolis and New York: Bobbs-Merrill, 1925), bk. 2, ch. 5, sect. 13, par. 1, p. 242. Grotius observed the difficulty, if not impossibility, of assigning "definite natural causes" for the unlawfulness of incestuous marriages within any degree of affinity or consanguinity (bk. 2, ch. 5, sect. 12, par. 1, p. 239).

8. Grotius, *The Law of War and Peace*, bk. 2, ch. 5, sec. 13, para. 5, p. 244.

9. Taylor, *Ductor Dubitantium*, 2.2.24–25.

10. Richard Cumberland, *De Legibus Naturae*, trans. as *A Treatise of the*

Laws of Nature by John Maxwell (London, 1727); facsimile reprint in *British Philosophers and Theologians of the Seventeenth and Eighteenth Centuries,* ed. René Wellek (New York and London: Garland, 1978), ch. 8, sec. 9, p. 338. The implications of this incipient questioning of the natural basis of the incest prohibition would be extended in the mid-eighteenth century by Henry St. John Bolingbroke, who went so far as to construe Eve as Adam's daughter: "Eve was in some sort the daughter of Adam. She was literally bone of his bone, and flesh of his flesh, by birth, if I may call it so, whereas other husbands and wives are so in an allegorical manner only. But to pass this over, the children of the first couple were certainly brothers and sisters, and by these conjunctions, declared afterward incestuous, the human species was first propagated" ("Fragments, or Minutes of Essays" in *Works,* 8 vols. (London, 1809), 7:497–98). Another instance where scripture seemed to sanctify parent-child incest on the grounds of necessity or good intentions was in its account of Lot's daughters. See, Bolingbroke, *Works,* 7:416–17; and Simon Patrick, *A Commentary Upon the Historical Books of the Old Testament* (London, 1727), Gen. 19:32.

11. Ruth Perry, *Women, Letters, and the Novel* (New York: AMS Press, 1980), p. 24.

12. René Girard, *Violence and the Sacred,* trans. Patrick Gregory (Baltimore and London: Johns Hopkins University Press, 1977), p. 74.

13. Such an association of seditious rebellion with incest was not unique in royalist discourse of the Restoration. Like sorcery, incest was associated with the sanctioning of alternative (and therefore illegitimate) sources of authority. Thus, for example, when George Hickes undertook in 1678 to recount the trial and conviction of the seditious conventicle preacher James Mitchell for his attempt on the life of the archbishop of St. Andrews, there seemed reason enough to feature Mitchell's tenuous association with the unsavory figure of Thomas Weir by appending to the record of Mitchell's trial the story of Weir's own earlier trial and execution for adultery, incest, sorcery, and bestiality. See *Ravillac Redivivus: Being a Narrative of the late Tryal of Mr. James Mitchel . . . , to which is Annexed, an Account of the Tryal of that most wicked Pharisee Major Thomas Weir . . .* (London, 1678). Weir had been tried and executed in 1670. Hickes, a nonjuror, was personal chaplain to the duke of Lauderdale. An expanded second edition of his narrative was published in 1682. In 1710, Curll also brought out an amplified version under the title "The Spirit of Fanaticism Exemplified." On the association of incest and sorcery (both of which figure significantly in *Love-Letters*), see Mary Douglas, *Purity and Danger: An Analysis of the Concepts of Pollution and Taboo* (London: Routledge and Kegan Paul, 1966), pp. 107–13; David M. Schneider, "The Meaning of Incest," *Journal of Polynesian Society* 85 (1976): 149–69; and Judith Lewis Herman, *Father-Daughter Incest* (Cambridge, and London: Harvard Univ. Press, 1981), p. 50.

14. Grey, his Whig allegiances notwithstanding, was also of royalist birth. "Consider, my lord," writes Sylvia, "you are born noble, from parents of untainted loyalty" (p. 33).

15. See, for example, Goreau, *Reconstructing Aphra,* pp. 272–73; Ballaster,

Seductive Forms, pp. 78–79; Robert Markley, " 'Be impudent, be saucy, forward, bold, touzing, and leud': The Politics of Masculine Sexuality and Feminine Desire in Behn's Tory Comedies," in *Revisionist Readings of the Restoration and Eighteenth-Century Theatre,* ed. J. Douglas Canfield and Deborah Payne (forthcoming); and Robert Markley and Molly Rothenberg, "Contestations of Nature: Aphra Behn's 'The Golden Age' and the Sexualizing of Politics," in this volume.

16. Janet Todd, *The Sign of Angellica: Women, Writing, and Fiction, 1660–1800* (New York: Columbia Univ. Press, 1989), p. 83; Maureen Duffy, Introduction to Virago edition of *Love-Letters,* pp. xi–xii.

17. Perry, *Women, Letters, and the Novel,* p. 25.

18. On the topic of self-preservation in seventeenth-century natural law theory, see Maximillian E. Novak, *Defoe and the Nature of Man* (London: Oxford Univ. Press, 1963).

19. Todd, *The Sign of Angellica,* pp. 79–82.

20. Judith Kegan Gardiner, "The First English Novel: Aphra Behn's *Love Letters,* the Canon, and Women's Tastes," *Tulsa Studies in Women's Literature* 8 (Fall 1989): 201–22.

21. Ibid., p. 207.

22. Ibid., p. 218. For a fuller discussion of oedipal models of the novel's origins, especially Ian Watt's, see also Laurie Langbauer, *Women and Romance: The Consolations of Gender in the English Novel* (Ithaca and London: Cornell Univ. Press, 1990), pp. 28–30.

23. See, for example, Judith Butler, "Prohibition, Psychoanalysis, and the Heterosexual Matrix," in her *Gender Trouble: Feminism and the Subversion of Identity* (New York and London: Routledge, 1990), ch. 2.

24. This question, in the form of debate about whether Henrietta Berkeley had been a consenting party in leaving her father's house, was also an important issue in Grey's trial. See Cobbett, *State Trials,* 9:127–86; and Price, *Cold Caleb,* pp. 98–100.

25. For a theoretical consideration of such destabilizing narrative strategies in twentieth-century women's writing, see Rachel Blau DuPlessis, *Writing beyond the Ending: Narrative Strategies of Twentieth-Century Women Writers* (Bloomington: Indiana Univ. Press, 1985).

26. Others have fruitfully discussed Behn's characteristic multiplying of subject positions. See, for example, Ballaster, *Seductive Forms,* ch. 3; and Jessica Munns, " 'I by a Double Right Thy Bounties Claim': Aphra Behn and Sexual Space," in *Curtain Calls: British and American Women and the Theater, 1660–1820,* ed. Mary Anne Schofield and Cecelia Macheski (Athens: Ohio Univ. Press, 1991), pp. 193–210.

27. Gardiner, "The First English Novel," pp. 212–13.

28. Duffy's assertion that Philander's impotence is a symptom of syphilis and thus a "tell-tale signal" of his sexual promiscuity (Introduction to *Love-Letters,* p. xii), a possibility Todd is also willing to entertain (*The Sign of Angellica,* p. 81), is an interesting but largely unfounded speculation.

29. Although I use it in a different sense, I borrow the impulse to characterize gender performance and cross-dressing as potential put-ons from Kristina Straub's recent work on female theatrical cross-dressing and the parodic performance of masculinity in the career and writing of Charlotte Charke in *Sexual Suspects: Eighteenth-Century Players and Sexual Ideology* (Princeton: Princeton Univ. Press, 1992), ch. 7; a version of this chapter, entitled "The Guilty Pleasures of Female Theatrical Cross-Dressing and the Autobiography of Charlotte Charke" also appears in *Body Guards: The Cultural Politics of Gender Ambiguity*, ed. Julia Epstein and Kristina Straub (New York and London: Routledge, 1991), pp. 142–66.

30. Gardiner simplifies what Behn makes problematic, it seems to me, when she reads these assertions by Sylvia as "subversive of traditional gender roles" in that they characterize the heroine as a desiring subject who "glories in her new desires" ("The First English Novel," p. 213).

31. This is not to deny Philander's account of his garden escapade either its comic hilarity or its status as Behn's satire of Philander/Grey. One cannot help but agree with Gardiner that Perry (who bases her reading solely on part one of the narrative) is wrong in her assertion that "there is no gaiety about [the] truancy" of Philander and Sylvia (Gardiner, "The First English Novel," p. 213; Perry, *Women, Letters, and the Novel,* p. 25). But is the gaiety of the episode generated solely or even primarily by Behn's wicked delight in humiliating Philander/Grey? Or is there some other, competing source of comedy at work? There is a question of audience at issue here, because Philander (to the extent that he functions as a character rather than a mere surrogate for Behn) controls the narration, which he offers as entertainment Sylvia. What is at stake for Philander in this relation? He claims a simple, practical motive—that of feeding Sylvia information Melinda will need to cover for him with the count. But if Philander were so utterly ashamed of the impotence Gardiner sees reenacted in the scene, why would he bother to give so elaborate an account of those events to Sylvia? Surely, if Beralti's garden tryst with the disguised Philander is a parodic repetition of the youthful upstairs encounter between Philander and Sylvia, its effect is less to burlesque Philander than the count.

32. That Sylvia and "the maid" are surrogates for one another is suggested at several other points, e.g., when Sylvia claims to be inditing for Melinda or when she puts (or at least attempts to put) Antonet to bed in her place with Octavio.

33. Once again, my reading here diverges from that of Gardiner, who insists that because Philander is Sylvia's brother "in law," as opposed to her father or her brother, he "has no authority over her," despite the fact that he is "politically more powerful" than she is ("The First English Novel," p. 218).

34. Eve Kosofsky Sedgwick, *Between Men: English Literature and Male Homosocial Desire* (New York: Columbia Univ. Press, 1985), p. 24.

35. Quoted ibid., p. 23.

36. Another such instance occurs when Philander attempts to secure control over Sylvia by staging a plot in which Brilliard, in effect, cuckolds him.

37. Sedgwick, *Between Men,* pp. 49–51.

38. On the function of cross-dressing in the eighteenth century, see Pat Rogers, "The Breeches Part" in *Sexuality in Eighteenth-Century Britain,* ed. Paul-Gabriel Bouce (Manchester, England: Manchester Univ. Press, 1982), pp. 244–58; Lynne Friedli, " 'Passing women': A Study of Gender Boundaries in the Eighteenth Century," in *Sexual Underworlds of the Enlightenment,* ed. G. S. Rousseau and Roy Porter (Chapel Hill: Univ. of North Carolina Press, 1988), pp. 234–60; and Straub, *Sexual Suspects.* For a more theoretical approach to the relationship between femininity and masquerade, see Mary Ann Doane's now-classic essay "Film and the Masquerade: Theorising the Female Spectator," *Screen* 23 (1982): 74–88. For another instance in Behn's text where female cross-dressing serves a specular and homosocial function, see Philander's reaction to Calista in male attire; drag increases Calista's likeness to Octavio and therefore enhances Philander's attraction to her (pp. 316–18).

39. Behn seems to comment indirectly on the ideological link between an ethics of sincerity and such a superabundance of father figures in her somewhat ironic portrayal of Octavio's initiation into a fraternal order of religious fathers.

40. The figure of Hermione interestingly reinvokes the theme of incest, because she is the former mistress of Cesario's father, the king.

41. It is perhaps significant that in her last cross-dressing escapade in the novel, Sylvia assumes a name, Bellumere, with an onomastic association to, among other things, maternity; the name suggests both a beautiful sight or luminary (Belle-lumière) and a beautiful mother (Belle-mère). Gardiner ("The First English Novel," pp. 215–16) faults Behn for her inadequate treatment of maternity in the novel in terms that seem to me to make a number of essentialist assumptions about female experience.

ROS BALLASTER

"Pretences of State":
Aphra Behn and the Female Plot

The Female Plot

Aphra Behn turned to fiction writing late in her literary career and only when she could no longer support herself by drama.[1] By the 1680s, the London theaters were in financial straits and ideological confusion. The mass paranoia that followed the "discovery" of the Popish Plot in 1678 (a supposed Catholic plot engineered by Pope Innocent XI, the King of France, the Archbishop of Dublin, and the Jesuits to murder Charles and crown the Catholic duke of York in his stead "exposed" by an Anglican clergyman turned Jesuit, Titus Oates), resulted in the king's departure to Newmarket, a succession of executions and purges of suspected Catholics, and, more importantly for Behn perhaps, a general decline in theatergoing.[2] Between 1678 and 1679, the King's Company closed down as a result of internal disputes, and the Duke's Company staged only six new plays.[3] Behn abandoned the stage for the novel.

Her success in this new medium was remarkable. Both her *Love-Letters between a Nobleman and His Sister* and the collected novellas entitled the *Histories and Novels* went into more than ten editions. It is not enough to explain this phenomenon as the simple effect of rising literacy among women and demands for fiction more suited to their taste, that is, centered on romantic intrigue. Rather, I would suggest, the figure of the woman, and in particular the female love victim, had a larger ideological significance than the appeal to women readers alone.

The execution of a king in 1649 was no easy event to purge from the public memory, even with the restoration of his son to the throne in 1660, and the hysteria that resulted from Oates's revelation of the Popish Plot was doubtless the result of renewed anxiety about the dangers of Catholic tyranny in England. In particular, the dynastic struggles of the Stuart sovereigns from Charles I's execution until the Hanoverian succession in 1714 seem to have thrown philosophical, literary, and political discourses into a profound crisis about the nature of authority and the means of its legitimation. Behn, a confirmed royalist, was no exception to this rule, and her location of authorial legitimation in a female narrative voice might be ascribed to a larger cultural movement toward locating moral value, law, and order in the individual, rather than directly feminist sentiment on her part.

As Susan Staves argues in her *Players' Scepters: Fictions of Authority in the Restoration,* a clear social consensus against the exercise of violence, whether manifested in the arbitrary tyranny of a king or the lawless behavior of the mob, seems to have emerged following Charles II's restoration in 1660. This ideological consensus generated a search for new models for social behavior in contemporary literature, to which the representation of heroic resistance through passivity in the figure of the sexually beleaguered woman seemed a particularly apposite response. Staves writes that "the late seventeenth century's interest in women was aroused by the usefulness of seeing women as models for men. As the culture became more a bourgeois culture of men who rejected the personal use of violence, where better to look for examples of how people manage without violence than among women?"[4] Ellen Pollak both reinforces the argument and notes the tensions it produced in contemporary accounts of the position of women. The feminocentric focus of much fiction in this period, she argues, did not produce an easy transition into the according of a full subjectivity and autonomy to women in general. Rather, artists, philosophers, and political theorists, Locke not least among them, sought to deploy the figure of the woman as a means of evolving a new concept of the masculine subject, while simultaneously maintaining a theory of natural female subordination to familial hierarchy and patriarchal rule:

> As patriarchal notions of divine-right monarchy were rejected by political theorists, as benevolist attitudes began to infiltrate religious thought, as empiricist philosophy increasingly designated the human subject as the locus both of psychic and of referential truth, new terms in keeping with these individualist traditions gradually evolved to accommodate the ongoing subordination of women to men in social, political, economic, intellectual and domestic life. Fuller and more complex strategies begin to emerge for resolving the increasing autonomy of the masculine subject, in a culture which increasingly affirmed the autonomy of individual desire, and the systematic denial of either desire or autonomy in women.[5]

Seen in this light, Behn's narrative strategies, whereby woman is represented as simultaneously subject (the female writer) and subjected (the female character) within the social order, are a register of this confusion, as well as an attempt to resolve it.

It is a critical commonplace to view Behn's feminist and party politics as deeply at odds. George Woodcock refers to her "radical and even revolutionary tendencies" and explains her "rather foolish loyalty to the reactionary Stuarts" as mere evidence of "the confusion of social ideas in that age."[6] Angeline Goreau asserts at one point in her "social biography" of Behn that "no two philosophical systems could be more opposed than Aphra's revolutionary [i.e., feminist] and Tory thinking."[7] According to these critics, Behn's commitment to authorizing a female narrative voice and her devotion to the authority of the king constitute an unresolvable contradiction in her writing. As the work of Staves and Pollak suggests, however, the ideological differences of Whig and Tory in the late seventeenth century were by no means as clear as they might at first appear. The correlation of Whig politics with bourgeois individualism and Tory politics with antiquated notions of hierarchy and patriarchy in the late seventeenth century is to a large extent a twentieth-century fiction.

Behn found a specific and progressive form of individualism in Tory myth and ideology, in contrast with the repression and egoism she commonly identified with the Whig politician. Following the Res-

toration in 1660, as Judith Kegan Gardiner argues, the sexual liber-
tarianism and cosmopolitan outlook of Tory royalism seemed to offer
new hopes for the revival of heroic individualism in contrast with the
supposedly worn-out dogmatism of the old Commonwealth.[8] It appears, then, that both Behn's and her readers' interest in giving public
validation to the authority of necessarily privatized female experience may have been a result of general political concerns rather than
specific feminist ones. Behn's success lay in her dual articulation of
Tory myth and feminocentric individualism.

Behn, I would argue, recognized at an early stage in her literary
career that the roles of woman writer and political commentator
were incompatible in the public mind and that if she was to make her
living by her writing and succeed in scoring political points for the
Tory camp, she would not be able to do so directly. An interesting
anecdote from her biographer, "One of the Fair Sex," illustrates the
restrictions Behn faced and the strategies of deceit she employed to
escape them. In the summer of 1666, Behn was commissioned on the
advice of her friend the playwright Thomas Killigrew, by Henry
Arlington, then secretary of state, to spy on the activities of English
insurrectionaries exiled in Antwerp during the second Anglo-Dutch
war. Her friendship and possible romance with William Scot, the son
of a regicide and a somewhat unreliable double agent for the English
government, made her an ideal choice for this sensitive mission.[9]
"One of the Fair Sex" claims that Behn sent information about a
planned Dutch attack up the Thames to destroy the English harbored
fleet, which was ignored. Clearly her spying role was to be solely that
of the woman behind Scot (who is satirized as the Dutchman Vander
Albert in the "Memoir"), because:

> all the Encouragement she met with, was to be laugh'd at by the
> Minister she wrote to; and her Letter shew'd by way of Con-
> tempt, to some who ought not to have been let into the Secret,
> and so bandy'd about, till it came to the Ears of a particular
> Friend of hers, who gave her an Account of what Reward she
> was to expect for her Service, since that was so little valu'd; and
> desir'd her therefore to lay aside her politick Negotiation, and di-
> vert her Friends with some pleasant Adventures of *Antwerp*, ei-
> ther as to her Lovers, or those of any other Lady of her
> Acquaintance; that in this she wou'd be more successful than in
> her Pretences of State, since here she wou'd not fail of pleasing
> those she writ to.[10]

Here then, Behn learns an important lesson about the woman writer's relation to audience and appropriate forms. A woman may write pleasant accounts of love affairs to her friends, but she will receive only contempt if she attempts to narrate political affairs to men of state.

Women's only political instrumentality was to be achieved by playing the role of seductress. Not only does the woman writer receive approval rather than scorn for her confinement of her interest to the sphere of love, she also receives financial remuneration. On her return from Antwerp, Behn's biographer tells us, the "rest of her Life was entirely dedicated to Pleasure and Poetry."[11] In fact, on her immediate return, Behn faced imprisonment for debts she had incurred in the king's service, as a passionate begging letter to Killigrew demonstrates.[12] This experience alone was doubtless enough to teach her that she could better make money by veiling her political interest in the appropriate female form of amatory fiction. Closer study of Behn's fictions reveals that these seemingly harmless and escapist fictions of seduction, betrayal, and tragic love do indeed address and rework a number of urgent ideological dilemmas in the period from the Restoration to the Glorious Revolution of 1688.

Oroonoko is the story of the life, romance, and death of an African prince who is tricked onto a slave ship, sold into slavery in the then English colony of Surinam, bitterly humiliated and tortured by the white male colonists following his attempt to lead a slave rebellion, and finally executed, having taken the life of his pregnant wife.[13] The pathetic story of an African prince is framed within a specific debate on the nature of kingly authority and passive valor. Oroonoko himself is presented as a natural prince. His enslavement is an indignity to his class rather than his race. Renamed Caesar by his considerate master, Trefry, Oroonoko is indeed the modern equivalent of a Roman hero, equalled only by his wife, Imoinda, "the beautiful Black *Venus* to our young *Mars*" (5:137). Behn's description of him places him firmly within the Roman analogy: "His Face was not of that brown rusty Black which most of that Nation are, but a perfect Ebony, or polished Jet. . . . His Nose was rising and *Roman,* instead of *African* and flat: His Mouth the finest shaped that could be seen; far from those great turn'd Lips, which are so natural to the rest of the Negroes" (5:136). Behn's description of her hero has generated a critical controversy about the extent of her anti-racism and/or abolitionist sympathies.[14] Behn goes out of her way to stress Oroonoko/ Caesar's distinctive difference from his fellow slaves, however. When they agree to a cowardly surrender following the slave rebellion he has led, Oroonoko declares himself "ashamed of what he had done in endeavouring to make those free, who were by Nature Slaves, poor wretched Rogues, fit to be used as Christian Tools; Dogs, treacherous and cowardly, fit for such Masters" (5:196).

It would seem then that Oroonoko serves less as a symbol of ethnic superiority than as a model of absolute virtue isolated in a politically and socially corrupt environment, and in this respect he has strong symbolic links with the suffering heroines of her other *Histories and Novels*. Behn's black hero is above all else a suffering king, like the Caesar he is named after, a victim of political corruption, abandoned by his own people and his enemies. Maureen Duffy suggests the novel might be read as a key novel, in which the exiled Duke of York, his wife Mary of Modena, and their son are cast as Oroonoko, Imoinda, and their unborn child,[15] while Laura Brown identifies Oroonoko as the martyred Charles I.[16] Whatever specific identification with the Stuart kings we choose to locate in the story of Oroonoko, it seems evident that the novel is deeply involved with contemporary political controversies despite its claims to romance.

A number of Aphra Behn's heroines, including Philadelphia in *The Unfortunate Happy Lady* (1698), Agnes de Castro in *Agnes de Castro* (1688), Arabella in *The Wandering Beauty* (1698) and Atlante in *The Lucky Mistake* (1698), share Oroonoko's symbolic function of representing virtuous merit that resists social or domestic tyranny by exhibiting a passive and even self-martyring heroism. Like her other fictions, *Oroonoko* takes the form of a sentimentalized romance; its political message is more evident only because of the masculine gender of its protagonist, which has inclined readers and critics to dismiss it less readily as a mere derivative of the French romance's feminocentrism.

The representation of passive heroism, embodied in the marginal figure of the slave or woman, is not the only covert means by which Behn allegorizes political agency. Susan Staves points out that several of the novels Behn wrote between the Exclusion Crisis and her death in 1689 address the acutely felt political dilemma over the value of oath-taking following the Popish Plot.[17] Perjurers—Catholics forced to disavow their church to escape persecution—became the recipients of public sympathy in this period. Thus, absolute moral justice became a problem, rather than a given, or, in Staves's words, the "Restoration understanding of oaths offers a particularly focused and elegant example of how a nominalist universe of force and passion triumphs over an idealist universe of words."[18]

With this ethical and epistemological contradiction in mind (whether to break a vow to the church or to the state to avoid political repression), Behn's frequent use of the plot convention of a heroine torn between vows (to a religious life and to a lover or to an old lover and a new) take on a newly political light. This is an acute psychological dilemma in *The Fair Jilt, The Perjur'd Beauty, The Impious Vow Punish'd*, and *The History of the Nun*. There can be little doubt that Behn's dramatization of the destructive effects of the confrontation between a concept of absolute moral justice, the inherent truth-telling capacities of the word, and the contingencies of political and social survival in the form of a feminocentric tale of love constituted one of the major causes of her popularity as a fiction writer in the late seventeenth century.

It has, then, become evident that the almost exclusive interest in feminine subjectivity in Behn's short novels of the late 1680s is, in many ways, a serviceable fiction. These novels provide rather a means of articulating party politics through the mirror of sexual politics, in which the feminine acts as substitute for the masculine, signifier to his signified. Embattled virginity, virtue rewarded or ravished, what we might call the female plot, serve to reflect and refract male plotting, or, in other words, the party, dynastic, and ideological conflicts of late Stuart government.

Mirroring Masculinity

Shoshana Felman, in a different context, has pointed out the metaphorical status of woman as love object in the rhetorical hierarchy of masculine and feminine that governs the amatory plot. Felman asserts:

> Defined by man, the conventional polarity of masculine and feminine names woman as a *metaphor of man*. Sexuality, in other words, functions . . . as the sign of a rhetorical convention, of

woman is the *signifier* and man the *signified*. Man alone has thus the privilege of proper meaning, or *literal* identity: femininity, as signifier, cannot signify *itself;* it is but a metaphor, a figurative substitute; it can but refer to man, to the phallus, as its proper meaning, as its signified. The rhetorical hierarchization of the very opposition between the sexes is then such that women's *difference* is suppressed, being totally subsumed by the reference of feminine to masculine identity.[19]

In the romantic plot, then, femininity serves to reflect masculine desire. Behn's plots are no exception to this rule, although her self-conscious and self-reflective deployment of the persona of the female narrator habitually problematizes the rhetorical function of femininity in relation to masculinity within her fiction.

Not surprisingly, then, sexual attraction in Behn's fiction is fundamentally narcissistic and frequently incestuous. Imoinda is the female mirror to Oroonoko, "Female to the noble Male; the beautiful black *Venus* to our young *Mars*" (5:137). The lovers' sibling likeness is reinforced by the fact that Imoinda's father, an army commander, has acted as a substitute father to the orphaned Oroonoko. In fact the lovers first meet in Coramantien as a result of Oroonoko's filial loyalty. On the general's death we are told that Oroonoko "thought in Honour he ought to make a Visit to *Imoinda,* the Daughter of his Foster-Father, the dead General" (5:137).

The incestuous innuendo of *Oroonoko* is not an isolated example in Behn's fiction. Sibling relations positively encourage love affairs in these novels, it appears, because they are not bound by the usual social separations and constraints enforced upon men and women. The most striking example occurs in a letter from Sylvia to Philander in the first part of the *Love-Letters between a Nobleman and His Sister* (1684), where she details her unwitting seduction through sibling closeness. Philander is Sylvia's brother-in-law, the husband of her sister Myrtilla, but Sylvia unequivocally condemns their liaison as incestuous. In what she calls "a fit of virtue," Sylvia chastises her lover for exploiting sibling familiarity to encourage incestuous desire: "Oh none, but under the intimate title of a brother, could have had the opportunity to have ruin'd me; that, that betray'd me; I play'd away my heart at a game I did not understand."[20] Philander's incestuous desire for his sister-in-law is represented as part and parcel of his Whiggish politics. Sylvia is, as Behn puts it, "a true Tory in every part,"[21] seduced away not only from her respect for her own father's authority but also, by implication, from that for her king's.

The siblings' "unnatural" rebellion against paternal authority is thus presented as analogous to the earl of Monmouth's disloyalty to his natural father and later to his uncle in successive rebellions. In indicting Cesario's (Monmouth's) behavior, Sylvia unwittingly condemns herself and foresees her own fate, for, like him, once she has broken her contract with paternal authority, she will embark on a steady decline into vice and manipulation. Seeking to persuade her lover to abandon Cesario's cabal, she warns: "No, no, *Philander;* he that can cabal, and contrive to dethrone a father, will find it easy to discard the wicked and hated instruments, that assisted him to mount it."[22] Sylvia's moral decline acts as a mirror to Cesario's increasing political corruption. Where the sexual plot dominates the first part of the novel, the third part is largely concerned with the political one. Thus, Behn's novel doubly articulates the political and the sexual, eroticizing the former while it politicizes the latter.

Behn's self-conscious use of femininity as a mirror to the masculine self and a register of both psychic and social disturbance is nowhere more evident than in the novella *The Dumb Virgin: or, the Force of Imagination* (1700). The story is a tragic one of unwitting incestuous desire between brother and sister. The hero, Dangerfield, is separated as a baby from his mother in a frustrated pirate attack upon a pleasure barge off the coast of Venice. Subsequently, she bears two girl children, one physically handicapped, the other dumb. Dangerfield is symbolically the father of his own sisters, in that his loss produces her sickness during both pregnancies and births. Upon her death we are told she "left the most beautiful Daughter to the World that ever adorn'd *Venice,* but naturally and unfortunately Dumb, which defect the learn'd attributed to the Silence and Melancholy of the Mother, as the Deformity of the other was to the Extravagance of her Frights" following the pirate raid (5:424). The two sisters, Belvideera and Maria, meet Dangerfield once they have all reached young adulthood. He comes to Venice having been raised as an English cavalier. Both sisters feel an instant attraction to him, and he in turn is captivated by the deformed Belvideera's wit and the dumb Maria's beauty.

Behn leaves us in no doubt that this sudden love for and from both women is mutually narcissistic and implicitly incestuous: "*Maria* . . . found something so Sweet in the Mien, Person and Discourse of this Stranger, that her Eyes felt a dazling Pleasure in beholding him, and like flattering Mirrours represented every Action and Feature, with some heightning Advantage to her Imagination: *Belvideera* also had some secret Impulses of Spirit, which drew her insensibly into a great Esteem of the Gentleman" (5:429). For Dangerfield, the two sisters act as twin distorting mirrors necessary to the erection of the perfect masculine self: "His Love was divided between the Beauty of one Lady, and the Wit of another, either of which he loved passionately, yet nothing cou'd satisfy him, but the Possibility of enjoying both" (5:431).

Not surprisingly perhaps, it is the dumb sister, Maria, whom he finally seduces. Maria is the consummate female object, the immaculate mirror to the masculine self because she cannot speak and, therefore, to the male gazer has no autonomy, no separate subjectivity. Behn explains why Dangerfield cannot resist temptation once he has gained access to Maria's bedroom: "He knew they were alone in the Dark, in a Bed-chamber, he knew the Lady young and melting, he knew besides she cou'd not tell, and he was conscious of his Power in moving" (5:440).

Behn provides us with one of her most highly eroticized depictions of femininity perceived through the male gaze when she describes Dangerfield's reading of the sight of Maria at her window in a nightgown just before the seduction. Maria's body is her only means of signification, because she cannot herself speak, and the passage reveals that she has no control over its messages. Like the pre-oedipal child of psychoanalytic theory, Maria is not a subject, but rather a mere agglomeration of bodily impulses. She simply mirrors the desire of her figurative author, Dangerfield. Without speech, locked in her pre-oedipal world of pulsions and needs, Maria can have no autonomous desire but can only mirror or mimic that of her lover, who

> saw her in all her native Beauties, free from the Incumbrance of Dress, her Hair black as Ebony, hung flowing in careless Curls over her Shoulders, it hung link'd in amorous Twinings, as if in Love with its own Beauties; her Eyes not yet freed from the Dulness of the late Sleep, cast a languishing Pleasure in their Aspect,

which heaviness of Sight added the greatest Beauties to those Suns, because under the Shade of such a Cloud, their Lustre cou'd only be view'd; . . . her Night-gown hanging loose, discover'd her charming Bosom, which cou'd bear no Name, but Transport, Wonder and Extasy, all which struck his Soul, as soon as the Object hit his Eye; her Breasts with an easy Heaving, show'd the Smoothness of her Soul and of her Skin; their Motions were so languishingly soft, that they cou'd not be said to rise and fall, but rather to swell up towards Love, the Heat of which seem'd to melt them down again; some scatter'd jetty Hairs, which hung confus'dly over her Breasts, made her Bosom show like *Venus* caught in *Vulcan's* Net, but 'twas the Spectator, not she, was captivated. (p. 433)

Maria's hair, eyes, clothing, and body itself all conspire to present her as an object to be possessed to complete the male gazer's selfhood by perfectly mirroring his desire. The nonsubject, the dumb virgin, simultaneously empty and whole (without speech she cannot enter subjectivity and thus does not know desire and, hence, the lack or separation that engenders desire), offers the possibility of wholeness to the oedipal lover. Expenditure of desire need not be loss because the smooth mirror will restore that same desire replete with selfhood to the lover.

Luce Irigaray, in theorizing the sexual economy of what she describes as a homosocial male imaginary, cites the virgin as the most valuable of all commodities in the masculine use of women for social exchange between men. It is this value that Maria, as her name (Mary the virgin) implies, quite literally embodies: "*The virginal woman . . . is pure exchange value.* She is nothing but the possibility, the place, the sign of relations among men. In and of herself, she does not exist: she is a simple envelope veiling what is really at stake in social exchange. In this sense, her natural body disappears into its representative function."[23] Dangerfield is on his way to visit with Rinaldo, his real father, when he is arrested by the sight of Maria. Rinaldo is called away on business, leaving the lovers in the same house. The sexual encounter between the brother and sister defers the acquaintanceship between the two men but also creates the conditions under which the encounter becomes one of recognition of their true relation to each other, that of father and son. Dangerfield's two rivals for Maria fight with him over his reported presence at the window of her bedroom;

his father intervenes in the fight, and both father and son are mortally wounded. Dangerfield's wig falls off to reveal a birthmark and Rinaldo dies recognizing his long-lost son. Maria promptly commits suicide, speaking her first and last words: "Oh! Incest, Incest . . . O my Brother, O my Love" (5:444). Maria's entry to subjectivity/speech is then coterminous with her death and her recognition of her desire as incestuous.

The plot of *The Dumb Virgin* is revealed to be constructed wholly in pursuit of the real identity of the male lover. It leaves, however, one loose end, precisely that of the speaking woman in the shape of Belvideera and, further, the figure of Behn herself, who is both narrator and character in this text. After the deaths of both men and the dumb virgin, who mediates their mutual recognition, the second sister Belvideera "consign'd all her Father's Estate over to her Uncle, reserving only a Competency to maintain her a Recluse all the rest of her Life" (5:444). Belvideera thus metaphorically substitutes for her dead sister, both virgin and dumb, but withdraws from society by handing over her newly conferred economic power to the legitimate male line. Belvideera's withdrawal appears to be both a gesture of submission to patriarchal power, by mediating the passage of familial wealth between her father and uncle, and of resistance, by refusing to participate any longer in a specularizing and objectifying male homosocial economy. Where she previously used voice and wit to negotiate that world, she now uses silence and virginity to deny it.

Behn does, however, leave us with the presence of a speaking, autonomous woman in the shape of her own character. Dangerfield dies trying to tell the narrator his real name so that she may tell their countrymen in England his tragic fate. He produces only the first three letters of his name, "Cla——," and "his Voice there fail'd him, and he presently dy'd; Death seeming more favorable than himself, concealing the fatal Author of so many Misfortunes, for I cou'd never since learn out his Name; but have done him the Justice, I hope, to make him be pity'd for his Misfortunes, not hated for his Crimes" (5:444). If all other voices fail in this narrative, that of its female teller survives to bear witness and to transform hatred into pity. It is, it appears, only from this contradictory position of the female subject, the woman who escapes the male subject/woman object dichotomy, that the story can be told. Although the ideology of the text seems to argue that the role of specularizer and speaker is only available to the masculine subject, that men make plots and women suffer under them, the emergence of the female narrator as closing character projects the possibility of occupying both sides of the dichotomy in the figure of the female artist.

The space that Behn negotiates for her female narrator is, however, not the transcendent one of muse or goddess that usually marks her poetic voice. It is, rather, a negotiation between masculine and feminine positions. Like the other women in the text, Behn as narrator still mediates or mirrors masculine identity to other men, in this case Dangerfield's history to his countrymen, converting criminal seduction into a tragic story of unwitting incest. The project of mirroring masculine heroism is to a certain extent, however, ironized by the very associations of the name Dangerfield in the late 1680s in England. Duke Dangerfield was a famous agent of anti-Catholic persecution in the years of the Popish Plot, posing first as an ardent Catholic named Willoughby to gain information to prosecute Mary Cellier, a Catholic midwife, for treason in 1680; he later posed as the Duke of Monmouth in Sheffield to pass fake coin during the duke's 1685 exile in Brussels. Dangerfield produced his own romance version of his biography, entitled *Don Tomazo,* in 1680; he described his exploits as a mercenary in Spain, making much of his sophisticated use of disguise.[24] In light of this history, Behn's seemingly innocent desire to clear her countryman's reputation becomes an ironic subversion of a political enemy's attempts at heroic self-representation and aggrandizement.

In *The Unfortunate Bride; Or, the Blind Lady a Beauty,* published in the same year as *The Dumb Virgin,* Behn once again presents physical disability in a woman as a means of dramatizing masculine specularity and narcissism. Here, too, Behn appears as an actor in the plot as well as the narrator but is incapable of averting the tragic denouement. The female narrator was, we are told, a "particularly intimate Acquaintance" (5:401) of the heroine, Belvira. She obtains some letters that reveal a plot to separate Belvira from her lover, but they arrive too late to prevent Belvira from marrying his best friend. The female narrator's power lies not in her actions within the plot but in her writing of it. Indeed it is her very lack of instrumentality in the real world she supposedly represents that gives her power and authority in the imaginary realm of art.

The Unfortunate Bride is a short romantic fiction that is dominated by tropes of vision and economic exchange. The hero, Frankwit, falls in love with Belvira, whose very name sets the symbolic language in motion—she is a beautiful vision. "Even from their Childhood," Behn tells us, "they felt mutual Love, as if their Eyes, at their first meeting, had struck out such Glances, as had kindled into amorous Flames" (5:403). When Belvira admits her love, they do not exchange words but loving looks: "Eager they looked, as if there were Pulses beating in their Eyes" (5:403–4). Frankwit indeed is so obsessed with his love that he neglects his financial concerns: "He fancied little of Heaven dwelt in his yellow Angels, but let them fly away, as it were on their own golden Wings; he only valued the smiling Babies in *Belvira's* Eyes" (5:404). Women's value, then, lies in their capacity to reflect and enlarge male desire.

Belvira's cousin, Celesia, is also in love with Frankwit, but it is clear that her love cannot be reciprocated because, as the blind lady of the narrative's title, she is incapable of reflecting his desire. Celesia is "the only child of a rich *Turkey* merchant, who, when he died, left her Fifty thousand Pound in Money, and some Estate in Land; but, poor Creature, she was blind to all these Riches, having been born without the use of Sight, though in all other Respects charming to a wonder" (5:405). Her financial value, then, is zero, because she lacks the only thing that Frankwit values, the capacity to mirror masculine desire. Her attempts to break in on the narcissistic closure of the lovers' looks are futile. When Belvira pities her cousin for her inability to see Frankwit, Celesia challenges their equation of desire and vision with the question: "If I fancy I see him, sure I do see him, for Sight is Fancy, is it not? or do you feel my Cousin with your Eyes?" (5:406).

Belvira shrewdly recognizes the nature and provisionality of her value in her lover's eyes. She is unwilling to marry him, arguing that "her Desires could live in their own longings, like Misers wealth-devouring Eyes" (5:405). A move out of the purely specular economy of love that they have previously inhabited into the legal and financial contract of marriage is a risk for the woman mirror. "Marriage

Enjoyments," she insists, "does but wake you from your sweet golden Dreams" (5:406). The possession as opposed to viewing of the image of desire may shatter the mirror and deprive the woman of her power.

Frankwit succeeds in persuading his mistress of the impossibility of living paralyzed in their specular economy and promptly breaks it by departing for Cambridge to set his financial affairs in order before their marriage. In his absence, Celesia's sight is providentially restored and Belvira informs her lover in a poem: "And yet, beyond her Eyes, she values thee,/'Tis for thy Sake alone she's glad to see" (5:409). The only value of Celesia's newly found sight is that it provides her with an opportunity to enter the sexual economy from which she was previously barred. Meanwhile, Frankwit falls ill and a black woman at his lodging house, Moorea, being infatuated with him, keeps back his letters to Belvira and writes anonymously to inform the latter of his death. In her grief, Belvira consents to be courted by Frankwit's best friend, Wildvil. On the wedding day, following the ceremony, both Frankwit and the letters the female narrator has retrieved and forwarded to their proper recipient arrive. The two men fight, Belvira seeks to intervene and she and her new husband are killed. On her deathbed, Belvira instructs Frankwit to marry Celesia, to whom she also leaves her fortune.

Through her complex and sometimes labored play with images of sight, expanding upon the well-tried metaphor of love's blindness, Behn sets up a tension between the power of vision and the power of writing. While the lovers can see each other, their love is inviolable, but the fixity of this mirroring relation is also revealed to be impossible to maintain. In psychoanalytic terms, the lover move from the nonverbal dyadic bonding that children experience with their mothers in the pre-oedipal imaginary to the symbolic world of paternal law and language as represented by the contract of marriage.[25] Belvira's consent to marry entails a separation; the symbolic rupture of their nonverbal visual exchange is accompanied by a literal separation with Frankwit's departure to Cambridge. From this point on, they have to rely on the much more perilous relation of writing. The letter is, it appears, a far more unstable means of communication than the eye; it can be lost, mislaid, misinterpreted, or suppressed. The lovers have to move out of the field of vision, but the substitution of writing is ultimately unsatisfactory. As the figure of Celesia proves, both vision and writing are vital to subjectivity. Deprived of her capacity for both because of her blindness from birth, Celesia accounts for nothing. Without sight and without writing, Celesia lacks the precondition and the capacity to signify meaningfully in the social order.

Feigning Femininity

Behn represents her own creative function in relation to the stories she tells as a complex interplay of these two poles of vision and writing. She not only narrates the stories but insists she was there. This narrative strategy is, of course, by no means unique to Behn in late-seventeenth-century fiction.[26] It is, however, in the stories discussed here, explicitly associated with the gender of the narrator in a formulation that is indeed novel in English prose fiction of the period. Behn's authority as narrator rests, then, on the authority of her presence at the scene itself; she both looks and tells. In her prefatory remarks to *Oroonoko* she insists, "I was myself an Eyewitness to a great Part of what you will find here set down; and what I could not be Witness of, I receiv'd from the Mouth of the chief Actor in this History, the *Hero* himself" (5:129). Almost exactly the same formulation appears in her dedication to Henry Pain prefixed to *The Fair Jilt*, the story of Prince Tarquin's fatal obsession with the manipulative Miranda, "Part of which [she] had from the Mouth of this unhappy great Man, and was an Eye-Witness to the rest" (5:70). Behn's stories, then, are supposedly a form of bearing witness, ensuring the posterity of her hero or heroine. If she does not claim to have been an eyewitness, her authorities are always those with special access to the subject matter. Thus, Philadelphia's story in *The Unfortunate Happy Lady* was delivered to the narrator by "one who liv'd in the Family, and from whom [she] had the whole Truth of the Story" (5:37), while that of Arabella in *The Wandering Beauty* was rendered by "a Lady of [her] Acquaintance, who was particularly concern'd in many of the Passages" (5:447). By this means, Behn successfully denies her own authorship of her stories. They are not, she claims, imaginative fiction but bare facts to which she simply testifies.

It is interesting to speculate what particular advantages Behn found in the novelistic strategy she so doggedly pursues. There could be no more definitive statement than that in the dedication to *The Fair Jilt,* where she writes: "However it may be imagin'd that Poetry (my Talent) has so greatly the Ascendant over me, that all I write must pass for Fiction, I now desire to have it understood that this is Reality, and Matter of Fact, and acted in this our latter Age" (5:70). Here, Behn distinguishes her poetic from her prose writing, representing herself as a scribe rather than artist, writer rather than author. By figuring herself as mere teller of tales, Behn presumably makes herself more acceptable to male critics, at least within the terms of her own fictional economy.

Behn's truth claims function as more than a protective cover from masculinist abuse to which she was by this late stage in her literary career, after all, well accustomed. Angeline Goreau points out that "there was some truth to her claim to truth: she was not, like other writers, merely repeating a story-telling convention, but signaling a new kind of relation of writer to narrative."[27] Behn's female narrator claims not only to be the author (imaginative creator) of her plots by virtue of her femininity but also excuses her lack of power as author of events in the plot by the same means. The lack of social power accorded to women excuses her lack of activity and intervention in the tragic stories she tells. This very inactivity endows her with a privileged position as writer. Her only power lies in her testificatory writing. In *Oroonoko,* the turn to writing as a result of practical impotence in the events she sees becomes a seizure of power, converting the enforced role of spectator into positive value in the scene of writing. Despite the claim to simply mirror or represent, writing comes to transform vision.

In *Oroonoko* Behn is at the greatest pains to analyze the position of the narrator in relation to the tragic action of which she is both part and not part. Despite her statement that it was her hero's "Misfortune . . . to fall in an obscure World, that afforded only a Female Pen to celebrate his Fame" (5:169), Behn's narrator constantly calls her reader's attention to her status in contemporary literary culture. Of another hero she also encountered in Surinam, one Colonel Martin, she comments in passing that she has "celebrated" him "in a Character of [her] new Comedy, by his own Name" (5:198).[28] Describing the English trading with native Indians in Surinam she slips in that she presented a set of feathers to the King's Theater that were used in a production of *The Indian Queen* and "infinitely admir'd by Persons of Quality" (5:130).[29] Behn's "Female Pen," then, as she makes perfectly clear, is by no means as obscure as her deprecatory comment might suggest. Her female pen is precisely the agent of her power.

The female narrator wins the affection and confidence of the proud and aristocratic slaves, Oroonoko and Imoinda, by her story-telling, tailoring her narratives towards their specific gendered interests: "I entertained them with the Lives of the *Romans,* and great Men, which charmed him to my Company; and her, with teaching her all the pretty Works that I was Mistress of, and telling her Stories of Nuns" (5:175). The full extent of Behn's authority both inside and outside the text lies in her authority as a fiction-maker, a role that is, in turn, intimately connected with her femaleness. Her relegation to the margins by the white male colonists, despite her claims to authority, put her in an analogous position to her hero, whose voice is also powerless. She is only useful to the white establishment, as she was in Antwerp, as a seductress, influencing an aberrant and politically dangerous man into cooperation with the rulers' political needs. Because Oroonoko only has eyes for his beautiful wife, Imoinda, Behn seduces him into the position of courtly lover through her stories. By telling his story after his death and elevating him to the status of hero, Behn claims, she is repaying her promise to him, exercising the power on his behalf that she was denied as an observer at the time.

Yet Behn is more than an observer in *Oroonoko.* She is, in the fullest sense of the word, a spectator, or rather, a specularizer. As I noted earlier, Behn customarily formulates sexual desire as a nar-cissistic investment in the other as mirror to the ego. She is thus as ambiguous about the Surinam natives' ignorance of the erotic joys of specularity, the scene of vision, as she is about the advantages of Oroonoko's inability to comprehend the ambivalent status of fiction, the scene of writing. Like her hero, the natives of Surinam are at first idealized for their natural innocence, which differentiates them from the corrupt and dissolute behavior of the white colonists.

However, two passages in *Oroonoko* problematize any inter-pretation of the novel as a nostalgic idealization of African and Indian cultures. In the first, with reference to their uninhibited nakedness, Behn explicitly identifies the Surinam Indian natives with pre-lapsarian innocence but appears to question the desirability of this quality, commenting that "they are extreme modest and bashful, very shy, and nice of being touch'd . . . and being continually us'd to see one another so unadorn'd, so like our first Parents before the Fall, it seems as if they had no Wishes, there being nothing to heighten Curiosity; but all you can see, you see at once, and every Moment see; and where there is no Novelty, there can be no Curiosity" (5:131). In courtship, the young man simply gazes on his love object "and sighs [are] all his language," while his mistress looks down "with all the blushing modesty . . . seen in the most Severe and Cautious of our World" (5:131). This is not, then, a world without sexual difference, but it is one in which no attempt is made to heighten sexual curiosity by exaggeration of that difference.

The importance of clothing in the business of erotic pleasure is highlighted in a second passage that sets about contrasting native Indian and white European culture. When an expedition visits a native Surinam community deep inland and as yet unexposed to white people, Behn insists on going ahead with her woman and brother, leaving Oroonoko and the others to hide in the reeds and observe the reaction to them. It is the white European's clothing, and particularly that of the women, that fascinates the Indians: "By Degrees they grew more bold, and from gazing upon us round, they touch'd us, laying their Hands upon all the Features of our Faces, feeling our Breasts, and Arms, taking up one Petticoat, then wondering to see another; admiring our Shoes and Stockings, but more our Garters. . . . In fine, we suffer'd 'em to survey us as they pleas'd, and we thought they would never have done admiring us" (5:185). In this passage, clothes are a means of enhancing difference, in this case, racial difference, by curiosity. And as in the sexual economy it appears that femininity is the signifier of difference. The women's clothing, the petticoat, the stocking, and the garter, all provide a means of prolonging (sexual) interest by withholding the discovery of the body beneath. Deferral brings pleasure. The pleasure is not solely, or even primarily, that of the gazer, however. Behn the storyteller has engineered this particular narrative scene to make herself the object of the gaze. The eroticism of these looks is doubled in that she has placed Oroonoko and the other companions to watch her being watched.

Thus, although the position of viewer is habitually a powerless one for the narrator in the plot of *Oroonoko,* the position of the viewed provides an opportunity for power. Just as she insists on Oroonoko concealing himself behind the reeds to display herself first, in her writing she repeatedly turns her reader's eye away from the royal slave to herself. The (erotic) center of this text is the female writer. The clothing that conceals her body, the writing that obscures the woman, only heightens the reader's pleasure, keeping possession out of reach and sustaining the libidinous drive of the text. Ultimately, *Oroonoko* bears witness to its author rather than to its eponymous hero.

Behn's teasing play with authorial presence, identified as a specifically feminine and fictional strategy, is, of course, intensely problematic in this early text of white colonialism. Artistic play and specularizing power seem to be won for the white woman writer at the expense of the black slave and the native, who are positioned, like Behn's female characters elsewhere, as naive victims. The knowledge of superior moral integrity or rectitude is little compensation for lack of political control and denial of self-representation.

With this in mind, however, Behn's foregrounding of the woman writer at the very inception of the novel was clearly a unique and sophisticated challenge to masculine dominance of the field of representation. Behn's troubled inquiry into the woman writer's relation to the amatory plot writes into the development of a new genre, new questions of gender. Vita Sackville-West, in one of the few early studies of Behn to take seriously her creative powers in fiction, complains that Behn allowed romance conventions to limit her explorations in realism: "We might have had the mother of Moll Flanders, and all we get is the bastard of Mademoiselle de Scudéry."[30] The contrast between Behn and Defoe, as cofounders of the early modern novel, is by no means a spurious one, but we might consider Behn's continued investment in the romance as more than a vestigial allegiance to a spent form. Defoe, although he shares with Behn the trope of claiming facticity and an interest in converting the private history into new models of public heroism, all too often presents himself as cultural policeman of female discourse. Thus, in his preface to *Moll Flanders* (1722), the editor informs us that he has placed an organizing structure and a moral awareness onto the anarchy and immodesty of the female narrator: "All possible Care however has been taken to give no leud Ideas, no immodest Turns in the new dressing up of this Story, no not to the worst part of her Expressions; to this Purpose some of the vicious Part of her Life, which cou'd not be modestly told, is quite left out, and several other Parts are very much shortn'd; what is left 'tis hoped will not offend the chastest Reader, or the modestest Hearer."[31] Thus, the editor metaphorically holds up his coat to conceal the blatant eroticism of the naked body of his heroine's text. Behn, in contrast, recognizes that the truly seductive form is the most clothed. Her rhetoric seduces by a complex system of concealment and display. The fascination with the female body lies precisely in seductive dress, not the body beneath.

Indeed, her text warns us, strip the woman and you find precisely nothing (visible) beneath, just as the attempt to strip away Behn's veils of writing to find out the real woman inevitably draws a blank. Sarah Kofman, in her rereading of Freud, has succinctly described the redundancy of the pursuit of true femininity: "to speak of a riddle of femininity and to try to solve that riddle are a strictly masculine enterprise; women are not concerned with Truth, they are profoundly skeptical; they know perfectly well that there is no such thing as 'truth,' that behind their veils there is yet another veil, and that try as one may to remove them, one after another, truth in its nudity, like a goddess, will never appear. Women who are truly women are perfectly 'flat.' . . . For 'truth,' the metaphysical lure of depth, of a phallus concealed behind the veils, that lure is a fetishist illusion of man."[32] Behn's writing has been veiled precisely by this pursuit in criticism and study of the truth of the woman as opposed to the complex truth of her texts' interaction with contemporary political and sexual ideology. Behn does indeed, through numerous autobiographical references in her fiction, poetry, and dramatic prologues and epilogues, construct herself as an enigma for the inquiring reader's consumption. Pursuit of these autobiographical traces reveals associations with the leading writers, politicians, and court figures of the late seventeenth century, as the work of William Cameron, Maureen Duffy, Angeline Goreau, and Germaine Greer has demonstrated. Given these material connections, I would suggest that we ought to assume ideological connections rather than a sad discrepancy between the sophistication of her feminism and the reactionary prejudice of her Toryism. I have attempted to point to ways in which

we might afford a wider historical interpretation of Behn's writing
that both incorporates and recognizes the limits of critical study to
date. As Michael McKeon has pointed out in his analysis of John
Dryden's *Absalom and Achitophel* (1681), "to historicize a literary
work is not just to situate it 'against' a 'background,' since this would
be only to provide a static focus on the work with a historical setting.
The aim of historicizing is instead to remind us that the literary
'work' itself partakes of historical process: that it is a strenuous and
exacting labor of discourse that seems thereby to detach itself from its
historical medium, but that bears within its own composition the
distinguishing marks of its continuity with the world it has ostensibly
left behind."[33] Historicizing Aphra Behn requires that the disclosure
of further details of her personal biography and the unfolding of her
powerful critique of Restoration constructions of female sexuality as
property be related to her powers as satirist and political commentator. As the comments of "One of the Fair Sex" suggest, Behn's
"pleasant Adventures" may be less a retreat from or substitute for her
"Pretences of State" than a covert means of ensuring political engage-
ment where it is most denied, in the domains of female sexuality and
writing.

Notes

1. Behn may have abandoned writing plays for four years because of political disfavor she incurred in August 1682. Behn had contributed a prologue and
an epilogue attacking the Duke of Monmouth for an anonymous play, *Romulus
and Hersilia; or, the Sabine War* (1682). On August 12, 1682, Charles II had
Behn and the actress Lady Slingsby, who had delivered the offending lines, taken
into custody by Arlington, the Lord Chamberlain. A broadside of the epilogue
and prologue was promptly published, entitled *Prologue to Romulus* (London,
1682).

2. See Angeline Goreau, *Reconstructing Aphra: A Social Biography of
Aphra Behn* (Oxford: Oxford Univ. Press, 1980), pp. 237–41.

3. Ibid., p. 241.

4. Susan Staves, *Players' Scepters: Fictions of Authority in the Restoration*
(Lincoln and London: Univ. of Nebraska Press, 1979), p. 186.

5. Ellen Pollak, *The Poetics of Sexual Myth: Gender and Ideology in the
Verse of Swift and Pope* (Chicago and London: Univ. of Chicago Press, 1985),
p. 2.

6. George Woodcock, *The Incomparable Aphra* (London and New York: T. V. Boardman, 1948), p. 151.

7. Goreau, *Reconstructing Aphra,* p. 268.

8. Judith Kegan Gardiner, "Aphra Behn: Sexuality and Self-Respect," *Women's Studies* 7 (1980): 69.

9. For Behn's activities in Holland, see William J. Cameron, *New Light on Aphra Behn* (Auckland: Univ. of Auckland Press, 1961). Cameron reproduces nineteen documents from and to Aphra Behn dated between July and December 1666 that are preserved among Williamson's state papers kept in the Public Record Office (pp. 34–86). Behn's letters are largely taken up by her financial concerns, because Arlington at no point provided her with any money for her spying activities. A letter from Byam to Sir Robert Harley in March 1664 makes it clear that Scot and Behn were friends in Surinam and suggests a romantic interest between them (p. 12).

10. Aphra Behn, "The History of the Life and Memoirs of Mrs Behn," in *All the Histories and Novels of the Late Ingenious Mrs. Behn,* 5th ed. (London, 1705), p. 7. An expanded version of the "Memoirs on the Life of Mrs Behn Written by a Gentlewoman of Her Acquaintance" was published in *The Histories and Novels of the Late Ingenious Mrs Behn* (London, 1696). "The History of the Life and Memoirs" was first published in the third edition of *All the Histories and Novels* (London, 1698).

11. Behn, The History of the Life," p. 28.

12. See *Calendar of State Papers,* Domestic Series, Public Record Office (London, 1668–69), p. 172. Behn had borrowed 150 pounds from one Edward Butler. When Arlington refused to pay it, Butler had her thrown into prison. Behn wrote two petitions asking for an order for payment of the money, the second accompanied by a covering letter to Killigrew written the day before she was taken to prison, saying that she had "cried [herself] dead" and was "sick and weak and ill" with worry. There is no record of how Behn obtained her release from prison.

13. Aphra Behn, *Oroonoko; or, the History of the Royal Slave,* in *The Works of Aphra Behn,* ed. Montague Summers, 6 vols. (1915; rpt. New York: Benjamin Blom, 1967), 5:125–209. Subsequent references to this edition will be cited parenthetically in the text by volume and page number.

14. For early critiques of Behn's palliation of antislavery discourse through her use of heroic romance conventions to depict her hero, see Hoxie Neale Fairchild, *The Noble Savage: A Study in Romantic Naturalism* (New York: Columbia Univ. Press, 1928), pp. 34–41; and Wylie Sypher, *Guinea's Captive Kings: British Anti-Slavery Literature of the Eighteenth Century* (Chapel Hill: Univ. of North Carolina Press, 1942), pp. 108–22. Laura Brown makes the reverse argument that Behn's appropriation of her hero to Western ideals is a means of negotiating racial difference for the purposes of antiracist polemic in her essay, "The Romance of Empire: *Oroonoko* and the Trade in Slaves," in *The New Eighteenth Century: Theory * Politics * English Literature,* ed. Felicity

Nussbaum and Laura Brown (New York: Methuen Press, 1987), pp. 41–62. Finally, Jerry C. Beasley has argued that Behn's novel is a subversive political allegory of British government with no interest in denouncing the slave trade. See "Politics and Moral Idealism: The Achievement of Some Early Women Novelists," in *Fetter'd or Free?: British Women Novelists, 1670–1815,* ed. Cecilia Macheski and Mary Anne Schofield (Athens: Ohio Univ. Press, 1986), p. 222.

15. Maureen Duffy, *The Passionate Shepherdess: Aphra Behn, 1640–89* (London: Methuen, 1989), p. 235.

16. Brown, "The Romance of Empire," pp. 59–60.

17. Staves, *Players' Scepters,* p. 193.

18. Ibid., p. 192.

19. Shoshana Felman, "Rereading Femininity," *Yale French Studies* 62 (1981): 25.

20. Aphra Behn, *Love-Letters between a Nobleman and His Sister,* ed. Maureen Duffy (London: Virago, 1987), p. 15.

21. Aphra Behn, "Dedication to Tho. Condon," in *Love-Letters between a Nobleman and His Sister* (London, 1684), n.p.

22. Behn, *Love-Letters,* p. 36.

23. Luce Irigaray, "Women on the Market," in *This Sex Which Is Not One,* trans. Catherine Porter (Ithaca: Cornell Univ. Press, 1985), p. 186.

24. On Dangerfield, see Philip W. Sergeant, "Duke Dangerfield," in *Liars and Fakers* (London: Hutchinson, 1926), pp. 133–98; John Kenyon, *The Popish Plot* (London: Heinemann, 1972), pp. 179–80; and Dangerfield's autobiography, *Don Tomazo, or the Juvenile Rambles of Thomas Dangerfield* (London, 1680). In the latter, Dangerfield makes much of his success in disguising himself as a Turk in Cairo. In his first encounter with his sisters at a masquerade, Behn's Dangerfield is dressed in a Turkish turban, which confuses the women in their attempts to meet with a famous English gentleman (5:427).

25. Jacques Lacan's theory of the mirror stage as a transitional moment in the pre-oedipal child's development toward the entry into paternal law and language that he terms the "symbolic" is particularly suggestive in this context. See "The Mirror Stage as Formative of the Function of I," in his *Écrits: A Selection,* trans. Alan Sheridan (London and New York: Norton, 1977), pp. 1–7. Lacan writes: "The jubilant assumption of his specular image by the child at the *infans* stage, still sunk in his motor incapacity and nursling dependence, would seem to exhibit in an exemplary situation, the symbolic matrix in which the I is precipitated in a primordial form, before it is objectified in the dialectic of identification with the other, and before language restores to it, in the universal, its function as object" (p. 2).

26. See Michael McKeon, *The Origins of the English Novel, 1600–1740* (Baltimore and London: Johns Hopkins Univ. Press, 1987), pp. 105–14. McKeon notes the recurrence of authenticating strategies, such as Behn's see-and-tell claim, in narratives in this period (particularly improbable tales of foreign lands or behavior) to distinguish them from the devalued "old Romance." He notes too the ultimate instability of such strategies in that they come

to function as rhetorical tropes in their own right, thus undermining their own claims to truth as opposed to art.

27. Goreau, *Reconstructing Aphra*, p. 287.

28. The comedy was *The Younger Brother,* not performed until February 1696, at Drury Lane, and published in the same year, adapted by Charles Gildon and accompanied by his "Memoir" of the author.

29. Sir Robert Howard's *The Indian Queen* was first produced by the King's Company in January 1664, while Behn must still have been in Surinam if she was ever there. The feathers would have had to have been used in one of the many revivals of this popular play.

30. Vita Sackville-West, *Aphra Behn: The Incomparable Astrea* (1927; rpt. New York: Russell and Russell, 1970), p. 73.

31. Daniel Defoe, *The Fortunes and Misfortunes of the Famous Moll Flanders, &c.,* ed. G. A. Starr (London and New York: Oxford Univ. Press, 1971), pp. 1–2.

32. Sarah Kofman, *The Enigma of Woman: Woman in Freud's Writings,* trans. Catherine Porter (Ithaca and London: Cornell Univ. Press, 1985), p. 105.

33. Michael McKeon, "Historicizing Absalom and Achitophel," in *The New Eighteenth Century,* ed. Nussbaum and Brown, p. 37.

CHARLOTTE SUSSMAN

The Other Problem with Women: Reproduction and Slave Culture in Aphra Behn's *Oroonoko*

Perhaps the most provocative aspect of Aphra Behn's contradictory account of slavery in her novel *Oroonoko, or the Royal Slave* is that Oroonoko rebels against his masters not when he himself is enslaved or when he finds his wife Imoinda in captivity, but rather when it becomes apparent that their child will be born a slave. Compounding the peculiarity of the novel's connections between familial relations and the relations of slavery, the failure of Oroonoko's rebellion occasions his murder of his wife and the child she is carrying in a scene of surprising and supererogatory violence. In this essay, I will use the historical context against which *Oroonoko* was written to explain both the emphasis the novel places on kinship ties and the brutality with which those ties are destroyed. Even a cursory examination of the socioeconomic structure of eighteenth-century English sugar colonies like Surinam, where *Oroonoko* takes place, reveals the overdetermined nature of the reproductive capacity of African slaves. Thus, it is possible to read Oroonoko's murder of his family to rescue them from slavery as symptomatic of the way that eighteenth-century discourse on slavery refigured the socioeconomic tensions of colonial slavery as a problem of biological reproduction.

For this reason, the yoking together of biological reproduction and slavery in Behn's novel is not surprising. Almost any discussion of slavery will eventually call into question the nature of family ties. What finally separates slavery from other kinds of servitude is that while a free person is born into a complex network of social ties and responsibilities, a slave is born into a single legal relationship—that of a servant to his master—over which he has no volition. The ordinary bonds that a slave might enter into, such as marriage or parenthood, have no force in the eyes of his master. The sociologist Orlando Patterson calls this characteristic of slavery "natal alienation." I quote his definition at length because of the insight it provides into the representation of slavery in *Oroonoko:* The phrase "goes directly to the heart of what is critical in the slave's forced alienation, the loss of ties of birth in both ascending and descending generations. It also has the important nuance of a loss of native status, of deracination. It was this alienation of the slave from all formal, legally enforceable ties of 'blood,' and from any attachment to groups or localities other than those chosen for him by the master, that gave the relation of slavery its peculiar value to the master."[1] Thus, part of the violence of slavery is the severing of family connections, however those ties are organized by a particular culture. In doing so, slavery also breaks the less obvious ties between people and the culture into which they are born. This peculiar horror of slavery is clearly illustrated in *Oroonoko:* The conflict between freedom and slavery is played out along the lines of family ties. Oroonoko reacts against slavery by fighting to reestablish his claim on his own child—to reinvolve that child in a heritage, in a history. It is, then, a measure of the brutality of the relation of slavery that the only way he can make the connection between parent and child evident is through murder.

The violence with which this sociological dynamic is played out in *Oroonoko* can be explained with regard to the particular problems of the eighteenth-century English slave trade. In the sugar colonies of the Caribbean, where *Oroonoko* takes place, the issue of reproduction involved not only the psychosocial dimension that Patterson illuminates but also the pragmatic ends of economics. Precisely because the slave trade was a trade in living human beings, the balance between births and deaths translated directly into economic profit and loss. In the Caribbean colonies, this relationship between people and profit was complicated by the fact that the population of slaves continually decreased despite constant importation of new African captives. This decrease was caused in part by a decision on the part of West Indian plantation owners that importing new slaves was cheaper and more efficient than inducing slaves to raise families. But even when masters tried to cultivate self-reproducing populations, they failed.[2] Death rates consistently outpaced birth rates, and the shrinking population resulted not only from the high mortality rate among slaves caused by impossible work in harsh conditions but also from a very low birth rate. Men far outnumbered women, and the healthiest women were chosen as concubines by white owners. These conditions were then exacerbated by malnutrition, frequent miscarriage, self-induced abortions, and infant mortality.[3] It is important to realize, however, that the appalling mortality of African slaves and the shrinking populations of the colonies are, in part, what made a profitable slave trade possible.[4] If the plantation owners had been able to establish groups of workers who renewed and increased their own number, the market on which the slave traders depended would have, to a large extent, dried up.

The relationship between the biological reproduction of slaves and the economic production of sugar was complicated: Plantation culture depended on the female capacity to reproduce, but female slaves were themselves workers, brutalized by a cruel economic system. As the eighteenth century wore on and the colonial structure of the English sugar colonies became more precarious, the responsibility of slave women for the low birth rate became a hotly debated issue. The controversy over whether black women willfully refused to reproduce or whether the slave system itself undermined their actual capacity to reproduce continues among historians today, and I will not resolve it here.[5] I will point out, however, that these problems eventually became a central battleground in the English imperial struggle to maintain a slave culture. Although this crisis did not become acute until the beginning of the nineteenth century, its importance is intimated in Behn's novel by the anxieties provoked by Imoinda's pregnancy. In the struggle over her unborn child, the historical specificity of Caribbean slavery surfaces, if briefly, in a text that otherwise almost completely elides the material facts of that institution. Imoinda's unborn child, made to motivate so much of the later action of *Oroonoko,* also bears with it all the problems of cultural as well as biological reproduction. If the child were to be born in the novel, that birth would signify both the continued captivity of Oroonoko's race and the continued viability of slave culture in Surinam. Its death, in contrast, indicates Oroonoko's continued, princely, control over his race.

Thus, although the problem of reproduction occupies a very small space in *Oroonoko,* it provides a crucial point of intersection between the historical context of the slave trade and an ahistorical heroic romance. Moreover, I choose to focus on this issue because it is a moment when a possible resistance to slavery is glimpsed within a text otherwise quite concerned with maintaining the status quo. The point of coincidence, which is also a window onto the possibilities for resistance, is the body of a woman. In this case, the woman is the black slave Imoinda.[6] To discuss how Imoinda's womb might be the focal point for a rebellion against slavery, this essay will investigate the two mutually exclusive descriptions of Imoinda that coexist within the novel. She is figured simultaneously as a passive piece of property and as an erotic, powerful agent. The strategic deployment of these images of femininity and the part the white female narrator plays in their organization reveals the larger ideological implications of the novel. In the interaction between these two images the erotic is used to elide the possibilities of resistance suggested by biological generation.

I

Imoinda is a possession even before she is a slave. She, and any children she might have, are inextricably bound by the property definitions of their native tribal culture. Imoinda's exile in Surinam, therefore, is not so much a transition from freedom to slavery as a transition from one code of property relations to another. Of course, the way she is "owned" by Trefry is very different than the way she is "owned" by the king of Coramatien, but in both cases Imoinda remains rigidly confined by codes of possession. The novel, however, represents Imoinda as holding a highly unstable position within both of those codes, an unstable position that constantly threatens to disrupt any social system. On the Gold Coast of West Africa, her marriagable body produces an important crisis in the political organization, as well as the family organization, of the tribe. In Surinam, her body as a reproductive vessel again provokes a violent confrontation, this time between Oroonoko's tribal values and slave culture itself. On both continents the crisis is solved in the same way; not by any change in existing conditions but through the elimination of the offending piece of property—Imoinda's body.

In Africa, the king is troubled by "having been forc'd, by an irresible Passion, to rob his son of a Treasure."[7] Erotic passion is directly linked to an acquisitive action; the king is moved to possess Imoinda in spite of the trouble it will cause within family power relations. Once she is taken by the king—"secur'd for the King's Use" (p. 12)—Imoinda is supposed to be his absolute property, a code she immediately violates by refusing to sleep with him. After Imoinda has been "possess'd" (p. 26) by the king's adoptive son, Oroonoko, however, property relations became even more strained. The king considers her a "polluted thing" (p. 26) and sells her into slavery: "the greatest revenge, and to which they a thousand times prefer Death" (p. 27). In this series of events, the conditions for Imoinda's value as property are laid bare; she must be possessed absolutely to be worth being possessed at all. Because of this system of value, Imoinda's chastity becomes an index of the king's authority; his power as a ruler depends on his ability to own the best things and to keep them for his own exclusive use. Imoinda's body also mediates the balance of power between father and son; the king's power over his adoptive son derives from his possession of Imoinda. Thus, in Africa, Imoinda's status as possession helps define the hierarchical relationship between king and subject as well as that between father and son.

Imoinda's very desirability, however, threatens to destabilize these relationships. When Oroonoko "possesses" her sexually he violates the tribal property laws along with familial sexual prohibitions. The legitimacy of these codes can only be restored by the removal of the property in question. Oroonoko and his king-father reconcile through the lie of Imoinda's honorable death and the truth of her disappearance. But, in fact, Imoinda and the crisis she provokes in power relations are simply exiled to the slave colony into which she is sold.

When Imoinda reappears in Surinam the crisis in property relations also reappears. This time, her progeny rather than her virginity becomes the property in question. Similarly, however, the desirability of this property threatens to upset the existing power structure. When she becomes pregnant "this new Accident made [Oroonoko] more impatient of Liberty . . . and [he] offer'd either Gold, or a vast quantity of Slaves, which should be paid before they let him go" (p. 45). His offspring and his wife, possessions that tribal law dictates should belong to him absolutely, do not.[8] Although slavery is acceptable in Oroonoko's eyes, in this case the wrong people are slaves. So he attempts to restore Imoinda to her rightful, inherited position of wife and mother by offering to fill her position on the plantation with "a vast quantity of Slaves." Imoinda will return to the property relationship of wife and no longer occupy the property relationship of slave. The slaves who would replace her would, presumably, be the people Oroonoko considers appropriate slaves, part of a class constituted by and within his own culture. In this moment, as in many other places within *Oroonoko,* the novel naturalizes the institution of slavery; the problem is not so much in the social structure of slavery itself, as in the way it is administrated.

Yet, because Imoinda is exempted from slavery at this point, her unborn child becomes the crucial instance of the conflict between two distinct codes of property relations: colonial slavery and a traditional tribal system, which, although it uses slaves, would never enslave the wife of its leader. At this juncture, however, the peculiarly rigid and demeaning nature of the property relation of colonial plantation slavery becomes apparent. Patterson once again provides a useful description of the difference between slaves and free persons with regard to property relations; he claims that "proprietary claims are made with respect to many persons who are clearly not slaves. Indeed any person, beggar or king, can be the object of a property relation."[9] The difference lies in the way that "the proprietor's power is limited by the fact that nonslaves always possess some claims and powers vis-a-vis their proprietor. . . . The slavemaster's power over his slave was total. Furthermore, with nonslaves, the proprietor's powers, however great, were usually confined to a specific range of activities; with slaves, the master had power over all aspects of the slave's life.[10] That is, even though Imoinda is the object of property relations in Africa, the property relationship of slavery in Surinam deprives her of any claims on other persons, even the person of her own child. Oroonoko, too, is the object of the exclusive property relationship of slavery. Slavery controls both of them, not only in their capacity as workers, but even in their capacity for biological reproduction.

Imoinda's pregnancy makes Oroonoko "even adore her, knowing he was the last of his great Race" (p. 45). And her pregnancy inspires his first plans for escape because "all the Breed is theirs to whom the parents belong" (p. 45). In Patterson's terms, Oroonoko rebels against the possibility that his child will be born into a natally alienated state. To Oroonoko's thinking, the child should be the next "of his great Race," born into the kinship network that makes Oroonoko a powerful prince. For the child to achieve such a status, however, the ties between parent and child as well as between husband and wife must be acknowledged. Only through the recognition of genealogical descent can the child receive its cultural inheritance. But slavery negates precisely those genealogical and cultural ties. If a child is born a slave, it will have no claim to its mother or father, and they will have no claims on it—the child will be alienated from the bonds that define community. Furthermore, the submission of his child to slavery will undermine Oroonoko's own status. His power as father and husband will be negated, leaving him also alienated from his traditional culture because he cannot bestow his paternity on his child.

The resolution to this crisis in property relations is brought about by extraordinary violence. The physical destruction of bodies is, at last, the only way to ascertain their true owners. Oroonoko decides that if he cannot escape he can at least revenge himself on his English captors. A crucial part of this plan to salvage his honor, however, involves Imoinda's death. He resolves to kill her himself rather than leave her to be "a Prey, or at best a Slave" to "nasty Lusts" (p. 71). Thus, he enforces his property claim to Imoinda's body—in both its sexual and its reproductive capacities—by murdering her. He kills this "Treasure of his Soul" by "first cutting her Throat, and then severing her yet smiling Face from that delicate Body, pregnant as it was with the Fruits of tenderest Love" (p. 72). Although the language here partakes of the nascent conventions of sentimentality, the very cuts between the pieces of her body become the inscription of his proprietorship.

In this scene, glory, violence, and property relations are inextricably intertwined. Although the vague category of glory seems out of place in the more precise mechanics of property relations, Patterson points out that qualities like honor, self-respect, and glory are often crucial indexes of actual power relations: "modern anthropologists have confirmed Thomas Hobbes' insight that the sense of honor is intimately related to power, for competing for precedence one needs power to defend one's honor."[11] This correlation between honor and power is illustrated in *Oroonoko* by the way in which the king of Coramantien's power depends on his control over Imoinda's honor/chastity. It is also evident in the way Oroonoko's struggle to redeem himself from slavery is intimately connected to his effort to redeem his honor.

Once Imoinda and the child are dead, Oroonoko does indeed seem to regain his honor, "that Glory which I have purchased so dear, as at the Price of the fairest, dearest, softest Creature that ever nature made" (p. 73). In Surinam, as on the Gold Coast, one's right to honorable treatment and one's position in property relationships are closely connected. Oroonoko's honor is, therefore, directly related to his ability to possess Imoinda as an unpolluted object. Oroonoko's glory is connected to his purchasing power, the degree to which he can exercise power over those things deemed to be his property. Imoinda's dead body thus becomes the price Oroonoko pays to make evident his status as her owner. She too appears willing to make her own dead body the evidence of her claim on Oroonoko's love, her own right, denied her in Africa, to "die by so noble a hand" (p. 72). It is representative of the restrictive nature of slave culture, however, that the only way these relations can be made manifest is through a self-directed, self-destructive violence.

Imoinda's murder, however, in no way changes the conditions of Oroonoko's captivity. The scene, instead, drains Oroonoko of the energy to carry out an actual rebellion. The violence of an uprising is thus absorbed into familial violence. The mayhem of this love scene only works to restore Oroonoko's personal honor, or glory.[12] Furthermore, Oroonoko's liberation from the demeaning conditions of slavery is carried out not against the slave-owners but on the body of a woman. Imoinda's dismembered body becomes, strangely enough, the sign of Oroonoko's nobility—of the spiritual liberty that must take the place, for him, of physical liberty.

This effect is most clear in the scene directly following Imoinda's death. When the plantation owners come to recapture Oroonoko, he is far too weak to hurt them; all he can do is hurt himself. The marks Oroonoko makes on his own body, however, mirror the injuries he has recently inflicted on Imoinda. First he cuts a piece of flesh from his own neck, just as he slit Imoinda's throat. Then, in an action that points to the underlying significance of Imoinda's murder, Oroonoko, rather than cutting off his own head, "rip'd up his own Belly, and took his Bowels and pull'd 'em out, with what strength he could" (p. 75). With this action he recalls that he has just effectively aborted Imoinda's child. Oroonoko is willing to do all this to avoid "the shameful Whip" (p. 75). Thus, the sign of Oroonoko's courage to choose a noble death over the shame of slavery is also a repetition of the sign of his absolute possession of wife and child. The code of nobility that Oroonoko writes on his own body signifies his power over a woman, not his emancipation from slavery.

Finally, then, the crisis in property relationships Imoinda provokes in Surinam is solved in much the same way the corresponding crisis is solved in Africa—by the elimination of the offending object, her body. But there are two crucial differences between Africa and Surinam. First, Imoinda's part in Coramantien property relations is not contingent on her race. In Surinam, however, the particular nature of the problems she causes result from her peculiar status as an African woman—caught between her property status as wife and her property status as slave. Also, in Africa the only piece of her body in question as property is her hymen, her virginity. But in Surinam at least three aspects of her body are at stake: its capacity to work, its capacity to have sexual intercourse, and its capacity to reproduce.

Still, Imoinda retains one peculiarly female quality on both continents. Crises in power are resolved through her powerlessness. In both cases her disappearance—effected by the exercise of masculine power—provides a solution that does not overturn the existing power structures. In Africa the ties between the king and Oroonoko are reestablished honorably through Imoinda's elimination. In Surinam, Imoinda's death paves the way for an ending that allows Oroonoko his glory without seriously challenging the existence of a slave culture. Her mutilation becomes a perfect substitute for violence against the slave owners. Woman's powerlessness seems to be culturally portable. She is a continual threat to the stability of power relations but also, because of her powerlessness, she serves as the ever-reliable instrument of their stabilization.

II

At the same time that the novel imagines Imoinda as a conveniently disposable possession, it also imagines her as an enormously powerful erotic figure. This figuration is achieved by assigning her the conventional features of a romantic heroine. Thus, Imoinda emerges as a character through the established codes of the heroic romance. Larger and more perfect than life, she is characterized not as an African woman of the seventeenth century but rather as the type of the heroine of heroic romance. She is "Female to the noble Male; the beautiful Black *Venus* to our young *Mars*" (p. 9)—an embodiment of a very western ideal. Within the codes of romantic love, however, Imoinda is a very potent figure, in direct contrast to the role she occupies in actual power relations. While still in Africa she carries out "a perfect Conquest over [Oroonoko's] fierce Heart, and made him feel the Victor cou'd be subdu'd" and proclaims "her eternal Empire over him" (pp. 9, 11). In the warlike vocabulary of love, Imoinda is an active campaigner in her own interest. She is an imperialist master, in total control of her territories.

Her power saps men's strength, rendering the most eminent submissive in her presence. In Surinam, "all the Slaves [were] perpetually at her feet" (p. 42), and the narrator claims to "have seen a hundred White men sighing after her, and making a thousand Vows at her feet, all in vain, and unsuccessful" (p. 9). The physical positioning of this scene—white men kneeling before a black woman— makes clear the extraordinary effect of Imoinda's erotic allure. In fact, the images describing this aspect of love directly contradict the images of property described earlier in this essay. In the conventional character of a romance heroine, Imoinda is not submissive but aggressive: dominating rather than dominated.

In terms of this set of conventions, Imoinda directs others' actions instead of being directed by others. She even has the capacity to render Oroonoko powerless by replacing his will with her image. In Africa "his Eyes fixed on the Object of his Soul; and as she turned or moved, so did they: and she alone gave his Eyes and Soul their

Motions" (p. 21). Imoinda's visual presence has the power to erase any other thought from his mind—his mental capacity does indeed shrink to the space of her body. This power appears inalienable in that the same scene takes place when the lovers meet in Surinam: "In a minute he saw her Face, her Shape, her Air, her Modesty, and all that call'd forth his Soul with Joy at his Eyes, and left his Body destitute of almost Life: it stood without Motion, and for a Minute knew not that it had a being" (p. 43). Insofar as she exists as an image of beauty, Imoinda's power is extraordinary. The power of love, here a purely erotic affect produced by the visual effect of her presence, is absolute. No other definition of self, no other possibility of action, can exist beside it.

Insofar as the novel describes Imoinda as a romantic heroine, she moves through *Oroonoko* in a kind of alternate universe, a world that runs parallel to the world of slavery and transcends it. Imoinda and Oroonoko "mutually protested, that even Fetters and Slavery were soft and easy, and would be supported with Joy and Pleasure, while they cou'd be so happy to possess each other, and to be able to make good their Vows. [Oroonoko] swore he disdained the Empire of the world, while he could behold his *Imoinda*" (p. 44). When Oroonoko discovers Imoinda again in Surinam, his physical captivity is elided as its characteristics are recoded in terms of the satisfaction of eros; he is able to replace each term of slavery with what seems to be the complementary term of love. His possession by Trefry is rendered "soft and easy" by his possession by Imoinda and his possession of her. The contracts and terms of slavery fade into unimportance beside the lovers' "Vows." The possibility of an "Empire" that could encompass the whole world pales next to the much smaller domain of Imoinda's body. The world of romantic love thus contains all the elements of the world of slavery but reorganizes those elements into "Joy and Pleasure." Imoinda's presence neutralizes, at least momentarily, the pains of slavery. Moreover, her love provides alternate definitions of the crucial terms of "possession" and "empire." As Laura Brown has pointed out, the emphasis on tragic love within *Oroonoko* works to cancel out any connection Oroonoko has to the actual trade in slaves.[13]

Yet, although the conventions of heroic romance allow Imoinda no feature that marks her as distinctly African, the context of slavery makes the erotic power of women seem coercive and constraining. For the alternate world that romantic love creates threatens to block any action in the real world of Surinam: Oroonoko "accus'd himself for having suffer'd Slavery so long: yet he charg'd that weakness on Love alone, who was capable of making him neglect even Glory it self, and, for which, now he reproaches himself every moment of the day" (p. 47). Despite Oroonoko's protestations of contentment in love, here the category of love becomes the ally of slavery. Suddenly love and slavery take sides against self and glory. Furthermore, in this passage love is personified, a rhetorical convention that might represent a third force interfering in Oroonoko's life but quite possibly refers to Imoinda herself.

Later, the figurative ties between love and slavery are even more closely related to Imoinda. After his abortive rebellion, as he debates whether or not to rebel again, Oroonoko "struggle[s] with Love for the victory of his Heart which took part with his charming *Imoinda* there" (p. 71). As in Africa, love is a warlike encounter, and Imoinda is figured as a combatant. In Surinam, however, the consequence of Oroonoko's loss of the territory of his heart is a continued existence in a state he considers degrading. Imoinda's extraordinary erotic allure is in the service of the coercive violence of slavery. The specific motion she stops with her presence is the action of rebellion.

This configuration—women and love aligned with slavers against men and glory—is acted out in *Oroonoko*. When Oroonoko tries to convince the slaves to rebel, one protests: "Were we only Men [we] would follow so great a Leader through the World: But Oh! consider we are Husbands and Parents too" (p. 61). Oroonoko assures the other slaves that the women will be able to join the escape, but the fears prove true: "The Women . . . being of fearful cowardly Dispositions . . . crying out *Yield!, Yield! and leave Caesar to their Revenge* . . . by degrees the slaves abandon'd *Caesar*" (p. 64). Imoinda, of course, does not act out the part she takes in Oroonoko's imagination, but remains with him until the end. Still, in this group of images, Oroonoko's romantic love for Imoinda is distinguished from his desire to establish and protect family ties. Although his desire to cement his property ties to her and his child motivates his original rebellion, in this instance the sentimental attachments between husbands, wives, and children work to keep the slaves in captivity. Romantic love is shown to be dangerous in a slave culture, an enemy to glory and to self-respect. Furthermore, women are the sole agents of this dangerous emotion, inflicting it on men. Imoinda's beauty is a double-edged sword: It makes slavery bearable, but it also prevents any action against slavery.

This second problem posed by women—the disturbing power of their erotic presence—is ultimately managed in the same way as the first problem, the way in which women's bodies threaten property relations. In short, Imoinda dies. She accepts her death quite willingly; "smiling with joy," she becomes the "ador'd Victim" (p. 72). Love effectively channels erotic power into submission. Still, by killing her, Oroonoko acts out his only revenge against slavery. Not only does he prove his power by taking her body out of the grasp of the slave owners, but he also proves his power against her body, insofar as that body has become a surrogate for the coercive power of slavery. The seemingly supererogatory brutality of this love scene is thus explained by the further overdetermination of Imoinda's body. That is, because the text figures Imoinda's sexual allure as complicit with slave culture, it is able to deflect political rebellion against slavery (what Oroonoko sets out to achieve) onto the defeat, or submission, of eros (what Oroonoko ends up achieving).

Cynthia Matlack claims that Imoinda's death scene in Thomas Southerne's dramatic adaptation of *Oroonoko* is only one of a number of similar scenes in heroic dramas of the period. In all the plays in which these scenes of willing sacrifice appear, "the political danger of women's erotic appeal can be seen in the extremely high incidence of metaphors describing the enslavement of the males by love."[14] The context of Behn's novel gives this conventional figure an added force: Imoinda's erotic appeal is figured by the novel to be the only slave-master against which Oroonoko can successfully rebel. Again, women's powerlessness becomes the convenient solution to the problem of slavery. Oroonoko does not have the power to challenge the larger social structures of slavery, but he does have the power to turn an adored "conqueror" into an "ador'd Victim." Sexual mastery over women is constructed as the perfect double to economic control over slaves.

III

At first glance, the only thing that these images of Imoinda—as a particularly valuable piece of property and as a heart-stopping beauty—have in common is their solution. Each poses problems that ultimately can only be solved by Imoinda's mutilation and elimination. Both images also function as surrogates for the problem of slavery. In either chain of association, Imoinda's murder holds the place that might be occupied by a full-scale rebellion against the plantation owners. The violence that might be directed toward white slavemasters is inflicted instead on the body of a black woman. But the two images are also involved on another level. Eros is used to mask the possibility of resistance that arises with Imoinda's pregnancy. It erases the disruption of stable property relations that Imoinda's capacity for generation causes.

Matlack notes the conjunction of politics, eros, and generation in her study of "erotic scenes in which the doomed women embrace their imminent death by willingly presenting their bosoms to the phallic dagger of authority." She claims that "at an elemental level of human semiotic exchange, this act of submission produces a transformation as the breasts which nourish progeny become the sign of domesticated eroticism."[15] We have already seen that erotic authority doubles for political authority in *Oroonoko* and that Oroonoko's power over Imoinda is a substitute for any power he might gain over the plantation owners. But Matlack's observation suggests that a double displacement might occur in the text. Although Imoinda does not present her breasts to be penetrated in the novel as she does in the play, we have already seen the importance of those parts of her body that "nourish progeny" in her mutilation. If Matlack is right, her body is eroticized both to absorb the political tension of the novel and to elide the fact that her body could be a reproductive vessel.

Why would it be important to deflect attention from the generative capabilities of a woman's body? At the beginning of this essay I alluded to the crucial place of reproduction in the slave economy of the Caribbean. Because of the need to reproduce labor through inherited status, a woman's womb played a central role in the economic organization of the slave colonies. And, in at least one instance, that womb became the site of resistance. Orlando Patterson, in the *Sociology of Slavery,* discusses the case of eighteenth-century Jamaica (an English sugar colony like Surinam), where "slave women absolutely refused to reproduce . . . as a form of gynecological revolt against the system."[16] Their refusal to reproduce was accomplished for the most part by self-induced abortion, complimented by widespread veneral disease and malnutrition. Patterson quotes a planter who claims that "they endeavour to obtain miscarriage either by such violences as they know to be generally effectual, or by some of the simples of the country which are possessed of forcible powers."[17] By the end of the eighteenth century the attitudes of the "considerable number of slave women [who] disliked the idea of having children"[18] were an established credo of the slave community, which continued to decrease.

More to the point, however, Patterson notes the case of an actual woman driven to the same extreme as her fictional counterpart, Oroonoko: "Sabina Park who was tried at the Half Way Tree slave court for the murder of her three-month-old child. . . . Sabina's complaint, according to the Crown witness was that 'she had worked enough for bukra (master) already and that she would not be plagued to raise the child . . . to work for white people.' Few slaves, of course, would go to this length, and the woman in question may well have been slightly mad; but there can be little doubt that her extreme attitude reflected a great deal of what a significant number of the slave women felt."[19] Eighteenth-century Jamaica, like Sabina Park herself, was an extreme example. In most cases, the slave populations of the Caribbean seem to have struck a balance between the hope of generation and the despair of slavery. But even one actual example is enough to suggest a constant threat. The possibility that captive women might take their biology into their own hands, either through abortion or the more extreme violence of murder, must have lurked in the imaginations of their white owners. For in this scenario, even the reproductive capacity of the womb—long thought to be the part of woman held in the strictest captivity by patriarchy—falls under suspicion for resistance. Even if the specter of infanticide is an imperialist fantasm, the mechanism through which the colonial mind projected responsibility for the brutality of slavery onto the very bodies it oppressed, the image becomes a sign of the colonist's fear of the consequences of slave culture. The persistence and force of this fear is perhaps best illustrated by the appearance of this gothic image of infanticide in a novel as little concerned with the realities of slavery as *Oroonoko*.

Thus, perhaps the desire to view Imoinda as a purely erotic creature derives in part from narrative's need not to see her capacity to direct her own biological functions. Sexual allure is, after all, a quality measured by the men who view her, not subject to her own control. Witness the erotic fate of those breasts that "nourish progeny" in the imagination of the seventeenth-century traveller, Richard Ligon: "The young [African] maids . . . have ordinarily very large breasts, which stand strutting out so hard and firm, as no leaping, jumping or stirring, will cause them to shake any more than the brawns of their arms."[20] These are breasts that clearly have never felt the weight of children, existing purely for the pleasure of the beholder. The elision of generation from the sexuality of black women might even explain the curious illogicality David Brion Davis notes in the thinking of eighteenth-century slaveholders. In the colonies "it could repeatedly be said that the low birth rate of West Indian slaves was due to the licentiousness of Negro women, though no one explained why a presumably equal licentiousness had the opposite result in Africa."[21] Perhaps for their own peace of mind, then, the slave masters concluded that the poor rate of reproduction resulted from the sexual proclivities of African women rather than from any conscious direction of their biology toward the political ends of resistance to slavery.[22]

We cannot be sure to what extant such historical material is relevant to *Oroonoko*, of course, but in Behn's text eros does indeed displace the representation of what I have been calling biology or women's capacity for reproduction—an elision that may be motivated by the desire to efface the womb as the site of resistance. Despite the length at which I have discussed them, Imoinda's pregnancy and the crisis in property relations it provokes take up a very small space in *Oroonoko*. In that small narrative space, though, the horrors of slavery surface for a short time. The fate of that unborn child brings the extraordinarily demeaning natal alienation of slavery to the foreground of the text. And through the highly unstable nature of Imoinda's body, the economic and ideological crisis brought about by the reproductive capacity of slave women in the Caribbean is brought briefly to bear on the novel.

Yet, when Imoinda is eliminated, all these other problems go with her. Like the child she bears, the baggage of cultural relevance that her pregnancy carries is effectively buried with her dead body. The battlefield of reproduction and the issues of cultural inheritance and power that it involves slide out of sight beneath conventional images of woman as a sexual icon. Throughout the novel the far more culturally accessible figure of a desirable woman is allowed to over-shadow the image of a black female slave and the contradictions she embodies. In fact, I have argued here that in *Oroonoko* romantic love generally effaces the other problem of women as reproductive ves-sels—the political problem of biological generation is deflected onto the more conventional problem of managing Imoinda's erotic power.

The narrative of *Oroonoko* mounts a concerted effort on many different levels to refigure what might be the feared consequences of a brutal slave culture (bloody rebellion, massive escape) as the ac-knowledged consequences of a doomed love affair (mutual suicide, tragic self-sacrifice). Imoinda, both as a piece of property and as an erotic icon, is the instrument the narrative uses to effect this reorgani-zation or even elision. Because her desirability is the cause of so many of the problems of the novel, the elimination or submission of her eroticized body can be constructed as the solution to both Oroo-noko's problems and the narrative's. The political issue of slavery is almost entirely deflected onto the more conventional, more tasteful, and more easily resolved problem of heroic romance.

IV

I would suggest that this deflection is carried out to a large degree by the other woman in *Oroonoko,* the narrator. Despite their overt friendship, the dynamics of representation in the text erode the soli-darity one might expect to find between two women in a novel written by a woman. In the midst of the brutal scene of Imoinda's murder—a scene in which I have claimed that cultural codes are forced to physical extremes—the narrator's voice observes: " 'Tis not to be doubted, but the parting, the eternal leave-taking of two such

Lovers, so greatly born, so beautiful, so young, and so fond, must be very moving, as the Relation of it was to me afterwards" (p. 72). The white female narrator steps in to provide a model for the reader's reception of the scene. The scene is reconstituted as a moving relation, a tragic love story that the narrator hopes will move her reader to sentimental response. In this perspective, Imoinda and Oroonoko are not captive people clinging to some remnant of cultural identity but rather any two noble, beautiful, young lovers doomed to a pitiful end.

The narrator steps in on at least two other occasions to receive, rather than give, an account of Oroonoko and Imoinda. The two other instances are, significantly, the lovers' meeting in Surinam and Oroonoko's death.[23] In each of these moments the mediation of the narrator serves both to remove all traces of slavery from the lovers and to channel the events into the conventional form of a romance. The narrator declares, in the last words of the novel, "I hope, the Reputation of my pen is considerable enough to make his glorious Name to survive to all Ages, with that of the brave, the beautiful, and the constant Imoinda" (p. 78). She plans for Oroonoko and Imoinda to survive as a couple, possessing only the attributes of a moving relation.

Thus, the narrator herself seems to side with the forces of romance in the conflict between love and rebellion; that is, she sides with the status quo of slave culture. Just as the slave women use love to dissuade their husbands from further bloodshed, the narrator consistently rechannels traces of the pain of a captive culture into romantic conventions. The context of slavery is never allowed to have disruptive power in the novel. There is a way, then, in which the self-consciously female speaker is complicit in Imoinda's oppression and death. Not only does the narrator never voice any opposition to slavery, but she also never allows the issue to be raised. In *Oroonoko*, conflicts that might involve slave culture are solved in terms of sexual and familial relations seen through the codes of heroic romance. The novel and its narrator consistently place Imoinda so that the African woman can absorb the incipient violence of a slave culture into the tropes of eros.

The relationship between the white female narrator and the black female slave resembles the relationship Gayatri Spivak describes between Jane Eyre and Rochester's Caribbean first wife, Bertha Mason. Spivak claims that Bertha Mason "must play out her role, act out the transformation of her 'self' into that fictive Other, set fire to the house and kill herself, so that Jane Eyre can become the feminist individualist heroine of British fiction. I read this as an allegory of the general epistemic violence of imperialism, the construction of a self-immolating colonial subject for the glorification of the social mission of the colonizer."[24] Although Imoinda is far more of an ideal for the narrator than a nemesis—exemplary rather than terrifying—the two women still exist in opposition within the text. The "reputation" of the narrator's "female Pen" (p. 40) is surely based on Imoinda as the "self-immolating colonial subject." Imoinda's glorious self-sacrifice and her perfect constancy and love provide the material for the construction of a self-consciously female narrator, a narrator, moreover, enshrined in feminist literary history as among the earliest of feminist individualist heroines. In this way the continual erasure of the African slave by the conventions of a romantic heroine forms the basis of a woman's literary voice, even as early as the end of the seventeenth century. The white woman speaks in the novel literally over the dead body of the black woman. And, it is perhaps not the least of the cruelties of colonial slavery that one woman's identity must be so constructed over and against another's. Thus, although we should see Behn's heroine as a crucial female voice in early modern English literature, we must also recognize the burden of racist discourse she must assume to speak as a white English woman.

Yet, the very need to kill Imoinda and the excessive violence of the series of mutilations her death inaugurates paradoxically allow into the text the issues they are designed to keep out. Imoinda's murder conjures up allusions to infanticide as the ultimate horror of slavery that must have been as much present in Behn's day as they are in ours. Furthermore, in the specific physical sites of mutilation— Imoinda's throat, Oroonoko's belly (and later his testicles[25])—the narrative points out possible sites of resistance. This kind of resistance, which is very different from the armed uprising the novel overtly treats, has nothing to do with conventional tropes of honor or glory. Instead, the circumstances of Imoinda's pregnancy and death demonstrate the lengths to which captive persons will resist the appropriation of their reproductive capabilities by their captors. The violence in *Oroonoko* does not spring from a conflict between freedom and slavery but rather from Oroonoko's and Imoinda's need to preserve the property relations of family and culture in a situation that all but destroys them. Theirs is a resistance that tests the limits of a slave's control over his or her own biology and the limits of the connections between body and culture. And, although it can only be expressed negatively in *Oroonoko,* the "gynecological revolt" Patterson records suggests that such control may be much less alienable than one would think and that such resistance can be very powerful. Behind the mask of eros, Behn's novel, perhaps despite itself, allows the threatening image of a rebellious womb to show.

Notes

I am grateful to Laura Brown for her help with earlier versions of this piece.

1. Orlando Patterson, *Slavery and Social Death: A Comparative Study* (Cambridge: Harvard Univ. Press, 1982), p. 7.

2. Orlando Patterson, *The Sociology of Slavery: An Analysis of the Origins, Development, and Structure of Negro Slave Society in Jamaica* (Kingston, Jamaica: MacGibbon and Kee, 1967), p. 109.

3. Cf. Rudolph Van Lier, "Negro Slavery in Surinam," *Caribbean Historical Review* 3–4 (1954): 139–40; Philip D. Curtin, *The Atlantic Slave Trade: A Census,* (Madison: Univ. of Wisconsin Press, 1969), p. 28; Eric Williams, *From Columbus to Castro: The History of the Caribbean, 1492–1969* (New York: Vintage, 1984), p. 146.

4. Williams, *From Columbus to Castro,* p. 146.

5. Cf. Barbara Bush, " 'The Family Tree is not Cut': Women and Cultural Resistance: Studies in the British Caribbean," in *In Resistance: Studies in African, Caribbean, and Afro-American History,* ed. Gary Okihiro (Amherst: Univ. of Massachusetts Press, 1986); Marietta Morrissey, *Slave Women in the New World: Gender Stratification in the Caribbean* (Lawrence: Univ. of Kansas Press, 1989).

6. At this point my argument closely resembles Laura Brown's discussion of the novel, in which she claims that "the figure of the woman in the imperialist narrative . . . provides the point of contact through which the violence of colonial history . . . can be represented," in "The Romance of the Empire: *Oroonoko* and the Trade in Slaves," in *The New Eighteenth Century: Theory * Politics * English Literature,* ed. Felicity Nussbaum and Laura Brown (New York: Methuen Press, 1987), p. 43.

7. Aphra Behn, *Oroonoko, or, the Royal Slave* (1688; rpt. New York: Norton, 1973), p. 15. Subsequent references to this edition will be cited parenthetically in the text by page number.

8. Cf. Bryan Edwards, *The History, Civil and Commercial, of the British Colonies in the West Indies* (Dublin: 1793), who notes the property status of children on the Gold Coast in his eighteenth-century discussion of slavery in the English Caribbean: "A power over the lives of slaves is possessed and exercised too, on the very frivolous occasions, without compunction or scruple, by every master of slaves on the Gold Coast. Fathers have the like power over their children" (p. 62).

9. Patterson, *Slavery and Social Death*, p. 21.

10. Ibid., p. 26.

11. Ibid., p. 79. Patterson further claims that "in all slave societies the slave was considered as a degraded person . . . the honor of the master was enhanced by the subjugation of the slave . . . and . . . wherever slavery became structurally very important, the whole tone of the slaveholder's culture tended to be highly honorific" (p. 79). Perhaps the most familiar instance in which all these claims are borne out as true is the American old South (pp. 94–97).

12. In a contemporary account, John Stedman also comments on the importance of honor in the economy of colonial violence: "Wonderful it is indeed, that human nature should be able to endure so much torture, which assuredly could only be supported by a mixture of *rage, contempt, pride, and the glory of braving his torments,* from whom he was so soon to escape," in *Narrative of a Five Years' Expedition against the Revolted Negroes of Surinam* (1796; rpt. Amherst: Univ. of Massachusetts Press, 1972), p. 383.

13. "In Behn's text, 'reductive normalizing' is carried out through literary convention, and specifically through the very convention most effectively able to fix and codify the experience of radical alterity, the arbitrary love and honor codes of heroic romance" (Brown, "The Romance of Empire," p. 49).

14. Cynthia S. Matlack, "Spectatress of the Mischief Which She Made: Tragic Women Perceived and Perceiver," *Studies in Eighteenth-Century Culture* 6 (1977): 319.

15. Ibid., 322.

16. Patterson, *The Sociology of Slavery*, p. 133.

17. Patterson, *The Sociology of Slavery*, p. 108. A fuller discussion of this material can be found in chapter 4, "An Analysis of the Slave Population of Jamaica," of *The Sociology of Slavery*. For a more general discussion of reproduction in slave communities, see *Slavery and Social Death*, pp. 132–35.

18. Patterson, *The Sociology of Slavery*, p. 106.

19. Ibid., p. 107.

20. Quoted in David Brion Davis. *The Problem of Slavery in Western Culture* (Ithaca: Cornell Univ. Press, 1969), p. 449.

21. Ibid., p. 470.

22. For another discussion of the extraordinary sexuality associated with black women, see Sander L. Gilman, "Black Bodies, White Bodies: Toward an

Iconography of Female Sexuality in Late Nineteenth-Century Art, Medicine, and Literature," in *"Race," Writing, and Difference,* ed. Henry Louis Gates, Jr. (Chicago: Univ. of Chicago Press, 1986), pp. 223–62.

23. After a description of Oroonoko's brutal execution, at which she is not present, the narrator closes the novel with the following summation: "I hope the Reputation of my pen is considerable enough to make his glorious Name to survive to all Ages, with that of the brave, the beautiful, and the constant *Imoinda*" (p. 78). Finally, she wants to end not with the "frightful Spectacles of a mangled King" (p. 77) but rather with an image of a loving couple.

24. Gayatri Chakravorty Spivak, "Three Women's Texts and a Critique of Imperialism," in *"Race," Writing, and Difference,* ed. Gates, p. 270.

25. When Oroonoko is executed, to inaugurate his dismemberment "the Executioner came, and first cut off his Members, and threw them into the Fire" (p. 77).

JACQUELINE PEARSON

The History of
The History of the Nun

Aphra Behn's life and work haunted writers for a century or more after her death in 1689.[1] *Oroonoko* in particular had a remarkable afterlife.[2] Her plots are told and retold, and her life too was reread and rewritten as a text. Women writers in particular needed to come to terms with Behn's work and her example as a way of understanding and negotiating their own place in the literary world. Many women writers of the late seventeenth and early eighteenth centuries read, enjoyed, and agonized over Behn; her imagination and her literary success attracted them, but because of her personal notoriety and the open eroticism of her work she also functioned as a "negative model."[3] Behn's adaptors, such as Catharine Trotter, Hannah Cowley, Jane Barker, or Thomas Southerne, reveal very clearly the post–1688 reaction against sexual explicitness and the development of a "new bourgeois ideology of femininity"[4] that increasingly confined women to a domestic sphere, so that paradoxically "at the same historical moment that women were . . . becoming visible as readers and writers, the literary representation of women . . . was producing an increasingly narrow and restrictive model of femininity."[5]

Particularly revealing is the posthumous history of *The History of the Nun; or, The Fair Vow-Breaker,* originally published in 1688.

This was dramatized by the most assiduous of Behn's adaptors, Southerne, as *The Fatal Marriage; or, The Innocent Adultery* in 1694; in the dedication he admits his debt to Behn but insists that he took from her "Novel" only a "Hint of the tragical part of this Play."[6] Southerne's play was later rewritten by David Garrick as *Isabella* in 1757.[7] Jane Barker's 1726 collection of linked stories, *The Lining of the Patch-work Screen; Design'd for the Farther Entertainment of the Ladies,* abridges and revises two of Behn's stories, *The Wandering Beauty,* which is reincarnated as "The Story of Tangerine, the Gentleman Gypsie," and *The History of the Nun,* which appears as "Philinda's STORY out of the BOOK" (pp. 59–64). Southerne's and Barker's revisions of *The History of the Nun* indicate the compelling power of Behn's imagination and especially of her depiction of female characters, but also a growing discomfort with Behn's reputation and the subversive unconventionality of her fictions. An examination of the alterations will reveal the changing views on female nature of the late seventeenth and early eighteenth centuries and will also cast light on the real nature of Behn's achievement.[8] It will also reveal the gendered ways in which Behn's successors read her texts (and read her as text) and how far the anxieties of influence she caused them were different for male and female writers. Southerne, for instance, shows none of the ambivalence about Behn that is at the heart of Barker's intertextual strategies. He can afford to take for granted his rights to literary creativity, which consequently does not seem for him problematic in the way that female creativity so often seems to Barker.

It may be useful to summarize Behn's plot because the novella is still little known. Its identity as the source of Southerne's play was not recognized until the publication of Montague Summers's edition of Behn's works in 1915.[9] *The History of the Nun* centers on Isabella de Vallary of Iper (Ypres, now in Belgium; Southerne relocates it in Brussels and Barker in Spain), who as a child enters a convent to please her father and becomes famous for her virtue and devotion. She is pursued by many lovers but rejects them all, including Villenoys. But she is not invulnerable to love and falls for Henault, eventually agreeing to flee and marry him. Although they gain a dispensation from the church, they are dogged by ill-luck and poverty, and despite Isabella's pleas, Henault tries to regain his father's support by going to the wars, where he is reported killed. Isabella mourns for a long time but ultimately agrees to marry Villenoys, now rich and independent, and they live happily together. One night when Villenoys is away, a strange man visits Isabella, who is horrified to discover that he is Henault, much altered by years of captivity. Terrified at the prospect of losing her comfortable life-style, her reputation, and the man she now loves, she smothers Henault as "the only means of removing all Obstacles to her future Happiness."[10] When Villenoys returns she reveals the body, pretending that he died of shock at hearing of her bigamous marriage. Villenoys decides to throw the body in the river. Isabella, however, is now afraid that he will despise and reproach her, so she sews the sack containing the body to his coat so that when he throws the body in the river he also falls in and drowns. Isabella's guilt is discovered and she dies bravely and penitently, after making an "Eloquent" (5:324) speech that interprets her story as an example of God's punishment of violated vows.

The Fatal Marriage was the earlier of Southerne's adaptations of Behn novellas into dramatic form, and both it and *Oroonoko* became hit plays that remained long in the repertoire and were allegedly especially popular with women theatergoers.[11] While Behn's narrative deals with Isabella's whole career, *The Fatal Marriage* compresses the time involved, concentrating on the events immediately surrounding her second marriage. We hear of her earlier life as a nun who breaks her vows, but this is very lightly sketched; indeed, this theme has been completely forgotten by the end of the play, whose moral emphasizes male tyranny rather than female guilt. Unlike Behn, who allows women the dignity of free will and of full moral parity with men, Southerne presents his play's heroine simply as a passive victim.

This is not, of course, the whole story of *The Fatal Marriage*'s images of women, for Southerne invents a comic subplot in which, to balance the tragic patriarch Baldwin in the main plot, a comic patriarch is reformed, and to balance the poignantly suffering Isabella, the bold witty heroine Victoria disguises herself as a man to escape her father and test her lover. Behn's single heroine is split apart, dismembered. The intelligence, self-assertiveness, and active desire that are essential parts of Behn's Isabella are imaged as masculine and embodied in Victoria's transvestite persona and in any case are confined to the inverted world of comedy. The privileged discourse of tragedy can, it seems, only function by establishing female goodness as synonymous with female passivity. Garrick's *Isabella* of 1757 carries even further this process of simplification, for by excising Southerne's comic plot without returning to the complexity of Behn's heroine, he suppresses altogether any sense of female autonomy and assertive desire and so reduces Behn's emotional outlaw to a respectable eighteenth-century matron.

Despite this important difference, there is a good deal of unanimity in Southerne and Garrick's revisions of the character of Behn's Isabella. Both at every point concentrate on her passive suffering and minimize, deny, or excuse her guilt. A complex and believable human being is transformed into an icon of virtue. For Behn, Isabella's capacity for guilt and her willingness to take full moral responsibility for her own actions are signs of her full human subjectivity; neither Southerne nor Garrick is willing to allow this full subjectivity to a woman. Southerne (and, following him, Garrick) exonerates Isabella by greatly expanding Behn's figure of Henault's "Cruel Father" (2:301), whose hatred and neglect of Isabella makes marriage with Villeroy an economic necessity. Southerne also invents Carlos, Biron's[12] villainous brother, who knows his brother is alive but conceals the fact out of envy and malice to further the bigamous marriage that he knows will result in tragedy. Abandoned or oppressed by the representatives of patriarchal power, Isabella is transformed from an active sinner to a passive sufferer. Unlike Behn's heroine, Southerne's (and following him Garrick's) murders neither her second husband, who survives the play, nor her first, who is killed by his own brother. Indeed, "innocent" and "innocence" become key words used of her (e.g., act 5, scene 2, lines 38a and act 5, scene 4, lines 15, 16, 28). Southerne has picked up these words from Behn, but whereas he invariably genders them as female and identifies them with female passivity, Behn had used them more evenhandedly to refer to either sex. In Behn's text Isabella's innocence is at best debatable, a fiction of conventional femininity that she acts out (5:317), while the men, Henault and Villenoys, are "Innocents" (5:320), allowed the lack of understanding and the passivity usually the woman's province. Whereas Southerne's dramatic world deals quite simply with a stereotypical distinction between active, experienced males and passive, innocent females, Behn interrogates and even inverts such distinctions.

The final scenes of Southerne's play reflect a detailed knowledge of Behn's original and an expectation that his audience will also know it and that this knowledge will color their expectations of the play. He is therefore more willing than Garrick to recall some elements in Behn's plot, while wholly altering their significance. Thus, Southerne's Isabella, like Behn's, prepares to murder Biron, but only in a fit of madness, and before it is too late she comes to her senses, is appalled by what she has almost done ("Murder my Husband!" [act 5, scene 2, line 60]), and repudiates the idea. Behn's Isabella directs a capacity for violence outwards, as murder: Southerne's (and Garrick's) more passive Isabella can only direct it inwards, as suicide, an act that, as an extreme version of approved womanly self-denial, clearly seemed to them the only authentic female heroism.[13] (Whereas Southerne allows Isabella to display the depth of her suffering by attempting murder, Garrick was clearly uncomfortable even with this much violence and self-assertion in a woman, and he tones the episode down considerably.) In addition, although Behn emphasizes Isabella's capacity for rational choices and her readiness to take the consequences, Southerne's Isabella is irrational, driven mad by her suffering. Picking up a word Behn uses once of Isabella in the middle of the novel (5:290), Southerne makes "distracted/ly" key words for Isabella (e.g., act 2, scene 3, line 17; act 4, scene 3, line 215; and act 5, scene 4, line 251). By showing her madness, Southerne can clinch his claim that she is innocent—not guilty by reason of insanity. Her "reas'ning faculties are all depos'd . . . / . . . This is the infant state/Of Innocence" (act 5, scene 2, lines 28, 37–38). Southerne's heroine is, morally, a child, and thus very different from Behn's guilty but morally adult heroine. As Ann Messenger has pointed out, Behn and Southerne here seem to "have reversed the cliché that men characteristically deal in abstractions and women in emotions and relationships,"[14] for Behn's text is complex, analytic, and even, I argue, ironic, while Southerne's concerns are less intellectual and more narrowly emotional.

Southerne and his adaptor, Garrick, alter Behn's original, then, by simplifying her complex and ambiguous protagonist into a female innocent driven by suffering into self-hatred, madness, and suicide.

The play hesitates between seeing Isabella as too passive, allowing herself to be coerced by all the men around her, and as not passive enough, because her final decision to remarry transgresses the boundaries of proper sexual behavior in a widow; somehow she is punished for two opposite failures simultaneously. The developing drama of sentiment, in the context of which *The Fatal Marriage* should be seen, "simultaneously glorified and debased" women,[15] creating extreme and lofty images of female virtue while debasing female characters by eroticizing their suffering. Because he aims to exonerate Isabella from any hint of blame, Southerne constructs her as an almost masochistically passive victim of male ill-treatment and of fate:

> I meet your Rage, and come to be devour'd:
> Say, which way are you to dispose of me?
> To Dungeons, Darkness, Death.
> (act 2, scene 3, lines 13–15)

In addition, he simplifies the passionately mixed feelings of Behn's heroine by showing her loving only her first husband; "My Soul is only Biron's" (act 5, scene 4, line 10).

Finally, to exonerate the heroine in 1694 and in 1757 it was necessary to present her not only as innocent, sexually unassertive, and passive but also as domestic. Where Behn's heroine is unable to have children after a miscarriage, Southerne's is equipped with a small, wise boy-child, whose presence gives an opportunity for a number of high emotional moments that emphasize her maternal qualities, her vulnerability, and the horrors of her poverty. (The child's role becomes even more prominent in Garrick's version.) The childlessness of Behn's heroine is used to legitimise an extradomestic role for women. "More are the Children of the Barren, than the Fruitful Woman" (5:310), and a woman's moral responsibility does not end at her own front door. In Southerne's world, however, a woman's place is in the family. He depicts but cannot fully articulate the contradiction that what causes Isabella's suffering and death is exactly the family within which she ought to confine herself.

Southerne's text in fact presents a number of unresolved contradictions. This becomes particularly clear in the epilogue. It is a conventional strategy for an epilogue to mock the absolutes the play has seemed to affirm, but this epilogue proves particularly problematic in its dismantling of the images of female innocence and self-punishment. Women who commit suicide to avoid rape are ridiculed: "'tis most egregious Nonsense,/To dye for being pleas'd, with a safe Conscience." Isabella's sufferings are here framed not as full subjectivity, but simply as erotic titillation for a male spectator/reader, and even rape, the most brutal expression of patriarchal power, is excused because it is what women really want.

In fact, the literary history of *The Fatal Marriage* reveals a growing ambivalence towards the play. Delariviere Manley in *The New Atalantis* sees it as really only legitimized pornography. An "Opera" or "Play" that sounds very much like *The Fatal Marriage* is instrumental in the seduction of Louisa by Hernando: "Louisa . . . became extremely mov'd. . . . Her young Breasts heav'd with Sorrow; the Tears fill'd her Eyes, and she betray'd her Sense of their Misfortune with a Tenderness that Hernando did not think had been in her; he was infinitely pleas'd."[16] Sensibility awakens sexuality, and she is rendered vulnerable to his adulterous advances. Southerne defines Isabella's suffering as erotic, and Manley shows the consequences of the habit of mind that accepts this: Women learn masochism and men learn sadism from the offered model, and the result is disastrous in their relations with each other. An even clearer allusion to *The Fatal Marriage* as the site of a dangerous eroticization of female suffering occurs in Henry Fielding's *Tom Jones*.[17] Sophia Weston, "alone and melancholy," is reading "a tragedy. It was *The Fatal Marriage;* and she was now come to that part where the poor distrest Isabella disposes of her wedding ring." She is much moved by it: "a shower of tears ran down into her bosom" (p. 706). Her reading of Southerne's tragedy, and her ready emotional response to it, frames Sophia as erotic, at least in the eyes of Lord Fellamar, who then attempts to rape her. Both Manley and Fielding reveal the ambivalence with which eighteenth-century audiences might have responded to *The Fatal Marriage*. On the one hand, Louisa and Sophia are treated with sympathy for their sensibility; but on the other hand, legitimate sensibility might easily pass over into transgressive sexuality, as it does for Louisa—or at least a male reader might anticipate the possibility that this might be so, as Lord Fellamar does as he observes Sophia. *The Fatal Marriage*'s praise of female passivity and its eroticization of female suffering are shown to have potentially dangerous consequences for female readers.

Southerne alters Behn's Isabella to assert and simplify her innocence and to equate this with passivity. Jane Barker alters her in the opposite direction, into an equally simple "Monster."[18] As a woman who has refused proper feminine passivity, she is unambiguously named as "wicked" (p. 61). Whereas Southerne minimizes Isabella's guilt, Barker maximizes it. Her nun (she is treated with so little sympathy that she is not even given a name) breaks her "solemn Religious Vow of Chastity" (pp. 59–60) to run away with a cavalier. The action, with one important exception, which I shall examine later, follows *The History of the Nun* closely. In general terms, Barker's major alteration is the use of a strong and unproblematic moral language: "Cruelty" (p. 62), "bloody and hateful" (p. 63), "wicked" (p. 61). Barker provides a strenuously moralized rereading of Behn's text: the nun's story is used to make very simple points about the destructive power of passion and to endorse the cliché "Marry in haste, and Repent at leisure" (p. 64).

Barker alters Behn's text as part of an ongoing process of assessment and criticism of Behn's work and the example she offered the woman writer. Barker's central female persona, Galesia, is herself a writer who exemplifies the eighteenth-century ideal of chaste, domestic, unassertive female authorship. Galesia and her creator are both disturbed by Behn's embodiment of a different image, free-speaking, assertive, and professional, and both are reluctant to risk associating herself with that image. In an earlier work, *A Patch-work Screen for the Ladies; or, Love and Virtue Recommended in a Collection of Instructive Novels* (1723), a lady, knowing of Galesia's "Bookish Inclinations," tries to divert her by asking "if I lik'd Mrs Phillips, or Mrs Behn best?" Katherine Philips, "the matchless Orinda," had become the approved model of the woman writer, the antitype of Behn. Galesia "reply'd, with a blunt Indignation, That they ought not to be nam'd together."[19] *A Patch-work Screen* and *The Lining of the Patch-work Screen* both display Barker's ambivalence about the precedent of Aphra Behn. Barker is excited by Behn's imagination and cannot stop retelling or imitating Behn's fiction, and yet she also feels called upon to condemn the example Behn provides for women writers, both overtly, as in the passage quoted above, or more indirectly, in the way she restructures and adds reassuring morals to stories by Behn.

Behn's cultural position in the 1680s allowed her to incorporate radical images of femininity into her work: Barker's in the 1720s did not, and as a result her textual strategies have to be more wily and covert. Although she seems highly critical of Behn, it would be wrong to consider her revisions wholly reactionary. "Philinda's STORY out of the BOOK" is embedded within a large fiction that casts light upon it. Galesia is visited by Philinda and Lady Allgood, who narrates Philinda's story while she reads a "little Old Book" (p. 52). Philinda's biography reveals the serious consequences faced by a woman writer if her texts are misinterpreted. (Philinda lends money to a male friend; when she writes asking him to meet her and return it the letter is intercepted by his wife, and her misunderstanding begins a chapter of accidents in which Philinda is imprisoned as a prostitute and misjudged by her husband.) Philinda then relates a story from "her old Book, in which she was much engag'd, in particular in one Story" (p. 58). Although Behn's name is not mentioned, this is presumably her *Histories and Novels* (which had editions of 1696, 1698, 1699, and 1700), the suppression of this fact a further sign of Barker's nervousness about her predecessor. The tale of the nun is moralized in a way that seems to castigate both its female protagonist and her female creator. But the frame story, with its warning that a woman's innocent writing may be misinterpreted, even used to define her unjustly as a whore, may be read to mitigate the anti-Behn thrust of the embedded fiction. Philinda (whose name, although conventional, recalls Philander, the male lead of Behn's most popular novel, *Love-Letters between a Nobleman and His Sister* [1684]), may represent Behn, falsely accused of sexual immorality and with her own words twisted against her, and may warn us of the possibilities that even Barker's own text may risk misinterpreting its Behnian source.

The Lining of the Patch-work Screen, like *A Patch-work Screen for the Ladies*, is a text about women negotiating roles as writers and as readers, and books, papers, and writing are important as props and symbols; and yet Barker's ambivalence is everywhere apparent. On the one hand she displays a knowledgeable interest in women writers,[20] which culminates in Galesia's dream in which Katherine Philips, the ideal woman author, is crowned Queen of Parnassus. On the other hand, tale after tale presents women's writing and reading as dangerous. Philinda's writing causes her to be defined as a prostitute, the Portuguese nun is enabled to break her monastic vows by smuggling letters to her paramour in "Books lent and return'd" (p. 78), and "secret correspondence" (pp. 137–38) endangers or compromises many women, like Favorella in "The Story of Belle-mien." Female reading may also be dangerous and certainly requires rigorous supervision and censorship. "The Story of Tangerine, the Gentleman Gypsie" retells Behn's story of *The Wandering Beauty*, but whereas Behn's Arabella Fairname is presented sympathetically as a delightful high-spirited heroine who refuses to marry for money, preferring "Nature and Inclination" to "Interest and Duty" (5:448), Barker's Lady Gypsie is "blamed" for such unrespectable and un-moral behavior and accused of being misled by "reading some ridicu-lous Romance or Novel" (p. 102). To an even greater extent the heroine of "The History of Dorinda" ruins her life because of the ridiculous "Freaks and romantick Frolicks" (p. 107) she has imbibed as she "had read Plays, Novels, and Romances" (p. 106). *The Lining of the Patch-work Screen* presents opposed images of woman readers (Dorinda corrupted by romances in contrast to Galesia's virtuous reading of religious texts like "Mr Dyke's Book" [p. 168]) and of women writers (Aphra Behn versus Katherine Philips). *The Lining* conveys the anxieties of being a woman reader and writer in the 1720s, especially a female anxiety of influence. Barker's female pre-decessors may legitimize her own literary ambitions, as does the ex-ample of Orinda, but they may equally well compound her dread of being misjudged or identified with their example. Behn in particular haunts the text, a writer to whose imaginative power Barker re-sponds but whose moral vision and example she finds intensely dis-turbing. Perhaps we should read these ambivalences in a Chodorov-ian sense, seeing her as attempting to create an identity separate from, and in opposition to, her literary mothers. As a means of achieving this end, the mother is split into two separate images, the good mother Orinda, chaste, modest, and nurturing, as contrasted with the bad mother Behn, sexual, imaginatively exciting, and assertive.

Southerne's and Barker's versions both show a fragmentation of Behn's complex heroine, a graphic demonstration of the so-called Augustan age's polarization of women into images of saints and whores. The work of these revisionists, however, helps us to get into focus the real achievements of Behn's narrative. Most important, by contrasting Southerne's and Garrick's Isabella and Barker's nun with

Behn's protagonist, we can appreciate to the full Behn's psychological and political complexity. Behn's Isabella unites the contradictory elements of Southerne's saint and Barker's sinner, providing a brilliant and convincing account of the paradoxes inherent in subjectivity itself and illustrating, as Behn puts it elsewhere, how "contradictory are we to our selves" (*The Unfortunate Bride,* 5:404). All motivation is seen as complex and paradoxical, and Behn works to reveal the means by which a woman of unusual virtue, piety and generosity becomes a vow-breaker, a bigamist, and "the Murderess of two Husbands (both belov'd) in one Night" (5:323).

Behn's use of framing devices is crucial to this project. A simple story of female vice and crime seems to be predicted by the subtitle (*The Fair Vow-Breaker*) and to be outlined at the beginning and end of the novella: "Of all the sins, incident to Human Nature, there is none, of which Heaven has took so particular, visible, and frequent Notice, and Revenge, as on that of Violated Vows" (5:263); "exhorting daily, the Young, and the Fair . . . never to break a Vow . . . 'She made a Speech . . . so Eloquent . . . a warning to the Vow-Breakers" (5:323–24). And yet this simple moralizing is repeatedly contained and subverted, so that the novella's whole significance is altered. This begins as early as the dedication, to Hortense Mancini, Duchess of Mazarin. Victim of an arranged marriage to a cruel, jealous, autocratic husband who frittered away the money she had brought him, Mancini tried in vain to effect a legal separation and when this failed fled to England and became one of Charles II's mistresses.[21] The dedication, with its convincing respect for Mancini, gives a different slant to a tale ostensibly about broken vows, suggesting that subjection to the church or to a husband need not necessarily be a virtue and that what the world calls female guilt may be understood in completely different ways. One of Mancini's sisters, Olympe, Comtesse de Soissons, had been banished in 1680 over the La Voisin affair and had even been accused of murdering her husband. Behn's dedication to Mancini must therefore be seen as ironic, as clumsily inappropriate, or else as helping to provide a frame that subverts the simple moral tale that the novella appears to offer.

That the last is most probable is suggested by the novella's other framing devices. The first four paragraphs of *The History of the Nun* in fact deserve close attention, for what they tell us about reading

the tale that follows is important and unexpected. Despite the subtitle, the novella actually begins, not with an exemplification of
female vice, but with a defense of women and an attack on male
infidelity: "What Man that does not boast of the Numbers he has . . .
ruin'd . . . ? Nay, what Woman, almost, has not a pleasure in Deceiv-
ing, taught, perhaps, at first, by some dear false one . . . ?" (5:263).
The hail of commas in the second sentence seems almost to disinte-
grate its account of female deceit, and it constantly qualifies an apparently simple statement—that men and women are equally guilty
of falsehood—with skeptical or ironic additions like almost and
perhaps. By this means a strong undercurrent is created that justifies
and sympathizes with female infidelity. Men's infidelity is biologically
programmed; women's is constructed by social circumstance: "For,
without all dispute, Women are by Nature more Constant and Just,
than Men" (5:263). Women are identified with a benevolent and
specifically female Nature, and apparent flaws are the creation of
patriarchy, for "Customs of Countries change even Nature her self"
(5:264). By a process of contextualization and a whole series of
frames a simple story about the punishment of broken vows—"perhaps, a moral tale"[22]—is subverted. A dedication to a woman who
has flamboyantly abandoned her husband and yet retains the admiration of the writer suggests unconventional ways of reading the tale's
female bigamist, as does the authoritative introduction in which male
example provides an alibi for broken female vows. But two further
important effects remain, as the fourth paragraph demonstrates—the
female narrator and her role and the nun as metaphor.

I have written elsewhere[23] about Behn's female narrators and
their functions in helping the reader to negotiate the ambiguities of
her fictions. In *The History of the Nun* the female narrator identifies
fruitfully and subversively with Isabella, so that a fiction that begins
by loudly declaring a moral purpose is deconstructed by the female-
identified voice of the narrator, which implies that this is too simple.
"I once was design'd an humble Votary in the House of Devotion,
but . . . I rather chose to deny my self that Content . . . than to languish . . . in a certain Affliction" (5:265). Women's power and inde-
pendence are rigidly limited, as is experienced by both the female narrator and the female protagonist. Isabella is forced to be "inclos'd . . .
making a Virtue of Necessity," and the female narrator is also meta-

phorically if not literally confined, unable to "alter Custom, nor . . . make new Laws, or rectify the old ones" (5:265). Their shared conventual background and their shared powerlessness within patriarchy create a strong sense of solidarity, even collusion, between the female narrator and the female protagonist, which also acts to complicate the apparently simple story offered.

Finally, in Restoration fiction as a whole, nuns feature as bizarre and eroticized exotics rather like the harem women who are in contemporary fiction not their opposites but their doubles. In Behn's fiction the nun instead becomes a metaphor for the female condition. Nuns and wives are openly identified as parallel instances of society's limitation of women's lives—"I could wish . . . that Nunneries and Marriages were not to be enter'd into, 'till the Maid, so destin'd, were of a mature Age to make her own Choice" (5:265). The "inclos'd Life" (5:268) of the nun figures the domestic life of all women, and Isabella is "inclos'd" not only as a nun but as a wife (5:306), and in her marriage as much as in the cloister she "liv'd . . . like a Nun" (5:309). Isabella is prevented from speaking of her love for Henault not only by her specific identity as nun ("my Vow") but also by her general identity as woman ("my Modesty" [5:292]), which serves as a synecdoche for femininity. For nuns, as for all women, "our Opportunities of Speaking are so few" (5:292). Even the limitations of the female narrator, compelled to restrict herself to certain topics—"It is not my business to relate the History of the War, being wholly unacquainted with the Terms of Battels" (5:304)—forms a parallel with the "inclos'd Life" of nuns and married women. This use of the metaphor of the nun as a means of understanding her own dilemma as a woman writer may help to explain the novella's unconventional sympathy for the guilty Isabella, whose transgressive desire to escape from confinement finds sympathetic echoes in the woman writer. All the metaphors in the opening paragraphs of the novella suggest that female powerlessness justifies female acts, so that vow-breaking, bigamy, and even murder are presented not as unproblematic sins but as horrific, extreme, but logical consequences of a social order that routinely allows women no freedom of choice over their own lives. Whereas Southerne's Isabella is a saint and Barker's is a monster, Behn's is Everywoman.

It is worth remarking on one further difference between Behn's novella and its later adaptations. While Southerne, Garrick, and Barker, at least within the confines of this tale, deal with conventional and repressive ideologies of gender difference, Behn works to complicate received images of gender. Henault in particular is feminized, "his Face exceeding beautiful, adorn'd with a thousand Graces" (5:274). He has been "kept at home" (5:274), like a woman, which has made him, again like a woman, "fit for soft Impressions," and "he car'd not for the Conversation of Men, because he lov'd not Debauch" (5:275); "lovely" recurs in descriptions of him (e.g., 5:282, 290). Behn replaces a conventional view of gender difference with a complex canvas of feminized men and women who are immasculated in their ability to take action and to take moral responsibility for their actions.

I will now discuss one final symbol that, perhaps more clearly than any other, points out differences between Southerne's, Barker's, and Behn's characterizations of Isabella: the metaphor of sewing. Needlework conventionally carries suggestions of approved female domesticity, tractability, meekness, chastity, and silence; it was a crucial element in the "creation of femininity," the lynchpin of a repressive ideology of gender difference.[24] It articulates a specifically female language that men only partially understand. Neither Shakespeare nor Congreve, it appears, uses the word "stich";[25] men watch female sewing from afar, observing, as it were, the *langue* but not the *parole* of needlework. Southerne does not show Isabella sewing at all. Her response to poverty is passive suffering and heartrending complaints. This contrasts forcefully with the stories of, for example, Jane Barker, whose impoverished women work to support themselves and their families, for instance as nurses (*Patch-work Screen*, p. 61), as small tradeswomen ("The Story of Mrs Goodwife," *Lining*, pp. 67–72), and especially as needlewomen ("The Story of Belle-mien" and "The Story of Mrs Castoff," both from *Lining*). It would not fit Southerne's dignified, suffering, leisure-class Isabella actually to work, and her lack of work, even the archetypal female needlework, again emphasises how passive she actually is.

As I have said, female sewing traditionally connotes female meekness and tractability. In *The History of the Nun*, Isabella spends her married life with Villenoys devoting herself to "Acts of Virtue" (5:310). When he goes hunting, she shuts herself up in the house with her "innocent Diversions of fine Work, at which she was Excellent" (5:311). It is the first time we have heard of her prowess as a needle-woman, and the detail is used here to present a conventional picture of Isabella as chaste, unassertive wife, framed by the comforting details of the domestic life. But its placing is fraught with irony, for it is prologue to the reappearance of her first husband and the revelation that this chaste unassertive married life is not at all what it seems. The scene, perhaps, is a reworking of the reunion of the chaste seamstress Penelope with the disguised, long-absent Odysseus, and this adds further ironies in the contrast between the faithful Penelope and the unintentionally faithless Isabella.

Behn typically places a time bomb under the conventionally repressive metaphor of sewing when she allows Isabella to use needlework as her weapon for the murder of her second husband. Villenoys, it will be remembered, has been recruited to dispose of the body of Henault. The body is bundled into "a Sack . . . whereon stuck a great Needle, with a Pack-Thread in it." Isabella is frantic with conflicting emotions, and Behn presents her state of mind with great subtlety and conviction. Because she fears that Villenoys will gain too much power over her, that he will cease to love her and "would be eternal reproaching her," she plans a second murder: "when Fate begins to afflict, she goes through stitch with her Black Work" (5:318). Fate, more usually imaged spinning, is here seen as a seamstress ironically like Isabella herself, and the idiomatic phrase "through stitch," meaning "thoroughly, completely," has its last element taken absolutely literally. "Black Work" may seem a general phrase to refer to the sinister activity of Fate, but more specifically it also refers to a fashionable kind of fine embroidery. By these puns, Fate is seen as a sewing woman like Isabella, and needlework, conventionally an image of female subordination, becomes a locus of female power. Such paradoxes emphasize Isabella's ambiguous status as virtuous murderess, innocent adulteress.

When Barker retells this story, the one important alteration she makes to the action is illuminating. Barker's heroine sews the sack containing the body to her husband's clothes by accident: "But in her Fright, by mistake, took hold of the Gentleman's Coat, and so fastned that into the Sheet" (p. 64). Behn's flawed, complex heroine sins deliberately and resolutely faces the consequences of her own free will; Barker's simpler villainess errs by accident, demonstrating the power of God to punish sinners. Where Behn radically subverts a conservative ideology of needlework, Barker in this instance uses it conventionally to punish female assertiveness.

Although Barker is critical of Behn's example, she is also drawn to her powerful depictions of outlaw women, and this ambivalence can be seen in the way that the image of sewing, although used repressively within Philinda's story, escapes out into the frame text in much more unconventional forms. Both *The Lining of the Patch-work Screen* and its earlier companion, *A Patch-work Screen for the Ladies,* describe themselves as the written equivalent of needlework and use sewing to provide rich and empowering metaphors for female creativity. The metaphor of needlework naturalizes women's writing, and a conventional contrast between legitimate female pastimes like needlework and potentially transgressive ones like reading and writing is deconstructed. But perhaps it also does more than that by implying that needlework, although conventionally a repressive image, might be used to present in coded form a potentially subversive female language. "The Heroick Cavalier; or, the Resolute Nun" in *A Patch-work Screen* may be influenced by Behn in its images of nuns and transvestites. A page boy is smuggled into a convent to further his cavalier master's liaison with a nun and smuggles out letters in a richly embroidered purse he has worked. The cavalier and nun are able to flee together, and the page is revealed as a girl in disguise, self-sacrificingly in love with her master. Needlework in this tale becomes a vehicle for women's language in the most literal way, and the whole tale demonstrates complex layers of female control, as the female author allows a female narrator to tell the female hero a story whose most ingenious and linguistically gifted character is, despite appearances, a woman. This tale is much more morally easy-going about romantic love versus monastic vows than "Philinda's STORY out of the BOOK," and this can be seen in the use of needlework, which is here celebrated as a locus of female virtue and power rather than enrolled as evidence of female vice and powerlessness. Perhaps her affirmative treatment of Behn-like elements in this tale prompts her guiltily self-correcting versions in her later collection. Barker is repeatedly drawn to images from Behn, and her overt resistance to Behn as a model is undercut by her covert acceptance of these Behnian images.

Behn's *The History of the Nun*, then, had a long and complex posthumous history. Southerne, Garrick, and Barker all rewrote the story in ways that demonstrate the backlash against feminism in the 1690s and early eighteenth century. All simplify the character of Isabella, although in contrary ways, so that she becomes in the hands of Southerne and Garrick a child-like secular saint and in the hands of Barker a didactic example of God's punishment of sinners. Southerne and Barker demand that a good woman should be passive and self-sacrificing, while Behn's sympathies are wider; she seeks to explain the social origins of what is conventionally read as female wickedness and to allow a woman to satisfy her own desires without necessarily being seen as evil. Alterations by Southerne, Barker, and Garrick highlight not only the complexity of character and of social context of Behn's Isabella but also the complexity of Behn's symbolism and narrative methods. Perhaps we can now accept as self-evident not only the complexity and originality of Behn's fiction but also her importance as a ghost haunting her seventeenth- and eighteenth-century successors in fiction and drama.

Notes

1. For example, Behn's novella *Agnes de Castro* inspired Catharine Trotter's hit play of the same name (London: 1696) and was later adapted as a tale in Elizabeth Griffith's *Collection of Novels Selected and Revised* (London, 1777), as well as David Mallet's play *Elvira* (London, 1763) and Charles Symmons' *Inez, a Tragedy* (London, 1796). Hannah Cowley's *A School for Greybeards* (London, 1786) adapts *The Lucky Chance,* Edward Young's *The Revenge* (London, 1721) is based on *Abdelazer,* and John Philip Kemble's *Love in Many Masks* (London, 1790) bowdlerises *The Rover.*

2. *Oroonoko* inspired another novel in Elizabeth Griffith's *Collection* and Thomas Southerne's immensely popular tragicomedy *Oroonoko* (London, 1696), which in its turn produced numerous progeny, including John Hawkesworth's *Oroonoko* (London, 1759); an anonymous adaptation (London, 1760) that cuts the comic scenes and introduces two new characters; Frank Gentleman's *Oroonoko* (Glasgow, 1760); John Ferriar's *The Prince of Angola* (Manchester, 1788); and *The Sexes Mismatch'd* in *The Strollers Pacquet Open'd* (London, 1742), which adapts Southerne's comic plot.

3. Jeslyn Medoff, "The Daughters of Behn and the Problem of Reputation," in *Women, Writing, History 1640–1740,* ed. Isobel Grundy and Susan Wiseman (London: B. T. Batsford, 1992), p. 43. For Behn's reputation, see also Jacqueline Pearson, *The Prostituted Muse: Images of Women and Women Dramatists,*

1642–1737 (Brighton: Harvester Press, 1988), pp. 143, 254. Nancy Cotton in *Women Playwrights in England, c. 1363–1750* (London: Associated Univ. Presses, 1980) usefully divides women writers into "Orindas" and "Astraeas" and describes the differences between women writers who were disciples of Behn and of Philips (pp. 194–212).

4. Jane Spencer, *The Rise of the Woman Novelist: From Aphra Behn to Jane Austen* (Oxford: Basil Blackwell, 1986), p. 15.

5. Kathryn Shevelow, *Women and Print Culture: The Construction of Femininity in the Early Periodical* (London and New York: Routledge, 1989), p. 1.

6. Thomas Southerne, *The Fatal Marriage*, in *The Works of Thomas Southerne*, ed. Robert Jordan and Harold Love (Oxford: Clarendon Press, 1988), 2:10, lines 18–19. Subsequent references to this edition will be cited parenthetically in the text.

7. For a fuller account of *Isabella* as an adaptation of *The Fatal Marriage*, see Harry William Pedicord, *The Theatrical Public in the Time of Garrick* (New York: King's Crown Press, Columbia Univ., 1954), pp. 87–94.

8. The fullest account to date of Southerne's revisions of Aphra Behn texts, especially of *Oroonoko*, can be found in Ann Messenger's "Novel into Play: Aphra Behn and Thomas Southerne," ch. 2 of her *His and Hers: Essays in Restoration and Eighteenth-Century Literature* (Lexington: Univ. Press of Kentucky, 1986).

9. See Paul Hamelius, "The Source of Southerne's 'Fatal Marriage,'" *Modern Language Review* 4 (1909): 353–56; corrected by Montague Summers, "The Source of Southerne's "The Fatal Marriage,'" *Modern Language Review* 11 (1916): 149–55.

10. Aphra Behn, *The History of the Nun; or, the Fair Vow Breaker*, in *The Works of Aphra Behn*, ed. Montague Summers, 6 vols. (1915; rpt. New York: Benjamin Blom, 1967), 5:315. Subsequent references to this edition will be cited parenthetically in the text by volume and page number.

11. See Pearson, *The Prostituted Muse*, pp. 38–39.

12. In Southerne's version, Behn's Villenoys becomes Villeroy, and Henault is renamed Biron (from the alias he uses in Behn's novella, Beroone).

13. Southerne adapts the career of the heroine of *Oroonoko*, Imoinda, in the same way. In Behn's novella, she is killed by her husband, whereas in Southerne's play she commits suicide.

14. Messenger, "Novel into Play," p. 55.

15. Janet Todd, introduction to *A Dictionary of British and American Women Writers, 1660–1800* (London: Methuen, 1984), p. 19.

16. Delariviere Manley, *Secret Memoirs . . . from the New Atalantis* (London, 1709), 1:218.

17. For the use of *The Fatal Marriage* in the eighteenth-century novel, see Robert Gale Noyes, *The Neglected Muse: Restoration and Eighteenth-Century Tragedy in the Novel (1740–1780)* (Providence: Brown Univ. Press, 1958), pp. 78–81.

18. Jane Barker, "Philinda's STORY out of the BOOK," in *The Lining of the Patch-work Screen; Design'd for the Farther Entertainment of the Ladies* (London, 1726), p. 63. Subsequent references to this edition will be cited parenthetically in the text.

19. Jane Barker, *A Patchwork Screen for the Ladies; or, Love and Virtue Recommended in a Collection of Instructive Novels* (London, 1723), p. 44. Subsequent references to this edition will be cited parenthetically in the text.

20. For example, she retells the famous *Story of the Portuguese NUN* (pp. 75–80) in a way that makes clear that she has gone to a written source, "her printed Letters" (p. 71). (*Seven Portuguese Letters* [1681] was widely believed to be the work of a woman, although Patricia Crawford, "Provisional Checklist of Women's Published Writings, 1600–1700," in *Women in English Society, 1500–1800*, ed. Mary Prior [London and New York: Methuen, 1982], pp. 261–62, doubts this attribution.) "The Cause of the Moors Over-running Spain" may be based on Mary Pix's *The Conquest of Spain* (1705). And Barker's praise for Katherine Philips ("Both improv'd Sexes eminently meet / They are than Man more strong, and more than Woman sweet" [p. 175]) paraphrases Cowley's commendatory ode to Philips's *Poems* (1664) and demonstrates that Barker had read this collection.

21. Mancini was also admired by Delariviere Manley, who praises her in the introduction to *The Adventures of Rivella* (London, 1714); Mancini's situation also inspired one of the age's most vigorous feminist polemics, Mary Astell's *Some Reflections upon Marriage* (London, 1700). See Ruth Perry, *The Celebrated Mary Astell: An Early English Feminist* (Chicago: Univ. of Chicago Press, 1986), pp. 150–56.

22. Paul Salzman, *English Prose Fiction, 1558–1700: A Critical History* (Oxford: Clarendon Press, 1985), p. 315.

23. Jacqueline Pearson, "Gender and Narrative in the Fiction of Aphra Behn," *Review of English Studies* 42 (1991): 40–56, 179–90.

24. Rozsika Parker, *The Subversive Stitch: Embroidery and the Making of the Feminine* (London: Women's Press, 1984), p. 1. See also Cecilia Macheski, "Penelope's Daughters: Images of Needlework in Eighteenth-Century Literature," in *Fetter'd or Free?: British Women Novelists, 1670–1815*, ed. Cecilia Macheski and Mary Anne Schofield (Athens: Ohio Univ. Press, 1986), pp. 85–100.

25. Shakespeare once uses *stitchery* (*Coriolanus*, act 1, scene 3, line 75) and once, in a metaphorical sense, *stitches* (*Twelfth Night*, act 3, scene 2, line 73). See Alexander Schmidt, *Shakespeare-Lexicon* (Berlin and London, 1886) and John Bartlett, *Concordance to Shakespeare* (London, 1894). Congreve has one use of *stitch'd* (*The Double Dealer*, act 5, scene 1, line 288). See David Mann, ed., *A Concordance to the Plays of William Congreve* (Ithaca: Cornell Univ. Press, 1973).

RUTH SALVAGGIO

Aphra Behn's Love:
Fiction, Letters, and Desire

As a premier Restoration playwright, Aphra Behn openly engaged the discourse of sexual intrigue—the topic of the day. But what did she have to say about love? We know that Behn was a great writer of romantic fiction, although we tend to associate these narratives with the writing she produced late in her career and less with her risqué dramas, which have brought her recognition and fame as the first professional woman writer in English. Yet Behn's turn to the subject of romantic love, in all its fantastic and often tragic dimensions, can tell us much more than her plays reveal about the predicament of women in love—and in Behn's case, about the ways in which this pivotal woman writer attempted to write the script of feminine desire.

The literary expression of love follows a long and varied history that has been intricately linked to the expression of male desire and sharply focused on a man's longing for a woman—a subject's desire for an object. Among the most intriguing questions asked by feminist critics and theorists in recent years are those that focus on women who act as subjects, who produce their own writing and desire: What happens, as Luce Irigaray asks, when the object begins to speak? Not surprisingly, this issue has proved pivotal in the reassessment of early women writers, especially those emerging in the late seventeenth and eighteenth centuries, when women began to write and publish in large numbers and change the shape of narrative. Indeed the emergence of women novelists and their preoccupation with romantic fiction has caused critics of early women writers to recast the whole question of romance in terms of the workings of feminine desire, a concern that has become the subject of such diverse studies as Peggy Kamuf's *Fictions of Feminine Desire,* Patricia Meyer Spacks's *Desire and Truth,* and Nancy Armstrong's *Desire and Domestic Fiction.*[1]

Aphra Behn rightly deserves a prominent position not only in the reassessment of early women writers but also in the ways that they can now be seen as reshaping the dynamics of romance and desire and thus transforming the love story. Narratives of desire are not themselves, strictly speaking, tales of love or sex. Although desire may propel the greatest love stories or sexual dramas, desire itself is the process of longing, of wanting. What distinguishes the love stories that consumed Behn's writing near the end of her career are the varied and often fantastic expressions of feminine desire. Her inscriptions of love lost and love thwarted give us a glimpse of a woman writer who was deeply dissatisfied with the plot of the conventional love story—as she both wrote and lived this narrative. Her fiction most certainly traces this process, notably as her heroines become subjects directing their desires in anything but conventional ways. Yet a crucial aspect of Behn's dissatisfaction with the love story is also to be found in her letter writing, specifically in a series of letters that her biographers believe she wrote and addressed to John Hoyle. These epistolary expressions of desire afford an intriguing example of what Linda Kauffman calls the "doubling" of "letter as literature, literature as a letter." But because for Behn these letters were not by any means purely literature, they also force us to come to terms with the letter as "female autograph," to use Domna Stanton's term—in this case, the letter as direct expression of a woman writer's own experience of desire.[2]

In both Behn's fiction and these personal letters, we can find remarkably complementary expressions of feminine desire. This is not to say that Behn's fiction should be reduced to autobiography, any more than it is to say that her personal letters should be read purely as fictive constructs. Yet the two forms of writing can mutually inform without collapsing into each other. For Aphra Behn, I will argue, the similar expression of feminine desire in her fiction and love letters shows her own attempt, often a frantic and desperate one, to make women into desiring subjects—to allow them to direct their own desire rather than to serve as objects of male desire. Yet this attempt was continually fraught with complications, as it likely was in Behn's own life, and as it remains in women's real and fictive scripting of themselves in the conventional plot of love.

In tracing this attempt, I will look closely at two of Behn's extreme and extremely different fictive accounts of love—*The Adventures of the Black Lady* and *The Fair Jilt*—and at her *Love-Letters to a Gentleman,* eight letters attributed to Behn by all of her biographers that were published shortly after her death. In simple terms we could say that these two works of fiction trace Behn's expression of desire as a woman who wrote about it, whereas her letters trace the expression of desire as a woman who actually experienced it. Useful as this distinction is to demarcate these texts, it nonetheless disguises the fact that all three are, after all, texts; that is, they are all pieces of writing through which Behn attempted to articulate feminine desire. I stress their connection as writing because the very process of writing becomes a crucial part of Behn's expression and experience of feminine desire. And here, I think, is where Behn's preoccupation with narrative becomes important. As Kauffman asks, "Is desire itself fundamentally fictive? Is artifice inseparable from longing, from language, from literature?"[3]

We know that Behn wrote nearly all of her fiction in the last few years of her life. Much of this fiction was not even published until after her death in 1689, and two of her more prominent narratives— *Oroonoko* and *The Fair Jilt*—were published the previous year. *The Adventures of the Black Lady,* one of her posthumous publications, was among Behn's first experimentations with fiction, probably written around or before 1685. Thus, although writing plays preoccupied Behn throughout virtually all of her career, writing fiction consumed her imagination during her last years. Although Behn's biographers have discussed several possible reasons for her shift in attention away from drama and toward fiction, it is understandable that Behn would turn to the writing of fiction, as so many women of her time did, to explore women's experience of love and desire not confined to the plot of Restoration comedy. The novel, after all, was fast establishing itself as the predominant literary genre, and romantic fiction in particular was fast becoming a genre dominated by increasing numbers of women writers. Because virtually all of Behn's writing in these last years—her fiction as well as her poetry and translations—focused on the subject of love, it is likely that Behn's turn to romance narratives signaled a search for different kinds of writing. In her fiction and her own love letters, this search led her through the world of longing and language—the writing of desire.

According to her biographers, Aphra Behn was at one time in love with John Hoyle, a lawyer and wit described by one of Behn's biographers as "a man of learning and brisk intelligence."[4] Behn addressed many of her love poems to Hoyle, and although we do not know how long their association actually lasted, we do know that it continued for many years, possibly beginning as early as 1670, when Behn was just turning thirty. The poem written to Hoyle in Behn's "Our Cabal," published in a collection of her poetry in 1684—five years before her death—seems written with enough distance and objectivity to suggest that the association was over with by then. Although the *Love-Letters to a Gentleman* were not directly addressed to Hoyle, virtually all of Behn's biographers have accepted Vita Sackville-West's belief that "these extraordinary documents" are indeed the record of Aphra Behn "in love, and most unhappily in love" with a man who did not return her passion.[5] George Woodcock, a later biographer, explains the matter this way: "Read in their entirety, these letters form an eloquent expression of a tragic and frustrating passion—the dark side of the mocking gaiety with which [Behn] faced the world of her plays."[6] The letters are indeed dark and heavy, especially compared to the lightness of the comedies that Behn produced for so many years. And they are, explicitly, love letters— not sexual play, not erotic flirtations. I turn to her love letters, then, to begin to explore this darkness, this story of unrequited love that narrates an intriguing script of feminine desire and shows a woman trying to write herself into a love story that resists her inclusion. How does one write this exclusion?

To answer this question, we need to understand the peculiar dynamics of Behn's connection with Hoyle. Throughout their relationship, Hoyle treated her with both affection and distance, and the letters are basically an account of Behn's response to his increasing coldness and unfaithfulness. What should be kept in mind from the very beginning—although it is usually mentioned at the end of biographical accounts of this relationship—is that John Hoyle was a homosexual and that at least part, if not much, of his coldness toward Behn derived from his sexual preference for other men. The story of their relationship and of Aphra Behn's experience of love may well be implicated in the dynamics of a sexuality in which men ultimately want to exchange pleasure with other men, although they may sometimes do so through the body of a woman. For Hoyle, this script of his homosexual relations, as much recent feminist theory suggests, may also describe the dynamics of heterosexual relations in which women are traded and exchanged among men. Although Behn continually sought a space for herself within these dynamics, her writing instead voiced the struggle she encountered in locating or occupying that space.

Behn's desire, as she writes it here, follows a heterosexual plot that is undermined by the homosexual and/or homosocial plot of men ultimately desiring each other. The woman finds no place for herself in this narrative, although she continually seeks one—as Aphra Behn did in her writing. Viewing the situation from this perspective, I must disagree with Woodcock's explanation of Behn's frustrations in love as resulting from what he calls her "ill-luck" in choosing "for the object of her deepest emotion a man who was probably psychologically incapable of any real or enduring love for a woman"—namely, a homosexual. Woodcock views Hoyle's attitude about love as "perverse—a desire to dominate combined with a desire to remain himself aloof and free."[7] Far from being perverse, such an attitude about love was quite common and in fact accounts rather precisely for the heterosexual attitudes of men during the Restoration: Whether their sexual exchanges were with wife or prostitute, they enjoyed the position of control and freedom. They could both dominate and remain independent. They were all, in a sense, John Hoyle. Several commentators on Behn, describing the crucial position she occupied as the first professional woman writer and the way in which her writing influenced the women who followed in her path, have said that if Aphra Behn did not exist, it would be necessary for us to invent her. I would add—describing the crucial role she plays in writing women's experience of love—that if her relationship with Hoyle had never happened, it would be necessary for us to invent it, for it explains perfectly the ways in which a woman's experience of love cannot fit the script of heterosexual relations built ultimately on homosocial and homoerotic desire directed by and circulating among men. Women have no place in this script, unless they at times serve as the passive object of the man's desire. For a woman to write about love, as Behn came to discover, meant that she was ultimately writing the story of her own displacement.

Reading through Behn's *Love-Letters to a Gentleman* involves one in the very experience of being displaced. Her emotions never seem to find a place. She goes back and forth, writing for this reason and then that reason, suggesting one motive and then another, knowing at first why she is writing and then finally not knowing. In fact, the first letter is about writing, so that writing itself and Behn's uncertainties about writing are intricately linked to her feelings of uncertainty and displacement in love.[8] "You bid me write," she says in this letter about Hoyle's unfaithfulness and promiscuity, "and I wish it were only the Effect of Complaisance that makes me obey you: I shou'd be very angry with myself and you, if I thought it were any other Motive." But then she quickly follows this with, "I hope it is not, and will not have you believe otherwise," as if to say that she is not really angry at his unfaithfulness, or at least that she does not want that to be her motive in writing. But then she turns again with "I cannot help, however, wishing you no Mirth, nor any Content in your Dancing-Design," though this is quickly followed with the qualification "this unwonted malice in me I do not like, and would have concealed it if I could, lest you should take it for something which I am not, nor will believe myself guilty of" (p. 54). Although Behn is ostensibly denying her guilt, I also sense an expression of her own feelings of displacement when she describes herself with the phrase "something which I am not." We might well wonder about Behn's conception of the something that she is—the woman who feels love or malice, who wishes him well or ill, who writes out of "Complaisance" or anger. Behn finds no place for herself in this love affair, in this writing that can only strive to suit itself to Hoyle's desire, not her own. She says, "I have so easily granted this Desire of your's, in writing to you" (p. 55), naming her very writing as her attempt to grant his desire. Behn's writing itself, the *Love-Letters* themselves, are the script of woman's love. It is a text in which Behn never found a place for herself, yet through which she continually wrote from her position of displacement. As in much romantic fiction, writing generates from the lack and longing experienced by the writer.

The letters are filled with descriptions of Behn's displacement, as if she occupied a kind of no-man's-land, or, more properly, a no-woman's-land in the territory of love. In a subsequent letter she speaks of being "surrounded with all the necessary Impossibilities of speaking to you" (p. 56), and it becomes clearer and clearer that the site of this impossibility is writing itself. "Possibly you will wonder what compels me to write; what moves me to send where I find so little Welcome; nay, where I meet with such Returns: it may be, I wonder too" (p. 58). Behn is writing to keep the love alive, to do the very thing that Hoyle wants her to do, and to do it exactly on his terms. For she is scripting herself into his love story—even though she knows that the writing is getting her nowhere, that she is creating no story of her own love. In another letter she tries to describe the "Secrets of my Soul," but quickly follows with "why I write them, I can give no Account: tis but fooling myself, perhaps, into an Undoing." This letter ends, "So much for Loving" (pp. 60–61). In yet another letter, she admits that her writing—caught in the expression of extreme emotions—can ultimately express none of these feelings: "My Soul is ready to burst with Pride and Indignation; and at the same Time, Love, with all his Softness, assails me, and will make me write: so that between one and the other, I can express neither as I ought" (p. 66).

Hoyle's game with Behn was a particularly insidious one to play with a woman who was so adept at writing and so obviously in love with him. He maintained his power in their relationship by insuring that she continually write to him. When she stops writing, he writes back to her claiming that he is hurt and disturbed, luring her back into the writing exchange that will sustain their connection and sustain as well his dominance. Although her carries on his sexual exchange with other women and men alike, he keeps Behn on hold through writing—through love letters in which she can say nothing about love, in which the subject of her writing becomes an "Impossibility." Thus she will write, then promise not to write, and then end up writing because all she can do is write: "I had To-night promis'd you should never have a tedious Letter from me more: I will begin to keep my Word, and stint my Heart and Hand. I promis'd tho' to write; and tho' I have no great Matter to say more, than the Assurance of my Eternal Love to you, yet to obey you, and not only so, but to oblidge my own impatient Heart, I must, late as 'tis, say something to thee" (p. 63). In her last letter to Hoyle, she asks, "Why, my dearest Charmer, do you disturb that Repose I had resolved to pursue, but taking it unkindly that I did not write? I cannot disobey you, because indeed I would not, tho' 'twere better much for both I had been for ever silent" (p. 68). The substance of these love letters was not the expression of love, but silence. But for a woman who wrote with such energy, with such fervor, as Behn did, could silence ultimately be the substance of her writing? Could writing about love, could the very writing of love, remain an "Impossibility?"

Behn's fiction, I believe, provided the space for her search for such possibilities. Not confined by the plot and structure of Restoration comedy, she could—as many women writers in fact did—create an assortment of scenarios for her female characters and in the process work through various scriptings of feminine desire. I read *The Adventures of the Black Lady* and *The Fair Jilt* as two particularly revealing plots that show Behn's struggle in writing the story of women and desire—stories of how women experience and express their love. A fuller understanding of this struggle, which I obviously cannot attempt here, would take us on a journey through Behn's world of fiction—from her first published work, *Love-Letters between a Nobleman and His Sister,* through *Oroonoko,* which I have come to regard as Behn's projection of her own thwarted desires onto the body of a black slave, indeed a tragic statement about the failure of love and woman's inevitable turning on her own body. I think we see this frustration express itself again and again in Behn's fiction, where woman either has no role at all in directing her desire (the role Behn herself assumed in her relations with Hoyle) or becomes a desiring subject by adopting positions of coldness, distance, and power (the role played by Hoyle in their affair). In suggesting this, let me again emphasize that I do not mean to confine Behn's writing to what we know about her biography. But I join with many recent critics of women's autobiographical writing in observing that a woman's writing is marked by her peculiar signature or autograph as a woman writer, in this case, by Behn's own experience of love—both its inexpressibility and, at the same time, Behn's determination to express the "impossibility of speaking."

Consider the predicament of Bellamora, the "Black Lady," who leaves the country and moves to the city in order to flee both her family and her lover.[9] Homeless and pregnant, Bellamora searches for a female relation of hers with whom she can live, undiscovered, for half a year. Instead of finding her relation, however, Bellamora meets a gentlewoman who listens to her sad story and takes her in. This gentlewoman seems to have a special interest in Bellamora's fate and particularly in reconciling her with her lover, Mr. Fondlove. And we soon discover why this is so—Fondlove, it turns out, is the gentlewoman's brother. The plot works itself out as you might expect. Fondlove arrives on the scene just at the moment when he is most needed—as the "Overseers of the Poor" threaten to claim Bellamora for a house of correction. He begs Bellamora to marry him, she finally consents, and they leave together.

It all seems like a typical love story or at least like one version of the typical love story. We have separated lovers coming together. We have a conventional fictional ending—marriage. We have a hero, Fondlove, who is very much in love with Bellamora, the object of his love. Only one thing is missing: Bellamora's love for Fondlove. There is no return. The circuit of desire moves from man to woman but does not circle back. When Bellamora first explains her predicament to the gentlewoman, she speaks of Fondlove as "one who, I dare believe, did then really love me" (5:6). He was, Bellamora says, full of "Passion" and "Sollicitations," and finding her "one Day all alone in my Chamber, and lying on my Bed . . . urged his Passion with such Violence" that, as she says, "I ruin'd my self" (5:6). That she perceives herself as initiating her own ruin is in itself curious, even more so when we keep in mind that she really has no affections for him at all. The fact of the matter is that her mother wanted her to marry someone else, a man who did not at all strike Bellamora's inclinations. It is "partly with my Aversion" to this man, and "partly with my Inclinations to pity" Fondlove, that she consents to his passion. Indeed, as she explains to the gentlewoman, Fondlove persists in his affections and wants to marry Bellamora. The gentlewoman is confused: "Why did you not, or why will you not consent to your own Happiness?" Bellamora's answer is the only statement we have of her desire: "Alas! . . . 'tis the only Thing I dread in this World: For, I am certain, he can never love me after. Besides, ever since I have abhorr'd the Sight of him" (5:7).

The reunion of Bellamora and Fondlove, far from proceeding from feelings of mutual love, proceeds instead from the desire of Fondlove, under the direction of his sister and the landlady of the house—both of whom facilitate this reunion by making it appear to Bellamora that she is destined to fall into poverty. Unknown to her, however, they have found Bellamora's lost "Money and Jewels" and of course have contacted Fondlove so that he can rescue Bellamora just as the city wardens threaten to take her away. Bellamora's desire, we can rightly say, is made possible through husband and money. Fondlove enters the plot near the story's end, "usher'd into *Bellamora's* Chamber by his Sister, his Brother-in-Law, and the Landlady" (5:9). We read much again about his tears and solicitations, his begging her to marry him with "a great many more pressing Arguments on all Sides." All we hear about Bellamora is contained in one statement: "To which at last she consented" (5:9).

But to what, exactly, does she consent? Clearly to the marriage and to Fondlove's arguments but not to love. Bellamora's own desire has no place in this story. Her condition remains dark; she is the "Black Lady." Her "adventure" records only one version of Behn's love story, but we find it repeated whenever she writes within what Rachel Blau DuPlessis calls the conventional endings for women in narrative—namely, marriage or death.[10] It constitutes the romance plot without the woman's passion for the simple reason that woman's passion had no way to direct its energies down the path of woman's desire. This is not to say that Behn did not write about passionate women, women who could indeed direct their desires and direct them powerfully. But when her women characters did so, they exceeded the plot of romance, and Behn herself ended up producing something more like the kind of sensational fiction that we find in *Agnes de Castro, The History of the Nun,* or *The Dumb Virgin.* These are not "boy meets girl, boy gets girl" narratives. These are not versions of "Reader, I married him." These are translations of a very different kind of darkness, one that Behn translated with a vengeance.

The Fair Jilt is a story of loving with a vengeance.[11] As Behn herself puts it, "I'll prove to you the strong Effects of Love in some unguarded and ungovern'd Hearts; where it rages beyond the inspirations of *a God all soft and gentle*, and reigns more like *a Fury from Hell*" (5:74). In many ways, this version of love is just the opposite of what we encountered in *The Black Lady*, for there love is nothing, and here it is too much. For Behn, the "Impossibility" of speaking about love, of writing love, meant that love was either lacking or excessive—that it was not there at all or that it reigned like a fury. In her *Love-Letters to a Gentleman*, Behn situated herself between saying this and saying that, proclaiming one thing and then another to Hoyle, ending up wondering if it " 'twere better" that "I had been for ever silent." In *The Fair Jilt*, we have a woman who, far from being caught in this impossible position, enjoys the position of Hoyle, the position of the man. Miranda, bringing both of her lovers to ruin and near death, finally comes out on top. In fact, she has it all, just as Behn imagined Hoyle had when she described him in her poem "Our Cabal" as "that haughty Swain, / With many Beauties in a Train," constantly preparing for "New Victories" while he "leaves the Old to its Despairs."[12] Love, in this poem, is envisioned as conquest, and Hoyle is the ultimate victor simply by virtue of what he has managed to conquer:

Success his Boldness does renew,
And Boldness helps him Conquer too,
He having gain'd more hearts than all
Th' rest of the Pastoral Cabal.

So with Miranda. A young maid in a convent, a dazzling beauty who quickly becomes the object of every lover's desire, she too is a "Black Lady" who haunts Behn's love stories. "She was tall, and admirably shaped; she had a bright Hair, and Hazle-Eyes, all full of Love and Sweetness. . . . Every Look, every Motion charm'd, and her black Dress shew'd the Lustre of her Face and Neck" (5:76). Yet although she is the object of every man's desire, her own love is fuelled by power: "thousands of People were dying by her Eyes, while she was vain enough to glory in her Conquests, and make it her Business to wound" (5:77).

Miranda's first conquest is a young friar (formerly dashing Prince

Hendrick) whom she tries to seduce through, interestingly, the writing of love letters. But as Miranda writes, the friar remains silent, making "no return," thus only urging her to write more, and to write more passionately: "she ceas'd not to pursue him with her Letters, varying her Style; sometimes all wanton, loose and raving; sometimes feigning a Virgin-Modesty all over, accusing her self, blaming her Conduct. . . . But still she writes in vain, in vain she varies her Style, by a Cunning, peculiar to a Maid possess'd with such a sort of Passion" (5:89). When the letters do not work, she decides to confront him openly in the confessional, where she presents herself "to his View the most wondrous Object of Beauty he had ever seen" (5:91). And there she tells him: "my dear Father . . . I love with a Violence which cannot be contain'd within the Bounds of Reason, Moderation, or Virtue. I love a Man whom I cannot possess without a Crime, and a Man who cannot make me happy without being perjur'd" (5:91). And here again, we hear echoes of the love letters to Hoyle: my love is impossible.

But the situation in *The Fair Jilt* is strikingly different. Now it is the woman who will openly direct her desire. When the friar refuses Miranda's solicitations, refuses to be the object of her desire, she "snatch[es] him in her Arms," giving him "a thousand Kisses." She then puts out all the candles, pulls the young friar into her lap, and cries "*A Rape!*" (5:93–94). The friar is imprisoned and brought to trial, condemned to be burned, then given a reprieve, and throughout the remainder of the narrative languishes "in Prison, in a dark and dismal Dungeon." Meanwhile "*Miranda,* cured of her Love, was triumphing in her Revenge, expecting and daily giving new Conquests" (5:97).

Miranda has it all—love, conquest, revenge, and more love. If her love letters to the friar did not secure her his love, the court has nonetheless—even with her letters as evidence against her—ruled in her favor. The text of love is the text of victory—exactly what it had not been for Behn herself in writing to Hoyle, exactly what it had been for Hoyle, who maintained his power over Behn by ensuring that she continually write to him. It is tempting to think that Behn took her revenge on Hoyle through Miranda, indeed through the friar himself, whose vows of chastity made him as inaccessible to Miranda as Hoyle's homosexuality made him inaccessible to Behn.

Strong as this biographical narrative may seem, the important message here, I believe, is that through Miranda, Behn was able to direct feminine desire differently, to rescript the love story so that writing itself is not only possible but victorious.

To use DuPlessis's terms, Behn's strategy here may well constitute a form of "writing beyond the ending"—beyond, that is, the conventional closures (death and marriage) reserved for women in narrative. If women cannot find a space for directing their desire in the conventional love story, indeed in life itself, then Behn will write them—or at least some of them—into the position of conqueror. Yet a woman's move from the position of object to subject is hardly an uncomplicated one, at least as Behn negotiated this move in her fiction. Other women characters appear on the scene, fracturing any unified entity of woman as subject and revealing the struggles Behn encountered in making women into subjects who direct their own desires. We see this happening throughout the remainder of *The Fair Jilt,* as Miranda pursues her next amour, Prince Tarquin, newly arrived from his travels throughout France and Germany—"a Prince of mighty Name, and fam'd for all the Excellencies of his Sex . . . a Prince young and gloriously attended" (5:97). They fall in love, Tarquin "entirely . . . conquer'd by this Fair One," and soon marry (5:100). When Miranda's father dies shortly thereafter, he leaves his fortune to both Miranda and her sister, the other woman to emerge in this love story. Alcidiana is "about fourteen Years of Age" and is now under the guardianship of her sister, Miranda, and the prince (5:101).

The relationship between the two sisters fast deteriorates—in part because of Miranda's squandering of their fortunes and in part because Miranda refuses to let her sister marry a young count. Meanwhile Alcidiana, refusing to remain a "Slave to the Tyranny of her Sister" (5:102), runs away to marry the count. Yet just as Alcidiana breaks through on her own, directing her own schemes and desires, Miranda vows to stop her at any cost and ultimately plans for her sister's murder.

After two unsuccessful murder attempts—one in which Miranda sets up a young page to poison Alcidiana, the other in which she begs her husband to shoot her sister at the theater—Miranda "at last confess'd all her Life" (5:117), including the truth about her deceit with the young friar, who happens to be with them in the same prison and is now happily released. Whereas Miranda now sinks in the public eye, Tarquin, condemned to death for his attempted murder of Alcidiana, rises, attracting "all the Compassion and Pity imaginable" (5:117). Alcidiana survives, yet Tarquin must face execution. And here the story takes some sensational twists.

For Prince Tarquin, it turns out, survives the attempted execution, the axe having struck him too low in the shoulder to have effectively beheaded him. He is carried off by a jubilant crowd. His friends promise him their assistance only if he will abandon Miranda, and although he secretly vows to himself never to do so, he complies with his friends' urgings. Meanwhile Alcidiana, "extremely afflicted for having been the Prosecutor of this great Man" (5:123), now seeks to gain his pardon and that of her sister. It seems she receives sufficient money from Miranda to marry after all and thus receives her happy ending.

And, in a sense, so do both Miranda and Tarquin, both finally receiving pardons. Publicly resolving "never to live with the Fair Hypocrite more," Tarquin nonetheless sends Miranda a letter before he departs, urging her to follow him to Holland, where, it seems, they will live happily ever after "retir'd to a Country-House" (5:123–24). We read very little about this happy ending except a few descriptive comments in the story's closing paragraphs, where we learn that Tarquin "liv'd as a Private Gentleman, in all the Tranquility of a Man of good Fortune" and that Miranda had "been very penitent for her Life past" and now lives in a "perfect State of Happiness" (5:124). If the story were to stop here, we would indeed have the ending of romance—not simply marriage, but happy marriage, happy ending. But the final line of Behn's story breaks through this closure: "Since I began this Relation," the narrator tells us, "I heard that Prince *Tarquin* dy'd about three Quarters of a Year ago."

Several important issues emerge here at the end of this narrative that can help us come to terms with Behn's struggle in writing the narrative of a woman's love. First, we need to return—again and again in Behn's fiction—to the troubling relationships among her female characters, especially when one betrays the other so powerfully as Miranda does Alcidiana. As I suggested earlier, there is a doubling of women characters that has the effect of fracturing female identity—that is, a division of women into different roles that allow them to assume different positions as subjects and objects in the love story. Just as Catherine Gallagher suggests that Behn had to forge an identity for herself in writing plays,[13] so I would suggest that Behn seeks various identities in her love stories. The problem, however, is that in these fictions of love, none of the identities prove entirely satisfactory. For if we position ourselves with Alcidiana, we are once again in the role of victim or, at best, of the young beauty who will find her place in the conventional ending of marriage. Then again, if we position ourselves with Miranda, we become victor; indeed, we become villain. In terms of the narrative, we assume the traditional male role in love stories built on conquest.

Second, the very theme of fracturing, indeed of mutilation, needs to be rethought in Behn. For while she certainly draws here on traditions in sensational romance and the revenge tragedy of an earlier age, much contemporary feminist theory posits that a woman's turning on her own body is a symptom of her very inability to express her body's urgings and desires. The hysteric rarely lashes out at her oppressor but instead turns her anger and frustration within, her body becoming the very site of her vengeance. In *The Fair Jilt*— indeed, as in *Oroonoko*—this scenario takes on a curious twist, for Behn projects the frustrations and sheer angst of her female characters onto the male's body. Thus it is Tarquin, not Miranda, who suffers bodily mutilation in his thwarted execution. This, too, seems to me to constitute yet a further fracturing of the female identity, for the most appealing and attractive character in *The Fair Jilt* is clearly Prince Tarquin. If I am correct in suggesting that Behn turned to fiction to explore the problematic dynamics of women's loving, then it is curious that the character who, in this story, is capable of enduring love is not the woman at all but the man. Could it be, then, that Behn's frustration about women's inability to direct their own desires was so intense that she finally had to project their desires onto men? This seems to be exactly what happens in both *The Adventures of the Black Lady* and in *The Fair Jilt*, where Fondlove and Tarquin (indeed, even the young friar) ultimately satisfy their desires.

In *The Fair Jilt*, however, I feel convinced that Behn was determined to write beyond this ending, and she does so by adding that rather shocking last sentence, "I heard that Prince *Tarquin* dy'd about three Quarters of a Year ago," ensuring Miranda's conquest after all.

But what happens to Miranda? Behn leaves her here, beyond the ending of this narrative, beyond any further authorial comment on this woman's desire. Just as Miranda's fate remains a question, so, I would argue, does Behn's struggle to create women as desiring subjects. Should Miranda be perceived as the victor or as a woman continually dissatisfied with her place in the script of love?

In one of her most admired poems, "Love Arm'd," Behn personifies love as a god surrounded by bleeding hearts that have fallen victim to his tyrannical power. Her vision of love as a ruthless conquerer is revealing enough, but what is just as revealing is Behn's vision of herself in this scene:

> Love in Fantastique Triumph satt,
> Whilst Bleeding Hearts a round him flow'd.
> For whom Fresh paines he did Create,
> And strange Tyranick power he show'd;
> From thy Bright Eyes he took his fire,
> Which round about, in sport he hurl'd;
> But 'twas from mine he took desire,
> Enough to undo the Amorous World.
>
> From me he took his Sighs and tears,
> From thee his Pride and Crueltie;
> From me his Languishments and Feares,
> And every Killing Dart from thee;
> Thus thou and I, the God have arm'd,
> And sett him up a Deity;
> But my poor Heart alone is harm'd,
> Whilst thine the Victor is, and free.[14]

Male and female roles in this story are very different from each other. For the man not only feeds love's power with his bright eyes, pride, and cruelty but himself gains just these offerings in return. The woman, however, ends up in a position of total loss. Love has taken from her sighs and tears, languishments and fears, has taken from her "desire" itself, and she receives nothing in return.

But what can she possibly receive in a game in which only the man can make the moves? What can she possibly say when only the man can assume the position of speaking? She can write and write— as Hoyle forced Behn to do, as many women writers have continually done—trying to retrieve what love has "undone" in her "Amorous World."

Luce Irigaray describes her own task in the "liberation of women" as an attempt "to go back through the masculine imaginary, to interpret the way it has reduced us to silence . . . [and] from that starting point and at that same time, to (re) discover a possible space for the feminine imaginary." She says that we need to do this so that women can "begin to escape from the spaces, roles, and gestures that they have been assigned and taught by the society of men."[15] Behn's message is that we need to go back through the feminine imaginary as well, especially now, when the feminist literary movement provides us with the means for reading and understanding women's texts and contexts. From this perspective, we can see Behn's romantic fiction providing her with generic opportunities to explore her own peculiar fictions of desire. Especially when read alongside her own narrative of love emerging in the letters to Hoyle, these fictions show women struggling with language and longing. They also trace the emergence of women as subjects—no matter how fractured—who attempt to direct their writing and desire. If we can discover possible spaces for the feminine imaginary, then Behn's fictions of women in love can show us how this particular female author, the first professional women writer in English, began to write from those impossible spaces.

Notes

1. See Luce Irigaray, *This Sex Which Is Not One,* trans. Catherine Porter (Ithaca: Cornell Univ. Press, 1985); Peggy Kamuf, *Fictions of Feminine Desire: Disclosures of Heloise* (Lincoln: Univ. of Nebraska Press, 1982); Nancy Armstrong, *Desire and Domestic Fiction: A Political History of the Novel* (New York: Oxford University Press, 1987); and Patricia Meyer Spacks, *Desire and Truth: Functions of Plot in Eighteenth-Century English Novels* (Chicago: Univ. of Chicago Press, 1990).

2. Linda S. Kauffman, *Discourses of Desire: Gender, Genre, and Epistolary Fictions* (Ithaca: Cornell Univ. Press, 1986), p. 17; Domna Stanton, *The Female Autograph* (New York: New York Literary Forum, 1984). See also Felicity Nussbaum, *The Autobiographical Subject: Gender and Ideology in Eighteenth-Century England* (Baltimore: Johns Hopkins Univ. Press, 1989).

3. Kauffman, *Discourses of Desire,* p. 17.

4. George Woodcock, *Aphra Behn: The English Sappho* (Montreal: Black Rose Books, 1989), p. 105. (Previously published as *The Incomparable Aphra* [London: T. V. Boardman, 1948]).

5. Vita Sackville-West, *Aphra Behn: The Incomparable Astrea* (New York: Russell and Russell, 1927), pp. 53–54.

6. Woodcock, *Aphra Behn*, p. 107. For further biographical information about Behn and Hoyle, see Maureen Duffy, *The Passionate Shepherdess: Aphra Behn, 1640–89* (London: Methuen, 1989); William J. Cameron, *New Light on Aphra Behn* (n.p.: Arden Library, 1979), and Angeline Goreau, *Reconstructing Aphra: A Social Biography of Aphra Behn* (New York: Dial Press, 1980).

7. Woodcock, *Aphra Behn*, p. 113.

8. *Love-Letters to a Gentleman*, in *The Plays, Histories, and Novels of the Ingenious Mrs. Aphra Behn* (London: John Pearson, 1871), pp. 54–72. Subsequent references to this edition will be cited parenthetically in the text by page number.

9. *The Adventures of the Black Lady*, in *The Works of Aphra Behn*, ed. Montague Summers, 6 vols. (1915; rpt. New York: Benjamin Blom, 1967), 5:1–10. Subsequent references to this edition will be cited parenthetically in the text by volume and page number.

10. See Rachel Blau DuPlessis, *Writing beyond the Ending: Narrative Strategies of Twentieth-Century Women Writers* (Bloomington: Indiana Univ. Press, 1985).

11. *The Fair Jilt*, in *The Works of Aphra Behn*, ed. Summers, 5:67–124. Subsequent references to this edition will be cited parenthetically in the text by volume and page number.

12. For the poem and a discussion of its context, see Woodcock, *Aphra Behn*, p. 106.

13. Catherine Gallagher, "Who Was That Masked Woman? The Prostitute and the Playwright in the Comedies of Aphra Behn," in *Women's Studies* 15 (1988): 23–42. (This essay is reprinted above in this volume.)

14. For the poem and a discussion of its context, see Woodcock, *Aphra Behn*, pp. 117–18.

15. Irigaray, *This Sex Which Is Not One*, p. 164.

Poetry

JUDITH KEGAN GARDINER

Liberty, Equality, Fraternity: Utopian Longings in Behn's Lyric Poetry

Aphra Behn was a poet of astonishing range and accomplish-ment.[1] In her own time she was praised primarily as a poet, and she hoped that posterity would place her with "Sappho and Orinda" in a female lineage of poetry and in the ageless pantheon of fame.[2] She awed men with her talent and fluency and inspired other women to write. Her later reputation is almost entirely as a playwright and pioneer novelist, however.[3] "With their feeble personification and insipid allegory, almost all" of her poems are "equally dull," com-plained critic Edward Wagenknecht in the early twentieth century. "And she—poor lady!—considered herself a poet first of all."[4] To-day's feminists prefer her vigorous polemics in behalf of herself and other women to her lyrics on more traditional topics.[5] However, her poetry forms a distinctive part of her oeuvre that should be more highly valued.

In this poetry, traditional tropes of heterosexual love present a longing for community, for a society in which the radical values of liberty, equality, and fraternity would be possible for women and defined in women's terms.[6] Of anomalous social position, Behn my-thologized her family of origin, her personal past, and her nation's history; her poetry created a world in which a woman like herself could flourish.[7] She contextualized her longings for a more just and fulfilling life not in Restoration England at large but only in a coterie of fellow poets and a realm of poetry, a pretty pastoral world that took shape in the printed book. In this as in many other respects, she is similar to the other best-known seventeenth-century woman poet, Katherine Philips—known as Orinda, as Behn was known as Astraea —and both women write within the traditions of seventeenth-century lyric established earlier in the century by the canonical male poets John Donne and Ben Jonson.[8] Such similarities between the more private and more public female poets help us understand how for the seventeenth century, the public and private were overlapping rather than polarized: Behn's poetry circulated in manuscripts among friends, was sung on the stage, and reappeared in published books.[9] Such poetry calls into question the categories of public and private often used to organize seventeenth-century literary history and also many conventional literary judgments, for example, those exalting the verisimilar over the artificial and the passionate over the playful.[10]

Behn's best known and most widely admired poem is "Love Arm'd," a song from her 1677 play *Abdelazar.*

> Love in Fantastique Triumph satt,
> Whilst Bleeding Hearts a round him flow'd,
> For whom Fresh paines he did Create,
> And strange Tyranick power he show'd;
> From thy Bright Eyes he took his fire,
> Which round about, in sport he hurl'd;
> But 'twas from mine he took desire,
> Enough to undo the Amorous World.
>
> From me he took his sighs and tears,
> From thee his Pride and Crueltie;
> From me his Languishments and Feares,
> And every Killing Dart from thee;
> Thus thou and I, the God have arm'd,
> And sett him up a Deity;
> But my poor Heart alone is harm'd,
> Whilst thine the Victor is, and free.[11]

The poem succeeds by the standards of cavalier poetry, expressing turbulent erotic passions in elegantly concise and self-contained tetrameter quatrains. The first quatrain paints an emblem. Personified love sits in a triumphal throne or chariot as in a classical victory pageant or a Renaissance masque, both spectacles of power. Love is a conquering hero at the expense of others who have lost. His "Fantastique Triumph" is both extraordinary and imaginary: The effective trisyllabic *fantastic* implies both the exaggerated power of love and its origin in the lovers' mental constructs. Love is the creator, although he creates pain rather than the universal harmony attributed to God by Milton's *Paradise Lost,* which appeared a few years before Behn began publishing. Therefore, love's alien and uncanny "strange" power is "tyrannic"—that is, both absolute and unjust. The seventeenth-century's frequent changes of political regime would certainly have left nearly everyone in Restoration England thinking that they had recently lived under a tyranny of one sort or the other, either Puritan or Royalist. "Tyranny" would not be a dead metaphor, then, but a lively reminder of being at the mercy of people and events beyond one's individual control, of political as well as personal passions. Milton makes Satan a grand tyrant, but Behn domesticates such cosmic references; similarly, she alludes to the baroque splendors of God enthroned and Christ's bleeding heart by painting images that recall contemporary baroque churches while keeping her lyric resolutely modest and secular.

The poem's great power derives from the contrast between its painful and exaggerated sentiments and a controlled and orderly form that seems to accept this situation as proper, normal, perhaps even necessary. The beloved's eyes are the source of love's fire, and love seems to enjoy the pure exercise of his power, hurling lightning bolts "in sport," a gesture huge and reckless enough to balance the lover's eyes, which are filled with enough "desire" to "undo the amorous world." The neat balances of "from me" and "from thee" break down, however. "To undo" is the opposite of creation, perhaps a synonym for the creation of pain, though unlike the woman undone by sexual indiscretion in Restoration London, the wounded lover is not abandoned and alone but is surrounded by bleeding hearts, as though the whole universe is wounded by love.

Similar patterns remain important throughout Behn's poetry: The woman always wants reciprocity, as does the lover of either sex; the man or the beloved wants freedom. Behn frequently depicts relationships of equality that degenerate, perhaps because it is so hard for her to imagine reciprocity and equality in a society devoid of them in which only sexual passion seems to offer the possibility of ecstatic reciprocity.[12] The carefully balanced "me" and "thee" in this poem seem to keep the relationship between the lovers as even as the meter, against the sense, so that the contrast between the poem's form and its emotional content reproduces the dilemma of the woman who is told that a relationship is equal at the same time that she feels more constrained than her lover both psychologically and socially. Equality is defined on his terms: Either lover can enter or leave the relationship at will, but the woman becomes emotionally more attached and more vulnerable because of possible pregnancy or loss of reputation—events such poems do not mention directly.

The phrase "thus thou and I" in the concluding quatrain works syllogistically in the fashion of the best seventeenth-century lyrics, although its conclusions do not spring logically from what has occurred before; instead, the logic is that implied simply by the combination "thou and I"—that is, by the desire that subordinates the lover to the beloved's power. "Thou and I" invent the god and shape its being. Without such deification, Love might be fair rather than tyrannical and sadistic. Once again the apparent union and reciprocity of the lovers breaks down into a power imbalance of female victimage. As Behn emphasizes by the pause late in the poem's last line, to be "free" from reciprocal claims is to be victorious over the committed. A poem written around the time of the English Revolution might well champion freedom although it appears equivocal about its meaning for women. Paradoxically, to be free may be possible only for the victorious, only for tyrants who keep others enslaved. Freedom may also only be possible for the dispassionate, those so cool that they do not care. Throughout her life Behn defended sexual passion as peremptory but also as central to human satisfaction. In a poem "To Desire" she could address it as an old but difficult friend, "thou haunts my inconvenient hours" (6:356), and, in her paraphrase of the Lord's prayer, she famously expected divine indulgence for an eroticism she could not seriously believe was sinful:

Of all my Crimes, the breach of all thy Laws
Love, soft bewitching Love! has been the cause
. . . That sure will soonest be forgiven of God.
(6:374)

In its original context, "Love Arm'd" opens Behn's heroic drama *Abdelazar*, where it is sung by the Queen of Spain, who is foolishly in love with a disdainful Moor who became her lover only for political reasons and who now rebuffs her (2:1–98). The song thus sets up Behn's goal of reciprocal emotion, indicated in meter and word patterning, against a context of power that vitiates reciprocity between men and women. Even though the woman is the active wooer and a queen, she is powerless against a foolish passion for a tyrannic man, and she thus colludes in the eroticizing of power on which this poem, and perhaps modern patriarchy, are based.

The context of that peculiar Restoration literary form, the heroic drama, mythologizes social contexts so that any heroine may be a queen; however, everyone in a play must be marked by class and gender, even if the classes and locale do not correspond to those of Restoration England. Lyric poems dissolve even this imaginary context into the freer space of the poetry anthology, in which "Love Arm'd" appears with no indication of who its speaker or beloved are. Even if love is tyrannical and unjust, such a world remains fair in the sense that the rules of love apparently apply to all lovers, whomever they may be. The roles are not gender-specific, and the lover clearly bears responsibility for the fix she or he is in because love's cruelty cannot exist without the cooperation of both parties. The miniature world of "Love Arm'd" is a cruel but meaningful one, potentially sex-egalitarian but confusing about the conventional alignments of gender.

If the central dynamic of Behn's poetry is the longing for reciprocity in a world in which men and women hold unequal power, then "The Disappointment" (6:178–82) is a humorous meditation and an ironic revenge on those conditions. "The Disappointment" may also be seen as an opposite to "Love Arm'd." Where "Love Arm'd" may display the woman suffering from a man's power over her, "The Disappointment" shows a woman suffering from the one form of powerlessness that is specific to men, sexual impotence. The perfect reciprocity that Behn implies ought to exist in sexual love is denied for the woman of "The Disappointment" in two apparently contrasting but reinforcing ways—the man's physical power over her and his lack of power over his own body, a debility Behn heightens in comparison to her source, whose hero later becomes vigorously successful with his mistress.[13] Thus, unlike Ovid's *Amores* book 3, poem 7, the classical precursor of such poems, or the French "L'Occasion Perdue Recouverte" that Behn's poem partly translates, or even the earl of Rochester's brutal "The Imperfect Enjoyment," Behn's poem does not contrast an incident of male impotence with his otherwise exaggerated virility.[14]

Whereas "Love Arm'd" paints an emblematic fiction of a personified god, "The Disappointment" revels in another artificial world, one Behn creates frequently in her nondramatic verse—that of precious pastoral. Seventeenth-century pastoral is often reviled as artificial and "effeminate," because we moderns prefer forms that seem closer to a direct transcription of social life, the novel aesthetic and aesthetic of the novel form that Behn helped shape in the 1680s.[15] In this poem, however, Behn moves away from social realism, changing its setting from an interior "appartement" in her source to an outdoor "lone Thicket made for Love." This transformation indicates that Behn positively embraced the pastoral; it was not just something she translated for quick cash.

One twilight afternoon "Amorous *Lysander*" surprises "fair *Cloris*" in that lonely thicket, and he immediately starts making love to her. The poem's only direct discourse, which is italicized, occurs when Cloris protests against her lover's advances, beginning "*Cease, Cease—your vain Desire, / Or I'll call out.*" Because we hear Cloris's words directly, we may feel that it is the woman's consciousness to which we are closest in the poem. Only she speaks directly in Behn's poem, although not in the source, where her lover is voluble; the rest of Behn's "The Disappointment" is reported via an apparently female narrator. Such phrasing highlights female agency in the poem, but the situation is complicated. Behn alters her source to emphasize Lysander's passivity despite the fact that he is the aggressor in the affair: He is "o'er-Ravish'd" and 'too transported"; "Excess of Love his Love betray'd." Conversely, Cloris's protests against an apparent rape underline that what a woman says is not necessarily what she means, a view that may alienate Behn from today's women: The narrator insists, like the male lover in the poem, that Cloris means yes when she says no. The narrator, another woman, can correctly read a woman who is either constrained from knowing her feelings or restrained from expressing them by conventional standards of female propriety. Thus, the poem gives us two contradictory ways of reading female reliability and the correspondence of speech to feeling, of expression to passion—Cloris's and the narrator's.

What Lysander seeks is less a particular woman than a cosmic power centered in the female body:

> His daring Hand that Altar seiz'd,
> Where Gods of Love do sacrifice:
> That Awful Throne, that Paradice
> Where Rage is calm'd, and Anger pleas'd;
> That Fountain where Delight still flows,
> And gives the Universal World Repose.

Immediately thereafter, in a passage that Behn expands from her source, the lovers enjoy a union that is reciprocal, passionate, and simultaneously physical and emotional.

> Her Balmy Lips incountring his,
> Their Bodies, as their Souls, are joyn'd;
> Where both in Transports Unconfin'd
> Extend themselves upon the Moss.

The body language of the poem hints at the possibility of true reciprocity; her hand touches his breast—a touch Behn adds to the original—then his hers. In the moments building up to the humorous climax, we hear of idyllic pleasures that cannot be sustained, a wordless reciprocity where his body and hers first mirror one another and then melt and blend. The language describing their rapture echoes that of Donne's poems like "The Extasie," describing a union that transcends the mere flesh. And Cloris and Lysander melt into just such a perfect, perhaps even idyllically infantile union, one that nostalgically recalls the poetry written before the English Civil War, the rosy Elizabethan bloom. This initial period of union in "The Disappointment" is mutual and consensual. The poem's references to higher loves and historical allusions help create its context, not a spiritually transcendent realm but a lost garden of earthly pleasures.

At the crucial moment, however, "The too transported hapless Swain / Found the vast Pleasure turn'd to Pain." The woman responds:

Cloris returning from the Trance
Which Love and soft Desire had bred,
Her timerous Hand she gently laid
(Or guided by Design or Chance)
Upon that Fabulous *Priapus,*
That Potent God, as Poets feign;
But never did young Sherpherdess,
Gath'ring of Fern upon the Plain,
More nimbly draw her Fingers back,
Finding beneath the verdant Leaves a Snake:

Than *Cloris* her fair Hand withdrew,
Finding that God of her Desires
Disarm'd of all his Awful Fires,
And Cold as Flow'rs bath'd in the Morning Dew.
Who can the *Nymph*'s Confusion guess?

Like Lightning through the Grove she hies,
Or *Daphne* from the *Delphick* God.

The diction here is both erotic and witty. The primary joke is that
the disappointed woman runs away like a frightened virgin. The en-
comium to Priapus, classical god of the phallus, unlike the earlier one
to Cloris's "altar" of love, is both exaggerated and ironically undercut. Internal rhyme makes the "Fabulous Priapus" already comic,
and the alliterations of "that potent god, as poets feign" link male
poetry, faking, and the myths or fables that govern society.

If male power is the dominating fact over female life, male impotence may seem a balancing justice, a kind of cheery revenge—even
though part of the joke is that male impotence becomes another kind
of power, that of withholding pleasure from the woman, for whom
heterosexual pleasure is only available when he wants and when he
can. In the double binds that Behn so frequently shows men putting
women in, the man may well treat the woman as an object to be
discarded when he has had his pleasure, but he blames her even more
severely when he cannot have his pleasure. This approach contrasts
with Behn's source, where Cloris is angry but Lysander pledges eternal love and apologizes for his failing, explaining that her "*Beauty*" in
his "*Soul . . . joynd Respect and Love in one*" to cause his embarrassment (pp. 6–7). As the woman speaker of Behn's lyric "To *Alexis* in

Answer to his Poem against Fruition" (6:348–49) complains, women can't win against their male lovers:

> They fly if Honour take our part,
> Our Virtue drives 'em o're the field.
> We lose 'em by too much desert,
> And Oh! they fly us if we yeild.

In Behn's version of "The Disappointment," the man's anger at the woman is just as strong as if his lost satisfaction sprang from the lady's denial rather than from his own impotence. The narrator claims, "The *Nymph's* Resentments none but I / Can well Imagine or Condole." Cloris keeps these imagined resentments to herself, in contrast to the French poem, in which she insults her lover's "*Scottish Lump*" and calls him "*weakly mann'd*" (p. 5). Behn's Lysander does not plead with his woman or languish in despair but "curs'd his Birth, his Fate, his Stars; / But more the *Shepherdess's* Charms." In the French source, he blames first the devil and then Cloris's heavenly beauty. In Behn, he charges that Cloris's "Charms" or spells have bewitched him to the "*Hell* of Impotence"—hardly a benign reference in an age when male impotence was a common complaint against witches and women were hanged for witchcraft. Even though the woman within the poem is disappointed and blamed, however, the female narrative voice seems just a bit gleeful at the philanderer's discomfort.[16]

Critic Richard Quaintance assumes that when Behn varies from her source, she errs, a victim of poetic incompetence: "Checked by indifference, inability, or the economy of the stanza form she chose, she totally missed some of the sense as well as the words of her original," he lectures. If we assume, however, not that she misunderstood the tradition but that she wished to redirect it, we can understand her relation to the male poetic tradition through her changes from her source. Quaintance laments that Behn "has turned a success story, prolix and jolly, into . . . an object lesson on the risk of self-absorption during love, a pragmatic warning against acting in love with love while Cloris is waiting." Behn "may be blaming" the man "out of a feminine sympathy," he says, apparently without realizing that his own disappointment with the poem may be the result of a masculine sympathy that Behn's poem deliberately invokes and then mocks.[17] This sympathy springs from an identification with the male hero so strong that it causes the modern male critic to misread Behn's poem, in which, unlike the source, Lysander does not noticeably act self-absorbed or in love with love at all as "Mad to possess, himself he threw / On the Defenceless Lovely Maid."

Pastoral settings were associated especially with women authors and audiences in the Restoration; they were considered effete and phony by many men.[18] It makes sense, then, to consider its advantages for a female author like Behn, who translated continental pastorals like "The Golden Age" and who transferred other poems into pastoral settings. One advantage of the pastoral is that it reformulates social class. Supposedly set in the lowest class of rural society and often in a purportedly primitive stage of social evolution, the pastoral masks the real class imbalances of the contemporary urban scene. The theatrical set to which Behn belonged was a privileged slice of London where the classes could mix—but only while following certain rules that traded female sexual respectability for access to men of rank and wit.[19] Behn's pastoral games and identifications by initials play peekaboo with social class—advertising their acquaintance with titled men and women by references to "My Lady Morland" or "Sir R.O." but teasing us about unknown others so that our sexual voyeurism about who is currently sleeping with whom is conflated with our print-reading outsiders' voyeurism about the upper classes.

Modern privacy was being invented in Behn's historical period, privacy with reference to one's relations to God, to bodily functions, to reading, and to sex. One might even argue that the conventions of literary voyeurism helped create conventions of privacy and that silently watching people became assimilated with that other private and recently silent activity, reading.[20] Pornography increased in the late seventeenth century, as did female literacy and misogyny. Earlier in the century John Donne wrote intense, passionate, and apparently private love poetry, yet in his lyrics passionate love for a woman was often predicated on the man's seduction being overheard, his erotic behavior overseen, by another man, the reader's surrogate—even in those poems that protest being looked at or talked about. "For God's sake hold your tongue and let me love," the lover tells his friend in "The Canonization." In Donne's "The Extasie," a pastoral lyric that had enormous influence on later seventeenth-century writers, the lover invokes a male spectator "by love refined" who would stand "within convenient distance" to view the lover and his beloved in an ecstatic embrace.[21] Only in terms of this voyeurism can the world-denying perfection of Donne's sexual love be affirmed. Behn makes such hidden voyeurism explicit, often to deliberately pornographic effect; at the same time, she reveals and alters its gendered dynamics. Although the seventeenth-century woman is already accustomed to being a spectacle for male viewers, Behn's poetry subjects both men and women to the scandalizing attention accorded sexual objects. "On a Juniper Tree, cut down to make Busks" (6:148–50) develops this erotic theme, covertly combining it with a convention of religious personification.

By adopting the persona of a juniper tree, Behn recalls Christian poems about the true cross while seeming to evade gender completely. The tree begins the poem by boasting that it was "The Pride and Glory of the Wood," then that its glory springs from its role in a sexual encounter between two lovers. "Beneath my shade the other day, / Young *Philocles* and *Cloris* lay." At one point the juniper sees itself as a "Rival Shade" to the lover and hence as male; it finds the woman desirable, steals kisses from her, and wants to be near her, echoing male erotic poetry from Catullus on. At another point it compares itself to women, however: "My Wealth, like bashful Virgins, I / Yielded with some Reluctancy." Insofar as Behn's voice sounds behind the personification, such allusions to virginity are ironized. The tree further claims to be the pander, duenna, and bridal chamber of the lovers all in one; the editors of *Kissing the Rod* note that in revising the poem, Behn made the woman's role more active.[22]

> Upon my Root she lean'd her head,
> And where I grew, he made their Bed:
> Whilst I the Canopy more largely spread.

Although by bending down its branches, the tree "had the blisse, / To rob the Shepherd of a kiss," Behn portrays the ideal sexuality between the lovers as completely mutual and reciprocal, not stealthy, a Donne-like merger of bodies and feelings:

> [The lovers] mingled melting Rays,
> Exchanging Love a thousand ways.

Kind was the force on every side,
. . .

His panting Breast, to hers now join'd,
They feast on Raptures unconfin'd;
Vast and Luxuriant, such as prove
The Immortality of Love.
For who but a Divinitie,
Could mingle Souls to that Degree;
And melt 'em into Extasie?
Now like the *Phenix,* both Expire,
While from the Ashes of their Fire,
Sprung up a new and soft desire.

(6:149–50)

The poem runs through a medley of motifs best-known from Donne's love poetry: melted souls, an ecstasy, a phoenix, and the play with religious language. In Behn's version, however, "immortality" alludes not to divine truth but simply to the renewed desire for sex: Her lovers "did invoke, / The God! and thrice new vigor took." After three bouts the woman humorously expresses doubts about her complaisance. Fortunately for her, her lover is still devoted to her. For him, "Loves sacred flame, / Before and after was the same"—clearly a utopian wish from Behn's viewpoint, as many of her poems register disappointment that men are so much less interested in women after than before the act.

After recording the lovers' perfect union, the tree returns to its perverse role: "The Shepherdess my Bark carest, / Whilst he my Root, Love's Pillow, kist." Andrew Marvell plays on such images of "vegetable love" more metaphysically in "The Garden," for example, in which the solitary speaker boasts that "Stumbling on melons, as I pass, / Ensnared with flowers, I fall on grass."[23] Whereas Marvell's speaker transcends the libertine garden tradition for the purer joys of contemplation, only sexual voyeurism provides Behn's tree a semblance of pleasure. Nature in Behn's poetry has no independent joys and needs human sexual love to animate it. Behn's pastoral is antinatural and thoroughly anthropomorphic. If, in the words that Pope so memorably rewrote, Behn calls "Wit . . . no more than *Nature* well exprest" (6:404), one might also say that for her, nature was little more than human wit well expressed in poetry.

After the lovers leave the woods, the juniper tree is desolate:

284

And if before my Joyes were such,
In having heard, and seen too much,
My Grief must be as great and high
When all abandon'd I shall be,
Doom'd to a silent Destinie
. . .
No more a joyful looker on.

Woefully isolated, the tree wants to participate not just in sex but in the human community. Bereft, the tree cries "Christal Dew" over Cloris. She responds as to a lover, with "Pity" because her "Soul is made of Love." Her loving response is ironic, however, that of a metamorphosing Ovidian god who objectifies lovers.

She cut me down, and did translate,
My being to a happier state.
No Martyr for Religion di'd
With half that Unconsidering Pride
[as the tree did].[24]

The tree's top is burned for incense, while its

body into Busks was turn'd:
Where I still guard the Sacred Store,
And of Loves Temple keep the Door.[25]

Thus the juniper ends up as part of a woman's corset, a homey, familiar, and humorous counterpart to other poetic metamorphoses or ways of getting near the beloved. Here the tree continues to act as pander or duenna, the complicit third to others' erotic coupling, or as a member of the woman's family, guarding her virtue.

The entire poem is an extended personification in tetrameter couplets, a light form appropriate for a bit of pastoral pornography. As a perversely enthusiastic voyeur, Behn's juniper is not simply part of a lush, natural setting, as we would expect from a tree, but participates, like the reader, in the pleasures of vicarious sex. As frequently happens in Behn's soft porn, the tree's voyeurism is satirically presented yet not undercut, and the poem invites the reader to engage in such dubious pleasures—admittedly weaker pleasures than those the lovers experience, but stronger and more pleasant fare than readers normally receive. Such pornography celebrates the joys of peeking more than the joys of sex; it depends on and incites a sense of sexual behavior as secret, forbidden, and titillating—more so, for example, than in erotic medieval fabliaux, where sexual couples are often humourously and publicly caught in the act.

Behn writes in one tradition of Donne, the tradition of witty erotic verse. This tradition is firmly androcentric, making women its objects, and hence it is difficult for women to take it seriously. Behn does not. Instead, she uses the pastoral setting to create alternatives to the world around her. One might argue that an identification with artifice works better than an identification with nature for women because women have too often been inscribed within a restrictive definition of nature, and the social as constituted in Behn's time was no better: Appeal to an artificial nature conspicuously unlike any nature one could see in contemporary London or in the countryside around it defines her pastoral.[26] In poems like "The Disappointment" and "On a Juniper Tree," Behn creates a nature that responds to women's as well as men's desires; however, it never aspires, as does the nature of some male Restoration writers, to the sublime. The limits against which her poetry strives are not those of the intractable flesh, because she implies that social restrictions, not those of nature, limit women most. To concede that the limits imposed on women were natural would be to give up the possibility of being a woman poet altogether.[27]

Behn in this respect differs dramatically from her friend and patron John Wilmot, the Earl of Rochester, a man who had everything except a conviction of the value of anything, a cynic who asked transcendental questions because social power was so clearly already his that his dissatisfaction had to reach beyond it. For Restoration women, who did not have everything and could not get it, Rochester's pose made no sense. Such women did not probe the paradoxes of embodiment in literature because they were always already assumed to be identical with their bodies; they therefore needed instead to explore the overcoming of embodiment. Moreover, women like Behn did not share male disgust with human flesh, although at the end of the century many women championed chastity over the difficulties of marriage. This disparity in the perspectives of male and female writers in the seventeenth century perhaps accounts in part for male critics' judgment that women's poetry of the period is shallow. Such critics may take the social order for granted and hence underestimate its restrictive powers on women, especially for women who do not respond to these restrictions by seeking social revolution. Restoration women did not, like some men of the time, need to seek in sexual experience a loss of identity they could find nowhere else, because they found loss of identity everywhere.[28] Like male poets erotic and mystic, women writers did seek ideal unions. They were much more likely than the men to dwell primarily on the reciprocity within union, however, perhaps otherwise fearing that in sex and religion as well as in marriage, the one flesh and one spirit of the joined couple would always be his. For a sense of reciprocity and fluidity, some religious women turned to a flexibly gendered God.[29] Secular women writers like both Behn and Phillips instead renamed themselves and others as a way of moving out of their defined social circumstances into new and ideal imaginary communities where they could be equal participants with other artists, lovers, and friends.

A crucial biographical fact about Behn is her social isolation from the usual familial supports at the time she became a professional author. Whereas other women writers relied on the categories of virgin, wife, or mother to provide them acceptability, Behn had no husband and no known husband's relatives, as other widows did, no children, and no known family of origin; this apparent familial vacuum indicates deliberate effort on her part to obfuscate those facts that would fix her social identity.[30] Instead, she springs from nowhere onto the stage, via South America, Continental spying, and jail. Gossips around her assumed that such a self-made woman must be man-made. Contemporaries alleged that her works were written by male lovers, and even some modern feminist editors cannot resist categorizing her as a prostitute: "There is no evidence that she chose the profession of writing: there is every sign that she was reduced to making a living by her wits. We may honour her for refusing the other obvious alternative, prostitution, if only we could be sure that she did."[31] If we look at the literary consequences of Behn's self-creation rather than worry its sexual economics, however, we see that such self-creation in a closed and hierarchical society demands the simultaneous creation of a new social order into which the new self fits. In their oriental courts, European carnivals, and American wildernesses, Behn's plays partially reformulate their societies, but the poetry is freer still to invent idealized, imaginary worlds.

In Behn's erotic poetry, sexual knowledge creates its own community of values. In "The Willing Mistress" (6:163), for example, after mutual kissing, the woman is "willing to receive / That which I dare not name." Her lover's eyes alone "tell their softning Tale" to woo her; without words he "lay'd me gently on the Ground, / Ah who can guess the rest?" The poem, an entirely verbal construction, describes an experience that claims to be entirely physical, unmediated by language. But the poem works only by its appeal to a linguistic community that can freely and easily translate the physical into a shared verbal world. We all already must know what "that which I dare not name" must be, and the final rhetorical question solicits the smug answer that all of us readers can "guess the rest." The shared joke requires shared knowledge, not of the idiosyncracies of any individual lover but of physical experience common to us all, and it expects us to laugh, too, at conventional verbal and social structures that pretend that we, including the women among the poem's readers, do not all know what sex is about and enjoy it equally well.

One possible community in opposition to patriarchal Restoration society was that of closely bonded women; that is, the society that Behn's poetic predecessor Katherine Philips tried to create in her poetry and in her life.[32] Like Philips, Behn eroticizes female friendships, most notably in "To the Fair *Clarinda,* who made Love to me, imagin'd more than Woman" (6:363). That poem, however, equates the "weak" with the "Feminine" and assumes a heterosexual norm so strong that female bonds are necessarily "innocent" and derivative on heterosexual models:

> without Blushes I the Youth persue,
> When so much beauteous Woman is in view,
> . . .
> In pity to our Sex sure thou we'rt sent,
> That we might Love, and yet be Innocent.

Apparent innocence, as always in Behn, nods to the community of readers in the know: "For sure no Crime with thee we can commit; / Or if we shou'd—thy Form excuses it."

More frequently, Behn expresses ties to women not through coupled relationships but indirectly through sexual triangles in which her female speakers typically cast themselves as the other woman, a discarded mistress. Older and less attractive than her rival, such a woman ingratiates herself with the rival by praising her and complaining about the man. Because she draws herself and the fickle male lover as morally equivalent, however, such praise ejects the rival into a superior but distant position above the speaker and her former lover. This sexual triangle made up of three people of both sexes allows Behn to shift positions and identifications; she does not, like so many male poets, simply use it to elide the sexual other and return to homosocial bonding.[33]

In "To My Lady *Morland* at Tunbridge" (6:175–77), Behn establishes a parallel between crowds who come out to admire the conquering hero who won a war and those that stare at the famous beauties of the hour: "I wish'd to see, and much a Lover grew / Of so much Beauty, though my Rivals too." Submitting to the woman rival, not the lover, the speaker judges that "Not to love you, a wonder sure would be, / Greater then all his Perjuries to me." Traditional male love poetry allows its characters only two positions, and only one of them gets to speak: Transfixed by a female beauty, the male lover gazes and spouts verse. For a woman to look at a woman's beauty in this convention turns the woman into an envious rival eager to replace the first woman. In "To Damon," (6:345–48), "Mrs. *A. B.*" rejects the position of being a sexual object lulled by "all those usual flatteries" praising her "face and Eyes" (6:346). Instead, the position of rival allows her to look actively at the other woman; as in other poems, like "To *Lysander* at the *Musick-Meeting*," the female speaker can gaze admiringly at a man, feeding her "greedy Eyes" with his "Heav'nly Form" (6:207–8). In "To My Lady *Morland*" the speaker moves from a male erotic pose to a male heroic one, echoing Caesar's famous boast only to reverse its narcissism and grandiosity; she becomes the conquered, not the conqueror. "I came and saw, and blest my Destiny; / I found it Just you should out-Rival me."[34] As she continues to praise the rival, however, she begins to undermine the rival's liaison with the lover to which at first she seemed to acquiesce. Claiming only the best of motives, she suggests that the rival deserves to have a better suitor than her own former lover; she deserves, in fact, a "Virgin-Heart," not that used-up old rake, who would be better off returning to the speaker, his discarded mistress. Shakespeare's sonnets accustom us to poems in which an aging lover harangues and excuses a dishonest beloved about a lovely rival, though he genders his more complicated triangles differently. Another Behn poem switches positions in the sexual triangle in comparison with "To My Lady *Morland*." In "Selinda and Cloris," Selinda asks Cloris whether her "Friendship" or her "Jealousie" led her to confide that Selinda's lover first belonged to Cloris (6:375–78). Thus, Behn's poems link their female speakers with other women by means of a chain of lovers that expands into a network of complex emotional relationships.

By adopting a heroic stance, that of the brave soul who comes to see what to conquer, Behn's speakers set their loyal feudal values against greedy, selfish, and implicitly capitalistic ones.[35] Like Donne, Behn chastises the turning of personal relationships into commodities at the same time that she uses the language of the market to denounce unfair competition: "I hate Love-Merchants that a Trade wou'd drive," the female speaker responds in "To *Lysander*, on some Verses he writ, and asking more for his Heart then 'twas worth" (6:202–4). She lectures him about the true value that love should have:

> A Heart requires a Heart Unfeign'd and True,
> Though Subt'ly you advance the Price,
> And ask a Rate that Simple Love n'ere knew:
> And the free Trade Monopolize.

In this poem the speaker is explicitly a jealous woman, furious that her equally jealous male lover imposes faithful isolation on her while having affairs with other women:

> And every Hour still more unjust you grow,
> Those Freedoms you my life deny,
> You to *Adraste* are oblig'd to show,
> And give her all my Rifled Joy.

Miserable and alone, the speaker says that she feels the "Fragments" of the lover's "Softness," while the other woman, the better capitalist, "takes the welcome rich Return" on what was originally the first woman's investment. The rules are unfair, and Behn does not know how to make them fair on a woman's terms. Unable to find a vocabulary of equality that does not assume a male norm, the poem attacks the double standard:

Be just, my lovely *Swain,* and do not take
Freedoms you'll not to me allow;
Or give *Amynta* so much Freedom back:
That she may Rove as well as you.

The liberal language of freedom, justice, and equality appears to establish a fair standard, a standard to be aspired to, and Behn was clearly fascinated by the Restoration "Rover" or heroic philanderer, like the hero of her best-known play. One could not simply reverse the double standard by giving women permission to be as bad as men, however. What Behn wants instead is a community on her terms, an equality of mutual devotion that she imagines as free of capitalistic "interest": "Let us then love upon the honest Square, / Since Interest neither have designd." But the poem ends anticlimactically because the speaker can blast the hypocrisy of the double standard only by falling herself into the male role of mercenary scoundrel. "For the sly Gamester, who ne'er plays me fair / Must Trick for Trick expect to find." And, as mercenary interests are anathema to true love in Behn's scheme, so is jockeying for power: "A Pox of Foolish Politicks in Love," as "An *Ode* to *Love*" expostulates (6:208–9).

Behn's love poetry expresses a longing for community that is more overt in what we might call her fraternal poetry, and she seeks ideal reciprocity not only through sex but through the writing of poetry. She does not elaborate on the stresses the solitary poet faces while toiling to find rhymes at her lonely writing table. Instead, she describes the poetic craft as a collective one. By making explicit the favors poets do one another to give all of them more work and more pleasure, Behn produces a community of egalitarian insiders, a mutual admiration society.[36] By publishing these poems about poetry writing, she then invites us outsiders to be provisional members of this inner community or to enviously define ourselves by our exclusion.

"A Letter to a Brother of the Pen in *Tribulation*" (6:185–86) addresses the "Brother" from the viewpoint of one of the boys. The speaker asserts that friendship and the confraternity of writing are more important than sexual difference, although she agrees that sex can get one into trouble and, under the circumstances, the brother who caught venereal disease has a right to be angry at women: " 'tis but Just thou shouldst in Rancor grow / Against that Sex that has Confin'd thee so," she comforts him, although she is a member of "that sex" herself. If liberty is a value, then, being confined is intolerable, especially being confined not to the love of one woman but to the love of none and the nasty *"Sweating-Tub"* used to cure such diseases. Although Behn commiserates with her friend, she is also razzing him about his unlucky disease, clearly the fault of his own habits as well as the woman's, and she is willing to tease him with a sibling-like rivalry that accepts the poem's readers as its confidantes. Her cozy footnotes explain the inside references to us readers: "I wanted a Prologue to a Play," she says of the occasion for the poem, and she teases the brother by revealing the secret she has just found out; "He pretended to Retire to Write" when he was really recuperating from "An Interlude of Whoring."

Another fraternal poem is more casual, less competitive. "To *Damon*. To inquire of him if he cou'd tell me by the Style, who writ me a Copy of Verses that came to me in an unknown Hand" (6:345–48) links the female speaker with a male friend in a union that is more intimate than the one she may establish with her unknown suitor, the writer of an anonymous poem in her honor. The title assumes that the speaker's friend Damon knows all the likely male poets well enough to tell by the style, not just the handwriting, whose verses pique her interest, and she therefore seems to share with Damon an easy camaraderie that is itself free of sexual tensions and full of mutual confidences. The unknown lover, in turn, deserves her interest and respect because he chose to woo her entirely and unphysically through disembodied words. She says that before the poem arrived to disturb her, she was "Free as the Air, and calm as that," a perfectly inhuman kind of freedom she does not really relish, although she enjoyed a sabbatical from thinking about "the faithless sex," as she calls men, reversing their criticisms of women. That stoic composure was only a pose, she admits:

> calm and innocent I sate,
> Content with my indifferent fate
> (A Medium, I confess, I hate.)

The anonymous poem attracts her, she says, not because it was "fill'd with praises of my face and Eyes, / My verse, and all those usual flatteries" but through the quality of its verse, which she thinks reveals the "Soul" of the man. Her artistry necessarily matches his: "I drew him all the heart cou'd move." Then she falls in love with the "dear Idea" she has formed, a love that allies her with the greatest, if most foolish, of male artists, "*Pigmalion,*" who "for the charms he made, he sigh'd and burn'd." So Behn eroticizes not merely the object of poetry but also its author and poetry-making in itself. She shares a community with the recipient of her poem while asking him about the man who sent her one. Poems circulate, and Behn is both poet and subject of poetry, sender and receiver in a community of interpretation that is the basis of both love and friendship and in which Behn imagines herself in both traditionally masculine and traditionally feminine roles. Other Behn poems, too, celebrate this poetic circulation, as in "The Sence of a Letter sent me, made into Verse; To a New Tune" (6:173) and "On a Copy of Verses made in a Dream, and sent to me in a Morning before I was Awake" (6:174–75).

In comparison to these playful and erotic poems of camaraderie, "To Mr. *Creech* (under the Name of *Daphnis*) on his Excellent Translation of *Lucretius*" (6:166–70) lifts the conventional pastoral disguise to praise her friend in his own name—and to comment directly on the impediments to women's equality that the other poems address imaginatively through their pastoral names and settings. Behn is unequivocal that women's faults are social rather than natural in origin, not universal but historically specific:

> Till now, I curst my Birth, my Education,
> And more the scanted Customes of the Nation:
> Permitting not the Female Sex to tread,
> The mighty Paths of Learned Heroes dead.

Taking seriously ideas about the enobling nature of literature, she once again connects the roles of poet and hero. To debar women from the one is to debase their chances of ever attaining the other. Like other feminists from the Renaissance through Virginia Woolf, she decries the meagerness of women's education, their relegation to inferior and disposable vernacular texts, and their exclusion from that classical culture that was coming to mark the English gentleman rather than the professional scholar: "The Fulsome Gingle of the times, / Is all we are allow'd to understand or hear." Then her friend Creech's translation of Lucretius

dost advance
Our Knowledg from the State of Ignorance,
And equals us to Man! Ah how can we,
Enough Adore, or Sacrifice enough to thee.

Cocky and self-confident with politicians or fellow playwrights, Behn shares some of the self-abasing admiration with which other seventeenth-century women writers treat male classicists, convinced by the culture around them that the lack of a classical education meant the lack not just of a body of knowledge but also of any possibility for full personal, intellectual, and moral development. Equality is obviously an unstable concept for Behn if women must "Adore" as a god the person who "equals us to Man" by sharing his learning.

This double assertion of equality and inferiority runs through Behn's poems to members of the nobility or clergy, like the earl of Rochester and Bishop Burnet. In thanking the poet Anne Wharton in "To Mrs. W. On her Excellent Verses (Writ in Praise of some I had made on the Earl of *Rochester*) Written in a Fit of Sickness" (6:171–73) Behn again praises "The Great, the God-like *Rochester*" who spoke to her "worthless" self:

With the same wonted Grace my Muse it prais'd,
With the same Goodness did my Faults Correct;
And careful of the Fame himself first rais'd,
Obligingly it School'd my loose Neglect.

(6:172)

The ideological barriers to her self-esteem clearly were formidable. She responded in part by adopting both sides of many contradictions, especially those that separated feminine attitudes from "my Masculine Part the Poet in me" (preface to *The Lucky Chance*, 3:187), but she had other defenses as well. One was to define herself as a woman who could simultaneously inhabit the usually masculine roles of both poet and hero, even if in subsidiary ways, a technique that resulted in Behn's seeing herself as perhaps lesser than, but not different from, the men.[37] Thus, she commends "the Honourable Sir *Francis Fane*, on his Play call'd the *Sacrifice*" (6:343–45) by saying that she read his poetry "with pleasure tho I read with shame" its superiority to her own. As with rival female beauties, she sustains community by praising the other and admitting her own inferiority of quantity but not of kind. When she reads his work, "the tender Laurels which my brows had drest / Flag, like young Flowers, with too much heat opprest." Bested, she is still crowned and garlanded, still one of the noble poet's guild.

In another poem celebrating a male translator of classical poetry, "A *Pastoral* to Mr. *Stafford*" (6:383–87), she is especially grateful for the translator's reclamation of female role models, and the classical precedent of female heroism allows her to display her own credentials as a female hero, a loyal royalist who has done her king dangerous public political service: "Once," she says

> by th' . . . Kings Commands,
> I left these Shades, to visit forein Lands;
> Imploy'd in public toils of State Affairs,
> Unusual with my Sex, or to my Years.

Her own unusual heroic experiences enable her to appreciate Stafford's translation of Virgil's Camilla, who "shews us how / To be at once *Hero* and *Woman* too." Camilla's heroism validates Behn's and makes it, though in an unbelieving and critical age, more plausible. For other models of how one can be a woman who is also a hero, Behn looks to classical history and myth, as the men did, and confirms her views by exchanging them with her brothers of the pen. Thus, she writes "To *Amintas*. Upon reading the Lives of some of the *Romans*" (6:360–61) to laud

> That age when valor they did Beauty name,
> When Men did justly our brave sex prefer,
> Cause they durst dye, and scorn the publick shame
> Of adding Glory to the conqueror.

If the erotic triangle of the fraternal band of poets provided Behn with her best model of community and her substitute for the marital family she did not have and apparently did not want, her Tory party allegiances provided her with a voluntary substitute for a family lineage and a family name, a family of descent that bestowed at once rank and history on its members. Behn's political poetry seems silly to us in part because it was silly; praising the unpopular James II as beloved by his people or the publicly philandering Charles II as a devoted husband who died like Jesus Christ, "A Bleeding Victim to *attone* for all," seemed fatuous then, as it does now.[38] "A Congratulatory Poem to her most Sacred Majesty on the Universal Hopes of all Loyal Persons for a Prince of Wales" celebrated hopes for the Roman Catholic James II's future progeny that were hardly universal in Protestant England.[39] Modern distaste for this political poetry may also result from the fact that the modern alignment of the political with the public was just beginning in the Restoration, yet bedroom politics still ruled the nation. Much of Behn's political verse celebrates personal female matters like pregnancy and childbirth that determined dynasties. Behn addresses royal women as wives and mothers and royal men as husbands and fathers; even her rather more successful political satire attacks political opponents through their sexual pecadilloes, as in the pleasant song "When *Jemmy* first began to Love" that alluded to Charles II's illegitimate son, the duke of Monmouth (6:165–66).[40]

In her last sick and painful hours, political loyalty seems to have sustained Behn's sense of herself as a poet identified with a bygone age and a cause nobly lost. Behn sets this personal loyalty to the Stuart family against political expediency in her "Pindaric Poem to the Reverend Doctor Burnet" (6:407–10), written when she was dying. Although Burnet urged her to celebrate William and Mary's assumption of the crown in the Glorious Revolution of 1689, she pleaded that "Loyalty Commands with pious force" and "stops" her pen. Even with history and possibly the good of the nation arrayed against her and the Stuarts, she founds her integrity on her loyalty to them:

> Tho' I the Wond'rous Change deplore,
> That makes me Useless and Forlorn,
> Yet I the great Design Adore.

Behn died as she had lived—a new woman longing for an imaginary past golden age and creating myths of a world where to be a public woman was not to be a whore but to be a hero and a poet, someone surrounded not by creditors or catcalls on a London street but by the utopian society organized through the communal dedications in a volume of her own lyric poems.

Notes

1. This essay builds upon and revises my earlier discussion of Behn's poetry, "Aphra Behn: Sexuality and Self-Respect," *Women's Studies* 7 (1980): 67–78.

2. Her poetic ambition is expressed in a passage of her own added to her version of Abraham Cowley's poem "Of Trees," in *The Uncollected Verse of Aphra Behn,* ed. Germaine Greer (Stump Cross, Essex: Stump Cross Books, 1989), p. 127.

3. See, for example, James Sutherland, *English Literature of the Late Seventeenth Century* (New York and Oxford: Oxford Univ. Press, 1969), pp. 132–33, 213–15. Sutherland does favorably mention "Love in fantastic triumph sat" (p. 169). Feminist Moira Ferguson praises Behn's "remarkable contributions to the rise of the novel" and her pioneering "niche in the theatre" but speaks of the poems in terms of their reference to "women friends" and "lesbian love," in Moira Ferguson, ed., *First Feminists: British Women Writers, 1578–1799* (Bloomington: Indiana Univ. Press; Old Westbury, N.Y.: Feminist Press, 1985), pp. 143–44.

4. Edward Wagenknecht, "In Praise of Mrs. Behn," *The Colophon* 18 (1934): 12.

5. For example, Angeline Goreau praises Behn's "bawdy poems" as "probably the first instance in which a woman dared to write openly about sex" in *The Whole Duty of a Woman: Female Writers in Seventeenth-Century England* (Garden City, N.Y.: Dial Press, 1984), p. 207.

6. For a view of why seventeenth-century protofeminist writers were politically conservative, see Catherine Gallagher, "Embracing the Absolute: The Politics of the Female Subject in Seventeenth-Century England," *Genders* 1 (March 1988): 24–39.

7. For biographical information on Behn, see Maureen Duffy, *The Passionate Shepherdess: Aphra Behn 1640–89* (London: Jonathan Cape, 1977); Angeline Goreau, *Reconstructing Aphra: A Social Biography of Aphra Behn* (New York: Dial Press, 1980); and Sara Mendelson, *The Mental World of Stuart Women: Three Studies* (Brighton: Harvester Press, 1987), pp. 116–84.

8. The two most important seventeenth-century female poets respond in many similar ways to a common literary tradition and to similar social constraints. It has been traditional to divide them according to sexual respectability and to divide their followers as well. See Marilyn L. Williamson, *Raising Their Voices: British Women Writers, 1650–1750* (Detroit: Wayne State Univ. Press, 1990).

9. For women's manuscript circulation, see Margaret J. M. Ezell, *The Patriarch's Wife: Literary Evidence and the History of the Family* (Chapel Hill and London: University of North Carolina Press, 1987).

10. I discuss transformations in the meanings of the public and the private in

"Add Women Who Stir: Rewriting Seventeenth-Century English Literary History," delivered at the University of Chicago Renaissance Seminar, May 1992.

11. All citations from Behn's works are taken from *The Works of Aphra Behn,* ed. Montague Summers, 6 vols. (1915; rpt. New York: Benjamin Blom, 1967), 6:163–64. Subsequent references to this edition will be cited parenthetically in the text by volume and page number.

12. For views on the importance of desire to Behn's poetry, see Gardiner, "Aphra Behn," and Carol Barash, "The Political Possibilities of Desire: Teaching the Erotic Poems of Behn," in *Teaching Eighteenth-Century Poetry,* ed. Christopher Fox (New York: AMS Press, 1990), pp. 159–76. According to Janet Todd, *The Sign of Angellica: Women, Writing, and Fiction, 1660–1800* (London: Virago, 1989), p. 71, Behn believes "against the odds" that "freedom and love can coexist."

13. The source poem is "L'Occasion Perdue Recouverte," in *Variantes d'après les Poésies Nouvelles et Autres Oeuvres Gallantes du Sieur de C . . ."* (Paris: Théodore Girard, 1662; rpt. 1862). The poem has been attributed to Pierre Corneille and to Benech de Cantenac. The poem is translated as "The Lost Opportunity Recovered" in *Wit and Drollery: Jovial Poems* (London: Obadiah Blagrave, 1682), pp. 1–16. I quote from this translation below. Subsequent references to this edition will be cited parenthetically in the text. I thank James Turner and Lise Leibacher for finding copies of these poems. On this genre of poems, see Richard E. Quaintance, "French Sources of the Restoration 'Imperfect Enjoyment' Poem," *Philological Quarterly* 42 (April 1963): 190–99.

14. Behn's poem was originally printed as by the Earl of Rochester. For the attribution, see David M. Vieth, *Attribution in Restoration Poetry: A Study of Rochester's Poems of 1680* (New Haven and London: Yale Univ. Press, 1963), pp. 448–50.

15. See Judith Kegan Gardiner, "The First English Novel: Aphra Behn's *Love Letters,* The Canon, and Women's Tastes," *Tulsa Studies in Women's Literature* 8 (Fall 1989): 201–22.

16. As is the case with Behn's detailed exposition of Philander's impotence in Behn's novel *Love-Letters between a Nobleman and His Sister,* ed. Maureen Duffy (New York: Penguin Books; London: Virago, 1987), pp. 50–51.

17. Quaintance, "French Sources," p. 198.

18. For women's use of pastoral, see Williamson, *Raising Their Voices,* pp. 290–306.

19. For Behn's milieu, see Goreau, *Reconstructing Aphra,* p. 211; more generally, see Allen Andrews, *The Royal Whore: Barbara Villiers, Countess of Castlemaine* (Philadelphia: Chilton Books, 1970).

20. On literary voyeurism, see Peggy Kamuf, *Fictions of Feminine Desire: Disclosures of Heloise* (Lincoln: Univ. of Nebraska Press, 1982).

21. This hypothetical person is referred to as "he." John Carey, ed., *John Donne: The Oxford Authors* (Oxford and New York: Oxford Univ. Press, 1990), pp. 95–96, 121–22.

22. Germaine Greer et al., eds., *Kissing the Rod: An Anthology of Seventeenth-Century Women's Verse* (London: Virago, 1988), p. 246.

23. Frank Kermode and Keith Walker, eds. *Andrew Marvell: The Oxford Authors* (Oxford and New York: Oxford Univ. Press, 1990), pp. 47–48.

24. Introducing her poetry with adulatory verse, Behn's friends adopted a facetious religious tone sometimes approaching blasphemy; for example, "The Beauties of her new Creation view'd / Full of content She sees that it is *good*," by J. Cooper, quoted in Summers edition of *Works*, 6:118.

25. A poem by Etheredge quoted by Quaintance as an analogue to "The Disappointment" has a lover unable to perform at the "sacred door" to love, cited in Quantance, "French Sources," p. 195.

26. On the disadvantages of being associated with the natural, see Donna Harraway, "A Manifesto for Cyborgs: Science, Technology, and Socialist Feminism in the 1980s," in *Coming to Terms: Feminism, Theory, Politics*, ed. Elizabeth Weed (New York and London: Routledge, 1989), pp. 173–204. For a view of the gendering of nature as female in the seventeenth century, see Carolyn Merchant, *The Death of Nature: Women, Ecology, and the Scientific Revolution* (San Francisco: Harper and Row, 1980).

27. Todd stresses Behn's view of femininity as socially constructed (*Sign of Angellica*, p. 1).

28. Perhaps more accurately we might say that women were not invited to form identities except under the gendered categories of virgin, wife, or whore.

29. For one discussion of such rhetoric, see Judith Kegan Gardiner, "Re-Gendering Individualism: Margaret Fell Fox and Quaker Rhetoric," in *Privileging Gender in Early Modern Britain*, ed. Jean R. Brink (Kirkland, Mo.: Sixteenth-Century Journal Publishers, 1993).

30. Her biographers still argue such matters as her natal name, her date of birth, and her religion.

31. Greer et al., eds., *Kissing the Rod*, p. 31.

32. See Harriette Andreadis, "The Sapphic Platonics of Katherine Philips, 1632–64," *Signs* 15 (Autumn 1989): 34–60.

33. For examples of such male bonding, see Eve Kosofsky Sedgwick, *Between Men: English Literature and Male Homosocial Desire* (New York: Columbia Univ. Press, 1985).

34. Behn recycles this poem as "To Mrs. *Harsenet*, on the Report of a Beauty, which she went to see at Church," (6:393–94). Here the wording is tighter and more epigrammatic: "I came, I saw you, and I must confess, / I wish'd my beauty greater, or yours less."

35. For a female heroism bound quite differently to female virtue in Renaissance women writers, see Elaine V. Beilin, *Redeeming Eve: Women Writers of the English Renaissance* (Princeton: Princeton Univ. Press, 1987).

36. Mendelson speaks of Behn both as part of a "poetic fraternity" and as having a literary "salon" (*Mental World*, pp. 152, 157).

37. The seventeenth century may begin a period of transition between a "one sex" model of women's inferiority and a "two sex" model of women's

complementarity to men. See Thomas Laqueur, *Making Sex: Body and Gender from the Greeks to Freud* (Cambridge and London: Harvard Univ. Press, 1990), and Gardiner, "Add Women Who Stir."

38. In "a Pindarick on the Death of Our Late Sovereign . . ." (Greer et al., *Kissing the Rod,* pp. 22–26).

39. Greer et al., *Kissing the Rod,* pp. 96–98.

40. The editors of *Kissing the Rod* say this poem is "clearly about Monmouth" (p. 254).

ROBERT MARKLEY
and MOLLY ROTHENBERG

Contestations of Nature: Aphra Behn's "The Golden Age" and the Sexualizing of Politics

Recent feminist critiques of early modern science by Carolyn Merchant, Brian Easlea, and Evelyn Fox Keller have argued for the foundational status of the popular analogy (used by Francis Bacon, Robert Boyle, and others) that identifies "man's" exploitation of a feminized nature with the patriarchal repression of women.[1] Although in the context of seventeenth-century natural philosophy, Aphra Behn's 1684 poem "The Golden Age" similarly offers a counter to masculinist constructions of nature and of women as passive sites for the inscription of male power, her idealization of a bountiful nature that exists prior to humankind's interventions ultimately reinscribes patriarchal structures even as it seeks to validate a "Golden Age" of unrepressed sexuality in which distinctions of gender, class, religion, and politics are subsumed within a vision of undifferentiated pleasure, plenitude, and fulfilled desire. As her introductory essay to her translation of Fontenelle's *A Discovery of New Worlds* demonstrates, Behn was well aware of the gendering of seventeenth-century scientific discourse and its implications for the disempowerment of women and the devaluation of nature.[2] The idea of an autonomous, self-sufficient realm of nature is crucial to feminist critiques of early modern science—in Behn's poem and in the work of twentieth-century critics and historians; if nature is independently "plentious," so the argument goes, then our self-imposed alienation from nature can and should be remedied by throwing off what Behn calls "those Politick Curbs" of both external and internalized repression.[3] Precisely because Behn's idealization of nature reproduces, as an oppositional strategy, the binary logic of Baconian exploitation, "The Golden Age" reinscribes hierarchical valuations of class status and property rights—and devalues labor—even as it ostensibly exposes them as ideological constructs. If nature is instead the site of complex cultural contestations, if nature is constantly in the process of being (re)produced by human interventions, then Behn's move to return to an unrepressed sexuality and a pristine natural world does not liberate either nature or sexuality from ideology but marks their further implication in the dialogically agitated discourses of seventeenth-century literature, natural philosophy, and politics. In this regard, Behn's poem provides an opportunity to explore the complexities of seventeenth-century constructions of nature that are marginalized in both traditional and revisionist accounts of the gendering of early modern science.[4]

"The Golden Age" ostensibly seeks to overcome the alienation of humankind from nature. In its evocation of a prefallen state, the poem describes "an Eternal Spring" where lovers "uncontroul'd did meet" with "unbounded Joyes" of sexual pleasure; a "bounteous Nature" provides a "kind increase" of "every necessary good," liberating "th'agreeing Swaines" from the need to work, to compete for food, or, significantly, to enter into a social order founded on "Right and Property." What differentiates Behn's Golden Age from the biblical Garden of Eden is precisely the absence of sin and of external forms of authority—"Monarchs" ("those Arbitrary Rulers over men"), "the Gods," and "Religion." Behn describes a post–Golden Age world in the same terms as the Christian perception of a postlapsarian world: alienation from nature, which produces the need to labor, and alienation from others, which produces the need for external forms of authority to police individual desires. Because she rejects the notion of sin, however, her analysis of the causes of the fallen states of both humanity and nature differs fundamentally from Christian narratives. In "The Golden Age," alienation, labor, and repression are not the consequences of an originary sin but are continually being reproduced by the repression of desire, by "Pride and Avarice," by the dissemination of "Honour" as a means to encourage individuals to police themselves in the names of religion and morality. The poem suggests that the conditions of the post–Golden Age world—individuals constrained by oppression and obedience to authority—*already* exist within the Garden of Eden in the form of divine prohibitions. In this respect, Behn's idealizing of unrepressed sexuality and pristine nature becomes a means to demystify forms of external and internalized repression that have been naturalized within religion and morality. As a counterstrategy, her poem must therefore hold open the possibility that somehow a way back to a state prior to repression can be found, that humankind is not irrevocably alienated from its desires by an originary sin. She must posit in her analysis an origin for repression that lies within the man-made realms of ideology and institutional authority.

However, Behn's idealization of sexuality and nature reveals a number of contradictions that arise from her linking of political and sexual repression. In a crucial sense, "The Golden Age" raises the question of whether humankind must unrepress sexuality to return to a pristine political state free from war, "Right and Property," honor, and so on, or whether a political revolution is necessary to restore humankind to a natural, unrepressed sexuality. In effect, Behn must insist on the causal link between politics and sexuality to ground her demystification of "Pride, Avarice" and "honour," but she must also separate sex and politics to avoid what, for her, would be dire social consequences: the fall from the benevolent—and ostensibly apolitical—Tory paternalism (envisioned in her comedies of the 1680s and other works) to the anarchy of a debased Hobbesian political realm, represented by her satire of the sociopolitical corruption of Whigs and Puritans in *The Roundheads, The City Heiress,* and *The Widow Ranter.*[5] As a professional woman writer, a proponent of women's sexual freedom, and a Tory apologist, Behn must draw on a variety of incommensurate discursive strategies and political values to ground her critique of repression in representations of a sexualized self that exists in an idealized form outside of the networks of ideological constraint. Therefore, her poem does not and cannot exhibit either a formal aesthetic unity or a coherent political ideology; in fact, its theoretical and historical significance lies in its disclosure of the necessarily fragmentary ideological conditions of its production, its registering of the discursive crises within late-seventeenth-century constructions of nature, politics, and sexuality.

The opening two stanzas of "The Golden Age" suggest the complications that arise from the arguments and strategies Behn uses to assert the foundational status of the connections among unrepressed desire, an idealized nature, and a nonhierarchical social order. What seems to begin as a description of the Golden Age becomes a polemic against repression. Yet because Behn conflates imagistically and conceptually the eternal state of nature and the historicopolitical realm, which is irrevocably marked by hierarchies of class and gender, she can define neither a method nor an agency for re-creating the "Blest Age":[6]

> . . . when ev'ry Purling Stream
>   Ran undisturb'd and clear,
> When no scorn'd Shepherds on your Banks were seen,
> Tortur'd by Love, by Jealousie, or Fear;
> When an Eternal Spring drest Ev'ry Bough,
> And Blossoms fell, by new ones dispossest;
> These their kind Shade affording all below,
> And those a Bed where all below might rest.
> The Groves appear'd all drest with Wreaths of Flowers,
> And from their Leaves dropt Aromatick Showers,
> Whose fragrant Heads in Mystick Twines above,
> Exchang'd their Sweets, and mix'd with thousand Kisses,
>   As if the willing Branches strove
>   To beautifie and shade the Grove
>   Where the young wanton Gods of Love
> Offer their Noblest Sacrifice of Blisses.

As the stanza progresses, nature increasingly takes on a personified sexuality that in lines three and four had been attributed, but only by negation, to "scorn'd Shepherds . . . Tortur'd by Love, by Jealousie, or Fear"; in fact, no shepherds, whether scorned or not, actually appear until stanza six. As nature assumes the erotic energy that Behn uses to distinguish the prelapsarian from the postlapsarian world, it becomes the necessary precondition for an undifferentiated social order from which all potential for conflict has been eliminated: "All below" share equally in the boughs' shade and the bed of blossoms. The lower classes, figured as the shepherds, are written out of the poem from the outset, so that the labor required to enable the existence of a leisured class is repressed in favor of an aestheticized labor ("To beautifie . . . the Grove") in which human agency has been displaced by nature's own activity ("the willing Branches strove"). The only inhabitants of the Golden Age are idealized aristocrats, apparently unsupported by any form of labor; these "Gods of Love" ostensibly neither have nor require any economic or political function.

The nature that Behn portrays in "The Golden Age," then, is not a pristine wilderness but an idealized vision of a bucolic English countryside that already has been acted upon (implicitly) by labor. Although blossoms fall in this "Eternal Spring," they are "by new ones dispossest"; this image of dispossession—of a violent renewal dependent on usurpation—marks the irruption of an economic and political lexicon ("affording," "Exchang'd," "Sacrifice") into an otherwise idyllic and ahistorical description of nature. In the next stanza, all human agency seems to disappear; even the deflected discourses of labor and politics are effaced until the closing lines of the stanza:

> While to their soft and tender Play,
> The Gray-Plum'd natives of the Shades
> Unwearied sing till Love invades,
> Then Bill, then sing agen, while Love and Musick makes the
> Day.

The birds' "Play" evades the negative consequences of labor (as their "Unwearied" singing suggests) until "Love invades," marking the return of the violence implied, as we discuss below, in the "Play" of unconstrained desire, in the maintenance of a hierarchical class structure and in the constant reconstruction and renaturalizing of nature.

Having described the idyllic natural conditions of the Golden Age in the first two stanzas, Behn attempts in stanza three to rewrite Genesis to promote her vision of an idealized nature prior to labor and repression:

> The stubborn Plough had then,
> Made no rude Rapes upon the Virgin Earth;
> Who yielded of her own accord her plentious Birth,
> Without the Aids of men;

As if within her Teeming Womb
All Nature, and all Sexes lay,
Whence new Creations every day
Into the happy World did come.

The issue of labor seems to be raised precisely so that it can be dismissed; labor functions as the excluded opposite—the devalued other—of an idealized earth that is at once virginal and polymorphously sexual and fecund. Behn appropriates the simple gendered oppositions of Baconian science that privilege man's labor over nature's plenitude, but she inverts this gender hierarchy in order to redescribe technological productivity as rape and to celebrate nature's self-sustaining generative powers. Although Behn retains the Baconian trope of a masculinized enterprise and a feminized and bounteous earth, she does not follow through on the binary logic implied by this inversion: in Behn's creation myth, earth's undifferentiated sexuality subsumes the sexual, specifically reproductive, functions of both men and women without privileging either: "within her Teeming Womb . . . all Sexes lay." This vision of an undifferentiated sexuality allows Behn to attack the sexually invasive and rapacious nature of Baconian industry and to resist traditional Judeo-Christian devaluations of female sexuality authorized, in the seventeenth century, by invocations of the myth of the Garden of Eden.[7] As part of her critique of the ideology represented by the "stubborn Plough," she explicitly revises the biblical story of Genesis in the second half of this stanza by displacing the opposition between masculine and feminine sexuality in favor of an opposition between two masculine sexualities—one aggressively phallic, the other noninvasive:

. . . the Snakes securely dwelt,
Not doing harm, nor harm from others felt;
With whom the Nymphs did Innocently play,
No spightful Venom in the wantons lay;
But to the touch were Soft, and to the sight were Gay.

Behn insists that we recognize the traditional moral implications of these lines and then (re)read them as a demystification of the repressive, masculinist sexuality that the biblical prohibitions enforce. But her redefinition of a noninvasive male sexuality requires a logical and temporal sleight of hand: the innocence of the nymphs and snakes defines itself in opposition to a phallic sexuality that is ostensibly a consequence of the fall from the Golden Age but that in these lines *already* is inscribed in the series of negations ("Not doing harm, nor harm from others felt") used to mark their "play." Symbolically, no erection ("soft") or ejaculation ("No spightful Venom") takes place and therefore neither can sexualized procreation; the nymphs' sexuality, described by touch and sight, removes them from an economy in which "labors" mark the consequences of unconstrained desire. Women are written out of this myth of undifferentiated procreation in the Golden Age because to foreground female sexuality in the late seventeenth century—to construct a positive image of an unrepressed female desire—is to be forced to confront the consequences of their sexual activity: pregnancy, the bearing of fatherless children, and resulting challenges to the hereditary distribution of wealth, power, and prestige. Behn's fiction of a Golden Age of undifferentiated sexuality, then, derives from and reinforces an idealized image of an aristocratic and patrilineal society that must seek both to control feminine desire through marriage and the laws of primogeniture and to naturalize the coercive means by which the exploitation of labor and natural resources maintains the hierarchies of class and gender.

In the poem's opening stanzas, Behn defines politics in terms of sexuality in order to suppress as well as to defer considering the consequences of unconstrained desire. What follows, then, is a sequence of attempts to locate an origin for repression by displacing these consequences into a past—her version of the Fall—as both the causes and the effects of everything that she tries to negate in the course of the poem: labor, the mystifications of "Honour," religion, war, politics, shame, avarice, ambition, and fame. Although she describes a temporal rupture between the Golden Age and the age of repression, she can neither locate historically nor define theoretically a structure of causation. In one respect, she suggests that a hierarchical social structure comes into being as a result of repression, but in another she implies that the inequities of power serve as the origin of repression:

> Monarchs were uncreated then,
> Those Arbitrary Rulers over men:
> Kings that made Laws, first broke 'em, and the Gods
> By teaching us Religion first, first set the World at Odds:
>   Till then Ambition was not known,
> That Poyson to Content, Bane to Repose;

Each Swain was Lord o'er his own will alone,
His Innocence Religion was, and Laws.
Nor needed any troublesome defense
  Against his Neighbors Insolence.

Monarchs are "uncreated" and "Arbitrary"; they seem to emerge from nowhere, without explanation. There is no history, no mythology, no logic to explain or to justify the "Arbitrary" exercise of power. Ambition, similarly, seems to be a progeny without a parent. Although Behn employs a rhetoric of origins and consequences— "first . . . first, first"—she describes no mechanism to account for the corruption of humankind and nature, that is, for the link between sexual and social repression.

Yet Behn's vision of unalienated sexuality depends on the prerequisites of social hierarchy: "Each Swain" must be "Lord" over his own "will," his own desire. The logic of this metaphor links the unconstrained exercise of pleasure to an idealized—and self-legitimating—aristocratic power, while in the next stanza Behn's attacks on "Right and Property," "Power," "Pride and Avarice" precisely recapitulate the self-aggrandizing and aristocratic values implicit in her evocation of the swain as "Lord." Her attack is based on the assumption that "Rapes, Invasions, Tyrannies" are products of the imposition of power on individuals who (then) learn to reproduce the repressions of "Tyrant Honour," internalizing them as a "Fond Idol." Her insistence on yoking power and pleasure in the figure of the swain presupposes a Hobbesian conception of atomistic individuals who are motivated by their inherent selfishness, which in Hobbes's view, leads inevitably to competition, to the conditions for "Rapes, Invasions, Tyrannies." In (re)creating the Golden Age, Behn denies both the assumptions and the consequences of the war of all against all by idealizing "bounteous Nature": in contrast to the Hobbesian state of nature, characterized by scarcity and therefore competition, Behn's prelapsarian world provides "every necessary good" as "a common Sacrifice to all th'agreeing Swaines." Behn mystifies the inequities of a hierarchical social structure predicated on coercion by idealizing the "common Sacrifice" of nature's "kind increase" in order to displace the political conflicts and sacrifices that occur when individuals act on the license of their own wills. The "common

Sacrifice" of nature also mystifies its appropriation—those "rude Rapes" that are necessary to an economy of "increase." The fiction of an infinitely bounteous nature, in turn, allows Behn to write out of her history the appropriation of the labor of commoners on which the economy of a hierarchical social structure depends. She uses the construct "all th'agreeing Swaines," then, to deny the Hobbesian premises that in a state of nature competition arises as a consequence of unchecked individual desires and that community can result only from coercion or from voluntary self-restraint. However, Behn's attack on the "needless use of Arms" and her insistent denial of the need for "any troublesome defense / Against [a] Neighbors Insolence" betrays her anxiety that the only basis for a hierarchical social structure lies in the use of force.

As Behn's revision of Hobbes suggests, unrepressed sexuality and an idealized nature are constituted in the poem by the very elements that Behn ostensibly rejects—property, pride, avarice, and "Trade." Consequently, the search for the origin of repression can lead only to the reinscription of the conditions of that repression and, significantly, to the reiteration of a language that presupposes humankind's alienation from nature and from the desires that the poet continually insists are natural. In the middle of stanza five, Behn's attack shifts from external forms of repression to "Honour" as both a mystification imposed on "the slavish Crowd"—"Nonsense, invented by the Proud"—and an internalized "Poyson" that teaches individuals to police their own desires. Again, however, the origin of honor is given incommensurate explanations: It was "not known in those blest days" of the Golden Age, and yet, when "the Amorous world injoy'd its Reign," "Tyrant Honour"—already present—"strove t'usurp in Vain," although it apparently was held in check by the exercise of individual desire. "Honour" deserves its derogatory personification, according to Behn, because it creates "those Politick Curbs to keep man in." Encompassing both external and internal forms of repression, honor apparently functions in opposition to desire. But the two are related dialectically: to justify its repressions, honor must presuppose the existence of a disruptive libidinal excess, and desire must be expressed in a language that defines itself by means of its resistance to an already existing state of repression.

In this regard, desire can be described only in terms that are parasitic on—and that seek to negate—the discourse of internalized repression: "The Nymphs were free, no nice, no coy disdain; / Deny'd their Joyes, or gave the Lover pain." Throughout stanza six, Behn relies on a vocabulary of invasion and conquest, even though she claims to be depicting mutual passion and unrepressed desire:

> The yielding Maid but kind Resistance makes;
> Trembling and blushing are not marks of shame,
>   But the Effect of kindling Flame:
> Which from the sighing burning Swain she takes,
> While she with tears all soft, and down-cast-eyes,
> Permits the Charming Conqueror to win the prize.

Nothing in these lines differentiates reciprocal love from rape except the poet's insistence that the maid's resistance is "kind" and her tears are "soft." Behn's language of negation works to mystify the power she herself assumes in order to render "kind Resistance" as a display of mutual passion rather than of masculinist violence. She uses two strategies to disguise the foundational status of violence, power, and repression in the construction of sexual and political relations. First, she creates the illusion of an "objective" stance from which she apparently derives her authority to interpret the semiotics of passion, to distinguish—albeit illegitimately—between "Trembling and blushing" produced by desire and these same physiological signs produced by fear. Her ostensible detachment covers for her imposition of an authoritative interpretation of the nymph's behavior. Then she mystifies this intrusive authority as the "soft power" of the voyeuristic cupids who watch and intervene only to encourage "a Shepherd uninspir'd" to amorous action; nonetheless, the cupid's power, as represented by his shooting an arrow at the swain, is both phallic and aggressive. In both cases, Behn relies on the very strategies of assertion that she previously had characterized as evidence of the illegitimate power she ascribes to the forces of repression. In the preceding stanza, she criticizes the arbitrary signification of "words since made" that allows "Rapes, Invasions, Tyrannies" to be "miscall'd" the "gaining of a Glorious Name"; in stanza six, however, she asserts her authority to interpret similarly "miscall'd" signs without acknowledging her appropriation of the linguistic and political power she has attacked.

Behn's efforts to distinguish between two kinds of language—a universal semiotic that, in the act of naming, discloses the essential natures of things and the socially constructed, politicized, and therefore mystified language of "Politick Curbs"—continue in the next stanza:[8]

> The Lovers thus, thus uncontroul'd did meet,
> Thus all their Joyes and Vows of Love repeat:
> 　　Joyes which were everlasting, ever new
> 　　And every Vow inviolably true:
> Not fear of Gods, no fond Religious cause,
> Nor in obedience to the duller Laws.
> Those Fopperies of the Gown were then not known,
> Those vain, those Politick Curbs to keep man in,
> Who by a fond mistake Created that a Sin;
> Which freeborn we, by right of Nature claim our own.
> 　　Who but the Learned and dull moral Fool
> Could gravely have forseen, man ought to live by Rule?

To maintain the fiction that a distinction exists between ideal and corrupt semiotics, Behn must posit the origin of repression as a "fond mistake" that gives rise to a system of morality, "obedience to the duller Laws." But the distinction itself depends on the temporal priority of this universal semiotic, a priority undermined by the contemporaneous existence of the "Learned and dull moral Fool," who "forsee[s]" the advent of the same moral codes that he himself already embodies. The truth of "every Vow"—the idealization of pristine language—depends on a strategy of negation ("Not kept in fear of Gods, no fond Religious cause") that allows Behn to idealize desire ("Joyes which were everlasting") as the basis of a community ("freeborn we") that can evade time and repression. In effect, love is described ideally and transhistorically in stanza seven precisely to mystify the Hobbesian self-interest and implicit violence of the "originary" seduction in stanza six.

The entire seventh stanza, then, ostensibly accounts for the origin of repression in terms of a historical movement from unrepressed desire to the repressions of religion and law, but this false history emerges as a displacement of the history of sexual and social violence always already present, a history Behn must deny in order to conduct her demystification of "Politick Curbs." The fallacy in her reasoning shows up in her logical and temporal markers: "The Lovers thus" seems to refer to a historical point after their initial meeting, so that "thus uncontroul'd" suggests that their sexual freedom is a result of their original encounter rather than its cause. If this is the case, then their love must exist in opposition to a state of repression that allows for the possibility of misinterpreting "kind Resistance" as a defense against rape. Or, if we accept Behn's assertion that the Golden Age did not have "Politick Curbs," then her repetition of "thus" lacks logical force. Any historical analysis of the power structure encoded in the lovers' relationship is deferred by the repetition of "thus" and the repetition of "Joyes and Vows of Love," both of which serve as a means to deny and to control the uncontrollable passion—the disruptive potential of passionate love and passionate violence—that the lovers represent. Behn's strategies of idealization and demystification are related dialectically: if the idealization of lovers and their joys and vows becomes a means to resist "duller Laws," it also describes processes of idealization that themselves repress the violence ("discord, noise, and wars") that maintains the social order. Behn's attempts to restrict the sociopolitical implications of her analysis by decoupling sexual from political repression continue to conflict with her efforts to locate a political origin for the policing of desire.

The tensions within Behn's analytic cannot be resolved because the myth of her egalitarian sexuality is founded on hierarchies of class, gender, and property. In stanza eight Behn tries to evade this contradiction by returning to an excoriation of "cursed Honour" that excludes its political dimension in order to focus on the internalizing of sexual repression. This redefinition of honor locates repression in the individual's sexual behavior rather than in cultural disseminations of power:

Oh cursed Honour! thou who first didst damn,
  A Woman to the Sin of shame;
    Honour! that rob'st us of our Gust,
    Honour! that hindred mankind first,
At Loves Eternal Spring to Squench his amorous thirst.
Honour! who first taught lovely Eyes the art,
  To wound, and not to cure the heart:
With Love to invite, but to forbid with Awe,
And to themselves prescribe a Cruel Law;

To Veil 'em from the Lookers on,
   When they are sure the slave's undone,
And all the Charmingst part of Beauty hid;
Soft Looks, consenting Wishes, all deny'd.

As in stanza five, honor is portrayed unequivocally as the source of all constraint, the unquestioned origin of repression, sin, and violence, but in these lines Behn represses the link between the sexual and the political upon which she had insisted earlier. The "Cruel Law" is shorn of its political implications; it is no longer a literal, external form of prohibition regulating relations among people but instead operates solely within an internal realm ("and to themselves prescribe") to create self-centered, atomistic beings. In effect, Behn argues that honor objectifies the coquette, transforming her from a desiring individual into a cipher embodying a corrupt language that cannot deliver what it promises. The coquette who learns "the art to wound" becomes a product of honor's ministry of perpetually deferred desire; with her "soft Looks, consenting Wishes, all deny'd," she is "drest to Tempt, not gratify the World." But like the "yielding Maid" of stanza six and the "bounteous Nature" of stanza four, she does not exist independently of the repressive forces that constitute her as an object of desire; even in the Golden Age, she would have no purpose other than to "gratify the World."

What are presented as the aftereffects of sexual repression—"the Sin of shame," wounding, cruelty, and slavery—in fact constitute "the Amorous world" as part of an already fallen and politicized realm. The portrait of the woman prior to her instruction in honor discloses what Behn seeks to hide—the implication of the world of politics and commerce in the construction of sexuality:

[Honour] gathers up the flowing Hair,
   That loosely plaid with wanton Air.
The Envious Net, and stinted order hold,
The lovely Curls of Jet and shining Gold;
No more neglected on the Shoulders hurl'd:
Now drest to Tempt, not gratify the World:
Thou, Miser Honour, hord'st the sacred store,
And starv'st thy self to keep thy Votaries poor.

The reification of the woman appears to be attributed to the workings of honor, that "Envious Net," but actually preexists them. Both her pre- and postlapsarian bodies are commodified: "The lovely Curls of Jet and shining Gold" define her in economic terms prior to the commercial interests of "Miser Honour" (stinting, hoarding, and storing) that postdate the Golden Age. By focusing on the woman as coquette, Behn displaces our recognition that, whether tempting or gratifying, the woman has value only within an exchange economy— the patrilineal system that objectifies her as a commodity on the marriage market. The coquette is constructed as a member of the landed classes, as her dress signifies; consequently, the temptation she offers—and the reward she withholds (until marriage, at least)—is not only sexual but also economic. Her culturally constructed motivation for frustrating the desires of men, for hoarding "the Charmingst part of Beauty," is to maintain her marketability. It is not honor that enslaves, impoverishes, and starves its victims but rather the very systems of exchange—commercial, political, and sexual—that ensure the transference of property from one generation of men to another by means of her body.

Although in the opening eleven lines of stanza nine Behn continues to revile honor (as the "base Debaucher of the generous heart" and a "Foe to Pleasure") and to define love implicitly in economic terms (as "a sacred Gift . . . made to be possest" that honor has "made a Theft"), by the middle of the stanza she has repoliticized honor ("tyrant over mighty Kings"), banishing it to "Princes Pallaces," leaving "Shepheards Cottages" free from its influence. Her insistence that honor "be gone!" marks her efforts to maintain the fiction that the Golden Age is nonpolitical and noncommercial, an idyllic space in which social status is naturalized ("the first rate of man / That nearest were to Gods Alli'd") and not a product of either the influence-peddling at the court or the vicissitudes of the market. In contrast to Behn's previous assertions that repression has a historical origin, this stanza suggests that unrepressed desire and honor exist contemporaneously but are located within different economies of political, commercial, and sexual exchange:

What mak'st thou here in Shepheards Cottages;
Why troublest thou the quiet Shades and Springs?
  Be gone, and make thy Fam'd resort
    To Princes Pallaces;
Go Deal and Chaffer in the Trading Court,
That busie Market for Phantastick Things;

Be gone and interrupt the short Retreat,
   Of the Illustrious and the Great;
   Go break the Politicians sleep,
   Disturb the Gay Ambitious Fool,
   That longs for Scepters, Crowns, and Rule,
Which not his Title, nor his Wit can keep;
But let the humble honest *Swain* go on,
In the blest Paths of the first rate of man;
   That nearest were to Gods Alli'd,
And form'd for love alone, disdain'd all other Pride.

Behn draws upon a traditional distinction between the values of the country and those of the court to identify the latter with trade, ambition, and the delusory satisfactions of "Phantastick Things." The country, on the other hand, is the home of the "humble honest *Swain*," who is "form'd for love alone" and rejects "Scepters, Crowns, and Rule." Historically, and implicitly within the poem, both the country and the court are the products of a patrilineal economy that must seek to repress desire to ensure the orderly transfer of land and money; the two realms, in this respect, are not sites of antithetical systems of value but projections of the same ideological imperatives of socioeconomic privilege. In the figure of the "Swain," Behn conflates two socioeconomic registers that heretofore she had kept implicitly distinct: laboring rustics and gentlemen-lovers.[9] The ambiguity of this figure allows her to mystify both the social hierarchy that creates shepherds, who are dispossessed from the power represented by the court, and the labor that is necessary to maintain the leisure of the country aristocracy so that its members can engage in "love alone" rather than in commerce or political intrigue. Despite Behn's attempt to describe the country as free from the interventions of trade and labor, it is as dependent upon the symbolic and practical "Market" as the court. In this poem, however, labor (in the senses of both the courtiers' business and the shepherds' work) can be only a "Phantastick Thing" because Behn's moves towards a liberatory rhetoric of desire always reinscribe the conditions of a social order that seeks to negate its dependence on and exploitation of the labor of the lower classes.

At the beginning of the final stanza Behn for the third time exclaims "Be gone!" The subject of her command is not simply "Honour" but the complexities and contradictions that continually reimplicate her vision of a nonhierarchical Golden Age in economies of privilege and repression. Behn's struggle throughout the poem has been to restrict the implications of her account of the origin of sexual repression and to naturalize desire as a communitarian ideal. At the end of her poem, she retreats to a version of the carpe diem motif as though it presented an escape from the problems of order and desire that she has dealt with in the previous nine stanzas. However, her use of this conventional motif forces her to introduce into the poem a seasonal conception of nature that is at odds with the "Eternal Spring":

> The Spring decays, but when the Winter's gone,
> The Trees and Flowers a new come on;
> The Sun may set, but when the night is fled,
> And gloomy darkness does retire,
> He rises from his Watry Bed:
> All Glorious, Gay, all drest in Amorous Fire.

Significantly, spring "decays" into the cycle of the seasons; although a renewal occurs, Behn emphasizes the inevitability of mortality in the very imagery she uses to describe Sylvia, the woman she addresses.

> But *Sylvia* when your Beauties fade,
> When the fresh Roses on your Cheeks shall die,
> Like Flowers that wither in the Shade,
> Eternally they will forgotten lye,
> And no kind Spring their sweetness will supply.

Sylvia is alienated from two natures—the "Eternal Spring" of the Golden Age and the cyclical seasons of renewal. Her sexuality and life irrevocably decay; her experience of the cyclical nature represented by the seasons is bounded by her mortality. In these lines, the implicit violence that had been figured in stanza one as the dispossession that allowed the "Eternal Spring" to renew itself is rendered imagistically as death and decay.

Behn's quest for an origin to explain humankind's fall into repression is displaced onto a nature that is continually in the process of decay and creation. From the point of view of postlapsarian humans, however, cyclical nature is experienced only as an inexorable movement towards death.

When Snow shall on those lovely Tresses lye,
And your fair Eyes no more shall give us pain,
   But shoot their pointless Darts in vain.
What will your duller honour signifie?
Go boast it then! and see what numerous Store
Of lovers will your Ruin'd Shrine Adore.
   Then let us, *Sylvia*, yet be wise,
   And the Gay hasty minutes prize:
The Sun and Spring receive but our short Light,
Once sett, a sleep brings an Eternal Night.

Significantly, the speaker's injunction, "the Gay hasty minutes prize," promises neither the satisfactions of sexual pleasure nor the rewards of idyllic existence in an eternal Golden Age; rather than emphasizing the eternity of sensual delight promised in earlier stanzas, Behn leaves Sylvia with the specter of her own mortality, whether or not she gives up the repressions of honor. Sylvia's beauties are cast in images of violence and pain that herald "an Eternal Night." In one sense, the pessimism of this stanza is a product of Behn's rejection earlier in the poem of the religion that "first set the World at Odds," leaving her in the position of a de facto mortalist.[10] Having defined the Golden Age as a negation of the various practices and strategies of external and internal repression, Behn leaves Sylvia no way to re-create the conditions of the Golden Age; she will either follow the dictates of "duller honour" or she will experience a few "Gay hasty minutes" of pleasure bounded temporally and physically by an "Eternal Night," by the decay of her body, which has been figured metaphorically in natural terms. The "Joyes which were everlasting, ever new" of stanza seven are predicated on a rejection of individual mortality and of a history that must always be figured as postlapsarian. The joys offered Sylvia, bounded by personal and cultural history, therefore reinscribe the conditions that exist throughout the poem—the "originary" alienation of a fallen sexuality.

Sylvia, then, is alienated from nature, alienated from her "numerous Store / Of Lovers," alienated from her own sexuality, and alienated from the very processes aging her body. Her alienation is not a function of honor's repressions but of Behn's reducing individuality to less than the sum of her physical parts. Whether Sylvia is repressed or unrepressed, she exists as nothing more than the fragments of cheeks, tresses, and eyes, like the objectified women of the Petrarchan sonnet tradition.[11] Even when Sylvia is granted the possibility of an unrepressed existence, her subjectivity is restricted to that of the atomistic, Hobbesian self whose pleasures, like her life, must be short because she has no access to an idealized, infinitely "bounteous nature." Instead, she is figured as a product of a postlapsarian and niggardly nature that "Stint[s] . . . short-liv'd joy." In previous stanzas, Behn represses the sociopolitical consequences of individualistic competition by denying the Hobbesian premise of nature's scarcity. In these lines, however, Behn acknowledges the conditions of Hobbesian conflict but depoliticizes them by displacing them onto a stinting nature. She can avoid dealing with the implications of the war of all against all, then, only by radically isolating Sylvia and by drastically limiting her agency: Sylvia's only choices are to wither and die or to have a few orgasms and then wither and die. Behn's exhortation to Sylvia to gather her rosebuds recalls the rape of the nymph in stanza six as well as the "Sacrifice" of bounteous nature in stanza four; far from empowering them, the limited agency Behn grants to Sylvia and to prelapsarian nature at best enables their "willing" complicity in their own exploitation.

The carpe diem motif with which Behn ends the poem suggests how thoroughly she has erased the possibility of recapturing a Golden Age; sociopolitical explanations of alienation are displaced onto a stinting nature, represented as the source of all dissatisfaction. Sylvia must be introduced in stanza ten precisely to define political problems solely in terms of individual choices and to foreclose the possibility of a political rather than biological analysis of an economy of scarcity that governs the distribution of everything from food to joy. In effect, Behn places Sylvia in a position analogous to that of many of the heroines in her comedies: the woman who is seeking sexual satisfaction and the socioeconomic legitimation of her desires. In plays such as *The Rover*, part II, Behn dramatizes the issue of women's desire as necessary to a "radical" questioning of gender roles because the liberatory potential of this desire does not extend to a questioning of "Right and Property" as the bases of a patrilineal society. But at the end of "The Golden Age," Behn does not have the generic trappings of comedy to distract our attention from the ways in which a seemingly "feminist" articulation of desire reinforces the processes by which the conservative political philosophy of right and property is—as it must be, in her mind—reinscribed. In this regard, Sylvia functions almost metonymically for the processes of political analysis that occur in the poem. Behn has no trouble in identifying the sources and causes of repression and human misery—religion, kings, unequal distributions of right and property, "Rapes, Invasions, and Tyrannies"—but her Toryism precludes her adding up these local analyses into a general critique of sociopolitical alienation. The move against which she guards ferociously is the move to a world in which property and power are leveled—the brief-lived experiments in 1649 and 1650 of the Diggers, which are appropriated and satirized in her plays as the grotesque self-aggrandizing of Puritans and Whigs.

Our reading of "The Golden Age" suggests that Behn's work in particular and the array of texts that, in the late seventeenth and early eighteenth centuries, have been identified as "feminist" cannot be read simply as ideological counters to a dominant masculinist ideology. Her poem is significant historically precisely because it discloses the contradictions within contemporary constructions of nature, politics, gender, and identity. In its efforts to celebrate prelapsarian nature as a mode of resistance to economies of repression, Behn's poem can generate only new strategies of implication, new modes of reinscribing an ideology that takes as fundamental humankind's alienation from nature, love, and labor. In this sense, her feminism, like that of her contemporaries, cannot be separated from the ideologies of privilege and power that map its limitations.

Notes

1. Carolyn Merchant, *The Death of Nature: Women, Ecology, and the Scientific Revolution* (San Francisco: Harper and Row, 1980); Brian Easlea, *Witch-Hunting, Magic, and the New Philosophy: An Introduction to the Debates of the Scientific Revolution, 1450–1750* (Brighton: Harvester Press, 1980); and Evelyn Fox Keller, *Reflections on Gender and Science* (New Haven: Yale Univ. Press, 1985).

2. On Behn's translation of Fontenelle, see Maureen Duffy, *The Passionate Shepherdess: Aphra Behn 1640–89* (New York: Avon Books, 1977), pp. 270–72.

3. All quotations are from *The Works of Aphra Behn*, ed. Montague Summers, 6 vols. (1915; rpt. New York: Benjamin Blom, 1967), vol. 6.

4. On constructions of nature in the seventeenth-century, see, Merchant, *Death of Nature;* Easlea, *Witch-Hunting;* Keller, *Reflections;* J. R. Jacob, "Restoration, Reformation, and the Origins of the Royal Society," *History of Science* 13 (1975): 155–76, and "Restoration Ideologies and the Royal Society," *History of Science* 17 (1980): 25–38; Paolo Rossi, *The Dark Abyss of Time: The History of the Earth and the History of Nations from Hooke to Vico,* trans. Lydia G. Cochrane (Chicago: Univ. of Chicago Press, 1984); and Michael Fores, "Constructed Science and the Seventeenth-Century 'Revolution,' " *History of Science* 22 (1984): 217–44.

5. See Robert Markley, " 'Be impudent, be saucy, forward, bold, touzing, and leud': The Politics of Masculine Sexuality and Feminine Desire in Behn's Tory Comedies," in *Revisionist Readings of the Restoration and Eighteenth-Century Theatre,* ed. J. Douglas Canfield and Deborah C. Payne (forthcoming). For other views of the link between politics and sexuality in Behn's works that emphasize her feminism, see Catherine Gallagher, "Who Was That Masked Woman? The Prostitute and the Playwright in the Comedies of Aphra Behn," *Women's Studies* 15 (1988): 23–42 (this essay is reprinted in this volume); Cheri Langdell Davis, "Aphra Behn and Sexual Politics: A Dramatist's Discourse with Her Audience," in *Drama, Sex, and Politics,* ed. James Redmond (Cambridge: Cambridge Univ. Press, 1985), pp. 109–28; Deborah C. Payne, " 'And Poets Shall by Patron-Princes Live': Aphra Behn and Patronage," in *Curtain Calls: British and American Women and the Theater, 1660–1820,* ed. Mary Anne Schofield and Cecilia Macheski (Athens: Ohio Univ. Press, 1991), pp. 105–19; Rose Zimbardo, "Aphra Behn in Search of the Novel," in *Studies in Eighteenth-Century Culture,* ed. Leslie Ellen Brown and Patricia Craddock (East Lansing, Mich.: Colleagues Press, 1989), 19:277–88; Dorothy Mermin, "Women Becoming Poets: Katherine Philips, Aphra Behn, Anne Finch," *ELH* 57 (1990): 335–55; Elin Diamond, "*Gestus* and Signature in Aphra Behn's *The Rover,*" *ELH* 56 (1989): 519–41.

6. On the problem of method in the Restoration, see Richard W. F. Kroll, *The Material Word: Literate Culture in the Restoration and Early Eighteenth Century* (Baltimore: Johns Hopkins Univ. Press, 1991).

7. There are a number of studies of the mythos of a patriarchal paradise in the seventeenth century; see particularly Christopher Hill, *Milton and the English Revolution* (New York: Viking Press, 1977), and Christopher Kendrick, *Milton: A Study in Ideology and Form* (New York: Methuen, 1986). On the relation of this tradition to the georgic revival in the seventeenth and eighteenth centuries, see Anthony Low, *The Georgic Revolution* (Princeton: Princeton Univ. Press, 1985), pp. 71–154.

8. On the significance of idealized and fallen semiotics in the Restoration, see Kroll, *The Material Word,* and Robert Markley, *Fallen Languages: Crises of Representation in Newtonian England, 1660–1740* (Ithaca: Cornell Univ. Press, 1993).

9. In her poem "A *Farewel to* Celladon, *On His Going into* Ireland" Behn consistently describes the aristocratic Celladon as a "Swain" who spent his life in

"Groves / Where unambitiously he lay, / And knew no greater Joyes, nor Power then Loves," until he is called to political service (as governor of Ireland) by his monarch.

10. On the mortalist heresy, see Christopher Hill, *The World Turned Upside Down: Radical Ideas during the English Revolution* (1971; rpt. Harmondsworth: Penguin, 1975).

11. On the implications of the Petrarchan sonnet tradition in the seventeenth century, see Laurie Finke, "Painting Women: Images of Femininity in Jacobean Tragedy," *Theatre Journal* 36 (1984): 357–70.

Contributors
Index

Contributors

ROS BALLASTER is a lecturer in English literature at the University of East Anglia, England. She is the author of *Seductive Forms: Women's Amatory Fiction, 1684–1740* (1992) and has cowritten *Women's Worlds: Femininity, Ideology, and the Woman's Magazine* (1991). She has published a number of articles related to Restoration and eighteenth-century women's writing.

LAURIE FINKE is an associate professor of Women's and Gender Studies at Kenyon College. She is the author of *Feminist Theory, Women's Writing* (1992) and has coedited *Critical Texts: Literary Theory from the Greeks to the Present* with Robert Con Davis and *Medieval Texts and Contemporary Readers* with Martin Shichtman.

CATHERINE GALLAGHER is a professor of English at the University of California, Berkeley. She is the author of *The Industrial Reformation of English Fiction: Social Discourse and Narrative Form, 1832–1867* (1985) and coeditor of *The Making of the Modern Body: Sexuality and Society in the Nineteenth Century* (1987) with Thomas Laqueur. Her work in progress, from which the essay in this volume is taken, is *Nobody's Story: The Appearance of Female Authorship in the Restoration and Eighteenth Century.*

JUDITH KEGAN GARDINER is professor of English and women's studies at the University of Illinois at Chicago. She writes about Renaissance English literature, twentieth-century fiction by women, and feminist and psychoanalytic theory, and she is currently working on a book about English women writers to be called *Add Women Who Stir: Rewriting Seventeenth-Century English Literary History.*

SUSAN GREEN is an assistant professor in the department of English at the University of Oklahoma, where she is an associate editor of *Genre*. She has published a number of articles on women's writing and is at work on a book on textuality and the body in women's writing of seventeenth-century England. With other members of the Folger Collective on Early Women Critics, she is editing a forthcoming anthology of early critical writing by women (1660–1820).

Contributors

HEIDI HUTNER is the author of "Aphra Behn's *Oroonoko:* The Politics of Gender, Race, and Class" in Dale Spender's *Early Women Writers: Living by the Pen* (1992) and "*Evelina* and the Problem of the Female Grotesque" (*Genre*, 1990). She is currently completing her dissertation, entitled "Representing the 'Other' Woman: Colonial Discourse in Restoration Drama," at the University of Washington.

ROBERT MARKLEY teaches English at the University of Washington. Editor of *The Eighteenth Century: Theory and Interpretation* since 1981, he is the author of *Two-Edg'd Weapons: Style and Ideology in the Comedies of Etherege, Wycherley, and Congreve* (1988) and of two forthcoming books on Restoration and eighteenth-century science as well as of numerous essays on literature, culture, and theory.

JESSICA MUNNS, educated at the universities of Essex and Warwick, has taught in England, Poland, and America and has previously published essays on Aphra Behn. She has completed a book on Thomas Otway and is co-editing the forthcoming *Cultural Studies: An Anglo-American Reader*.

JACQUELINE PEARSON is a lecturer in English literature at the University of Manchester, England. She is the author of *Tragedy and Tragicomedy in the Plays of John Webster* (1980), *The Prostituted Muse: Images of Women and Women Dramatists, 1642–1737* (1988), and a number of articles, primarily on Renaissance and Restoration drama and on seventeenth-century women writers, including Aphra Behn, Margaret Cavendish, and Aemilia Lanier. She is presently at work on a history of women's reading from the late sixteenth to the early nineteenth centuries.

ELLEN POLLAK is associate professor of English at Michigan State University and author of *The Poetics of Sexual Myth: Gender and Ideology in the Verse of Swift and Pope* (1985). The essay in this volume grows out of current work in progress for a book-length study tentatively entitled "Theaters of Desire: Gender, Incest, and Representation in the Eighteenth-Century British Novel."

MOLLY ROTHENBERG is associate professor of English at Tulane University. She is the author of "*Chaos Brightend*": *Rethinking Blakean Textuality* (1992), and she has published a number of articles on eighteenth-century literature and historiography.

RUTH SALVAGGIO is the author of *Enlightened Absence: Neoclassical Configurations of the Feminine* (1988) and *Dryden's Dualities* (1983) and is a member of the Folger Collective on Early Women Critics for the forthcoming anthology *Early Women Critics, 1660–1820*. She teaches in the American studies department and in women's studies at the University of New Mexico.

Contributors

JANE SPENCER is a lecturer in English literature in the School of English and American Studies, University of Exeter. She is the author of *The Rise of the Woman Novelist: From Aphra Behn to Jane Austen* (1986) and *Elizabeth Gaskell* (forthcoming). She is editing four of Behn's plays, *The Rover, The Feigned Courtesans, The Lucky Chance,* and *The Emperor of the Moon* and is researching the stage history of Behn's dramatic work.

CHARLOTTE SUSSMAN is an Assistant Professor of English at the University of Colorado, Boulder. She recently received her Ph.D. in English from Cornell University.

Index

Abolitionism. *See* Colonial discourse
Achilles, 24
Adams, Hazard, 17, 39n. 1
Adams, Parveen, 121, 122, 143n. 3,
    146n. 17
Aldridge, Alfred Owen, 182n. 3
Andreadis, Harriette, 299n. 32
Andrews, Allen, 298n. 19
Anti-Semitism, 113, 118n. 4
"Ariadne," 88; *She Ventures and He
    Wins*, 91
Arlington, Henry, Lord Cham-
    berlain, 190, 208n. 1, 209n. 9
Armstrong, Nancy, 119n. 8, 146n.
    14, 254, 269n. 1
Arnold, Matthew, 20, 21, 40n. 6
Astell, Mary, *Some Reflections upon
    Marriage*, 252n. 21
Atack, Margaret, 127, 146n. 18
Atkins, J. W. H., 62n. 28
Austen, Jane, 156; *Lady Susan*, 179

Bacon, Francis, 301, 302
Bakhtin, Mikhail, 104–5, 120n. 12
Ballaster, Ros, 6, 9, 10, 13n. 18,
    118n. 4, 182n. 2, 183n. 15,
    184n. 26
Barash, Carol, 298n. 12
Barker, Jane, 7, 234, 244, 247, 252n.
    20; "The History of Dorinda,"
    243; *The Lining of the Patch-
    work Screen*, 235, 242, 243,
    249, 252n. 18; *A Patchwork
    Screen*, 241–42, 247, 249,
    252n. 19; "Philanda's STORY
    out of the BOOK," 235, 242,
    249, 252n. 18; "The Story of a
    Tangerine," 235, 243; "The
    Story of Bellemien," 243; "The
    Story of Mrs Castoff," 247;
    "The Story of Mrs Goodwife,"
    247; "Story of a Portuguese
    NUN," 252n. 20

Barry, Elizabeth, 117
Bartlett, John, 252n. 25
Beasley, Jerry C., 210n. 14
Beaumont, Francis, 20
Behn, Aphra: biographical back-
    ground of, 2, 3–4, 190, 207,
    209n. 9, 234, 255–58, 260–61,
    287, 299n. 30; *Abdelezar*, 250n.
    1, 274, 277; *The Adventures of
    the Black Lady*, 255, 260, 261–
    63, 267, 270n. 9; *Agnes de Cas-
    tro*, 192, 250n. 1, 262; *All the
    Histories and Novels of the Late
    Ingenious Mrs. Behn*, 209n. 10;
    The Amorous Prince, 139; *The
    City Heiress*, 92, 303; "A Con-
    gratulatory Poem," 296; "The
    Disappointment," 277–82, 286;
    The Dumb Virgin, 195–99, 262
    The Dutch Lover, 8, 48, 122–42,
    143n. 5, 144n. 7; "Epistle to
    the Reader," 21, 32–37, 44–
    49, 54, 122–23, 124, 145n.
    11
    The Fair Jilt, 193, 255, 260, 263–
    68, 270n. 11; dedication,
    202–3
    The False-Count, epilogue, 56;
    "A *Farewel* to Celladon," 320n.
    9; *The Fatal Marriage*, 215n. 17;
    The Feigned Courtesans, 91–
    100, 101n. 10
    The Forced Marriage, 84n. 2, 88;
    prologue, 51, 66–67
    "The Golden Age," 7, 10, 103,
    301–19, 319n. 3; *Histories and
    Novels*, 187, 192, 209n. 10,
    242; *The History of a Nun*, 193,
    234–50, 251n. 10, 262; *The Im-
    pious Vow Punish'd*, 193; "A
    Letter to a Brother," 291–92;
    "Love Arm'd," 268, 274, 277–
    78

Behn, Aphra (*cont.*)
  *Love-Letters between a Nobleman
    and His Sister,* 3, 8, 12n. 11,
    151–81, 187, 194–95,
    210nn. 20, 21, 22, 242, 260,
    298n. 16; dedication, 210n.
    21
  Love-Letters to a Gentleman,
    255–60, 263, 270n. 8
  The Lucky Chance, 3, 12n. 11,
    73–84, 129–31, 146n. 23,
    250n. 1; prologue, 17, 26, 27;
    preface, 17, 32, 38–39, 53,
    294; dedication, 32, 36, 49–
    50
  The Lucky Mistake, 192; "On a
    Copy of Verses made in a
    Dream," 293; "On a Juniper
    Tree," 283, 285, 286;
  Oroonoko, 1, 3, 5, 6, 12n. 11,
    102, 191–92, 194, 202–4,
    209n. 13, 212–31, 231n. 6,
    232nn. 7, 13, 233nn. 23, 25,
    234, 250n. 2, 255, 260, 267;
    "Our Cabal," 256, 263; "A Pas-
    toral to Mr. Stafford," 295; *The
    Perjur'd Beauty,* 193; "A Pin-
    darick Poem on the Death,"
    300n. 38; "Pindaric Poem to the
    Reverend Doctor Burnet," 296;
    *The Plays, Histories, and Novels
    of the Ingenious Mrs. Aphra
    Behn,* 270n. 8; *Prologue to
    Romulus,* 208n. 1
  The Rover: part I, 3, 4, 6, 12n. 11,
    13n. 21, 27–29, 86–88, 91,
    92, 100n. 1, 100–101n. 6,
    101n. 13, 105–11, 118nn. 2,
    3, 135, 139, 250n. 1, 291;
    parts I and II, 50, 10, 102–5,
    111–18, 118n. 1, 118–19n.
    4, 303; part II, 318; dedica-
    tion, part II, 50
  *Selected Writings of the Inge-
    nious Mrs. Aphra Behn,* 145n.
    11
  The Roundheads, 303; dedication,
    21–22

"Selinda and Cloris," 290; "The
  Sence of a Letter," 293
Sir Patient Fancy, 89, 100n. 3,
  143n. 4, 147n. 26; preface,
  25, 51, 53; "To the Reader,"
  100n. 3
"To *Amintas:* Upon reading the
  Lives," 295; "To Damon," 289,
  292; "To Desire," 276; "To *Lysander* at the *Musick-Meeting*,"
  289; "To *Lysander,* on some
  Verses," 290; "To Mr. *Creech,*"
  293; "To Mrs. *Harsenet,*" 299n.
  34; "To Mrs. W. On her Excellent Verses," 294; "To My Lady
  Morland at Tunbridge," 289–
  90; "To the Fair Clarinda," 61n.
  12, 288; *The Unfortunate Bride,*
  199, 202, 244; *The Unfortunate
  Happy Lady,* 192, 202; *The
  Wandering Beauty,* 192, 202,
  235, 243; "When *Jemmy* first
  began to Love," 296; *The
  Widow Ranter,* 73, 102, 303;
  "The Willing Mistress," 288;
  The Younger Brother, 211n. 28;
  The Young King, dedication, 26,
  56
Beilin, Elaine V., 299n. 35
Bentley, Mr. (bookseller), 57
Berggen, Paola S., 145n. 9
Berkeley, Lady Henrietta, 152, 172,
  181, 184n. 24
Berkeley, Lord, 152
Bernbaum, Ernest, 2, 12n. 7
Betham, Matilda, 2, 11n. 4
Bevis, R. W., 101n. 13
Bhabha, Homi K., 120n. 16
Bible, 86, 154, 305, 306
Binns, J. W., 145n. 9
Bloch, Howard, 41n. 18
Boehrer, Bruce, 182n. 3
Bolingbroke, Henry St. John, 183n.
  10
Boothby, Frances, *Marcelia: or the
  Treacherous Friend,* 88
Bourdieu, Pierre, 23, 40n. 9
Brontë, Charlotte, *Jane Eyre,* 230

Brown, Beverley, 121, 122, 143n. 3, 146n. 17
Brown, Laura, 5, 13nn. 16, 17, 18, 20, 100n. 4, 101n. 13, 119n. 4, 192, 209–10n. 14, 210n. 16, 222, 231n. 6, 232n. 13
Brown, Thomas, 2, 11n. 1, 56, 61n. 20
Buckhurst, Lord (Charles Sackville), 2, 23, 24; *Pompey,* 24
Buckingham, Duke of, 2
Burke, Carolyn, 146n. 13
Burnet, Bishop Gilbert, 294
Burney, Frances, 18; *Evelina,* 179
Bush, Barbara, 231n. 5
Butler, Edward, 184n. 12, 209n. 12
Butler, Judith, 151, 184n. 23
Byam, 209n. 9

Calendar of State Papers, 209n. 12
Cameron, William J., 12n. 7, 207, 209n. 9, 270n. 6
Carey, John, 298n. 21
Carey, Lady Elizabeth, 70, 71; *The Tragedy of Miriam,* 85nn. 6, 7
"The Cause of the Moors Overrunning Spain," 252n. 20
Cavendish, Margaret, 88
Cellier, Mary, 199
Centlivre, Susannah, 88; *The Wonder: A Woman Keeps a Secret,* 91
Certeau, Michel de, 41n. 17
Charke, Charlotte, 185n. 29
Charles I (king of England), 188, 192
Charles II (king of England), 3, 24, 28, 41n. 12, 122, 187–88, 208, 244, 295–96
Chartier, Roger, 61n. 17
Chodorow, Nancy, 243
Christine de Pisan, *Roman de la Rose,* 18
Cixous, Hélène, 126, 146n. 16
Clifton, Sir William, 22
Colonial discourse, 1, 6, 9–10, 104–5, 112–18, 118–19n. 4, 119n. 5, 120n. 16, 191–92, 206, 212–33, 260

A *Comparison between the Two Stages,* 57, 61n. 19, 61n. 23
Congreve, William, 247; *The Double Dealer,* 252; *The Way of the World,* 61n. 18
Copeland, Nancy, 118n. 3
Cotton, Nancy, 42n. 20, 48, 251n. 3
Cowley, Abraham, "Of Trees," 297n. 2
Cowley, Hannah, 34, 252n. 20; A *School for Greybeards,* 250n. 1
Crawford, Patricia, 60–61n. 10, 252n. 20
Creech, Thomas, 42n. 34, 60n. 3; *Lucretius,* 293
Cumberland, Richard, 154; *Legibus Naturae,* 182–83n. 10
Currer, Betty, 99
Curtin, Philip D., 231n. 3

Daly, Mary, 127
Dangerfield, Duke, 199, 210n. 24
Davis, Cheri Langdell, 320n. 5
Davis Robert Con, 40n. 2, 42n. 33
Defoe, Daniel, 159, 160–61, 211n. 31
de Lauretis, Theresa, 142–43n. 2
Dennis, John, 143n. 4
De Ritter, Jones, 118n. 3
Diamond, Elin, 5–6, 13n. 18, 101n. 14, 103, 119n. 6, 320n. 5
Diggers, 319
Doane, Mary Anne, 186n. 38
Dobree, Bonamy, 100n. 4
Donne, John, 274, 283–84, 286, 298n. 21; "The Canonization," 282; "The Extasie," 279, 282
Doran, John, 2, 11n. 5
Douglas, Mary, 183n. 13
Dryden, John, 2, 9, 18, 39, 40n. 4, 58, 60n. 7, 62nn. 27, 28, 73, 85n. 9; "Absalom and Achitophel," 152; "Annus Mirabilis," preface, 40n. 4; "An Essay of Dramatic Poetry," 19–20, 23–25, 31–32, 33–39, 41nn. 10, 11; *An Evening's Love,* preface, 40n. 4; *The Rival Ladies,*

Dryden, John (*cont.*)
dedication, 31, 40n. 4; "Tyran-
nick Love," 62n. 27. *See also*
Howard, Sir Robert, *The Indian
Queen*
Duffy, Maureen, 3, 12n. 9, 85, 92,
101n. 11, 118nn. 1, 2, 155,
181n. 1, 184n. 16, 184n. 28,
192, 207, 210n. 15, 270n. 6,
297n. 7, 319n. 2
Dugaw, Dianne, 120n. 17
Duncombe, John, *The Feminiad*, 2,
11n. 3
DuPlessis, Rachel Blau, 41n. 13,
184n. 25, 262, 265, 270n. 10
Durfey, Thomas, 61n. 19
Dusinberre, Juliet, 145n. 9
Dutch Wars, 24, 41n. 12
Dyce, Alexander, 2, 11n. 4

Easlea, Brian, 301, 319n. 1, 320n. 4
Eco, Umberto, 145n. 12
Edwards, Bryan, 232n. 8
Elam, Keir, 145n. 12
Eliot, George, "Silly Novels by Lady
Novelists," 18
Ellenhauge, Martin, 147n. 27
Ellman, Mary, 26, 41n. 16
Engell, James, 40n. 3
English Civil War, 30, 279
English Revolution, 276
Etherege, Sir George, *The Man of
Mode*, 89, 144n. 7
Exclusion Crisis, 3, 32, 37, 92, 103,
192
Ezell, Margaret J. M., 297n. 9

Fairchild, Hoxie Neale, 209n. 14
Farquhar, George, *The Recruiting
Officer*, 61n. 19
Fauré, Christine, 146n. 13
Felman, Shoshana, 193, 210n. 19
Feminism, 88, 91, 252n. 21; back-
lash against, 250; Behn's, 1, 3–
11, 25, 121, 188–90, 207, 318–
19, 320n. 5; feminist criticism of
Behn, 3, 5–11, 25, 103–4, 156–
57, 273, 287, 320n. 5; feminist
criticism and theory, 17–18,

121–22, 124–28, 130–31,
142–43n. 2, 253, 257, 267, 269,
293, 301
Ferguson, Moira, 12n. 9, 13n. 12,
297n. 3
Ferriar, John, *The Prince of Angola*,
250n. 2
Fielding, Henry, *Tom Jones*, 240
Finch, Anne, 18
Finke, Laurie, 5, 8–9, 40nn. 2, 5,
42n. 33, 321n. 11
Fitz-roy, Henry, 22, 37
Fletcher, John, 20, 124
Fontenelle, Bernarde, *A Discovery of
New Worlds*, 301
Fores, Michael, 320n. 4
Forsyth, William, 2, 11n. 6
Foucault, Michel, 4, 13n. 14, 104,
108, 117, 119n. 8, 120nn. 10,
11
Freud, Sigmund, 160, 207
Fuss, Diana, 121, 125, 142n. 1

Gallagher, Catherine, 7, 28, 29,
41nn. 15, 17, 42nn. 22, 29, 51,
59–60n. 2, 60n. 6, 61n. 11, 103,
119n. 6, 129–31, 146n. 22, 267,
270n. 13, 297n. 6, 320n. 5
Gardiner, Judith Kegan, 7, 119n. 9,
156–58, 161–62, 165, 167,
176, 185nn. 30, 31, 33, 186n.
41, 209n. 8, 297nn. 1, 10,
298nn. 12, 15, 300n. 37
Garrick, David, *Isabella*, 235, 237–
39, 243, 247, 250, 251n. 7
Gentleman, Frank, *Oroonoko*, 250n.
2
Gilbert, Sandra M., 12n. 10
Gildon, Charles, 73; 211n. 28
Gilman, Sander L., 232–33n. 22
Girard, René, 155, 183n. 12
Glorious Revolution, 296
Goody, Jack, 182n. 5
Goreau, Angeline, 12n. 9, 13n. 12,
41nn. 14, 15, 42nn. 23, 32, 43n.
36, 60n. 10, 84–85n. 5, 181n. 1,
183n. 15, 189, 203, 207, 208nn.
2, 3, 209n. 7, 211n. 27, 270n. 6,
297nn. 5, 7, 298n. 19

Index

Gosse, Edmund, "Mrs Behn," 2, 12n. 7

Gould, Robert, *Satirical Epistle to the Author,* 84

Green, Susan, 7, 8, 124, 145n. 10

Greenblatt, Stephen, 144n. 8, 147n. 27

Greer, Germaine, 12n. 10, 207, 283, 299n. 31, 300nn. 39, 40

Greimas, A. J., 8, 124–28, 132–34, 145n. 12

Grey, Lord of Werke, 152, 161, 172, 183n. 14, 184n. 24, 185n. 31

Griffith, Elizabeth, *Collection of Novels Selected and Revised,* 250nn. 1, 2

Grotius, Hugo, 154; *The Law of War and Peace,* 182nn. 7, 8

Gubar, Susan, 12n. 10

Gwynn, Nell, 37, 62n. 27

Hamelius, Paul, 251n. 9

Hanovarian succession, 188

Harbage, Alfred, 147n. 28

Hargreaves, Henry Allen, 143n. 4, 147n. 26

Harley, Sir Robert, 209n. 9

Hawkesworth, John, *Oroonoko,* 250n. 2

Hawkins, Harriet, 37, 43n. 37

Hays, Mary, "Aphara Behn," 2, 11n. 4

Haywood, Eliza, *Female Spectator,* 18

Herman, Judith Lewis, 183n. 13

Hickes, George, 183n. 13

Hill, Christopher, 320n. 7, 321n. 10

Hobbes, Thomas, 219, 308, 309, 318

Hobby, Elaine, 3, 12n. 9

Hodge, Robert, 40n. 7

Holland, Peter, 117, 120n. 19, 143n. 4, 147n. 26

Homer, *The Odyssey,* 248

Horace, 35, 38; *Art of Poetry,* 34

Howard, Sir Robert, 24; *The Indian Queen,* 204, 211n. 29

Hoyle, John, 3, 26, 254, 256–60, 263–64, 268–69

Hudson, William Henry, 2, 11n. 6

Hughes, John, 9

Hume, R. D., 92, 100n. 4, 101nn. 12, 13, 144n. 6

Hunt, Leigh, "Poetry of British Ladies," 2, 11n. 6

Hutner, Heidi, 10, 119n. 5

Hyland, Peter, 145n. 9

Irigaray, Luce, 126, 131, 145–46n. 13, 146n. 15, 147n. 24, 197, 210n. 23, 253, 269n. 1, 270n. 15

Jacob, J. R., 320n. 4

James II (king of England), 2, 295–96

Jamieson, Michael, 145n. 9

Jardine, Lisa, 144n. 8

Johnson, Barbara, 40n. 1

Jonson, Ben, 20, 274

Jose, Nicholas, 5, 13n. 16

Kamuf, Peggy, 254, 269n. 1, 298n. 20

Kaplan, Charles, 39n. 1

Kauffman, Linda, 254, 255, 269nn. 2, 3

Kavanagh, Julia, *English Women of Letters,* 2, 11n. 4

Kavenik, Frances, 123, 144n. 7

Keller, Evelyn Fox, 30, 42n. 26, 301, 319n. 1, 320n. 4

Kemble, John Philip, *Love in Many Masks,* 250n. 1

Kendrick, Christopher, 320n. 7

Kenyon, John, 210n. 24

Killigrew, Thomas, 118n. 1, 190, 191; *Thomaso,* 91, 102, 105–7, 109–16, 118n. 3, 120n. 13

Klein, Richard, 169

Kofman, Sarah, 211n. 32

Kolodny, Annette, 6–7, 13n. 19

Korshin, Paul, 40n. 9

Kress, Gunther, 40n. 7

Kristeva, Julia, 127, 128, 136, 146n. 17

Kroll, Richard W. F., 5, 13n. 16, 320nn. 6, 8

Krysinski, Wladimir, 145n. 12

Lacan, Jacques, 5, 210n. 25
Langbauer, Laurie, 184n. 22
Laqueur, Thomas, 300n. 37
Lee, Nathaniel, 2
Lennox, Charlotte, 18
Levine, Laura, 144n. 8
Libertinism, 26–31, 42n. 23, 103–4, 153, 168, 172, 180, 190, 284
Ligon, Richard, 227
Link, Frederick, 3, 12n. 7
Lipking, Lawrence, 17, 39n. 1
Locke, Thomas, 188
"L'Occasion Perdue Recouverte," 278, 298n. 13
London Chronicle, 2
Low, Anthony, 320n. 7
Lowe, Robert W., 143n. 4
Lucretius, *De Rerum Natura,* 42n. 24, 293

McCarthy, William, 3, 12n. 10
Macheski, Cecilia, 252n. 24
McKeon, Michael, 5, 13n. 16, 208, 210n. 26, 211n. 33
Mallet, David, *Elvira,* 250n. 1
Mancini, Hortense, Duchess of Mazarin, 244, 252n. 21
Manley, Mary Delariviere, 88; *The Adventures of Rivella,* 252n. 21; *The New Atlantis,* 240, 251n. 16
Mann, David, 252n. 25
Markley, Robert, 4, 5, 6, 7, 10, 13nn. 5, 16, 40n. 4, 42n. 27, 103–4, 119n. 7, 184n. 15, 320nn. 5, 8
Marvel, Andrew, "The Garden," 284
Maus, Katherine Eisaman, 41n. 15, 101n. 15, 143n. 4, 144n. 8
Marx, Karl, 5
Matlack, Cynthia, 224–25, 232n. 14
Medoff, Jeslyn, 250n. 3
Mendelson, Sara, 297n. 7, 299n. 36
Merchant, Carolyn, 30, 31, 42n. 28, 116, 301, 319n. 1, 320n. 4
Mermin, Dorothy, 320n. 5
Messenger, Ann, 238, 251nn. 8, 14
Milton, John, *Paradise Lost,* 275
Mitchell, James, 183n. 13
Modena, Mary of, 192
Moi, Toril, 146n. 13

Monmouth, Duke of, 28, 152, 199, 208n. 1
Morris, Meaghan, 127, 146n. 19
Morrissey, Marietta, 231n. 5
Munns, Jessica, 8, 29, 41n. 15, 42n. 25, 62n. 30, 144n. 6, 184n. 26

New historicism, 5, 6
Novak, Maximillian E., 184n. 18
Noyes, Robert Gale, 251n. 17
Nussbaum, Felicity, 5, 13nn. 16, 17, 20

Oates, Titus, 187–88
O'Donnell, Mary Ann, 13n. 12
Oedipus, 169
"One of the Fair Sex," 2, 12n. 7, 190, 209nn. 10, 11
Orgel, Stephen, 123, 143n. 4, 144nn. 8, 9
Orinda. *See* Philips, Katherine
Orrery, Earl of, 31, 40n. 4
Otway, Thomas, 58, 61n. 21, 62n. 22; *Don Carlos,* preface, 56; *The Souldiers Fortune,* dedication, 56, 57
Ovid, *Amores,* 278

Pajaczkowska, Claire, 146n. 17
Palmer, John, 100n. 4
Park, Sabina, 226
Parker, Rozsika, 252n. 24
Patrick, Simon, 183n. 10
Patronage, 22–23, 26, 33, 37–38, 40n. 9, 50, 119n. 6
Patterson, Orlando, 213, 218, 225, 231, 231nn. 1, 2, 232nn. 9, 11, 16, 17, 18, 19
Payne, Deborah C., 23, 26, 40n. 9, 41n. 17, 42nn. 19, 30, 31, 43n. 36, 60nn. 2, 9, 119n. 6, 320n. 5
Pearson, Jacqueline, 7, 90, 101nn. 6, 7, 250n. 3, 251n. 11, 252n. 23
Pedicord, William Harry, 251n. 7
Perry, Ruth, 12n. 9, 155, 156, 183n. 11, 184n. 17, 185n. 31, 252n. 21
Peters, Julie Stone, 5, 13n. 16
Philips, Katherine [pseud. Orinda],

241, 242, 243, 251n. 3, 252n.
20, 273, 274, 287, 288; *Horace,*
88; *Pompey,* 88; *Poems,* 252n.
20
Pix, Mary, 88, 90; *The Conquest of
Spain,* 252n. 20; *The False
Friend,* prologue and epilogue,
100n. 2; *Queen Catherine,* prologue, 101n. 8
Pollak, Ellen, 7–8, 188–89, 208n. 5
Polwhele, Elizabeth, *The Faithful Virgins,* 88
Poovey, Mary, 42n. 20
Pope, Alexander, *The First Epistle of
the Second Book of Horace Imitated,* 2, 11n. 2
Popish Plot, 92, 99, 187–88, 192,
199

Quaintance, Richard E., 281, 298nn.
13, 17

Race, racism. *See* Colonial discourse
Rich, Adrienne, 40n. 1
Richardson, Samuel, 99; *Clarissa,*
91, 178–79
Richter, David H., 40n. 1
Roberts, David, 61n. 13
Rochester, Earl of (Lawrence Hyde),
2, 27, 36, 37, 50, 84n. 3, 102,
286, 294, 298n. 14
Rogers, Katharine M., 3, 12n. 10,
100
Rogers, Pat, 186n. 38
Rojas, Fernando de, prologue to *Ce-
lestina,* 61n. 17
Romulus and Hersilia, 208n. 1
Rossi, Paolo, 320n. 4
Rothenberg, Molly, 4, 5, 7, 10, 184n.
15
Rothstein, Eric, 123, 144n. 7
Rousseau, Jean-Jacques, *Discourses
on Inequality,* 3
Rowe, Nicholas, *The Fair Penitent,*
91
Royalism, 108, 116, 155, 181, 183n.
14, 275
Rye House Plot, 152
Rymer, Thomas, 9

Sackville-West, Vita, 2, 12n. 7, 206,
211n. 30, 256, 270n. 5
Salisbury, Earl of, 25
Salvaggio, Ruth, 9
Salzman, Paul, 252n. 22
Sappho, 72, 273
Schleifer, Ronald, 128, 145n. 12,
146n. 21
Schneider, David M., 183n. 13
Scot, William, 190, 209n. 9
Scudéry, Madeleine de, 206
Sedgwick, Eve Kosofsky, 169, 171,
185nn. 34, 35, 186n. 37, 299n. 33
Sedley, Sir Charles, 2, 24
Settle, Elkanah, *Empress of Mo-
rocco,* 61n. 19
Seven Portuguese Letters, 252n. 20
The Sexes Mismatch'd, 250n. 2
Shadwell, Thomas, *The True Widow,*
85n. 9
Shakespeare, William, 20, 31, 137,
138, 139, 247, 252n. 25, 289–
90; *All's Well That Ends Well,*
139; *As You Like It,* 124; *Corio-
lanus,* 252n. 25; *Measure for
Measure,* 139; *Midsummer
Night's Dream,* 139; *Othello,*
139, 143n. 4; *Twelfth Night,*
123–24, 252n. 25; *Two Noble
Kinsmen,* 124
Shevelow, Kathryn, 251n. 5
Sidney, Sir Philip, "An Apology for
Poetry," 35, 43n. 35
Slavery. *See* Colonial discourse
Slingsby, Lady (actress), 208n. 1
Smith, Hilda Lee, 3, 12n. 9
Soissons, Comtesse Olympe de, 244
Southern, Richard, 143n. 4, 147n. 26
Southerne, Thomas, 7, 234, 243; *The
Fatal Marriage,* 235–41, 243–
44, 246, 247, 250, 251nn. 6, 7,
12; *Oroonoko,* 224, 236, 250n.
2, 251nn. 8, 13
Spacks, Patricia Meyer, 254, 269n. 1
Spencer, Jane, 3, 7–8, 12n. 9, 251n. 4
Spender, Dale, 12n. 9, 13n. 12
Spivak, Gayatri Chakravorty, 54, 59,
61nn. 15, 16, 62n. 29, 143n. 2,
229–30, 233n. 24

Staël, Madame (Anne-Louise-
　　Germaine) de, 39–40n. 1
Stallybrass, Peter, 60n. 4, 106, 120n.
　　14
Stanton, Domna, 254, 269n. 2
Staves, Susan, 153–54, 182nn. 3, 5,
　　6, 188–89, 192–93, 208n. 4,
　　210nn. 17, 18
Stedman, John, 232n. 12
Steele, Richard, *The Spectator*, 2,
　　11n. 1
Straub, Kristina, 43n. 38, 185n. 29,
　　186n. 38
The Strollers Pacquet Open'd, 250n. 2
Summers, Montague, 235; "Memoir
　　of Mrs. Behn," 2, 12n. 7
Sussman, Charlotte, 10
Sutherland, James, 60n. 7, 297n. 3
Symmons, Charles, *Inez, a Tragedy*,
　　250n. 1
Sypher, Wylie, 209n. 14

Taylor, Jeremy, 154; *Ductor Dubi-
　　tantium*, 182nn. 5, 9
Todd, Janet, 4, 12n. 9, 13n. 13, 155–
　　56, 183nn. 16, 19, 28, 298n. 12
Tory, 1, 3, 4, 6, 9, 21, 103, 104, 189,
　　190, 195, 207, 295, 303, 319
Traci, Phillip, 145n. 9
Trotter, Catharine, 69, 234; *Agnes de
　　Castro*, 250n. 1
Trumbach, Randolph, 42n. 21
Turner, James G., 42n. 21
Tuve, Sir Samuel, *Adventure of Five
　　Hours*, 101n. 13

Van Lier, Rudolf, 231n. 3
Venereal disease, 72
Vieth, David M., 298n. 14
Virgil, 295

Wagenknecht, Edward, 273, 297n. 4
Watt, Ian, 184n. 22
Weir, Thomas, 183n. 13
Wellek, René, 183n. 10
Wharton, Anne, 294
Whig, 21, 104, 118, 155, 158, 167,
　　181, 183n. 14, 189, 195, 303,
　　319

White, Allon, 60n. 4, 106, 120n. 14
Whitford, Margaret, 146n. 13
William and Mary (king and queen
　　of England), 296
Williams, Eric, 231nn. 3, 4
Williams, Jane, 2, 11n. 4
Williamson, Marilyn, 297n. 8, 298n.
　　18
Wilson, John Harold, 143n. 4
Wilson, W. Daniel, 182n. 3
Wolfram, Sybil, 153, 182n. 5
Wollestonecraft, Mary, 39n. 1; *Vin-
　　dication of the Rights of
　　Woman*, 18
Women and slavery. *See* Colonial dis-
　　course
Women's education, 34, 35, 42nn.
　　32, 34, 48–49, 293
Women writers, 1, 6, 18, 26, 40n. 1,
　　53, 56, 65, 69, 84, 84n. 1, 88,
　　90–91, 190–91, 206, 234–35,
　　242–43, 246, 253–54, 256,
　　268–69, 286, 294, 297nn. 8, 9,
　　303; woman writer as pros-
　　titute, 25–26, 50–51, 57, 66,
　　68–69, 71, 73, 85n. 9, 119n. 6,
　　242, 287, 296
Woodcock, George, 12n. 7, 143–
　　44n. 5, 189, 209n. 6, 256, 257,
　　270nn. 4, 6, 7, 12, 14
Woolf, Virginia, 2, 40n. 1, 293; *A
　　Room of One's Own*, 12n. 7,
　　65, 84n. 1
Wycherley, William, 2, 58, 62n. 26,
　　71–72, 85n. 8; *The Country
　　Wife*, 89, 100n. 4; *The Plain
　　Dealer*, 62n. 24; dedication to
　　The Plain Dealer, 57–58, 61n.
　　13; "To the Sappho of the Age,"
　　11n. 1

Yaeger, Patricia, 128, 146n. 20
York, Duke of, 28, 37, 50, 92, 187,
　　192
Young, Edward, *The Revenge*, 250n.
　　1

Zimbardo, Rose, 320n. 5